CRITICAL CITIZE

Critical Citizens

Global Support for
Democratic Government

EDITED BY

Pippa Norris

OXFORD

UNIVERSITY PRESS

Great Clarendon Street, Oxford OX2 6DP

Oxford University Press is a department of the University of Oxford.
It furthers the University's objective of excellence in research, scholarship,
and education by publishing worldwide in

Oxford New York

Athens Auckland Bangkok Bogotá Buenos Aires Calcutta
Cape Town Chennai Dar es Salaam Delhi Florence Hong Kong Istanbul
Karachi Kuala Lumpur Madrid Melbourne Mexico City Mumbai
Nairobi Paris São Paulo Shanghai Singapore Taipei Tokyo Toronto Warsaw
with associated companies in Berlin Ibadan

Oxford is a registered trade mark of Oxford University Press
in the UK and in certain other countries

Published in the United States
by Oxford University Press Inc., New York

British Library Cataloguing in Publication Data
Data available

Library of Congress Cataloging in Publication Data
Critical citizens: global support for democratic government / edited
by Pippa Norris.
Includes bibliographical references and index.
1. Democracy—Public opinion.   2. Legitimacy of governments.
3. Comparative government.   4. World politics—1989-   I. Norris,
Pippa.
JC421.C79   1999   320.9'09'049—dc21   98-40751
ISBN 0-19-829568-5 (pbk)

5 7 9 10 8 6 4

Printed in Great Britain
on acid-free paper by
Biddles Ltd., Guildford and King's Lynn

FOREWORD

JOSEPH S. NYE, JR.

The mission of the John F. Kennedy School of Government is to train people for public service and to conduct policy-relevant research that contributes to the solution of public problems. To carry out that mission, we needed a better understanding of how government and governance in democracies was changing. Soon after I arrived at the Kennedy School at the end of 1995, I asked an inter-disciplinary group of faculty to work with me on a multi-year project called 'Visions of Governance for the Twenty-First Century'. Politicians were telling us that the era of big government was over, but they said little about what would take its place. We do know that markets and non-profit organizations are filling functions once considered the province of government, and that there have been some trends towards devolution from federal to state governments in the United States. And as we enter the Information Age—sometimes referred to as the Third Industrial Revolution— we know that the first and second industrial revolutions at the turn of the last two centuries had profound centralizing effects on government. What we do *not* know is whether the twenty-first century will produce equally enduring decentralizing effects, and what will be the implications for democratic governance. The Visions project is designed to explore such questions and suggest new directions for policy-makers.

We began by looking back at what has happened to views of government over the past thirty years. The results were set forth in *Why People Don't Trust Government*, published in 1997. In brief, we found that confidence in US government has sharply declined. In 1964, three-quarters of Americans said that they trusted the federal government to do the right thing most of the time. Today only a quarter do so. The numbers are only slightly better—about 35 per cent—for state and local government. Some polls show even lower levels.

Government is not alone. Over the past three decades, in America, public confidence had dropped by half or more for many major institutions: from 61 to 30 per cent for universities; 55 to 21 per cent for major companies; from 73 to 29 per cent for medicine; and from 29 to 14 per cent for journalism. In 1996, 30 per cent of the public said they had hardly any confidence in the leaders of the press—about the same as Congress. Our first book focused on the United States, with only passing glances at what appeared to be similar experiences in other developed countries. Now, in the second volume of the project, Pippa Norris and her colleagues have helped to fill that gap. The chapters that follow show that the United States is not alone.

Does it matter? Is it possible that the current symptoms are, in fact, a sign of health? After all, the United States was founded with a mistrust of government. A long Jeffersonian tradition says that we should not worry too much about declining confidence in government. If the polls reflect wariness rather than cynicism, the result maybe healthy. 'Critical citizens' are good for democracy.

As we discussed in our first volume, and as this volume further elaborates, there are various dimensions of political systems. If one looks at the underlying constitutional framework, rather than the day-to-day operations of government, public opinion polls are more positive. Today 90 per cent of Americans say that they like their democratic system of government. In European countries, similar figures appear. At the constitutional level, the current situation is not like France in 1968—much less 1789! There is no 'crisis of democracy' as some predicted in the 1970s. On the other hand, there is widespread erosion of support for *institutions*, both public and private, that have under-girded democratic governance in the past.

Thus, there remains cause for concern. Loss of confidence can harden into cynicism and hatred. Since Jimmy Carter's 1976 campaign, presidential candidates in the United States have tended to 'run against Washington'. Now most politicians do. Studies show that, over the past three decades, the American media generally report on politics and government with a much more negative slant. It might not matter if the only casualty were the vanity of politicians, but, over long periods, a high degree of citizen disaffection can weaken democratic institutions. Voluntary compliance with the law, the public's willingness to pay tax dollars, and the eagerness of bright young people to enter government service are three ways in which institutional confidence and faith in government may be vitally connected. Without these critical resources, government cannot perform well, and people will become even more distrustful and disaffected. Such a cumulative downward spiral could erode support for democracy as a form of governance.

The underlying causes are complex. Our first volume examined seventeen different hypotheses and discarded many. Some, such as the end of the Cold War, failed the 'time test' since the Cold War ended long after confidence had begun to decline in the mid-1960s. Similarly, the view that 'it's all the economy, stupid', ignored the fact that in the United States this decline began during a period of prosperity, and loss of confidence is reported equally among economic winners and losers. Indeed, one of our project's more striking findings, which corroborated earlier work by Lipset and Schneider (1987), is that loss of confidence is a social rather than a personal phenomenon. Few people report that their views of government derive from personal experience with it; rather, such attitudes are informed by the media and politicians.

The following chapters place these questions of diagnosis, causation, and consequences in a comparative perspective. They do not pretend to have all the answers. Further work will be needed as we try to understand the evolution of democratic governance. But no one can afford to move along that path without benefiting from the important insights reported by this book.

PREFACE

This book arose as part of an ongoing project on 'Visions of Governance for the Twenty-first Century', initiated in 1996 by Dean Joseph S. Nye at the John F. Kennedy School of Government. This project explores what people want from government, the public sector, and from non-profit organizations. The first volume from the Visions project, focusing primarily on the United States, *Why People Don't Trust Government* (Cambridge, Mass.: Harvard University Press, 1997) was edited by Joseph S. Nye, Philip D. Zelikow, and David C. King. This book generated a lively debate about whether trends towards declining confidence and trust in government evident in the United States were *sui generis* or whether similar patterns were evident in many established, and emerging, democracies.

To examine this issue the Kennedy School gathered together some of the foremost scholars of comparative politics in a workshop on *Confidence in Democratic Governance: America in Comparative Perspective*, sponsored by the Pew Charitable Trust, which met in Washington 25–7 August 1997. This brought together a distinguished group of international participants to compare citizens' attitudes towards governance in democracies world-wide. We are most grateful to Paul Light and the Pew Charitable Trust for facilitating this workshop and to everyone who participated as paper-givers, discussants, or chairs, including: Suzanne Berger, Russell Dalton, James A. Davis, Wolfgang Donsbach, Geoffrey Evans, Peter Hall, Soren Holmberg, Ronald F. Inglehart, David Jones, Marvin Kalb, Lucinda Kennedy, Anthony King, Hans-Dieter Klingemann, Marta Lagos, Juan Linz, Seymour Martin Lipset, Ian McAllister, Arthur Miller, William Mishler, Kenneth Newton, Joseph S. Nye, Jr., Claus Offe, Thomas E. Patterson, Barbara Pfetsch, Paul Pierson, Theda Skocpol, Jacques Thomassen, and Sidney Verba.

Moreover during the Fall Semester 1997 we followed the workshop by inviting colleagues to present some of their research at lectures and seminars held at the Kennedy School of Government and the Minda de Gunzburg Center for European Studies. This included visits by Geoffrey Evans, Dieter Fuchs, Richard Rose, Ola Listhaug, and Ronald Inglehart. We are most grateful to colleagues who visited us and to Charles S. Maier, Director of the Minda de Gunzburg Center for European Studies, and Abby Collins for supporting this series from the 1997 Program to Study Germany and Europe.

The book also benefited from the support of many colleagues at the Shorenstein Center on the Press, Politics and Public Policy and the Kennedy School of Government, particularly from Marvin Kalb, Elaine Kamarck, and Shirley Williams, as well as from the invaluable administrative and editorial assistance of David Jones, now at James Madison University, who played a critical role during his time at Harvard in completing the manuscript. I am also most grateful for all the students who participated in my class at the Kennedy School on Democracy and Democratization, generating a stimulating discussion of draft chapters from the book on the basis of their experience of democratization in countries as diverse as Spain, the Philippines, South Korea, Burma, Tibet, Pakistan, Mexico, and Brazil. Lastly we owe a large debt to the rich and extensive cross-national data-sets, notably the *World Values* and *Eurobarometer Surveys*, and from the literature on political culture and democratization which has been generated during the last decade. By updating the previous literature to examine trends since the end of the Cold War, as well as moving beyond advanced industrialized societies, the book aims to provide a systematic analysis comparing global patterns of political support in transitional, consolidating, and established democracies at the end of the twentieth century.

Pippa Norris

Harvard University
May 1998

CONTENTS

LIST OF FIGURES

LIST OF TABLES

LIST OF CONTRIBUTORS

Pippa Norris is Associate Director (Research) of the Joan Shorenstein Center on the Press, Politics, and Public Policy and Lecturer at the Kennedy School of Government at Harvard University. She focuses on comparative political behaviour and recent publications include *The Politics of News* (1998), *Passages to Power* (1997), *Britain Votes 1997* (1997), *Politics and the Press* (1997), *Electoral Change Since 1945* (1997), and *Comparing Democracies* (1996). She is currently working on books analysing voting behaviour and political communications.

Russell Dalton is Professor of Political Science at the University of California, Irvine. His scholarly interests include comparative political behaviour, political parties, social movements, and political change in advanced industrial societies. Publications include *The Green Rainbow: Environmental Groups in Western Europe* (1994), *Citizen Politics in Western Democracies* (1996), *Politics in Germany* (1992), *Germany Transformed* (1981), *Electoral Change in Advanced Industrial Democracies* (1984), *Challenging the Political Order* (1990), and *Germans Divided* (1996). He is now working on a comparative study of electoral choice in advanced industrial democracies and a new book on the causes and consequences of party decline.

Dieter Fuchs is Associate Professor of Political Science, Free University of Berlin, and Senior Research Fellow, Science Centre Berlin. Among his publications are *Die Unterstutzung des politischen Systems der Bundesrepublik Deutschland* (1989) and *Citizens and the State* (1995) co-edited with Hans-Dieter Klingemann.

Sören Holmberg is Professor of Political Science at Göteborg University, Sweden and Director of the Swedish Election Study Programme. Recent publications include *Representation from Above: Members of Parliament and Representative Democracy in Sweden* (1996).

Ronald F. Inglehart is Program Director, Center for Political Studies, Institute for Social Research at the University of Michigan. He is chair of the steering committee of the *World Values Surveys* and was co-investigator of the *Eurobarometer* surveys from 1970 to 1990. His books include *The Silent Revolution* (1977), *Culture Shift in Advanced Industrial Society* (1990), *Value Change in Global Perspective* (1995), and *Modernization and Postmodernization* (1997).

Hans-Dieter Klingemann is Director of the Research Unit on Social Institutions and Social Change at the Wissenschaftszentrum für Sozialforschung (WZB), Berlin. Recent books include, among others, *Citizens and the State* (1995), *A New Handbook of Political Science* (1996), and *Parties, Policies, and Democracy* (1994). His current research focuses on democratic transition and consolidation, including a major study on values and value change in Central and Eastern Europe with Ronald Inglehart and Max Kaase.

Ola Listhaug is Professor of Political Science at the Norwegian University of Science and Technology, Trondheim. He is author of *Citizens, Parties and Norwegian Electoral Politics 1957–1985* and articles on political behaviour and comparative politics. He is currently directing an international group of scholars on the Foundations of Public Opinion at the Centre for Advanced Study at the Norwegian Academy of Science and Letters.

Ian McAllister is Director of the Research School of Social Sciences at the Australian National University, Canberra. His books include *Political Behaviour* (1992), *Dimensions of Australian Society* (1995), *The Australian Political System* (1995), *How Russia Votes* (with Richard Rose and Stephen White, 1996), and *The Loyalties of Voters: A Lifetime Learning Model* (with Richard Rose) (1990). Previously he held appointments at the University of New South Wales, the University of Strathclyde, and the University of Manchester. His research interests are in comparative political behaviour, political parties, voters, and electoral systems.

William Mishler is Professor of Political Science at the University of Arizona, Tucson. Books include *The Resurgence of Conservation in Anglo-American Democracies* (1998), *Representative Democracies in the Canadian Provinces* (1982), and *Political Participation in Canada* (1979), along with *Democracy and its Alternatives: Understanding Post-Communist Society* (1998) written with Richard Rose.

Neil Munro is a graduate of Russian and Chinese from the University of Queensland. He is a research fellow at the Centre for the Study of Public Policy, University of Strathclyde.

Kenneth Newton is Professor of Government at the University of Essex and Executive Director of the European Consortium for Political Research. Recent publications include *Beliefs in Government* (with Max Kaase, 1995), *Political Data Handbook* (with Jan Erik Lane and David McKay, 1997), *The Politics of the New Europe* (with Ian Budge, 1997), *The New British Politics* (with Ian Budge, Ivor Crewe, and David McKay, 1998), and *Social Capital and European Democracy* (edited with Jan van Deth, Marco Maraffi, and Paul Whiteley, 1998).

Joseph S. Nye, Jr. is Dean of the Kennedy School of Government, Harvard University and Don K. Price Professor of Public Policy. He joined the Harvard faculty in 1964 and served as Director of the Center for International Affairs, Dillon Professor of International Affairs, and Associate Dean of Arts and Sciences. He has also served in government, including September 1994–December 1995 as Assistant Secretary of Defense for International Security Affairs. His most recent books include *Why People Don't Trust Government* (1997), *Bound to Lead* (1990), and *Understanding International Conflicts* (1993).

Richard Rose, FBA, is Director of the Centre for the Study of Public Policy, University of Strathclyde, and international scientific adviser of the Paul Lazarsfeld Society, Vienna. Since 1991 he has directed a programme of survey research in fifteen post-communist democracies and South Korea. He has written more than three dozen books and his work has been translated into sixteen languages. Recent related publications include *What is Europe?* (1996), *How Russia Votes* (1997), and *Democracy and its Alternatives in Post-Communist Europe* (1998).

Doh Chull Shin is Professor of Political Science at the University of Illinois, Springfield. He has published widely on comparative democratization in *World Politics*, *Comparative Politics*, *Social Indicators Research*, and other journals.

1

Introduction: The Growth of
Critical Citizens?

PIPPA NORRIS

THIS book brought together a network of international scholars to address a series of interrelated questions. The first are *diagnostic*: how far are there legitimate grounds for concern about declining public support for representative democracy world-wide? Are trends towards growing cynicism with government in the United States evident in many established and newer democracies? The second concern is *analytical*: what are the main political, economic and cultural factors driving the dynamics of support for democratic government? The last questions are *prescriptive*: what are the consequences of this analysis and what are the implications for public policy and for strengthening democratic governance? Chapters in this volume critically explore these issues seeking to establish a world-wide audit of public support for representative democracy at the end of the twentieth century.

Certain common themes have emerged from this volume which can be highlighted here. The first is to emphasize that the concept of political support is *multi-dimensional*. Rather than talking about 'political trust', in every case we need to specify its object. Just as 'social trust' can refer to trust towards one's family and friends, one's neighbours and community, or to citizens in different countries, so political trust depends upon the object. The Eastonian classification draws a valuable distinction between support for the political community, regime, and authorities. Building upon this foundation, the five-fold conceptualization used within this volume draws a line between the political community, regime principles, regime performance, regime institutions, and political actors. Much confusion surrounding this topic results from neglecting these distinctions.

This expansion of the Eastonian schema is long overdue because the second major theme which emerges from this book concerns divergent trends in support for regime principles and institutions. At the turn of the millenium most citizens in well-established and in newer democracies share widespread aspirations to the ideals and principles of democracy. The end of the Cold War has produced crumbling adherence to the old nostrums of authoritarian regimes.

By the end of the twentieth century overwhelming support is given to the principle of democracy as an ideal form of government, even among citizens living under flawed regimes characterized by widespread abuse of human rights and civil liberties, such as in Nigeria, Peru, and Turkey. Such adherence may be purely symbolic, like abstract support for the principles of freedom and equality, or it may be more deeply grounded. At the same time citizens draw a clear distinction between which type of government they would choose as their ideal and the performance of current regimes. At the end of the twentieth century citizens in many established democracies give poor marks to how their political system functions, and in particular how institutions such as parliaments, the legal system, and the civil service work in practice. This pattern has long been evident in Italy and Japan, but as Dalton demonstrates in Chapter 3 of this volume the erosion of support for core representative institutions has spread to many more advanced industrialized societies. Other chapters illustrate the conflict between democratic ideals and reality evident in many newer or incomplete democracies such as South Korea, Russia, and East Germany.

The last theme which emerges concerns how we interpret the consequences of these developments. Classic theories of political culture have long suggested that if the structure of government conflicts with the political culture, then regimes lack legitimacy to tide them over bad times (Almond and Verba 1963). This may produce serious problems of government stability which may hinder the process of consolidation in newer democracies. If people become disillusioned with the perceived performance of democratic governments, over successive administrations, then in time this might erode their belief in democracy itself. In this perspective failure of performance will flow upwards to undermine democratic values. In Chapter 4 Rose and Mishler stress that the publics in Central and Eastern Europe do not hanker nostalgically to return to the old regimes of the communist era. Nevertheless there are indicators that the public remains dissatisfied with its forms of governance in many newer democracies. Parliaments and parties provide some of the most important channels of linkage between citizens and representative government yet the evidence in this book demonstrates a widespread lack of confidence in these institutions throughout Latin America as well as in many Central and Eastern European countries. Without a deep reservoir of public support to bolster regimes through economic crisis or external shocks, semi-democracies may revert to their authoritarian legacy. The potential problem is less that the public actively desires the return of old regimes, than that new democracies, lacking legitimacy, may be undermined by leadership coups, by ethnic conflict, by extreme nationalist parties, or by a more gradual erosion of political rights and civil liberties. In this view the sky is not falling down for democracy, as Chicken Little claimed. But neither is the Panglossian view true that all remains well in the body politic.

Yet other authors in this volume provide an alternative interpretation which regards the tensions between ideals and reality as essentially healthy for the future of democratic governance, since this indicates the emergence of more 'critical citizens', or 'dissatisfied democrats', who adhere strongly to democratic values but who find the existing structures of representative government, invented in the eighteenth and nineteenth centuries, to be wanting as we approach the end of the millenium. In established democracies this may increase the pressures for structural reforms, to make elected governments more accountable to the public. For advocates of direct democracy, the forms of governance in the nation-state need to evolve to allow more opportunities for citizen decision-making than an election for government every few years. Proponents argue for increased use of referendums and initiatives, devolution to community organizations, and grassroots mobilization to solve local problems. In this perspective, the challenge is to reform existing institutions and to widen citizen involvement in governance, with the evolution of new channels to link citizens and the state.

In addressing these issues this book aims to steer a course between the Scylla of crisis theories and the Charybdis claiming that all's right with the world. There are genuine grounds for concern about public support for the core institutions of democratic government, in established and newer democracies, but too often 'crisis' accounts are broad-brush and exaggerated when the diagnosis needs to be careful, systematic, and precise. To examine these issues this introduction falls into four parts. We start by reviewing the previous literature on democratic crisis and stability. We then outline the conceptual framework and data sources used throughout the book. On this basis we highlight the major findings about global trends in support for democratic governance. The last part outlines the plan of the book and summarizes the contents in subsequent chapters.

Theories of Democratic Crisis and Malaise

The 1960s and 1970s: A Crisis of Democracy?

Theories of democratic crisis have gone through periodic cycles of hope and fear. The politics of the late 1960s and early 1970s led several theorists to predict a 'crisis' of Western democracy (Crozier, Huntington, and Watanuki 1975; Huntington 1981). Exuberant democracy was believed incompatible with effective governability (Brittan 1975; King 1975). These accounts struck a popular chord because many contemporaries felt that riots over civil rights, violent protest over Vietnam, and the trauma of Watergate seemed to be tearing America apart, the antithesis of the quiescent Eisenhower years. Similar echoes were heard in Europe rattling off the cobblestones of Paris, London, and Bonn, reflecting the 1968 student radicalism and industrial strife in Europe. Crozier, Huntington, and Watanuki (1975) argued that weakening confidence in government leaders and political institutions in Western Europe, the United

States, and Japan was due to increasing demands from interest groups and new social movements, the rise of protest demonstrations and civil disobedience, more polarized ideological and issue cleavages, combined with the apparent incapacity of national governments to mitigate the consequences of the international economic recession produced by the OPEC oil shocks. Nineteenth-century institutions of representative democracy seemed unable to cope with twentieth-century demands, producing what appeared to be the crisis of the overloaded state.

Similar anxieties were heard about problems facing newer democracies in this period: O'Donnell claimed that the process of democratization in Latin America contained internal contradictions, producing rising public demands which ultimately undermined economic development and weakened state management, producing a reversion to authoritarian rule (O'Donnell, Schmitter, and Whitehead 1986). This account seemed to fit the reverse wave of democratization from 1958 to 1975. Fledgling democracies crumbled throughout Latin America with a succession of military coups: Peru (1962), Brazil and Bolivia (1964), Argentine (1966), Chile and Uruguay (1973). Authoritarian rule was ascendant in Asia (Pakistan, South Korea, Indonesia, the Philippines, India), Southern Europe (Greece, Turkey) and Africa (Nigeria). Some of these countries had just been decolonized, others had been democracies for many years, fuelling a wave of concern about the future stability of democracy and its applicability to developing societies.

The 1980s: Confidence in Democracy Regained?

'Crisis' theories tended to fall out of intellectual fashion during the 1980s, as they appeared to have underestimated the adaptive capacities of the modern state. In established democracies the resurgence of confident conservatism blue in tooth and claw, led by Reaganism and Thatcherism, seemed to lower public expectations simultaneously, reduce government services, and reverse the 'politics of decline' (Hoover and Plant 1989; Krieger 1986; Norpoth 1992). During the 1980s the Left lost political and intellectual ground in many OECD countries (Fox Piven 1992; Anderson and Camiller 1994; Kitschelt 1994). Far from being a threat, new types of direct action like demonstrations quickly became part of the conventional repertoire of middle-class political participation (Barnes and Kaase 1979; Topf 1995). New social movements like environmentalism and feminism became absorbed into the mainstream policy process (McAdam, McCarthy, and Zald 1996; Dalton and Kuechler 1990). In America, despite the anti-government rhetoric, the sunny economic can-do optimism of Reaganism dispelled the shadows of Carteresque malaise.

The evidence for the 'crisis' thesis came under strong challenge from a network of scholars focusing on trends in political support in Western Europe. The five-volume *Beliefs in Government* project provided a thorough examination of public opinion in Western Europe based primarily on analysing the series of *Eurobarometer Surveys* from 1973 to 1990 (Klingemann and Fuchs

1995; Kaase and Newton 1995). A wide range of contributors to this project found little systematic evidence for widespread signs of growing malaise during these decades. Instead, diverse patterns of political support were found in different European societies, whether measured by trust in politicians (Listhaug and Wiberg 1995), satisfaction with the workings of the democratic process (Fuchs 1995), institutional confidence (Listhaug and Wiberg 1995), or electoral turnout (Topf 1995). The only trend consistent with the 'crisis' thesis was a general cross-national weakening in attachment to political parties (Schmitt and Holmberg 1995). As one account summarized these conclusions: 'There is little evidence to support the various theories of crisis, contradiction and catastrophe. There are few signs of a general decline in trust, confidence in public institutions, political interest, or faith in democracy; nor is there much evidence of an increase in apathy, alienation, or faith in democracy' (Budge and Newton 1997: 132). From this perspective the overall pattern of change in democratic attitudes during the 1970 and 1980s in Europe was one of trendless fluctuations, not secular decline, so why worry? Crisis theories seemed to have gone the way of bell-bottoms, Afghan coats, and patchouli oil.

World-wide the transition from authoritarian rule received a new burst of life with the third wave of democratization. This process started in the mid-1970s with the restoration of elected civilian administrations in Portugal, Spain, and Greece (Morlino and Montero, 1995). The surge of democratization gathered pace in Latin American and Asia, followed by historic developments with the end of the Soviet empire in Central and Eastern Europe, which brought a heady mood of optimism in the West. By the end of the twentieth century around 40 per cent of states around the world can be classified as fully democratic (or 'free'), according to Freedom House's classification of political rights and civil liberties (Karatnycky 1997). As Huntington described the era between the end of the Portuguese dictatorship and the fall of the Berlin Wall: 'Although obviously there were resistance and setbacks, as in China in 1989, the movement towards democracy seemed to take on the character of an almost irreversible global tide moving on from one triumph to the next' (Huntington 1991: 21).

1990s: Malaise Redux?

Yet by the early to mid-1990s many commentators sensed, if not a crisis of government, then at least a more diffuse mood of *Angst*. Like a mid-life divorce, the end of the Cold War proved unsettling. Democracy seemed to have triumphed and yet to become absorbed by self-doubt. Popular accounts stressed widespread signs of democratic malaise, claiming that the electorate in many industrialized societies, but particularly in the United States, had become deeply disengaged. Voters were commonly described as 'ready to revolt', 'angry', 'disgusted', and 'frustrated' (Tolchin 1996; Dionne 1991; Craig 1993). In America the stereotype of the 'angry white male' was discovered in 1994. Yet the popular *Zeitgeist* in America seemed more anxious than angry, immobilized on the couch by ennui more than energized by radical energy. As one commentator put it, Europe and America seem to have experienced '. . . a flight from politics, or what the Germans call *Politikverdrossenheit*: a weariness about its debates, disbelief about its claims, skepticism about its results, cynicism about its practitioners' (Maier 1994: 59).

Studies confirm the long-term slide in political trust for federal government and many major institutions in America over the last three decades (Lipset and Schneider 1987; Nye *et al.* 1997). According to NES data, in 1958 almost three-quarters of citizens said that they trusted the federal government 'most of the time' or 'just about always'. By 1980 only a quarter proved as trusting. Since then trust has remained low compared with earlier decades, although there was a modest recovery in 1996 (see Figure 1.1).

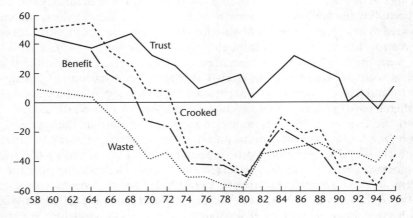

Fig. 1.1. Confidence in politicians in the United States, 1958–1996.
Source: NES Percentage Difference Index.

Many established democracies seemed to share an underlying unease about a long-term decline of public confidence in government and anxieties about a growing disconnection between citizens and the state. Britain experienced the rise of a more sceptical electorate (Curtice and Jowell 1997). Swedish surveys monitored a thirty-year erosion of trust in politicians, paralleling trends in the United States (see Holmberg, Chapter 5 this volume). Widespread cynicism about government remained embedded in the Italian and Japanese political cultures, fuelling pressures in the early 1990s for major reforms of the electoral and party systems in both countries (Morlino and Montero 1995; Morlino and Tarchi 1996; Pharr 1997). Echoes of earlier crisis theories were used to describe public discontent in established democracies as diverse as Canada (Delacourt 1993), India (Kohli 1990), Israel (Avishai 1990), and Britain (Sampson 1993), as well as the European Union (Hayward 1995; Koechler 1987). Some went so far as to claim a 'moral crisis' afflicting Europe and North America, with citizens increasingly polarized, divided, and mistrustful of political leaders and institutions (Maier 1994).

Since 1973 the 'third wave' of democracy has transformed the geopolitical map and greatly expanded the universe of 'electoral democracies'. Nevertheless the heady mood of optimism following the fall of the Berlin Wall was succeeded by a more cautious ambience. During the mid-1990s the surge in the number of democratic states worldwide stabilized rather than expanded. In semi-democracies the consolidation stage proved sobering and fraught with obstacles, especially throughout much of Africa and Asia. Semi-democracies faced the challenge of the triple transformation of their nation-state, economic structures and political systems. Outside of wealthy industrialized nations the quality of democratic government often remains flawed, poorly institutionalized, and insecure.

The consolidation literature stresses that many 'incomplete', 'partly-free' or 'semi-democracies' continue to be plagued by problems of ethnic conflict and religious polarization, widespread administrative corruption, intimidation and dishonesty at the ballot box, severe socioeconomic inequalities, constraints on the press and coercion of opposition movements, weak legislatures, highly fragmented or predominant party systems, rising levels of violent organized crime, and executive arrogation of power against representative institutions (Diamond, Linz, and Kipset 1995; Diamond, Plattner, and Chu 1997; Hadenius 1997). Occasionally semi-democracies revert to authoritarian rule, as in Nigeria and Algeria, but more commonly they fail to become fully consolidated. Rose and Mishler's studies of public opinion in Central and Eastern Europe since the fall of the Berlin Wall shows that although many citizens remain highly sceptical about democracy nevertheless they prefer the new regimes to the old, and there are few grounds to believe that the public desires a return to authoritarianism (Rose *et al.* 1998; Mishler and Rose, Chapter 4 this volume). Despite occasional reversions, notably in Africa, and the lack of progress in regions like the Middle East, the critical problem facing most semi-democracies at the end of the twentieth century concerns the flawed and incomplete quality of democratic government, more than its persistence or stability.

Understanding Trends

The twentieth century has therefore experienced periodic cycles of hope and fear about the state of popular support for democratic government. We need to re-examine this issue because understanding trends has important implications for explaining the causes of this phenomenon. If we establish a similar pattern of growing scepticism about government across established democracies then plausibly this may be due to common structural and secular trends shaping public opinion in advanced industrialized societies. In this case, we might look for explanations such as social capital theory focusing on a decline in civic engagement and social trust (Putnam 1994, 1995a, 1995b); or post-materialist theory emphasizing changing value orientations (Dalton 1996; Inglehart 1977, 1990, 1997a).

Alternatively if we find different trends across different democracies then the pattern of deepening cynicism in the United States and Sweden, and enduring alienation with government in Italy and Japan, may reflect country-specific factors. In this case we should search for explanations based on specific historical traditions, the performance of governments, or the workings of particular political systems. Path-dependent theories, for example, suggest that countries and regions drawing on different historical roots may continue to display markedly different attitudes towards government today. In this view our institutions, norms, and values are conditioned to an important degree by earlier patterns. If true, then even two neighbouring countries as superficially similar as Canada and the United States may maintain different public philosophies towards the state (Lipset 1990, 1996).

Establishing the pattern of basic trends in public support for democracy is also critical for understanding their possible consequences. If disenchantment with representative government has become widespread this can be regarded as worrying in itself, as an indicator of the health of democracy. But this is also a matter of serious concern if significant consequences flow from this development. As discussed in the final chapter of this book it is commonly claimed that in established democracies growing cynicism may produce declining electoral turnout and political engagement (Teixeira 1992); may facilitate the growth of protest politics and extreme anti-state parties (Craig and Maggiotto 1981; Muller 1979; Muller, Jukam, and Seligson 1982; Cheles, Ferguson, and Vaughan 1995) and at elite level may perhaps deter the best and brightest from entering public service (Nye et al. 1997; Norris 1997).

Even greater concern has focused on the effects of widespread cynicism in newer and more fragile democracies such as Russia, South Africa, and Taiwan. The quality of democracy in many incomplete, partial, or semi-democracies has often proved deeply flawed. Widespread cynicism about democratic government may exacerbate this situation. Adherence to a democratic political culture has long been thought a necessary (but not sufficient) condition for the consolidation of newer democratic governments (Lipset 1959; Almond and Verba 1963; Dahl 1971; Linz and Stepan 1978; O'Donnell et al. 1986; Lipset 1993; Diamond et al. 1995, 1997; Linz and Stepan 1996). The conclusion of the book considers the consequences of falling faith in government and the implications for democratization.

The first challenge for this volume is therefore to sort out the claims and counter-claims about the breadth and depth of any erosion of public confidence in representative government within established and newer democracies. To consider these issues Part I of this volume describes the extent of cross-national support for democratic government and the dynamics of public opinion over time. Certain methodological observations are helpful in sorting out the evidence. Consistent and systematic comparison depends upon five factors:

- the conceptual framework;
- suitable sources of survey *data*;
- the selection of time *periods*;
- the choice of countries; and
- the choice of appropriate measures.

Let us consider each in turn.

The Conceptual Framework for Critical Citizens

The most critical step in our analysis is the use of a consistent conceptual framework. One important theme to emerge from this volume is that political support needs to be understood as a multi-dimensional phenomenon. This book develops a fivefold conceptual framework distinguishing between the different levels or objects of political support. These distinctions are often blurred in practice, when popular discussions about declining confidence in legislatures, trust in politicians, and support for democratic values are treated as though interchangeable. This practice has led to considerable confusion about claims and counter-claims in the literature. One of the most useful analytic frameworks is provided by David Easton (Easton 1965, 1975) who distinguished between support for the community, the regime, and the authorities.

These distinctions provide an essential starting-point but this book suggests that greater refinement of categories is necessary since there are significant theoretical and empirical gradations within different parts of the regime. In Easton's conception the regime constituted the basic framework for governing the country. People could not pick and choose between different elements of the regime, approving of some parts while rejecting others. Yet in practice citizens do seem to distinguish between different levels of the regime, often believing strongly in democratic values, for example, while proving critical of the way that democratic governments work in practice. People also seem to make clear judgements concerning different institutions within the regime, expressing confidence in the courts, for example, while disapproving of parliament. Accordingly, strongly influenced by the arguments of Russell Dalton (Chapter 3 this volume) and Hans-Dieter Klingemann (Chapter 2 this volume), the authors in this volume expanded the classification into a fivefold framework distinguishing between political support for the community, regime principles, regime performance, regime institutions, and political actors (see Figure 1.2). These levels can be seen as ranging in a continuum from the most diffuse support for the nation-state down through successive levels to the most concrete support for particular politicians.

The first level concerns diffuse support for the *political community*, which is usually understood to mean a basic attachment to the nation beyond the present institutions of government and a general willingness to co-operate together politically. As Linz and Stephan emphasize (1996), agreement about the boundaries of the political community is the essential precondition for the foundation of any stable nation-state. 'Without the existence of a state, there cannot be a consolidated modern democratic regime' (Linz and Stephan 1996: 7). But the boundaries of the political community can be defined more narrowly in terms of a local or regional community, or a community defined by

Diffuse Support

Object of Support	Summary of Trends
Political Community	*High* levels of support.
Regime Principles	*High* levels of support.
Regime Performance	*Varied* satisfaction with the workings of the regime.
Regime Institutions	*Declining* confidence in government institutions; *low* levels of support in many newer democracies.
Political Actors	*Mixed* trends in trust in politicians.

Specific Support

Fig. 1.2. The conceptual framework for the book.

political cleavages based on ethnic, class, or religious identities, as much as by physical geography. As discussed by Newton in Chapter 8 of this volume, these boundaries are important for social-capital theories concerned with issues of social trust and civic engagement. Attachment to the nation is conventionally measured by items tapping a sense of belonging to the community, national pride, and national identity.

The second level refers to support for the core *regime principles* representing the values of the political system. In democratic states this dimension refers to what Rose (1997*a*) has termed 'idealist' definitions of democracy derived from classical liberal theory. Since democracy remains an essentially contested concept, open to multiple meanings, there is no consensus about which values should be nominated as most important. Empirical studies about what people understand by the term suggests that democracy means different things to different people in different societies (Thomassen 1995; Simon 1996; Miller, Hesli, and Reisinger 1997). Nevertheless, the basic principles of democratic regimes are commonly understood to include such values as freedom, participation, tolerance and moderation, respect for legal-institutional rights, and the rule of law (Beetham 1994; Simon 1996). Surveys can tap agreement with these specific values, or more commonly general agreement with the idea of democracy as the best form of democracy (Fuchs 1995).

The third level concerns evaluations of *regime performance*, meaning support for how authoritarian or democratic political systems function in practice. This taps a 'middle level' of support which is often difficult to gauge. In *Eurobarometers* this is commonly measured by '*satisfaction with the performance of democracy*', that is, how democracy functions in practice as opposed to the ideal (Fuchs 1995). Yet this measure is ambiguous, and as contributors note, alternative interpretations of this item are possible. This survey item taps both support for 'democracy' as a value (which might be expected to rise gradually over time), and also satisfaction with the incumbent government (which might be expected to fluctuate over time). But as Klingemann argues the focus on 'how democracy is working' does seem to make it a suitable item to test public evaluation of democratic performance more than principles. One can believe strongly in democratic values yet feel that the way democracy functions in a country leaves much to be desired. In newer democracies, Mishler and Rose suggest that we need to compare the current against the older regime, since this provides a common standard, rather than comparing the current regime with an idealized conception of representative democracy.

The fourth level focuses on support for *regime institutions*, tapping what Rose (1997*a*) terms a 'realistic' view of democracy. This includes attitudes towards governments, parliaments, the executive, the legal system and police, the state bureaucracy, political parties, and the military (Listhaug and Wiberg 1995; Lipset and Schneider 1987). These studies seek to measure generalized support for the institution—that is approval of the powers of the Presidency rather than support for Bill Clinton, and support for parties rather than particular party leaders—although in practice the dividing line between the office and incumbents is often fuzzy. We also commonly make a conventional divisions between 'public' and 'private' institutions, although this line may vary depending upon the degree of state control. As Hibbing and Theiss-Morse argue (1995: 23), much can be learnt by examining the dynamics of support for individual institutions, such as Congress and the courts, because evidence suggests that the public distinguishes between them.

Lastly, we are also interested in comparing specific support for *political actors* or authorities, including evaluations of politicians as a class and the performance of particular leaders. Studies have compared popular support for different presidents or prime ministers, whether satisfaction with leadership has declined since the post-war period, and the dynamics of support such as 'rally round the flag' effects (Brace and Hinckley 1992; Clarke and Stewart 1995; Rose 1995). More often, analysis at this level has focused on trust in politicians as a class, using items first developed by the NES in 1958 (summarized in Figure 1.1) and adopted later by some other national election studies (see Dalton, Table 3.3 and Holmberg, Fig. 5.1 in this volume). Indeed many previous studies of political trust have often relied exclusively on these measures, as though there were no other indicators of support, even though it is possible to deeply mistrust politicians and yet to continue to have confidence either in the institutional structures or in particular representatives.

One long-standing controversy surrounding the original NES measures of political trust has its origins in the Miller–Citrin debate in 1974 (Miller 1974*a*, 1974*b*; Citrin 1974). This debate revolved around whether, as Miller argued, the results measured by the NES index indicated a profound loss of diffuse support for the political system as a whole, or whether, as Citrin suggested, it indicated more specific approval of the performance of political leaders. In the conceptual framework used in this study we come down strongly in favour of understanding the NES measures as referring to trust in political actors, *not* the political regime *per se*. The items derived from the NES index, subsequently used in Scandinavian and European surveys, explicitly ask about support for 'politicians', including 'MPs', 'people running the government', 'officials', 'parties', 'political leaders', 'people in government', 'people in parliament', 'politicians in general', 'members of parliament', and similar phrases (see Dalton, Table 3.3; Holmberg, Fig. 5.1 in this volume). As Citrin argued (1974) many Americans who scored low on trust in the NES index expressed pride in 'our system of government'. These stimuli therefore probably provoke short-run evaluations of current office-holders more than diffuse support for the political system as a whole: 'The cynical responses to the CPS political trust items are hardly extreme. To believe that the government wastes "a lot" of money, can be trusted "to do what is right only some of the time", and includes "quite a few" people who are "crooked" or "don't know what they're doing" need not speak of a deep-seated hostility towards the political system at the regime or community levels' (Citrin 1974: 975). Moreover these items are rarely about 'government' in the sense used by most parliamentary democracies, where this term is usually reserved for the party or parties in office more than the system of government including the executive, judiciary, and legislature. These types of items will therefore be understood in this book as monitoring 'trust in politicians', which is only one component of the regime as a whole.

As discussed by Dalton and Klingemann in subsequent chapters, the book adopts this fivefold classification of political support because factor analysis strongly suggests that the public makes these distinctions, and there are divergent trends over time in support for different levels. One reason for the confusion in the literature between those who see a pattern of declining confidence in established democracies and others who see only trendless fluctuations is the reliance on different indicators relating to different levels of support. It is rational and consistent, for example, for citizens to believe in democratic values but to remain critical about the way democratic governments actually work in practice, or to have confidence in political institutions but no faith in politicians, or to disparage most politicians but to continue to support a particular leader, or to trust each other but not elected officials. Evidence in subsequent chapters suggests that political support is not all of one piece. If the public can and does distinguish between different objects of support, our analysis needs to be aware of these distinctions.

Sources of Comparative Survey Data

The conceptual framework is critical but to move beyond this towards empirical analysis we need suitable sources of data. In developing societies until recently, in the absence of systematic surveys of public opinion, the importance of cultural factors has traditionally been examined by tracing the influence of particular religious traditions or historical experiences gauged at the national or macro level. It has commonly been found, for example, that post-colonial states which experienced Anglo-American rule were more likely to prove stable democracies than those once colonized by France, Portugal, the Netherlands, Spain, or Belgium (Hadenius 1994; Lipset 1993). Other work on political culture in developing societies has commonly been more interpretative and qualitative (Diamond 1994). Only in recent years have we started to develop more systematic data comparing public opinion at individual level across newer democracies.

Much of this work has focused on understanding the dynamics of public opinion in Central and Eastern Europe and the political culture in the former Soviet Union (Finifter and Mickiewicz 1992; Gibson, Duch, and Tedin 1992; Duch 1993; Miller and Gronbeck 1994; Evans and Whitefield 1995; White, Rose, and McAllister 1997; Rose, Mischler and Haerpfer 1998; Mishler and Rose 1995a; Mishler and Rose 1995b). But a growing literature in the last few years has started to analyse public opinion in other new democracies, for example data in Latin America (Booth and Seligson 1994; Linz and Stephan 1996), South Africa (Gibson 1996, 1997) and Asia (Shin 1998).

In mapping political support in the major regions of the world the book draws on multiple sources of data. Due to an extensive international network of survey researchers we now have access to a wider range of evidence than ever before. Sources of comparative public opinion data include Almond and Verba's path-breaking *Civic Culture* study, a five-nation survey in 1959/60; the Political Action Study carried out in five nations in 1974; *Eurobarometers* conducted twice yearly since 1973 among the expanding universe of member states of the European Union; the International Social Science Programme (ISSP) monitoring social and political attitudes every year since 1985; the *World Values Survey* (WVS) undertaken in 1981–4, 1990–3, and 1995–7; the *Central and Eastern Eurobarometer* started in 1989; the *New Democracies Barometer* operating since 1991; and the *Latinobarometro* started by MORI in 1995. These sources are supplemented by occasional international surveys by major polling companies including Harris, Times-Mirror, MORI, and Gallup. We also draw on national surveys, such as election studies, where there are comparable time-series data. These multiple sources have been produced by an extended network of political scientists, drawing on similar concepts and methods. With regional and worldwide surveys we have started to move from comparing 'countries' and 'regions' to types of political, social, or economic system as the common unit of analysis.

Analysing Time-Series Trends

When understanding time-series data we need care to compare items during similar periods, since different starting or ending dates may be critical for our understanding of causal relationships. For example, if the major decline in confidence in government occurred during the mid- to late 1960s, as suggested by Crozier *et al.* (1975), this could not be tested by examining evidence from the *Eurobarometer Surveys*, which only started in 1973. Careful attention must also be paid to matching measurement periods to our hypotheses about patterns of change. If television is largely to blame for political cynicism, for example, ideally we need to examine survey indicators before this media became well established during the late 1950s in developed societies. Unfortunately in most countries few consistent items stretch back to surveys before the 1970s. The first items on political trust, for example, were asked in 1948 in West Germany, in 1958 in the United States and in 1968 in Sweden, but only later in many established democracies. Despite the richness of recent cross-national data-sets, much survey evidence in newer democracies only started in the 1990s.

In assessing trends over time, multiple indicators are better than single ones but often we have only two or three observation points. If so, we need to consider whether the observations occurred during 'typical' periods. Evidence from national election studies, for example, may monitor higher levels of political efficacy than periods of normal politics. Many chapters analysing causal explanations rely upon the second wave of the *World Values Survey*, conducted in 1990–3, but we need to note that this was a time of major transition in many newer democracies. The focus on more recent evidence is critical for understanding trends, using the third wave of the *World Values Survey* conducted in 1995–7, because the last decade provides important insights into the process of democratic transition and consolidation.

In time-series analysis where we have more regular measurements we need to distinguish between alternative patterns. Often studies search for linear secular trends, which show a consistent and steady decline in support over successive periods. But we need to be open to alternative patterns over time including 'stepped' or period-specific shifts, cyclical waves of ebb and flow in support, and trendless fluctuations around the mean. Each of these may offer different interpretations.

The Selection of Countries

The selection of countries is also critical for systematic comparison. We have now accumulated a rich body of comparable survey evidence in established democracies in North America and Western Europe. But even with the World Values Study consistent evidence globally remains limited. We lack systematic cross-national data for many countries in Africa, the Middle East, and South Asia, in part because surveys often follow, rather than precede, the process of democratization. Nevertheless this book contains some of the broadest evidence which has recently become available. Drawing on the *World Values Survey*, Hans-Dieter Klingemann (Chapter 2) provides a wide-ranging comparison of attitudes towards democracy in many countries world-wide. Subsequent chapters go on to compare public opinion across advanced industrialized societies (Dalton) and in seven newer democracies in Central and Eastern Europe (Mishler and Rose). Contributors have also focused in depth on selected case-studies chosen to illustrate different facets of the issues under consideration, including Sweden (Holmberg) as a smaller, affluent welfare state where there has been growing disengagement with government, South Korea (Rose, Shin, and Munro) as an East Asian society in the throes of the democratization process, and Germany (Fuchs) as a single country deeply divided by its recent historical traditions between East and West. The advantages of the case-study approach is that chapters can look at a single nation, or compare subcultures within countries, to provide a richer and more detailed understanding of public opinion within its specific historical and institutional context.

Measures of Trends in Political Support

Political Community

Turning to the available evidence, we should bear in mind that there is often a significant gap between our concepts and measures. Contributors are dependent upon the available survey items, which were often designed for different analytical purposes than those we most want to tap. Nevertheless a shared consensus about many measures has developed in survey research. Support for the political community is conventionally gauged by indicators of national identity and pride. The latter is measured in the *World Values Survey* by the following item: '*How proud are you to be (British/American/German, etc.)? Very proud, quite proud, not very proud or not at all proud?*'

Many long-established nation-states such as Canada, Belgium, Italy, and Britain are believed to be under threat in the late twentieth century, threatened by global and international forces on the one hand and by the fissions of regional and/or linguistic political identities on the other. Yet evidence in this book suggests that in the mid-1990s indicators of national pride remained relatively high with no consistent secular decline across nations. Drawing on the mid-1990s *World Values Survey*, Klingemann demonstrated that more than three-quarters of all citizens expressed pride in their country in 17 out of the 24 nations under comparison. Those who proved 'very' or 'quite' proud of their country ranged from a low of West Germany (57 per cent) and Japan (62 per cent) up to a remarkable 98 per cent of all citizens in the United States (Klingemann, Table 2.3). National pride demonstrates considerable fluctuations over time but no secular decline compared with either the early 1980s (Dalton, Figure 3.2 in this volume), or the early 1990s (Klingemann, Table 2.5 in this volume).

An alternative indicator of national support in the *World Values Survey* asks respondents about willingness to volunteer for military service: '*Of course we all hope that there will not be another war, but if it were to come to that, would you be willing to fight for your country?*' Klingemann demonstrates that a high proportion of citizens remained 'willing to fight for their country', with Germany and Japan, with their historical legacies, again at the bottom of the league (Klingemann, Table 2.6). This evidence suggests that in the countries under comparison there has been no consistent decline over time in support for the political community at national level.

Regime Principles

Studies also tapped support for the overall values and principles of democracy. This provides insights into the perceived moral legitimacy of the government—i.e. whether it is seen as authorized to exercise power—which is usually regarded as essential for long-term political stability. Public opinion surveys have commonly measured support for democratic values by gauging agreement with the idea of democracy, approval of democracy as the *'best form of government'* and as *'a good way of governing'*, and preference for democratic over authoritarian regimes.

Evidence presented by Klingemann (Table 2.7) demonstrates that by the mid-1990s democracy as an ideal form of government was supported by the overwhelming majority of the public in nearly all countries (with the exception of Russia where it was supported by only a bare majority). Based on *Eurobarometer* data, Dalton (Table 3.5) also confirms overwhelming and widespread approval of the idea of democracy (over 90 per cent), and positive attitudes towards democracy as the best form of government, throughout Western Europe. In the mid-1990s democratic values were also supported by the majority of citizens throughout Latin America, although with some variations between the most positive countries including Argentina and Uruguay, and the less positive such as Brazil and Chile (Klingemann, Table 2.7). Lastly Rose *et al.* asked citizens in South Korea to indicate their views of democracy as an ideal and in reality. Using a 10-point scale ranging from complete dictatorship (1) to complete democracy (10), respondents were asked *'Where would you place the extent to which you personally desire democracy for our country?'* and *'Where would you place our country at the present time?'*. The results (Chapter 7, this volume) demonstrate the tensions between ideal and reality: people thought the government in power was less democratic than their aspirations. South Koreans demonstrated overwhelming support for democracy as an ideal but serious doubts about how far their government met this ideal.

This body of evidence suggests there are few grounds for concern about the widespread adherence to the principle of democratic values, measured at this abstract level, in the countries under comparison. By the mid-1990s democracy has come to be widely regarded as the ideal form of government in the countries where we have evidence in Western and Eastern Europe, North and South America, and Asia. If not the 'end of history' this seems to represent the triumph of liberal democracy against any ideological alternative form of government. Yet we need to register two important qualifications to these observations: we lack equivalent survey data in large parts of the world with authoritarian regimes, such as many countries in the Middle East, Africa, and East Asia. Moreover, abstract approval of the broad ideals and principles of democracy may be rooted in shallow support for particular aspects, like tolerance of dissenting views or minority rights (McClosky and Brill 1983; McClosky and Zaller 1994). As well as broadening our cross-national comparison, in subsequent surveys we need to go much further to deepen our analysis of what people understand by the principles and values of democracy.

Regime Performance

The chapters in this book also tap evaluations of the way the regime works, and particularly satisfaction with the way the democratic process functions in practice. The evidence for South Korea presented in Chapter 7, which we have already discussed, confirms the pattern found in previous studies in Central and Eastern Europe where there remains a marked gap between evaluations of the ideal and the practice of democracy (Evans and Whitefield 1995). In Western Europe, where we have the longest time-series data in the *Eurobarometer*, studies have relied upon the standard question: '*Are you very satisfied, fairly satisfied, not very satisfied or not at all satisfied with the way democracy is functioning (in your country)?*'. This measure has been extensively analysed and Fuchs (1995) demonstrated that satisfaction with the working of democracy, monitored regularly by this item since 1973, shows a pattern of trendless fluctuations over time. Nevertheless there are persistent cross-national differences within Western Europe, with the lowest satisfaction commonly expressed in Italy and Greece contrasted with the most positive responses recorded in Denmark and Norway (Klingemann Table, 2.11). In the *Latinobarometro*, using the same item, Klingemann found that in the mid-1990s two-thirds or more of citizens in Latin America were dissatisfied with regime performance, with public opinion particularly critical in Mexico, Colombia, and Brazil (Table 2.9).

In Chapter 4 of this volume Mishler and Rose use an alternative measure in the *New Democracy Barometer* in Central and Eastern Europe (1991–6) making a direct comparison between newer and older regimes without reference to democracy per se: '*Here is a scale for ranking governments: the top, +100, is the best, and the bottom, −100, the worst. Where would you put (a) the former Communist regime; (b) the present system with free elections and many parties; (c) our system of governing in five years time?*' This is designed to avoid idealistic evaluations of principles, and measures past and current regimes on a common metric. The results demonstrate that during the 1990s the emerging democracies in Central and Eastern Europe have experienced a modest rise in support for the new regimes compared with their communist predecessors (Mishler and Rose, Figure 4.1). Nevertheless this pattern does vary among different countries and support for current regimes remains far stronger in the Czech Republic and Poland than in Hungary and Slovakia.

An alternative perspective is provided by Fuchs in Chapter 6 of this volume which compares support for the system of government in the unified Germany. He found that Germans in East and West shared similar normative conceptions of the meaning of democracy: both emphasized that democracy required liberal and social rights. Nevertheless citizens in both regions differed sharply in their evaluations of the performance of democracy in the German government. Respondents were asked: '*Do you believe that we in the Federal Republic have the best form of government, or is there a form of government that is better?*' He found a large and persistent gap from 1990 to 1995 in evaluations of the system across both regions: more than 70 per cent of respondents in the West believed that Germany had the best form of government compared with less than 40 per cent in the East. The evidence presented in the first section of this book therefore strongly suggests that patterns of satisfaction with the performance of democracy varies substantially cross-nationally and that in general this shows no clear decline over time. One plausible explanation to account for variations between countries, explored in subsequent chapters, is that these evaluations reflect different experiences of governments in transitional, consolidating and established democracies.

Regime Institutions

Chapters have also compared support for the core institutions of the state, along with attachment to political parties as one of the key linkages between citizens and the state. We can draw a distinction between 'public' institutions, including parliaments, the civil service, the judiciary, the legal system, the armed forces, and the police, and 'private' institutions like trade unions and companies, although the precise boundary varies between different systems (for example, whether the church is established or disestablished, whether companies are nationalized or private). This book focuses on the central institutions of government, with private institutions providing a point of comparison. The institutional focus looks at the formal structures, not the specific incumbents or office-holders. It emphasizes evaluations of the office of the presidency, parliament, and politicians/MPs in general, for example, not the performance of particular leaders or representatives. Studies have commonly confirmed a significant gap between trust in institutions like the US Congress and trust in particular members (Parker and Parker 1993).

The most striking finding to emerge from this comparison, and the most convincing evidence supporting the malaise thesis, is the declining support for public institutions demonstrated in many of the chapters. The *World Values Survey* can be used to compare attitudes towards authority, based on approval or disapproval of the statement '*More respect for authority would be a good thing*'. Comparing the *World Values Survey* in 1981 and 1997, Inglehart found that respect for authority declined in 28 out of the 36 countries for which we have time-series data. He argues that this shift in values is associated with a broader pattern of declining respect for authoritarian and hierarchical institutions. The *World Values Survey* shows that from 1981 to 1997 two-thirds or more of the countries under comparison experienced declining confidence in the armed forces and police, and this fall was especially strong among postmaterialists. The *Latinobarometro* compared public opinion in 17 countries in Latin America and found that in the mid-1990s on average only a fifth of the public expressed '*a lot*' or '*some*' confidence in political parties, and less than a third reported confidence in the national parliament, civil service, government, police or judiciary (Lagos 1997). Among the more affluent OECD countries Ian McAllister (Chapter 9 this volume) also noted a modest decline from 1981 to 1991 in public confidence towards parliament and the civil service. In Chapter 11 of this volume Norris confirmed this pattern based on a combined index of institutional support, including confidence in parliament, the civil service, the police, army, and legal system, using the *World Values Surveys*. Confidence in this combined institutional index declined from 1981 to 1991 across all 17 countries with time-series data, although the fall was sharpest in South Korea, Argentina, and Finland.

Much previous work has compared support for political parties, associated with theories of de-alignment (Dalton *et al.* 1984; Crewe and Denver 1985; Franklin *et al.* 1992; Schmitt and Holmberg 1995; Norris 1997*a*). There is a long-standing debate about whether trends in partisan identification signify party decline or evolution (Mair 1997). In this book Russell Dalton (Table 3.2) provides the most detailed long-term evidence of the proportion of people with a party identification, especially strong identifiers, across 18 nations. Dalton confirmed declining party attachments across nearly all advanced industrialized societies, although the exact timing and strength of the decline varied between nations.

Finally, in Chapter 2 of this volume Klingemann demonstrates a remarkable degree of cross-national variation in evaluations of the performance of the governmental system, parliament, and confidence in government, with highly negative responses in most countries in Central and Eastern Europe (with particularly critical responses in Russia, the Ukraine, and Belarus) as well as in Latin America. The first part of this book indicates that support for public institutions, notably for parliaments and parties, does seem to have fallen during the 1980s in many, though not all, established democracies. Moreover, levels of support for the institutions of representative democracy seem low in many newer democracies. Although the problem should not be exaggerated, given the limited evidence of time-series trends, if we had to specify the most important concern about support for government, the cross-national evidence points towards this institutional level.

Political Actors

Lastly studies have focused on support for political actors (or 'authorities'). This is most commonly measured by generalized trust for politicians and public officials, and by evaluations of the performance of particular presidents, prime ministers, party leaders and representatives monitored in regular opinion polls. In Chapter 3 of this volume Dalton compared the evidence for generalized trust in politicians and government, where NES items are replicated in national election studies and similar mass surveys. The standard NES items on trust in politicians provide the longest time-series available but they do not necessarily translate well into other contexts, their meaning is open to different interpretations, and alternative indicators have been used elsewhere, so the comparative time-series analysis remains limited across countries.

Nevertheless as Dalton shows (Table 3.3), the disenchantment with politicians in the United States seems to be reflected in trends in Sweden and Canada, although there is a mixed pattern elsewhere. This pattern was confirmed by Sören Holmberg (Figure 5.1) who looked in more detail at trends in the smaller welfare-states in Scandinavia and the Netherlands. He found that Sweden is the only country in the comparison which has experienced a steady long-term decline in trust for politicians similar to that found in the United States: 'Generalized political trust has been plummeting more or less constantly for the last thirty years in Sweden' (Holmberg, Chapter 5, this volume). In contrast trust in politicians has actually increased in the Netherlands, and remained stable in Norway and Denmark. This evidence suggests that generalized trust in politicians varies substantially across nations, although the comparative evidence remains patchy.

From the available evidence the mapping exercise in the first part of the book suggests the broad picture outlined in Figure 1.2. The general diagnosis from Part I therefore confirms that there has been an erosion of public support for the core institutions of representative government, including parties and parliaments, in recent decades. Yet this is insufficient, by itself, to support the crisis of democracy thesis. The public's evaluations of how regimes function varied substantially between newer and established democracies. Moreover there was little systematic evidence for a long-term crisis in support for democratic principles or for the nation-state. Democratic values now command widespread acceptance as an ideal, but at the same time citizens have often become more critical of the workings of the core institutions of representative democracy.

Explaining the Dynamics of Political Support

If this represents a broad consensus about the diagnosis of the problem, how do we explain this pattern? Why should confidence in government and democratic institutions vary cross-nationally? The *Visions of Governance* project developed a series of alternative hypotheses (Nye *et al.* 1997) which can be tested through cross-national comparisons. Subsequent chapters analyse the most plausible explanations for the decline in institutional support including the impact of social trust, government performance, institutional designs, and shifts in cultural values.

Declining Social Trust and Civic Engagement?

In recent years there has been increased interest in theories of social capital. The work of Robert Putnam, in particular, has re-emphasized the importance of social trust for civic engagement, in Italy (Putnam 1994) and the United States (Putnam 1995a, 1995b). This theory suggests that in recent decades there have been significant changes in patterns of social interaction in the United States, as face-to-face activities within the local community have been falling. Many activities common in the 1950s have been in steady decline, whether in terms of local political activities (going to PTAs, attending political meetings, helping candidates), working with neighbours on local issues, joining social clubs and leisure societies, and even entertaining friends and family at home. Many factors have contributed towards these developments, including generational shifts and patterns of women's employment. But it is the possible consequences which we will address. These changes in lifestyles, Putnam argues, have led to a steady secular decline in social trust with important consequences for civic engagement and for good government.

To reconsider these issues Kenneth Newton (Chapter 8, this volume) examines the nature of the relationship between social and political trust, and in particular whether theories of social capital help explain declining support for governmental institutions and generalized political trust in established democracies. The chapter discusses the conceptual meaning of social trust and considers the available survey evidence in Europe. Newton concludes that there is not a close or consistent association between social and political trust, nor between social trust and political behaviour, nor between activity in voluntary associations (civic engagement) and political attitudes and behaviour. In short, Newton dashes cold water on social-capital theory and stresses that political trust seems to be more a product of political rather than social factors.

Political Explanations: The Failure of Government Performance?

As discussed earlier, one of the most common perspectives draws on the 'crisis of government' literature of the 1970s (Crozier *et al.* 1975) and locates the primary explanation in terms of relative expectations of government compared with its actual performance (Lawrence 1997; Bok 1997). In this view the heart of the problem lies in increasing expectations of government due to the expanded role of the state in the post-war period and new demands by citizens, and the inability of government to meet these expectations given the globalization of the economy, problems of government overload, and hence the 'crisis of the state'. Studies in political economy have argued that regime support is influenced by public evaluations of government performance (Weil 1989; Weatherford 1984, 1987, 1992; Clarke, Dutt, and Kornberg 1993; Lockerbie 1993; Anderson 1995; Weisberg 1996). Although there is a growing body of literature, much of this concentrated on the United States, studies often use a limited time-period, and there is no consensus about the most appropriate way to compare government performance on a consistent and meaningful basis.

To explore these issues further, in Chapter 9 of this volume Ian McAllister considers the evidence for performance-based explanations. The study focuses on confidence in political institutions (parliament and the civil service) in advanced industrialized societies, comparing the universe of 24 OECD countries. McAllister first analysed the macro-level impact on institutional confidence of alternative objective indicators of economic and social policy outputs, such as levels of adjusted GDP, life expectancy, education, and unemployment. He then went on to examine the influence of the social and economic factors on institutional confidence at individual-level. McAllister concluded that there was a modest yet consistent relationship between support for political institutions and subjective economic satisfaction, but institutional support seemed unaffected by objective indicators of economic performance. Overall the impact of the political economy on institutional confidence proved more limited than the influence of deep-rooted cultural values, especially the length of time which a country had been democratic.

For another perspective on this issue Arthur Miller and Ola Listhaug (Chapter 10, this volume) set out to compare the relationship between institutional confidence and the economic performance of governments. The study first examines the direct link between government performance, as measured by objective indicators of inflation, unemployment and government deficits, and institutional confidence in two dozen countries. Miller and Listhaug conclude that institutional confidence is not influenced by either recent levels of inflation and unemployment or recent changes in those conditions. The only measure of economic performance which did seem to be correlated with institutional confidence concerns the size of the government deficit as a percentage of GDP. Miller and Listhaug go on to examine expectations of government and the dynamics of institutional confidence in three countries with suitable time-series data: Norway, Sweden, and the United States. The study concludes that failure of economic performance is one factor which does undermine trust in government although changes in citizen's expectations about government also play a role.

Institutional Explanations: The Failure of Constitutional Design?

Another body of literature has suggested that we may have been experiencing a growing 'democratic deficit' as significant changes in the political process may have widened the gap between citizens and the state. In particular the linkages between representative elites and public opinion—provided by the intermediary institutions of political parties, interests groups, and parliament—may have weakened over time (Hayward 1995, 1996). Both Holmberg and Dalton stress that the role of parties may be regarded as particularly critical linkage mechanisms, especially in theories of responsible party government. The most plausible explanations here focus on the lack of accountability of political leaders in countries with either predominant one-party governments, or semi-permanent coalitions, or divided governments. Under such systems it is extremely difficult for citizens to use elections as an opportunity to 'kick the rascals out', if dissatisfied with government performance (Powell 1989). Other factors hindering accountability may include the professionalization of legislatures and low levels of incumbency turnover, insulating politicians from electoral defeat (Norris 1997b). The increasing globalization of governance, and the weakening independence of the nation-state, may also reduce the ability of citizens to use party choice in national elections as a mechanism to determine public policy. The lack of minor 'protest parties', especially those on the right, may fail to provide a channel for disaffected voters (Miller and Listhaug 1990). Some, or all, of these factors may have made governments, and legislators, increasingly unaccountable and unresponsive to public opinion, and therefore may have increased disillusionment with government performance.

In Chapter 11 of this volume Norris examines institutional explanations for system support, in particular whether certain sorts of constitutional arrangements generate stronger levels of institutional confidence. The study compared countries in terms of their political rights and civil liberties, executive–legislative relations, party systems, state structures and electoral systems, and the winners and losers from the system. Since institutions are largely stable phenomenon, the most effective research design to test this thesis requires comparison across a wide range of different types of political systems, rather than a comparison of trends over time. The study found that winners who backed the party in government expressed significantly more institutional confidence than losers. Institutional support also tended to be higher in states characterized by a wide range of political rights and civil liberties, as well as 'Westminster' rather than consociational democracies. The chapter concludes by considering the implications for issues of constitutional design in newer democracies.

Cultural Explanations: Modernization and Changing Values?

Lastly cultural explanations, notably Inglehart's theory of post-materialism (Inglehart 1977, 1990, 1997a), suggest that value change in post-industrial societies has encouraged the development of more critical citizens who question traditional sources of authority, including government. During the post-war decades, Inglehart argues, post-industrial societies have gradually experienced a major shift in their basic values. The growth of post-materialist values among the younger generation has been marked by a gradual decline in support for traditional sources of political authority, including representative government, and established, hierarchical institutions such as the army, police, and church (Inglehart 1997a). Moreover, Inglehart suggests, modern societies have seen a slump in conventional forms of political participation, such as membership in political parties and voting turnout. Older forms of representative democracy have declined but at the same time Inglehart finds an increase in new forms of self-expression and political participation, such as activism in social movements. If so, trends in confidence in government should be closely related to the process of modernization.

Post-materialist theory emphasizes that the modernization process has undermined support for traditional, hierarchical institutions and authoritarian values, producing a crisis of confidence in government, but this should not be understood as a crisis of confidence in democracy per se. Rather, Inglehart argues that this signifies the growth of post-material values among the younger generation, with increased demands for new forms of political engagement via new social movements and direct action, to replace the older channels of participation via parties and interest groups. The implications of generational value change is that, if correct, the erosion of faith in government is a process which is difficult, if not impossible, to reverse. There may be certain fluctuations due to 'period effects', for example blips upwards or downwards following eras of economic boom or bust, but the general trend should be a slow but steady secular erosion of faith, in government as in God.

Interpreting the Consequences

While we have established a broad consensus about trends in system support, and some clarification of the major explanations, there is little agreement about their consequences. As Easton pointed out (1965) the implications of any erosion of support may vary depending upon the level. As discussed in the conclusion, support for specific political leaders, for elected representatives in parliaments, for particular parties and for governments in office, can be expected to ebb and flow as part of the normal process of democratic politics. At regular intervals, so long as representatives and parties in office are not insulated from defeat, dissatisfied citizens can use elections as the safety-valve in the system to 'throw the rascals out'. Anger or disaffection with government may spur civic engagement as much as disengagement. Of course elections may fail to function as an effective safety-valve under certain conditions: in party systems with predominant parties in government for decades such as (until recently) the position of the Japanese LDP or Italian Christian Democrats; where there are semi-permanent coalition partners in government, such as in Switzerland; or where incumbent representatives are insulated from high turnover, as in the US Congress (Powell 1989). In these systems, without an outlet, public disaffection may strengthen and accumulate.

More significant systemic effects can be expected if there is growing disillusionment with the performance of the major civic institutions in representative government, including parliaments, the legal system, parties and the civil service. Citizens may become disaffected with the political system if they feel that the courts are untrustworthy, elected representatives pay them no heed, and the administrative process is rife with corruption and clientalism (Gamson 1968; Miller and Borrelli 1991). A steady drumbeat of criticism, such as an onslaught of Congress-bashing or a presidential media feeding frenzy due to accusations of sexual or financial ethical violations, may drain the 'reservoir of public good will' over the long haul. If enough popular disaffection accumulates this may help to generate major constitutional changes, particularly if public opinion can be expressed through channels like referendums, as with the electoral reforms introduced in the recent years in New Zealand and Italy (Norris 1995), or the term limits movement in the US (Craig 1993). There may be more systemic effects on the regime: Harmel and Robertson found a significant association between levels of satisfaction with democratic processes and cabinet stability in Western Europe (1986). If popular pressures lead to institutional reforms this can be understood as a demand-side process which helps resolve tensions between democratic ideals and reality (see Chapter 7, this volume).

The consequences for the political system may be even more serious if citizens do not adhere to the basic principles and values of the regime, like tolerance of minorities, since then there is no consensus about the rules of the game. Nevertheless as Rose argues (1997) because democracy is a symbol, approval of democracy as 'the best form of government' in the abstract may tell us little unless we probe further to understand what people understand by this statement (Simon 1996; Thomassen 1995).

Lastly, if there are deep divisions about the national identity of the political community—if there is no agreement about the boundaries of the state and deep ethnic, religious, or regional/linguistic conflict—then ultimately this can have serious consequences (Taras and Ganguly 1998). This can result in a renegotiation of the constitutional settlement such as in the UK and Canada, incidents of violent terrorism by breakaway groups like the Basque separatists, persistent and bloody civil wars such as those in Northern Ireland, Somalia, and Bosnia, or even in the breakdown of the nation-state and regional succession such as the velvet revolution experienced by the former Czechoslovakia.

Conclusions

Close reading of the available evidence in many countries around the world provides convincing evidence for certain core contentions. These assertions are sketched in bare-boned fashion here and the supporting evidence will be argued, developed, and qualified throughout this book.

The first is that political support is not all of one piece and to make progress we need to disentangle its different components and objects. The argument in this book is that we need to distinguish between support for the community, regime principles, regime performance, regime institutions, and political actors. We have considerably more evidence about some levels than others but the evidence in this book strongly suggests that the public makes clear distinctions between these objects, and so should we.

The second claim flows from the first, namely that in established democracies, during the last decades of the twentieth century, growing numbers of citizens have become increasingly critical of the major institutions of representative government. The evidence presented by different contributors to this volume suggests that in most countries support for the community and for democratic principles remains overwhelming. Evaluations of regime performance, and trust in politicians, varies substantially from one country to another. But public support for the core institutions of representative government—including parties, parliaments, and governments—has fallen in many, but not all, established and newer democracies. Moreover, in newer democracies support for the current regime and for representative institutions often remains remarkably shallow, which may create serious problems for the stability of these systems during the consolidation process.

Lastly, while there is broad agreement among the book's contributors about these patterns, and some common ground concerning their explanation, nevertheless as we shall see considerable controversy remains concerning the interpretation of their consequences. In many countries during recent years political support has eroded most sharply and consistently for government institutions, but not for democratic values and principles. Moreover, in many emerging and transitional democracies, as well as in some established democracies, citizens are highly critical in their evaluations of how well regimes work. There is growing tension between ideals and reality. This may have produced the emergence of more 'critical citizens' or perhaps 'disenchanted democrats'.

As discussed further in the conclusion these results are open to at least two alternative interpretations. If 'the fish rots from the head' then the erosion of support for the core institutions of representative government may be seen as a worrying development which may gradually undermine faith in democratic values. If people cannot trust parliaments, public officials, parties or the police, and the regime performs poorly, then they may come in time to be disillusioned with democracy as an ideal. This may have serious consequences since public adherence to democratic values is usually regarded as a necessary, but not sufficient, condition for the long-term stability of democracies, to tide regimes over bad times.

Alternatively these trends may prove a more positive development which will ultimately strengthen democratic government if this signifies the growth of more critical citizens who are dissatisfied with established authorities and traditional hierarchical institutions, who feel that existing channels for participation fall short of democratic ideals, and who want to improve and reform the institutional mechanisms of representative democracy. Criticism does not necessarily imply disengagement. It can mean the reverse. We need to explore further the consequences of this development. It is too easy to link trends like the decline of trust in America with the fall in turnout, without seeing whether these phenomena are actually causally connected. Established democratic regimes, and core institutions like parties and parliaments, may be adopting and evolving to meet new challenges, not declining. In newer democracies dissatisfaction with the performance of regimes characterized by widespread corruption, abuse of power and intolerance of dissent, can be regarded as a healthy reaction. Too much blind trust by citizens and misplaced confidence in leaders, for good or ill, can be as problematic for democracy as too little. The consequences of declining support for government institutions therefore remains open to debate. The conclusion considers the implications of this analysis for public policy reforms, for strengthening transitional and consolidating democracies, and for new channels of public participation in governance.

PART I

Cross-national Trends in Confidence in Governance

2

Mapping Political Support in the 1990s: A Global Analysis

HANS-DIETER KLINGEMANN

OVER the past quarter-century, an unprecedented and often unantici-
pated wave of democratization has spread over large parts of the world.
While some scepticism is reasonable regarding both the level and durability of
many of the new experiments within the 'third wave' of democratization
(Huntington 1991), the direction and scope of these developments are largely
beyond dispute. One need not adhere to the premiss that this movement is an
inevitable endpoint (Fukuyama 1991) in human governance in order, none
the less, to acknowledge the current historical reality. The breadth and depth
of the trend need not, however, carry with it the presumption of permanence.
The previous two waves of democratization over the past century were followed by considerable backsliding. Evidence of similar retrogression is evident
within the third wave. Some countries, such as Nigeria, have been participants
in both the second and the third wave, and have already fallen back. Others,
such as Turkey and various Latin American cases, continue to struggle with an
apparently tenuous grasp on the climb to status as stable democracies. Most
democratic theorists would argue that the success or failure of such experiments is in large part a function of the support built among the citizenry, support that lends *legitimacy* to the regime. It is further asserted that legitimacy is
heavily influenced by, or almost a function of, the *performance* of the regime
(Lipset 1959, 1993, 1994).

The main goal of this chapter is to use an extensive body of comparative survey research to map patterns and forms of political support across a wide range
of political conditions. While the goal is primarily descriptive, at least two
interesting themes emerge. First, there are no major trends suggesting a
decline in support for democracy as a form of government in the abstract or
as applied to existing democratic experience. Certainly, there is no evidence of
a crisis of democracy (see Klingemann and Fuchs 1995; in contrast, see
Crozier, Huntington, and Watanuki 1975). There are, to be sure, citizens of

Richard I. Hofferbert has helped to cut and substantially rewrite an earlier draft of this chapter. I
want to gratefully acknowledge his generous help.

established and of fledgling democracies who express considerable dissatisfaction with the performance of their regimes. But—and this is the second theme that emerges from this chapter—the fact of dissatisfaction does not imply danger to the persistence or furtherance of democracy. A significant number of people spread around the world can be labelled 'dissatisfied democrats'. They clearly approve of democracy as a mode of governance, but they are discontented with the way their own system is currently operating. The dissatisfied democrats can be viewed as less a threat to, than a force for, reform and improvement of democratic processes and structures as the third wave continues to flow.

Since the beginning of the 1990s an unprecedented number of countries have implemented some variant of a democratic political structure. However, while formal institutions of representative democracy are in place, their likely persistence is subject to dispute. This is true for both the old and the newly established democratic regimes. As discussed in the introduction, during the 1960s and mid-1970s crisis theories dominated the debate. Fuchs and Klingemann (1995) reviewed and evaluated major hypotheses on why public support for democratic politics may be eroding. The *Beliefs in Government* project did not find much empirical evidence in the Western European countries in the 1970s and 1980s for any of the crisis theories. Overall, citizens of EU states had not withdrawn support for their democracies. Crisis theorists seemed to have underestimated the adaptive capacities of these countries' democratic institutions. In possible contrast, however, the newer democracies, and especially those in Central and Eastern Europe, are suffering stress because they have to cope with simultaneous political and economic transformations. Under these circumstances, arguments that predict a return to authoritarian rule or anarchy command some plausibility (for example, Ekiert 1991). Despite this, empirical analyses (especially those reported by Mishler and Rose 1994, 1996, 1997; Rose and Mishler 1996) demonstrate that citizens of Central and Eastern European countries are prepared to face that double challenge. At least they do not want to give up their newly established democratic structures or return to the old regime. Mishler and Rose (1997: 447) summarize the results of their most recent survey analysis as follows: 'There is little basis in this analysis to fear that the collapse of democracy is imminent or that a return to authoritarianism is inevitable. To the contrary, as long as the new democracies of Central and Eastern Europe protect the individual liberties that citizens so highly value, scepticism is unlikely to degenerate into distrust.'

Most scholars agree that the survival of democracies rests on a broad and deep foundation of support among the citizenry. Democracies lacking such a foundation of legitimacy are at risk. Political systems, and in particular democracies, that are ineffective in meeting public expectations over long periods of time can lose their legitimacy, with consequent danger to the regime. As broad theoretical assertions, at a high level of abstraction, this chain of reasoning is largely accepted by systems analysts and democratic theorists alike. But operationalization and measurement of concepts, as well as sufficient historical and comparative data to test the key linkages, have proved largely elusive. Political and academic developments in the late twentieth century have provided an opportunity to begin remedying these shortcomings.

This chapter exploits the impressive resources of the *World Values Surveys* to map certain key elements of political support among the mass publics in established, experimental, and would-be democracies. Specifically, this chapter develops indices fitted reasonably well to three forms of support: support for the political community; for regime principles or democracy as an ideal form of government; and approval of the regime's performance. Support along these three dimensions is examined by means of comparable national surveys.

The argument here is that ordinary people can differentiate between different objects of support—between the political community, the desirability of a democratic regime, and actual performance of the regime. Further, they can be critical of how well the regime functions without necessarily concluding that the democratic form of government needs to be abandoned as an ideal. Dissatisfaction with the regime's effectiveness does not necessarily translate into the delegitimation of democracy.

The Concept of Political Support

Scholarly insistence on the need for congruence between the form of governing institutions, on the one hand, and political culture, on the other, can be traced in an unending stream back at least to Aristotle. Among modern democratic theorists, the concept of political support and its component elements is most commonly discussed with reference to the work of David Easton. As discussed in the Introduction, Easton distinguishes between the *objects* of support and the *types* of support. Within objects, he distinguishes support for the political community, the regime, and the incumbent authorities.

The political community is the cultural entity that transcends particularities of formal governing structures and enscribes the elemental identity of the collectivity constituting the polity. The regime is constituted of those principles, processes, and formal institutions that persist and transcend particular incumbents. And the political authorities are those officials occupying governmental posts at a particular time. Thus a citizen might have adhered strongly to her or his status as a member of the Soviet Union as a political community without necessarily holding to the particular institutions of that political regime or even to the particular territorial definition of the polity. However, when a self-definition, such as 'Russian' takes precedence over an alternative attitude object, such as 'Soviet', then the definition of political community is likewise different. One can also identify with the political community and still advocate a substantially different regime. A Pole, strongly identified with the Polish political community may none the less have been an ardent member of *Solidarity* and thus sought to depose the pre-1989 regime. And, finally, one could well accept the current Polish regime but campaign vigorously for the electoral victory of the opposition.

Data from the *World Values Surveys* allow for measurement of these forms of political support, namely: identification with the political community, as well as the legitimacy of democratic principles, and the effectiveness of the regime performance. These attitudinal constellations can be mapped across countries by geographic regions, by the age and level of democracy, and by the general level of economic development. Mapping these components is a significant start toward comparative understanding of the breadth and forms of political support across the world of established, fledgling, and would-be democracies near the turn of the millennium.

Surveys, Timepoints, and Indicators

Today, in many countries, the attitudes of citizens are monitored routinely but comparable data across countries and time are not easily available. Such efforts as the International Social Survey Programme (ISSP) and of the *New Democracies Barometer* (NDB), sponsored by the Austrian Paul Lazarsfeld Society, have done a lot to improve the situation.

This study relies mainly on the *World Values Surveys* (WVS).[1] This study, co-ordinated by Ronald Inglehart, is still the only comparative survey project that, in principle, aims at global coverage.[2] Surveys during the mid-1990s from the *World Values Surveys*, appropriate for measuring the relevant aspects of political support, were available for 39 states. They include countries in North and Central America (4), South America (6), Australia (1), Asia (5), Africa (2), Western Europe (8) and Eastern Europe (13).[3] In addition, differing levels of political support in the mid-1990s can be compared to those at the beginning of the 1990s in 25 countries. Since not all of the indicators selected for analysis are available in every survey, the exact number of countries on which specific analyses are based are reported for each table. In addition to the *World Values Surveys*, the chapter also draws on three regional comparative surveys monitoring satisfaction with the democratic process, an important indicator of regime performance.[4] Based on these sources, in total 87 surveys are avail-

---

[1] Data collection in the former republics of the Soviet Union and in West and East Germany has been supported by a grant from the VW Foundation.

[2] For the first major analyses of the early waves of the *World Values Survey*, see Ronald Inglehart (1977, 1990, 1997a).

[3] For our purposes, West and East Germany were analysed separately and counted as two cases.

[4] These are (1) the *1996 Latinobarometer Survey* co-ordinated by Marta Lagos which covers 11 countries; (2) the West European *1995 Eurobarometer Survey* carried out on behalf of the European Commission which together with an associated Norwegian survey comprises 18 countries (Great Britain and Northern Ireland as well as West and East Germany counting as separate cases); and (3) the *1996 Central and Eastern Eurobarometer Surveys* (19 countries) also sponsored on a regular basis by the European Commission. Cross-time comparisons for the performance indicator with the early 1990s are possible for subsets of countries both for the *Western European Eurobarometer Surveys* (15 countries) and the *Central and Eastern Eurobarometer Surveys* (18 countries).

able for 63 countries for the mid-1990s. These countries include about 45 per cent of the world population. Yet, as already noted, limited availability of specific, comparable indicators restricts the number of countries included in different aspects of the analysis.

Large-scale cross-national surveys are, by necessity, co-operative projects. Funding by a single source is virtually impossible to obtain. This implies that indicators which finally enter the questionnaire are a result of much discussion and some compromise or they are, as is the case of the surveys paid for by the European Commission, beyond control by academic researchers. For this reason analysts face problems of secondary analysis. They are obliged to use those indicators that finally entered the questionnaire, even though alternatives might have been preferred. This should be kept in mind when it comes to the choice of indicators for the different types of political support.

The immediate task is to test how far key theoretically posited dimensions of political support can be identified within the available data.

Political Community

Two indicators are available for the measurement of support for political community:

- 'How proud are you to be a [citizen of this country]? (4) Very proud, (3) quite proud, (2) not very proud, (1) not at all proud.'
- 'Of course we all hope that there will not be another war, but if it were to come to that, would you be willing to fight for your country? (1) yes, (0) no.'

Democracy as an Ideal Form of Government

It is basic to my thesis that citizens can compare and evaluate alternative types of regimes, beyond merely assessing the immediate attractiveness of the particular regime under which they are currently living. Thus, inquiry into the attractiveness of *democracy* is possible (assuming authorities allow the research to be conducted) even among populations living under non- or quasi-democratic regimes. In the same sense that people can discriminate between specific incumbent authorities and the regime, so they can discriminate between their current regime and conceivable alternatives. Thus, the respondents in the *World Values Surveys* were asked the following two questions regarding democratic principles:

- '*I am going to describe various types of political systems and ask what you think about each as a way of governing this country. For each would you say it is (4) a very good, (3) a fairly good, (2) a fairly bad, or (1) a very bad way of governing this country?* Having a democratic system.'[5]

[5] The item has been asked in the context of a four-item battery. The additional three items read as follows: 'Having a strong leader who does not have to bother with parliament and elections'; 'Having experts, not government, make decisions according to what they think is best for the country'; 'Having the army rule'.

- *'I am going to read off some things that people sometimes say about a democratic system. Could you please tell me if you (4) agree strongly, (3) agree, (2) disagree, or (1) disagree strongly, after I read each of them?* Democracy may have many problems but it's better than any other form of government.'[6]

These questions tap the extent to which people find democracy as a form of regime attractive. The assumption is that people can distinguish between the moral propriety of the regime and its empirical performance.

Regime Performance

Three questions are used to measure the performance of the regime:

- *'People have different views about the system for governing this country. Here is a scale for rating how well things are going: (1) means very bad and (10) means very good. Where on this scale would you put the political system as it is today?'*
- *'How satisfied are you with how the people now in national office are handling the country's affairs? Would you say you are (4) very satisfied, (3) fairly satisfied, (2) fairly dissatisfied, or (1) very dissatisfied?'*
- *'I am going to name a number of organizations. For each one, could you tell me how much confidence you have in them: is it (4) a great deal of confidence, (3) quite a lot of confidence, (2) not very much confidence, or (1) none at all?'*
  - *The Parliament*
  - *The Government in (Capital City)*

In addition to these questions one widely used indicator for regime performance is available in the three regional surveys mentioned above. The reference object is the quality of the democratic process, that is the constitutional reality in the citizen's country. For the Western European and the Latin American surveys the relevant question reads as follows:

- *'On the whole, are you (4) very satisfied, (3) fairly satisfied, (2) not very satisfied, or (1) not at all satisfied with the way democracy works (in your country)?'*

The question wording is slightly different for the Central and Eastern European surveys:

- *'On the whole, are you (4) very satisfied, (3) fairly satisfied, (2) not very satisfied, or (1) not at all satisfied with the way democracy is developing in (your country)?'*

Despite the difference, these latter two indicators are treated as equivalent because of the specific historical contexts in which they have been used.

---

[6] This item, too, has been asked as part of a four-item battery. These are the additional three items: *'In democracy, the economic system runs badly'*; *'Democracies are indecisive and have too much squabbling'*; *'Democracies aren't any good at maintaining order'*.

The Dimensionality of Political Support

From what has been argued above we would expect dimensional analysis to yield the following three distinct factors:

- Support for political community,
- Support for democracy as a form of government, and
- Evaluation of the current performance of the regime.

The dimensionality is tested by (confirmatory) factor analysis both for the pooled data and for each single country. Table 2.1 shows that the pooled analysis strikingly bears out our expectation. The pattern which was predicted for theoretical reasons is clearly there.[7] This means that the analytically defined distinct types of political support are also kept apart in the minds of the citizens. This is an important finding. It means that one may meaningfully discuss identity with the political community independently of the form of government or its performance. Further, it enables the identification of people who are dissatisfied with the actual performance of the regime but at the same time support democracy as a form of government: 'the dissatisfied democrats'.

Table 2.1. Dimensions of political support

	Political community	Democracy as an ideal form of government	Performance of the regime
Fight for country	.81	–.06	.03
National pride	.71	.12	.15
Democracy: Good way of governing	.02	.83	.10
Democracy Best form of governing	.03	.84	.04
Performance of system	.01	.14	.69
Performance of people in national office	.07	.10	.67
Performance of parliament	.09	.01	.77
Performance of government	.12	–.04	.82
Eigenvalue	1.20	1.46	2.24
% Total variance	15	18	28

Note: Pooled Analysis of *World Values Surveys*, 1994/7 (38 countries) (Rotated Factor Matrix).

---

[7] All eight indicators are available for 37 of the 39 WV-surveys taken in the mid-1990s. Part of the relevant questions are missing in the Chinese and in the South Korean surveys. The single-country analyses confirm the general pattern in 30 out of the 37 cases. The deviant cases are Taiwan, the Philippines, Nigeria, Estonia, Russia, Belarus, and the Ukraine. In 5 out of these 7 cases the

The analyses reported in Table 2.1, thus, clearly confirm that these three dimensions are present and distinct across a multi-country (pooled) set of respondents. Given, however, that the general fit and specific factor loadings vary somewhat from country to country, it is less cumbersome to use the factor analysis to guide the construction of simpler, additive indices.[8] Thus, I have constructed three such indices—one for each of the three concepts.[9]

(1) Support for political community: The variables *'fight for country'* (0/1) and *'national pride'* (recoded 1,2 = 0; 3,4 = 1) are added to form a three-point scale of support for the political community: 1 = low support; 2 = medium support; and 3 = high support. Proportion of citizens with high support for political community are displayed in the respective tables.

(2) Support for democracy as a form of government: The variables *'democracy best form of government'* and *'democracy good way of governing'* are added to form a seven-point scale, ranging from 1 = low support to 7 = high support. Proportion of citizens with scale values 5–7 are displayed in the respective tables.

(3) Performance of the regime: The variables *'performance of the system for governing'* (recoded 1–3 = 1; 4–5 = 2; 6–7 = 3; 8–10 = 4), *'performance of people in national office'* (1–4), *'confidence in parliament'* (1–4), and *'confidence in government'* (1–4) are added to form a 13-point scale: 1 = low performance to 13 = high performance. Proportion of citizens with scale values 8–13 are displayed in the respective tables.

Support for Political Community

An expressed willingness to fight for one's country, combined with a high degree of national pride might be variously labelled. Here we use these ques-

dimension of democracy as a form of government stands out as it should. In Nigeria and Russia the same is true for the political community dimension. However, although the general hypothesis is not borne out in all countries, it holds in the overwhelming majority.

[8] I could have used factor scores from the pooled analysis; however, those scores for any single country would be directly weighted by the overall distribution across countries. An additive score avoids this statistical encumbrance.

[9] I have checked the intercorrelations of the variables involved and found them satisfactory in the cases of support for democracy as a form of government (pooled correlation .44, average of single country correlations .39) and evaluation of performance of democracy (pooled correlations system for governing: people in national office .40; system for governing: confidence in parliament .30; system for governing: confidence in government .37; people in national office: confidence in parliament .32; people in national office: confidence in government .37; confidence in parliament: confidence in government .63; averaged single country correlations correspond in all cases to those reported for the pooled analysis). The intercorrelation between the two indicators forming the dimension of support for the political community, however, were considerably weaker (pooled correlation .19) and not significant at the .001 level in 2 of the 38 countries (Philippines and Taiwan; average single country correlation .19).Thus, in addition to discussing scale distributions we might wish to look at the two indicators forming the scale also separately.

tions for an index of 'support for the political community'. At least on the surface, it would not seem to be much of a shift to label such attitudes either 'patriotism' or 'nationalism'. Often, in discussions of the positive aspects of political community it is indeed the case that the other side of the coin could be negatively assessed under the label 'nationalism'. Whether or not one attaches a pejorative valence to the phenomenon depends, in part, on the context in which it is being used. However, it is indeed the case that, in the pooled analysis of all respondents over all of the countries included, the index retains its orthogonality with both approval of democracy and assessment of performance (Table 2.1). The index of support for political community at least is statistically independent of and not antithetical to support of democracy as a form of government. Thus, the concept of political community, as conceptualized and measured here, may denote a benign form of patriotism and not necessarily carry a pathological connotation.

Support for the political community scale values range from 1 (low support) to 3 (high support). To aid in mapping from a cross-country perspective the countries are displayed and arrayed in Table 2.2 by the proportion of citizens with a high level of support for political community, divided in columns across regions. On average the mean level in 38 countries is 68 per cent.[10] This average disguises a very high range of 75 per cent points. It is not a goal of this essay to evaluate alternative explanations for the cross-national distributions along the dimensions of political support, however, some comment on the distribution in Table 2.2 is not out of order. Azerbaijan and Turkey rank highest; the two parts of Germany and Japan trail the distribution, with a level of support of 37 and 18 per cent respectively. The latter finding confirms a well-known pattern which has often been related to the World War II experiences of these countries. While in all other countries at least half of its citizens identify with their political community, the German and Japanese citizenry carry the burden of their nationalistic past quite visibly, resisting even what might be considered a form of salutary patriotism. As far as support levels for Azerbaijan and Turkey are concerned these two countries have to cope with challenges to a redefinition of their respective political communities. However, the same is true for a number of the other newly formed Central and Eastern European states. In these cases the findings are mixed. Of the 14 countries included in the survey 7 range above average and an equal number range below average.

The number of countries varies across regions not only because of the varying number of nation states in each region but also because of the relative success in organizing the *World Values Surveys* in different countries. With these cautions in mind, there are no striking differences in support for the political community across regions that are comparable to those within the regional groupings themselves. Thus, the Asian range is from Japan's uniquely low 18 to China's relatively high 84 per cent support for the political community.

[10] The relevant indicators are missing for South Korea.

Table 2.2. Support for the political community

Country	Global regions						
	Western Europe	Eastern Europe	Asia	Africa	North & Central America	South America	Oceania
Azerbaijan		93					
Turkey		92					
Peru						86	
Venezuela						85	
Slovenia		85					
Sweden	85						
China			84				
Philippines			83				
Norway	81						
Finland	78						
USA					76		
Dominican Rep.					75		
Australia							73
Belarus		72					
Croatia		71					
Mexico					71		
Puerto Rico					71		
Yugoslavia		70					
Armenia		70					
Georgia		69					
South Africa				69			
Chile						67	
Brazil						64	
Moldova		63					
Argentina						63	
Ukraine		62					
Taiwan			62				
Russia		62					
Nigeria				61			
Switzerland	60						
Estonia		58					
Spain	58						
Uruguay						56	
Lithuania		54					
Latvia		52					
East Germany		37					
West Germany	36						
Japan			18				
MEAN	66	67	62	65	73	71	73

Note: Support for political community: the variables '*fight for country*' (0/1) and '*national pride*' (recoded 1,2 = 0; 3,4 = 1) are added to form a three-point scale of support for the political community: 1 = low support; 2 = medium support; and 3 = high support. The proportion of citizens with high support for the political community are displayed in the table.

Source: World Values Surveys, 1994/7.

Eastern European countries range from 37 to 93 per cent, and so on—a range far greater than the modest differences between regional means.

Table 2.3 offers a different view of the map of support for political community. It arrays countries in three columns: older democracies, younger ('third wave') democracies, and what might be entitled younger 'would-be' democratic systems. The age of the system does of itself seem to discriminate between the democratic systems, with the mean of the older systems at 64 and the younger at 61 per cent high support for the political community. The countries with lower democracy scores, however, exhibit a rather higher mean score (69) than either the older or the younger democracies. Whether or not this is a reflection of the darker side of a sense of political community cannot be determined until more time passes during which progress toward democratization may, or may not, be registered in the currently low democracy countries.

The political turbulence beneath the third wave of democratization heightened the sense of possible political change around the world. As interesting as the cross-national distribution of political attitudes at a single time, such as

Table 2.3. Support for the political community by type of democracy, 1996 (%)

Systems over 40 years*, High Democracy**		Systems under 40 years, High Democracy		Systems over 40 years, Low Democracy	
Country	High support for political community	Country	High support for political community	Country	High support for political community
Sweden	85	Slovenia	84	Azerbaijan	93
Norway	81	Croatia	71	Turkey	92
Finland	78	South Africa	69	Peru	86
USA	76	Chile	67	Venezuela	85
Australia	73	Brazil	64	Philippines	83
Puerto Rico	71	Argentina	63	Dominican Rep.	75
Switzerland	60	Estonia	58	Belarus	72
West Germany	36	Spain	58	Mexico	71
Japan	18	Uruguay	56	Yugoslavia	70
		Lithuania	54	Armenia	70
		Latvia	52	Georgia	70
		East Germany	38	Moldova	63
				Ukraine	62
				Taiwan	62
				Russia	62
				Nigeria	61
MEAN	64		61		69
Mean 1995 per cap GDP (1990 US$)	26,808		6,978		2,190

* System Age: Gurr, POLITY III Dataset (ICPSR No. 09263).
** High Democracy = Freedom House 1996 Rating =/> 2.
   Low Democracy = Freedom House 1996 Rating < 2.

Note: China, Mexico, Puerto Rico, and Venezuela do not fit any of the 3 categories.

Source: World Values Surveys, 1994/7.

the publics' support for their respective political communities, may be the likely changes in distribution of such attitudes. Certainly in light of the scholarly scepticism cited in the introductory section of this essay, any general downward trend would be cause for grave concern. The data for monitoring and mapping those changes, while far from ideal, are unprecedented in the history of social science. Thus, it is possible, for a large number of the countries included in the *World Values Surveys* not only to examine cross-national distributions, but also to plot changes in certain attitudinal configurations. There is not a full complement of items included in the various scales for all multiple times across all 39 countries in this study, but some of the items have been repeated for several. Because most analyses claim that standards of comparison have changed we restrict cross-time comparisons to the period from shortly after the breakdown of the former communist regime to the most recently available data.

Are there any patterns of change in the mid-1990s, compared to a few years earlier? National pride can be compared over time for 24 countries, as reported in Table 2.4. There is an increase in the proportion of citizens who are '*very proud*' or '*quite proud*' of their country in 9 countries (average increase 5 per cent points), no change in six countries (+ or – 2.5 per cent points), and a decline in national pride in 9 countries (average decline 11 per cent points). No country stands out with respect to increasing levels of national pride. As far as decline is concerned, it is most expressed in the three Baltic countries as well as in the two parts of Germany. There is a tendency of further increase in countries which are already high in national pride and a tendency of further decrease where national pride is already low.

Data on changes in the readiness to fight, perhaps the more nationalistic of our two indicators, are available for the same 24 countries (Table 2.5). The proportion of citizens ready to fight for their country has gone up in 10 countries (average increase 10 per cent points), has been stable in 4 countries (+ or – 2.5 per cent points), and gone down in 10 countries (average decrease 10 per cent points). The average figures hide large country differences. A particularly large increase in the readiness to fight could be observed in two South American countries (Brazil + 37, Argentina + 20 percentage points); the largest decrease occurred in the three Baltic states (Latvia – 30, Estonia – 16, Lithuania – 16 percentage points). However, unlike the apparent broadening of the range of national pride, there is no obvious general pattern to these changes in willingness to fight for the country.

Support of Democracy as an Ideal Form of Government

The factor analyses reported in Table 2.1 reinforce the argument that the public's support for democracy as a form of government can be separated both analytically and empirically from the evaluation of performance of the

Table 2.4. Change in national pride in the 1990s (%)

Country	Very proud, or quite proud (mid-1990s)	Pattern of change as compared to the early 1990s		
		Increase	No change	Decline
USA	98		−0.1	
Australia	97		−1*	
South Africa	97	+5		
Mexico	94	+5		
Turkey	94		+2	
Spain	92	+5		
Slovenia	92		+1	
Finland	89	+7		
Norway	89	+6		
Sweden	89	+5		
Argentina	89	+3		
China	88	+6		
Chile	87		+1	
Nigeria	85		−1	
Brazil	84			−3
Belarus	79			−3
Switzerland	78			−3
Russia	71	+6		
Lithuania	69			−18
Latvia	67			−24
Estonia	67			−17
East Germany	62			−12
Japan	62			−4
West Germany	57			−11

* In Australia change is measured as compared to 1981.

Note: Question: 'How proud are you to be a [citizen of this country]? (4) Very proud, (3) quite proud, (2) not very proud, (1) not at all proud'.

Source: World Values Surveys, 1990–3, 1994–7.

regime. It should be clear where this is leading. It is leading to the suggestion, offered in the Introduction, that persons dissatisfied with the current performance of the regime, especially in fledgling democracies, do not necessarily constitute a reservoir of anti-democratic sentiment. In fact, it may well be the case that those who support democracy as a form of government but also give a poor score to current performance of the regime in their own country—those whom I label as the 'dissatisfied democrats'—may well constitute a potential force for improving rather than for abandoning the democratic experiment.

Support for democracy as a form of government is measured by a seven-point scale. The country mapping in Table 2.6 reports the proportion of citizens with a positive attitude (scale values 5 to 7). Support for democracy as a form of government is generally rather high in the 38 countries for which data are available. Interestingly, the range is anchored and fully covered by the post-communist countries of Central Europe and the former USSR. As a set,

Table 2.5. Change in willingness to fight for country in the 1990s (%)

Country	Would fight for my country (mid-1990s percentage 'yes')	Pattern of change as compared to the early 1990s (%)		
		Increase	No change	Decline
Turkey	96.3	+4.3		
China	93.4			−3.6
Sweden	92.1	+3.6		
Slovenia	89.8	+7.5		
Norway	88.6	+3.4		
Belarus	87.8			−2.8
Finland	84.2			−3.3
Russia	82.2		−1.3	
USA	77.4		−0.4	
Australia	74.6		−0.4*	
Estonia	74.6			−17.5
Chile	74.0			−8.9
Mexico	73.0	+3.3		
Brazil	71.8	+36.5		
South Africa	70.4			−6.7
Switzerland	70.3	+4.4		
Nigeria	69.5			−10.4
Lithuania	68.1			−15.6
Latvia	67.6			−29.8
Argentina	67.0	+20.1		
Spain	58.8		−0.1	
East Germany	49.9			−3.0
West Germany	49.2	+7.5		
Japan	24.2	+3.9		

* In Australia change is measured as compared to 1981.

Notes: Questions: 'Of course we all hope that there will be not another war, but if it were to come to that, would you be willing to fight for your country? (1) yes, (0) no.'

Sources: World Values Surveys, 1990–3, 1994–7.

these countries are not distinctive; nor are other geographic regional patterns apparent, other than the clustering of the Western Europeans on the higher end of the scale. The mean value for all 38 countries is 84 per cent. Eleven countries, most of them West European states, have over 90 per cent support for democracy as a form of government, suggesting that experience with functioning democratic regimes, with all their blemishes, far from leading to cynicism and rejection, reinforces citizens' commitment to that ever more widely accepted form of government. In another 16 countries democracy is supported by 8 out of 10 citizens. Russia shows the lowest level of support. Among the 11 countries where support ranges from 71 to 79 per cent are another 5 Eastern European countries, 3 South American states, Finland, and the Philippines.

No additional insight emerges readily when, as in Table 2.7, the countries are arrayed by system age and level of democracy. The high level democracies have not apparently disappointed their citizens, but the mean difference

Table 2.6. Support for democracy as an ideal form of government (%)

Country	Global regions						
	Western Europe	Eastern Europe	Asia	Africa	North & Central America	South America	Oceania
Azerbaijan		97					
Croatia		95					
Uruguay						94	
West Germany	93						
Norway	93						
Sweden	93						
Spain	92						
Switzerland	91						
East Germany		91					
Argentina						90	
Dominican Rep.					90		
Turkey		89					
Japan			88				
Yugoslavia		88					
USA					88		
Nigeria				87			
Puerto Rico					87		
Lithuania		86					
Peru						86	
South Africa				85			
Estonia		85					
Georgia		85					
Venezuela						85	
South Korea			84				
Taiwan			83				
Australia							83
Slovenia		82					
Latvia		79					
Chile						79	
Brazil						78	
Belarus		75					
Finland	75						
Armenia		75					
Ukraine		75					
Philippines			72				
Mexico					71		
Moldova		71					
Russia		51					
MEAN	90	81	82	86	84	86	83

Note: The variables '*democracy best form of government*' and '*democracy good way of governing*' are added to form a seven-point scale, ranging from 1 = low support to 7 = high support. Proportion of citizens with scale values 5–7 are displayed in the table.

Source: World Values Surveys, 1994/7.

between the older (88 per cent mean) and younger (86 per cent) democracies is hardly noteworthy. Some doubt is spread among those not attaining a high democracy score, but still a large majority of the citizens of these countries approve of democracy as a form of government, thus perhaps warranting the reference to them as 'would-be' democracies.[11]

Table 2.7. Support for democracy as an ideal form of government by type of democracy, 1996 (%)

Systems over 40 years*, High Democracy**		Systems under 40 years, High Democracy		Systems over 40 years, Low Democracy	
Country	High support for democracy	Country	High support for democracy	Country	High support for democracy
West Germany	93	Croatia	95	Azerbaijan	97
Norway	93	Uruguay	94	Dominican Rep.	90
Sweden	93	Spain	92	Turkey	89
Switzerland	91	East Germany	91	Yugoslavia	88
Japan	88	Argentina	90	Nigeria	87
USA	88	Lithuania	86	Peru	86
Puerto Rico	87	South Africa	85	Georgia	85
Australia	83	Estonia	85	Venzuela	85
Finland	75	South Korea	84	Taiwan	83
		Slovenia	82	Belarus	75
		Latvia	79	Armenia	75
		Chile	79	Ukraine	75
		Brazil	78	Philippines	72
				Moldova	71
				Mexico	71
				Russia	51
MEAN	88		86		80

 * System Age: Gurr, POLITY III Dataset (ICPSR No. 09263).
 ** High Democracy = Freedom House 1996 Rating =/> 2.
   Low Democracy = Freedom House 1996 Rating < 2.
Source: *World Values Surveys*, 1994/7.

Evaluations of the Performance of the Regime

Data for evaluation of regime performance are available for 37 countries. The additive scale ranges from 1 (low) to 13 (high). In the mapping exercise, Table 2.8 displays the proportion of citizens with scale values 8 to 13. Compared to support for democracy as a form of government, evaluation of performance of the regime is considerably lower in all countries (average 26 per cent). Only in such diverse countries as Azerbaijan, Norway, and South Africa do more than half of the citizens evaluate performance highly. There is, in Table 2.8, some evidence of a regional pattern, with the Western Europeans again, as a set,

---

[11] No indicators are available to assess change over time with respect to support of democracy as a form of government.

Table 2.8. Evaluations of regime performance

Country	Global regions						
	Western Europe	Eastern Europe	Asia	Africa	North & Central America	South America	Oceania
Azerbaijan		77					
Norway	70						
South Africa				54			
Switzerland	46						
Taiwan			42				
Philippines			41				
Chile						38	
Croatia		38					
Puerto Rico					34		
Sweden	33						
Peru						32	
Brazil						28	
Yugoslavia		26					
USA					25		
Turkey		25					
Finland	23						
Australia							23
Estonia		22					
Mexico					22		
West Germany	22						
Slovenia		21					
Uruguay						21	
Georgia		21					
Spain	18						
Armenia		17					
Lithuania		17					
Argentina						16	
Latvia		16					
East Germany		15					
Moldova		12					
Japan			12				
Nigeria				11			
Ukraine		10					
Belarus		8					
Venezuela						6	
Dominican Rep.					6		
Russia		4					
MEAN	35	20	38	32	22	23	23

Note: Performance of the regime: the variables '*performance of the system for governing*' (recoded 1–3 = 1; 4–5 = 2; 6–7 = 3; 8–10 = 4), '*performance of people in national office*' (1–4), '*confidence in parliament*' (1–4), and '*confidence in government*' (1–4) are added to form a 13-point scale: 1 = low performance to 13 = high performance. The proportion of citizens with scale values 8—13 are displayed in the table.

Source: World Values Surveys, 1994/7.

manifesting high assessments although, even there, the spread from Spain's 18 to Norway's 70 per cent, is much wider than the interregional means.

No doubt, democracy thrives and can be built on a widespread, healthy dose of scepticism. And it is not at all clear where the bottom is for positive benefit. But surely in some cases these surveys must be tapping more than scepticism and moving more into the zone of dismay. There must be some concern for the situation in Russia (4 per cent), the Ukraine (10 per cent) and Belarus (8 per cent), as well as in Venezuela (6 per cent) and the Dominican Republic (6 per cent). In these countries taken together only 1 citizen out of 10 is satisfied with the performance of the respective political regime.

Again, I must stress the value of separating support for democracy as an ideal form of government from citizens' evaluations of the contemporary performance of their particular political regime, however much it may meet or stray from democratic norms. Thus, for example, 87 per cent of Nigerians hold to the belief that democracy is the desired form of government, even though only 11 per cent of them approve of the performance of their troubled political system (realistically, most would argue, in this time period). Likewise, over 89 per cent of Turks support the principles of democracy, while barely a quarter assess contemporary performance highly. Such disparities are not confined to polities having long experience with such dramatic regime changes as military coups, as have both Nigeria and Turkey. There is likewise a broad difference in the support for and evaluation of democracy in both Germanys. Support for democracy as a form of government in the recently reunited parts of that country is 93 and 91 per cent, West and East respectively, while evaluation of current performance is only 22 per cent in the West and 15 per cent in the East.

Table 2.9, arraying the countries again by system age and level of democratization, is perhaps more revealing in the case of evaluations of system performance than were its counterparts for support for the political community (Table 2.3) or for democracy as a form of government (Table 2.7). There is a clear stepwise decline in the mean evaluations as one moves from the older (mean = 32 per cent) to the younger democracies (27 per cent), and from these to the 'would-be' democracies (23 per cent).[12]

'Satisfaction with the way democracy works' has long been used as an indicator for the citizens' evaluation of the performance of democracy in their respective countries (Fuchs, Guidorossi, and Svensson 1995) and it correlates .46 with the performance of democracy scale discussed above.[13] The indicator is not available for most of the *World Values Surveys*. However, it has been widely included in the three regional surveys mentioned earlier. This database allows for cross-national comparison for the mid-1990s for 50 countries

[12] The interesting case of Azerbaijan, of course, broadens the range in the set of younger, low-scoring political systems.

[13] The association of the index 'performance of democracy' and the indicator 'satisfaction with the democratic process' can be assessed for 10 Eastern European countries and West Germany. The intra-country correlations range from .30 for Belarus and .55 for East Germany. The mean of the intra-country correlations is .43 which is only slightly lower than the pooled correlation (.46).

Table 2.9. Evaluations of regime performance by type of democracy, 1996 (%)

Systems over 40 years*, High Democracy**		Systems under 40 years, High Democracy		Systems over 40 years, Low Democracy	
Country	High regime performance	Country	High regime performance	Country	High regime performance
Norway	70	South Africa	54	Azerbaijan	77
Switzerland	46	Chile	38	Taiwan	42
Puerto Rico	34	Croatia	38	Philippines	41
Sweden	33	Brazil	28	Peru	32
USA	25	Estonia	22	Yugoslavia	26
Finland	23	Slovenia	21	Turkey	25
Australia	23	Uruguay	21	Mexico	22
West Germany	22	Spain	18	Georgia	21
Japan	12	Lithuania	17	Armenia	17
		Argentina	16	Moldova	12
		Latvia	16	Nigeria	11
		East Germany	15	Ukraine	10
				Belarus	8
				Dominican Rep.	6
				Venezuela	6
				Russia	4
MEAN	32		27		23

* System Age: Gurr, POLITY III Dataset (ICPSR No. 09263).
** High Democracy = Freedom House 1996 Rating =/> 2.
  Low Democracy = Freedom House 1996 Rating < 2.
Source: World Values Surveys, 1994/7.

(Table 2.10). Among these are 17 Western European countries, 22 from Central and Eastern Europe, and eleven South American countries. Satisfaction with the democratic process has not been particularly stunning in the mid-1990s. The average proportion of those who are very or fairly satisfied is only 40 per cent. But again the average hides much difference across countries. While the Western Europeans, with the exception of the southern countries (Spain, Portugal, and Italy, in particular) are on the higher side (the average, including the southern countries, is 56 per cent), the Latin Americans are certainly on the lower end (average 29 per cent). Of the Central and Eastern Europeans, Hungary, Slovakia, Belarus, Ukraine, Armenia, Russia, Moldova, and Bulgaria score very low indeed.

Change over time in performance is difficult to assess. In part, because the respective indicators are not available in a large number of cases, and in part because the indicators which are available are not exactly comparable. Tables 2.11–2.14 present information about the publics' evaluations of different facets of regime performance, including confidence in parliament and government, and satisfaction with the democratic process, with the results summarized in Table 2.15. In general, the common theme of declining assessment of political institutions is reflected, with both the number of countries

Table 2.10. Satisfaction with democratic performance in the 1990s

Country	Percentage very or fairly satisfied		
	Western Europe (1995)	Eastern Europe (1996)	Latin America (1996)
Denmark	83		
Norway	82		
Luxemburg	77		
Albania		76	
Netherlands	71		
Ireland	70		
West Germany	67		
Austria	63		
Northern Ireland	57		
Romania		56	
Sweden	55		
Belgium	54		
Finland	52		
Uruguay			52
Poland		48	
East Germany		48	
France	47		
Great Britain	46		
Georgia		44	
Azerbaijan		43	
Slovenia		43	
Spain	41		
Estonia		41	
Czech Republic		41	
Yugoslavia		41	
Macedonia		41	
Portugal	40		
Croatia		39	
Ecuador			35
Argentina			35
Lithuania		33	
Paraguay			31
Venezuela			30
Peru			30
Chile			29
Greece	28		
Latvia		28	
Bolivia			25
Brazil			22
Hungary		22	
Slovakia		21	
Belarus		20	
Ukraine		20	
Armenia		19	
Italy	19		
Colombia			16
Mexico			12
Russia		8	
Moldova		6	
Bulgaria		6	
MEAN	56	34	29

Note: EB Question: 'On the whole, are you (4) very satisfied, (3) fairly satisfied, (2) not very satisfied, or (1) not at all satisfied with the way democracy works (in your country)?'

Sources: Eurobarometer, Latinobarometer, Central and Eastern Eurobarometer. Data for Azerbaijan (Feb. 1997) and Moldova (Dec. 1996) are taken from the World Values Surveys (Eastern Europe).

experiencing decline and the average percentage of declines generally exceeding increases. Lack of confidence in parliaments is particularly pronounced, with 15 of 22 countries showing decline, and an average cross-national average of – 12 per cent points.

Satisfaction with the 'democratic process', however, which already was at a low level at the beginning of the 1990s, showed fewer cases of decline than of increase, and the cross-national average was an inconsequential –.3 per cent points. More noteworthy, given their dramatic regime changes in the early 1990s, the Central and Eastern European countries experience equal numbers of increases as declines, with no net change—even given the much vaunted difficulties of readjustment, breakdown of law and order, corruption, dual economic and political transformations, and widespread governmental instability. It might be expected that the disappointment would be concentrated in the countries of the former USSR, compared to the others (perhaps placing the three Baltic countries in the latter set, as well). However, the surveys reveal no such—or any other obvious—pattern. Increases in confidence in the democratic process are registered in Albania, Romania, Poland, Estonia, Latvia, Belarus, and Armenia, with declines in Georgia, Slovenia, Russia, Moldova,

Table 2.11. Confidence in parliament in the 1990s (%)

Country	A great deal or quite a lot of confidence (mid-1990s)	Pattern of change as compared to the early 1990s		
		Increase	No change	Decline
Norway	69	+10		
South Africa	60			–6
Turkey	48			–9
Sweden	45		–2	
Estonia	44			–25
Mexico	43	+8		
Chile	38			–25
Nigeria	37			–17
Spain	37		–1	
Brazil	34	+10		
Finland	33			–3
Australia	30			–25*
Belarus	30		+0.5	
USA	30			–15
West Germany	29			–21
Japan	27			–3
Lithuania	26			–39
Latvia	25			–47
Slovenia	25			–11
Russia	23			–24
East Germany	17			–24
Argentina	15		–1	

* In Australia change is measured as compared to 1981.

Sources: World Values Surveys, 1990–3, 1994–7.

Cross-national Trends in Confidence

Table 2.12. Confidence in government in the 1990s (%)

Country	Citizens with a great deal or quite a lot of confidence (mid-1990s)	Pattern of change as compared to the early 1990s		
		Increase	No change	Decline
Chile	53			–6
Estonia	50			–14
Turkey	47	+15		
Mexico	42	+17		
Latvia	38			–19
Lithuania	36			–22
Spain	31	+3		
USA	31			–11
Nigeria	27		+0.6	

Sources: World Values Surveys, 1990–3, 1994–7.

Table 2.13. Satisfaction with the democratic process in Western Europe in the 1990s (%)

Country	Very or fairly satisfied in May 1995	Pattern of change compared to Nov. 1991		
		Increase	No change	Decline
Denmark	83	+9		
Norway	82	+9		
Luxemburg	77		+0.3	
Netherlands	71	+9		
Ireland	70	+14		
West Germany	67		+1	
Northern Ireland	57	+14		
Belgium	54		+2	
East Germany	48	+4		
France	47	+4		
Great Britain	46			–14
Spain	41			–15
Portugal	40			–35
Greece	28			–6
Italy	19		–0.3	

Note: May 1995 is the latest satisfaction with democracy measurement available.
Sources: Eurobarometer Surveys.

and Bulgaria. The absence of clear patterns is itself useful information. It suggests that there are no evident pathologies of confidence, across the board, uniquely challenging the new or 'would-be' democracies. Their problems, to the extent that they are grave, seem to be specific rather than general. They point to the importance of political processes within countries. This turns the

Table 2.14. Satisfaction with the democratic process in Central and Eastern Europe in the 1990s (%)

Country	Very or fairly satisfied in Nov. 1996	Pattern of change compared to Nov. 1992		
		Increase	No change	Decline
Albania	76	+34		
Romania	56	+27		
Poland	48	+12		
Georgia	44			−7
Slovenia	43			−6
Estonia	41	+12		
Czech Republic	41		+2	
Macedonia	41			−10
Lithuania	33			−18
Latvia	28	+10		
Hungary	22		−2	
Slovakia	21		−2	
Belarus	20	+9		
Ukraine	20		−0.4	
Armenia	19	+6		
Russia	8			−5
Moldova	6*			−32
Bulgaria	6			−33

Note: Nov. 1996 is the latest measurement available.

Sources: *Central and Eastern Eurobarometer Surveys*. Data for Moldova (Dec. 1996) are taken from the *World Values Survey* (Eastern Europe).

Table 2.15. Changes in evaluations of regime performance in the 1990s

Object of evaluation	Increasing (no. of countries)	Decreasing (no. of countries)	Overall mean % change
General system performance (N = 12)	4	8	−7
Confidence in parliament (N = 22)	3	15	−12
Confidence in government (N = 9)	3	5	−12
Satisfaction with the democratic process (N = 15, EB)*	7	4	−0.3
Satisfaction with the democratic process (N = 18, Central & Eastern EB)**	7	7	0.0

Sources: *World Values Surveys* data, unless otherwise noted. Not included are cases where no change was evident. Timing of surveys varies somewhat, but change is generally measured from the early 1990s to about 1995 or 1996. Details and specific country listings and distributions are documented in Appendix 2.

 * EU countries, based on *Eurobarometer Surveys* (EB). The mean is heavily skewed downward by Portugal's 35.5 per cent drop. Excluding this case, the mean would be a 2.4 per cent increase.

 ** *Central and Eastern Eurobarometer Surveys*. Moldovan data (1996) are from the *WVS*.

attention to the macro level. Let us conclude by highlighting a few critical macro observations that bring the threads of this discussion somewhat together.

Conclusions: The Relationship Between Community, Democracy, and Performance

The factor analysis reported in Table 2.1 supported the utility of at least a part of the taxonomy of system support. We have compared measures constructed out of surveys from dozens of countries to gauge:

- Support for political community
  Attitude object—the political community
  Mode of attitude—expressive
- Approval of democracy as an ideal form of government
  Attitude object—the regime
  Mode of attitude—moral
- Evaluation of the current performance of the regime
  Attitude object—the regime
  Mode of attitude—instrumental

The factor analysis (Table 2.1) demonstrated that the indices used for these three concepts tapped clearly distinguishable and distinct dimensions at the level of individual survey respondents. That micro distinctness, however, does not rule out the possibility of interesting relationships between these three phenomena at the macro level. Two figures demonstrate the extent to which such relationships may prove interesting.

By way of introducing the relevant figures of the different attitudes, we can return to the phenomenon of the 'dissatisfied democrats'. This is the label applied to people who put a high rating on the attractiveness of democracy as a form of government but at the same time place a low rating on the performance of their particular democratic regime. For the present, I shall not distinguish between dissatisfied democrats in established, fledgling, or 'would-be' democracies. Of course, extrapolations as to the systemic consequences of actions based on such a disjunction between desired and actual states would need to account for the setting in which the disjunction occurs. The likely actions of mobilized dissatisfied democrats in pre- or non-democratic systems would, no doubt, take very different form from their counterparts in functioning democracies. The former could be hypothesized, for example, as having a high revolutionary potential, while the latter might be expected to serve a reforming and enhancing role in their respective democracies. Some insight may be suggested by the aggregate relationships.

Figure 2.1 plots the percentage of high support for the political community on the vertical axis. The horizontal axis is an aggregate relative of the 'dissatisfied democrats', in that it is the difference in the percentage of respondents

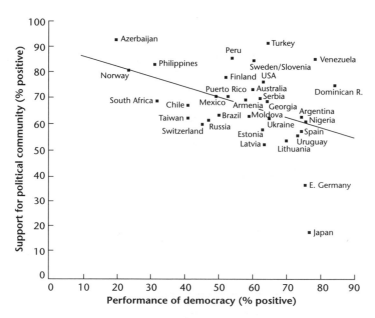

Fig. 2.1. Support for political community.

Source: *World Values Surveys* 1994–7.

expressing support for democracy as a form of government and the percent-age evaluating the regime's current performance positively. Thus, the figure tells us that countries with a wide disparity between the moral assessment of democracy and the instrumental performance of the regime are also likely to be countries with a relatively low support for the political community. Thus, there is indeed a potential for erosion of the broadest, perhaps most basic iden-tity within a polity that can be linked to the extent to which its performance matches the moral aspirations of the population. However, there is sufficient ambiguity in the fit of my measure to the concept of political community (as noted in the earlier discussion of 'patriotism' and 'nationalism') and sufficient spread in the relationship to put this proposition on the agenda as just that— a proposition, worthy of further exploration.

Similar material for further exploration is presented in Figure 2.2, plotting countries according to the percentage approving democracy as an ideal versus the performance of their particular system. Again, good performance, at the system level, is associated with increased approval of democracy as an abstraction. Performance cannot be ignored. The evidence of Figure 2.2, to be sure, is consistent with the standing claim that effectiveness is a condition for

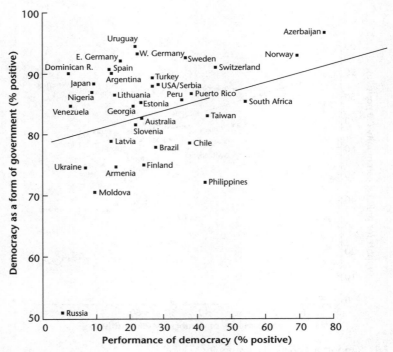

Fig. 2.2. Support for democracy as an ideal form of government.
Source: *World Values Surveys* 1994–7.

legitimacy. However, I think the evidence is sufficiently mixed to underscore the need for considerable refinement, especially now that the range of national political experience has been broadened so dramatically and now that there is a growing body of heretofore hardly imaginable evidence available for more detailed exploration of the inner workings of embryonic, adolescent, and mature democracies.

The data, remarkable as they are, do not provide all the answers to the questions posed here. However, the evidence is sufficient to invite a great deal more exploitation. My effort at mapping should serve as an introduction. But it also is consistent with other recent inquiry in casting doubt on the much-acclaimed 'decline' or 'crisis' critiques of modern democracy. I can find no evidence of growing dissatisfaction with democracy as a form of government. Further, there is no apparent evidence that the dissatisfied democrats across the globe constitute a danger to democracy. Quite the contrary, they may well be the hope for the future of democratic governance.

3

Political Support in Advanced Industrial Democracies

RUSSELL J. DALTON

TWO decades ago political analysts worried about the fragility of democracy. Governments were struggling with new issue demands, and political institutions were having difficulty adjusting to calls for a more participatory democracy. As discussed in the Introduction to the book several scholars described this situation as a 'crisis' of Western democracy (Crozier *et al.* 1975; Huntington 1981).

The end of the Cold War has given rise to a new euphoria about democracy and the democratic process, including by some who had earlier trumpeted the warning calls (Huntington 1991; Fukuyama 1992). And yet, as democracy celebrates its triumph over communism, there are continuing signs of public doubts about the vitality of the democratic process. Joseph Nye and his colleagues (1997) demonstrate that low levels of political trust among the American public have continued into the 1990s. The large protest vote for Perot in 1992 and the term-limits movement signal Americans' continuing political doubts. Several cross-national analyses suggest this is not a distinctly American phenomenon (Dalton 1996). This chapter builds on Hans-Dieter Klingemann's global analysis (Chapter 2 of this volume) by focusing on political support in advanced industrial societies. Our goal is to determine how citizens in these nations judge the democratic process today. Is there a popular crisis of democracy? We face two challenges in answering this question. First, there is the conceptual problem about what is meant by 'political support' or 'support for democracy'. Second, there is the empirical problem of assembling the appropriate cross-national and cross-temporal data to evaluate claims about changes in public opinion. This chapter addresses both of these topics to provide a framework for assessing public support for democratic politics in advanced industrial societies.

I would like to thank Clive Bean, Harold Clarke, David Easton, Mark Gray, Olafur Th. Hardarsson, Ian McAllister, Rolf Röntgen, Risto Sänkiaho, Carole Uhlaner, Peter Ulram, and Martin Wattenberg for their contributions to this research.

The Meaning of Political Support

One of the basic difficulties in studying political support is that the term has many possible meanings. The theoretical distinctions between different levels of political support are well known, but these are often blurred (or ignored) in the debate over public trust and confidence in democracy. Sometimes evidence of public discontent is no more than dissatisfaction with the incumbents of office—a normal and healthy aspect of the democratic process. In other instances, the theoretical significance of public opinion findings are uncertain because the wording of the survey questions is ambiguous. As discussed in the Introduction we believe it is essential to distinguish between at least five objects of political support, and in reality this is a continuous dimension from evaluations of the immediate actions of government officials to identifying with the nation state.

Table 3.1. Levels of political support

Level of analysis	Affective orientations	Instrumental evaluations
Community	National pride National identity	Best nation to live in
Regime		
Principles	Democratic values	Democracy best form of government
Performance	Participatory norms Political rights	Evaluations of rights Satisfaction with democratic process
Institutions	Institutional expectations Support for parties Output expectations	Performance judgements Trust in institutions Trust in party system
Authorities	Feelings towards political leaders Party Identification	Evaluations of politicians

In addition to the objects of political support, it is important to distinguish between two types of political beliefs that are represented by the two columns of Table 3.1. Almond and Verba (1963), for example, distinguished between affective and evaluative beliefs. Affective beliefs involve an acceptance or identification with an entity; evaluative beliefs involve a judgement about the performance or appropriateness of the object. Similarly, Easton (1965) distinguished between diffuse and specific support (also see Muller and Jukam 1977). According to Easton, diffuse support is a deep-seated set of attitudes toward politics and the operation of the political system that is relatively impervious to change. Diffuse support has also been interpreted as measuring the legitimacy of a political system or political institutions. In contrast, specific support is closely related to the actions and performance of the government or 'political elites'. Table 3.1 makes the distinction between general *affective orientations* that represent adherence to a set of values (what Easton labels diffuse support), and *evaluations* that reflect judgements about political phenomena (specific support).

If we combine these two dimensions—political level and the type of belief—this gives us a familiar map of public orientations toward politics and the political system. To illustrate this framework in more detail, the cells of Table 3.1 contain typical public opinion questions that might measure each type of belief. Affective orientations to the community might be tapped by questions such as feelings of national pride or a sense of national identity. Evaluations of the nation and political community might be measured by questions that ask which is the best nation in which to live. At the other end of the continuum, affective feelings toward political incumbents might be measured by feeling thermometers concerning leaders. By comparison, questions on leadership performance tap evaluative feelings toward presidents and prime ministers.

This is certainly not an original framework—but it is necessary to emphasize the distinction between various measures of political support. These differences are sometimes blurred, and these differences are politically significant in interpreting our findings.[1] The distinction between diffuse and specific support is important in understanding the significance of public attitudes toward the political process. Democratic political systems must keep the support of their citizens if they are to remain viable. Yet, since all governments occasionally fail to meet public expectations, short-term failures to satisfy public demands must not directly erode diffuse support for the regime or political community. In other words, a democratic political system requires a reservoir of diffuse support independent of immediate policy outputs (specific support) if it is to weather periods of public dissatisfaction.

Comparisons across levels of support also are important. Discontent with political authorities normally has limited systemic implications. Citizens often become dissatisfied with political office-holders and act on these feelings to select new leaders at the next election. Dissatisfaction with authorities, within a democratic system, is not usually a signal for basic political change. Negative attitudes toward political officials can exist with little loss in support for the office itself or the institutional structure encompassing this office. As the object of dissatisfaction becomes more general—the performance of the regime or attachment to the political community—the political implications increase. A decline in support for the political process might provoke a basic challenge to constitutional structures or calls for reform in the procedures of government. Weakening ties to the political community in a democratic system might foretell eventual revolution, civil war, or the loss of democracy. Therefore, 'not all expressions of unfavorable orientations have the same degree of gravity for a political system. Some may be consistent with its maintenance; others may lead to fundamental change' (Easton 1975: 437). Having introduced this framework, we will draw together a variety of public opinion

---

[1] Two good examples of close attention to the theoretical and empirical differences between these various aspects of political support are Muller and Jukam (1977) and Fuchs (1989).

data to determine how contemporary publics view the political process in advanced industrial democracies.

Assembling the Empirical Evidence

It is not our goal to review the rival hypotheses on why public support for democratic politics may be eroding (see Klingemann and Fuchs 1995; Nye *et al.* 1997). The general features of these theories, however, have implications for the types of empirical evidence that should be collected. Thus, we want briefly to discuss these theoretical explanations in the context of our data collection needs.

Many of the 'crisis of democracy' theories link the decrease in public support for democracy to broad, ongoing changes in the nature of advanced industrial societies. As subsequent chapters explore, if there is an extensive and long-term shift in public attitudes toward government, then it presumably results from equivalent processes of social and political change—and not coincidental political scandals or episodic policy problems.[2] For instance, some analysts have argued that the public's expanding issue interests have involved governments in new policy areas, such as protecting the quality of the environment, arbitrating moral issues, and assuring equality for minorities and women (Inglehart 1990, 1997*a*). This was coupled with popular demands for a more open and participatory style of democracy. From this perspective, the challenge to democracy arose because established institutions did not respond effectively or efficiently to long-term changes in public expectations for government. An alternative approach has focused on this same process, albeit with a different interpretation (Crozier *et al.* 1975; Huntington 1981). These scholars claimed that advanced industrialism weakened the ability of social groups to guide and moderate the demands of individual citizens. Furthermore, the mass media became critics of government and stripped away the cloak of anonymity that once shielded government actions from popular scrutiny (Patterson and Donsbach 1997). Governments consequently were being 'overloaded' by the demands of citizen action groups and issue-based politics (see the Chapters by McAllister and by Miller and Listhaug in this volume). As Samuel Huntington succinctly stated, the crisis of democracy arose from an excess of democracy on the part of the citizenry (1975, 1981). Yet another approach to this topic stresses the change in social and political patterns of advanced industrial societies. For example, Robert Putnam's research (1995*a*) suggests that changing social relations, the decline in social capital, and the intrusive influence of the media have contributed to a new political isolationism.

---

[2] We agree with Nye *et al.* (1997) that performance-based theories seem insufficient to explain a broad scale and continuing trend of declining political support (also see Clarke *et al.* 1993).

These explanations are very different in their theoretical premisses and the causal processes they emphasize, but they all suggest that long-term changes in the social and political conditions of advanced industrial societies may be eroding public support for the political process. If we accept this brief review of the literature, it suggests the type of empirical evidence we should collect. Ideally, we should assess these theories with long-term trend data, especially data which begin in the more halcyon period of the late 1950s and early 1960s. Although data from the 1980s and 1990s are relevant to the research question, they may come too late to test (or track) changes in public sentiments. In addition, we should be sensitive to the various levels and types of political support as outlined in Table 3.1, and we would like to collect varied measures of authority, regime, and community support. It would be ideal if comparable measures were available cross-nationally as well as cross-temporally.

These data needs are difficult to fulfill. There is a very long series of election studies and other opinion surveys for the United States that provides a rich, though not ideal, database for studying political support. In many other nations, however, the data-series is normally much thinner. The most extensive data are available for more recent years, but the baseline measures from earlier periods are often lacking. Within these constraints, we have attempted to assemble long-term trends in political support from the national election study series, or a comparable data series, for as many advanced industrial democracies as possible. We emphasized the temporal dimension over the cross-national dimension. The results, we believe, provide a comparative overview of trends in political support in advanced industrial democracies.

Confidence in Political Authorities

Public concerns about the democratic process normally begin with questions about the holders of power. Americans might not doubt the institutions of governance, but they might criticize Richard Nixon's actions during Watergate, George Bush's involvement in the Iran–Contra negotiations, or Bill Clinton's multiple indiscretions. Questions that focus on specific politicians illustrate the public's doubts. For example, the American National Election Study (ANES) found that feeling thermometer ratings for both the Republican and Democratic candidates in 1992 had decreased to nearly historic low points. This may be a problem with the candidates themselves. However, there are also signs that the public has become more focused on leaders and more demanding in judging them (Wattenberg 1991: ch. 4). As an illustration, during a modest recession in 1992 Bush's popularity hit a low point that nearly matched Nixon's worst approval rating during the Watergate crisis or Harry Truman's in the midst of the Korean War (*Public Perspective*, April/May 1995: 42).

Greater scepticism and doubts about political elites seem to be a common development in other advanced industrial democracies. In Britain, for instance, the low points of prime ministerial popularity have sunk steadily lower over the last five decades. At his nadir, John Major received lower approval ratings than any British PM in the post-war era (Rose 1995a). We can point to similar developments in other nations,[3] although the nature of such patterns tends to be cyclical. When incumbents lose favour, they are replaced by new political figures who restore public confidence at least temporarily— this is the nature of democratic politics. We would argue, however, that there appears to be a greater emphasis on individual politicians in contemporary politics, increased volatility in leadership evaluations, and increased public scepticism about the holders of office (e.g. Wattenberg 1991). Evaluations of individual politicians or public support for particular political parties is the most specific and short-term measure of political support (Table 3.1).

Trust in Authorities

The most extensive evidence on public evaluations of political actors comes from the United States with its long series of American National Election Studies. A variety of evidence, described in Nye, Zelikow and King (1997), points to growing American scepticism of their government over time (Figure 1.1). The early readings described a largely supportive public. Most Americans believed that one could trust the government to do what is right, that there are few dishonest people in government, and that most officials know what they are doing. These positive feelings remained relatively unchanged until the mid-1960s and then declined precipitously. Conflict over civil rights and Vietnam divided Americans and eroded public confidence in their leaders; Watergate and a seemingly endless stream of political scandals may have pushed support even lower over the next decade.

Distrust of government officials reached a low point in 1980 when the upbeat presidency of Ronald Reagan temporarily reversed these trends. Reagan stressed the positive aspects of American society and politics—and opinions rebounded in 1984. However, further declines continued in later elections. By 1994 these indicators had hit historic lows. Only 22 per cent of the American public felt one could trust the government to do the right thing most of the time, only 20 per cent believed the government is run for the benefit of all, and only 48 per cent thought most government officials were honest.

Cross-national evidence similar to these US time-series is relatively rare (Miller and Listhaug 1990; Dalton 1996: ch. 12). The most extensive effort to document cross-national feelings of trust in politicians was Ola Listhaug's (1995) analyses in *Citizens in the State*. Listhaug presented similar time series from Denmark, the Netherlands, Norway, and Sweden that yielded mixed patterns. He concluded that the data 'do not justify . . . a uniformly pessimistic—

---

[3] For instance, Falter and Rattinger (1997) show that public evaluations of all three 'established' German political parties has decreased from 1977 to 1994; there has also been a trend of decreasing trust in Canadian politicians (Clarke *et al.* 1992).

nor an excessively optimistic—picture of developments in political trust' (1995: 294).

We have built on Listhaug's analyses for a larger set of advanced industrial democracies, and with a longer data-series when available. We have focused on what might be considered evaluations of political authorities, including measures of trust in MPs, evaluations of politicians as a group, and feelings of confidence in government. We excluded measures that tap feelings of political efficacy, which are sometimes intermixed with confidence measures.

Table 3.2 presents measures of trust in politicians from 14 nations. The table presents the regression coefficients for each time trend. Many of these items use similar wording because they were influenced by the ANES series and the University of Michigan's pioneering studies in electoral research. Individual nations sometimes include a slight variation on these standard questions, and new items to measure political support.[4]

Again, we find that by expanding the cross-national and cross-temporal breadth of the empirical data, there is clear evidence of a general erosion in support for politicians in most advanced industrial democracies.[5] The patterns of decreasing confidence in the United States are well-known, and the regression coefficients show significant decreases in each of these trust measures. There is also strong evidence of decline in Canada, Finland, and Sweden (see, e.g. Kornberg and Clarke 1992; Borg and Sänkiaho 1995; Holmberg in this volume). Long-term trends for Austria similarly point to a long-term and deepening erosion in political confidence (Ulram 1994). Previous research found that political support grew during the postwar decades in Germany (Baker *et al.* 1981); but political trust has decreased since the late 1960s and early 1970s.

Table 3.2. Trends in trust in politicians by nation

	Trend	Standard error	Time period	Number of timepoints
Australia				
Trust government	.000	—	1979–88	(2)
Politicians knowledgeable	–3.556	—	1979–88	(2)
Austria				
Only interested in votes	–.385	(.228)	1974–96	(4)
MPs lose touch	–.577	(.101)	1974–96	(4)
Politicians don't care	–.297	(.114)	1974–96	(4)
Canada				
Government doesn't care	–.541	(.199)	1965–93	(7)
MPs lose touch	–.524	(.149)	1965–93	(7)

[4] For the specific question wordings and data sources please contact the author.

[5] Listhaug (1995) studied support trends in only four nations (Denmark, Netherlands, Norway, and Sweden). In a broader cross-national context, we can now see that these four nations are not representative of advanced industrial democracies. Moreover, even in these nations the addition of later timepoints showed decreasing trust in Denmark, Norway and Sweden (Borre and Andersen 1997; Holmberg in this volume).

Table 3.2. *cont.*

	Trend	Standard error	Time period	Number of timepoints
Denmark				
Politicians don't care	−.185	(.194)	1971–94	(9)
No principles	.610	(.327)	1971–84	(5)
Make right decisions	−.169	(.281)	1971–94	(11)
Finland				
Only interested in votes	−.389	(.261)	1978–91	(11)
MPs lose touch	−.495	(.158)	1974–94	(11)
A party furthers interests	−.891	(.421)	1974–91	(15)
Germany				
Officials don't care (a)	−1.270	(.249)	1969–94	(5)
Officials don't care (b)	−.661	(.505)	1974–94	(4)
MPs lose touch	−.525	(.318)	1974–91	(3)
Great Britain				
Only interested in votes	−.339	(.268)	1974–96	(6)
MPs lose touch	−.292	(.262)	1974–96	(6)
Party over nation	−.748	(.257)	1974–96	(6)
Improve government	−.636	(.284)	1973–96	(6)
Iceland				
Politicians trustworthy	−.850	(.613)	1983–95	(4)
Italy				
Officials don't care	−.235	—	1975–91	(2)
MPs lose touch	−.118	—	1975–91	(2)
Japan				
Many dishonest politicians	−1.943	(.942)	1976–92	(3)
Netherlands				
Only interested in votes	.785	(.200)	1971–94	(8)
MPs don't care	.903	(.189)	1971–94	(8)
Promise too much	−.653	(.102)	1977–94	(5)
MP friends	−.325	(.151)	1977–94	(5)
Personal interest	.150	(.188)	1977–94	(5)
Norway				
Only interested in votes	.115	(.284)	1969–93	(4)
MPs don't care	−.286	(.763)	1969–89	(3)
Trust politicians	.010	(.280)	1973–89	(5)
Waste taxes	.143	(.398)	1973–93	(6)
Politicians smart	.025	(.320)	1973–89	(5)
Sweden				
Only interested in votes	−1.326	(.161)	1968–94	(9)
MPs don't care	−.815	(.100)	1968–94	(9)
United States				
Politicians don't care	−.940	(.157)	1952–94	(12)
Trust government	−1.417	(.275)	1958–94	(10)
Leaders crooked	−.553	(.155)	1958–94	(10)
Waste taxes	−.553	(.232)	1958–94	(10)
Govt. benefits all	−1.176	(.330)	1964–94	(9)

Note: Table entries are unstandardized regression coefficients of time on each variable; the associated standard errors are in parentheses. The original variables are coded so that negative regression coefficients indicate a decrease in trust over time.

Sources: The respective national election study series in each nation; details are available from the author.

Shorter time-series for Australia, Britain, Iceland, Italy, and Japan also point to growing public disenchantment with politicians. Furthermore, many of these opinion-series begin fairly recently; in several nations there are indirect indications from other data sources that trust in politicians was higher before these data series began (Curtice and Jowell 1997; McAllister 1992).[6]

The sharpest deviation from the pattern of declining trust is the Netherlands. The two longest Dutch opinion-series—MPs don't care and politicians are only interested in votes—show statistically significant improvements between 1971 and 1994. These are the only two statistically significant positive coefficients in the table. However, two of the three additional measures that are available for the 1977–94 period display a decline. We can speculate on why the Netherlands differs from other nations, but without further empirical evidence this will remain merely speculation.[7] Norway and Denmark also display a mixed pattern, which justified Listhaug's early caution. However, when we examine support measures across this larger set of nations, there is a pattern of spreading public distrust of politicians.

Declining party identification

It is important to determine whether apparent dissatisfaction with specific politicians has generalized to broader, affective orientations such as feelings of party identification. The concept of party identification has reached such a prominent position in electoral research because scholars see these orientations as key determinants of many different aspects of political behaviour. In terms of our research interests, partisanship encompasses normative attitudes regarding the role that political parties should play in the democratic system. The formal theory for this view has been best expressed by Herbert Weisberg (1981), who argued that among its several dimensions of meaning, party identification taps support for the *institution* of the party system in general, as well as support for a specific party.

Earlier research suggested a trend of decreasing partisanship, but the pattern was described as mixed (Schmitt and Holmberg, 1995: 101). As part of a collaborative project on party change in advanced industrial democracies, we have collected long-term series on the levels of party identification in 19 nations.[8] By extending the time-span and the cross-national breadth of the data, the empirical evidence now presents a clear and striking picture of the

[6] For example, if the American time-series had begun in 1976, as do many other national series, the marked drop in trust would be much less evident. The respective 1976–92 coefficients would be: trust (–.337); crooked (–.182); waste taxes (–.556); and benefits all (–.241).

[7] We suspect that the Dutch time-series begins too late to capture the stable period of Dutch politics before the end of pillarization and the realignment of the party system in the late 1960s (equivalent to US opinion levels before the drop in trust in the late 1960s). A Dutch series beginning in the early 1960s might follow the pattern of other advanced industrial democracies.

[8] I would like to acknowledge my collaboration with Ian McAllister and Martin Wattenberg in the collection and interpretation of these party identification data. One reason for the difference from Schmitt and Holmberg (1995) is the inclusion of eight additional nations (Australia, Austria, Canada, Finland, Iceland, Japan, New Zealand, and the United States), and each of these nations displays a pattern of decreasing partisanship. In addition, extending the time-series in several other nations

erosion of partisan attachments among contemporary publics (Table 3.3). In 17 of the 19 nations, the regression slopes for overall party identification are negative—a striking consistency for such a diverse array of nations. Similarly, all of the coefficients for the percentage of strong partisans are negative, albeit of different strength and statistical significance. The United States, Britain and Sweden continue to display the decrease in partisanship that has long been observed in the literature, but now these cases are joined by most other advanced industrial democracies. If party attachments reflect citizen support for the system of party-based representative government, then the simultaneous decline in party attachments in nearly all advanced industrial democracies offers a first sign of the public's affective disengagement from politics.

Confidence in Political Institutions

To see whether institutional confidence has spread beyond parties the best evidence again comes from the American National Election Studies. A series of questions suggests that the decline in public confidence is broader than just dissatisfaction with the party system. For example, several questions from the

Table 3.3. Trends in party identification over time

Nation	% with PID	% Identifiers		% Strong identifiers		Period	(N)
		b	Sig.	b	Sig.		
Australia	92	−.146	.35	−.620	.00	1967–96	(7)
Austria	67	−1.120	.00	−.777	.00	1969–94	(9)
Belgium*	50	.039	.85	−.290	.07	1975–94	(20)
Great Britain	93	−.225	.02	−1.098	.00	1964–92	(8)
Canada	90	−.113	.09	−.066	.57	1965–93	(8)
Denmark	52	.126	.60	−.189	.57	1971–90	(7)
Finland	57	−.293	.49	−.147	.61	1975–91	(4)
France*	62	−.860	.04	−.600	—	1975–94	(20)
Germany	78	−.462	.02	−.449	.01	1972–94	(7)
Iceland	80	−.750	.02	−.449	.01	1983–95	(4)
Ireland*	61	−1.700	.00	−.950	.00	1978–94	(17)
Italy*	78	−1.300	.00	−.970	.00	1978–94	(17)
Luxemburg*	61	−.580	.02	−.470	.00	1975–94	(20)
Japan	70	−.386	.06	—	—	1962–95	(7)
Netherlands	38	−.199	.44	−.142	.45	1971–93	(8)
New Zealand	87	−.476	.01	−.750	.01	1975–93	(7)
Norway	66	−.220	.34	−.280	.18	1965–93	(8)
Sweden	64	−.690	.00	−.473	.01	1968–94	(10)
United States	77	−.409	.00	−.225	.05	1952–92	(11)

Note: The % with party identification in column two is the average of the percentage expressing an identification in the first two surveys in each series.

Source: Nations marked with an asterisk are based on the *Eurobarometer Surveys*; other nations are based on the respective National Election Studies (Dalton 1998).

strengthened ongoing patterns of dealignment. For more extensive analyses of the party identification trends and their sources see Dalton (1998).

ANES examine the perceived responsiveness of government and political institutions (Dalton 1996: 271). These questions show a trend of decreasing belief that parties, elections, and the government are responsive to the public's interests. Another battery of questions taps confidence in political and social institutions and shows a similar decline in support from 1966 to the 1970s and 1980s, with new low points scored in the early 1990s (Dalton 1996: 267–9; Blendon *et al.* 1997)[9]. Americans' dissatisfaction with government now extends beyond just the incumbents in office to the institutions themselves.

This erosion of public confidence in political institutions does not appear unique to the United States. British citizens are well known for their support of democratic institutions. Yet these aspects of the British political culture also have eroded. The democratic political consensus has weakened among signs of growing popular dissatisfaction with political parties and the other institutions of government (Curtice and Jowell 1997; Topf 1989). As one illustration, in 1987 less than half of Britons believed that either civil servants, the national government, or local councils could be trusted to serve the public interest (Jowell and Topf 1988).

Unfortunately, comparable long-term cross-national data on trust in political institutions are not available. The best available evidence comes from Ola Listhaug and Matti Wiberg's analysis of the 1981–4 and 1990–3 *World Values Surveys* (Listhaug and Wiberg 1995; Inglehart 1997*a*). They analysed public confidence in government institutions and found a general pattern of decline for European publics[10]. Table 3.4 extends their analyses to a larger set of advanced industrial democracies. Although this data-series begins after the drop in political support that occurred before the 1980s, we still find a general decline in confidence in government institutions. Averaged across five different institutions, confidence decreased an average of 6 per cent over this decade. Ronald Inglehart's analyses in this volume reaffirm and expands this point: support for institutions of political authority has weakened in advanced industrial democracies.

When the signs of growing popular scepticism first appeared in American surveys during the late 1960s and early 1970s, there were reasons to link these findings to the immediate problems of American politics (Miller 1974*a*, 1974*b*; Citrin 1974). These were exceptionally turbulent years for the United States. A decade of social protest, a divisive and costly war, economic recession, and unprecedented corruption by government officials strained the fibre of American politics far beyond its regular bounds. And yet, the continuation of these American trends into the 1990s, and parallel evidence from other advanced industrial democracies suggests that we are witnessing more than a

---

[9] For the specific question wordings and data sources please contact the author.

[10] Listhaug (1995) studied support trends in only four nations (Denmark, Netherlands, Norway, and Sweden). In a broader cross-national context, we can now see that these four nations are not representative of advanced industrial democracies. Moreover, even in these nations the addition of later timepoints showed decreasing trust in Denmark, Norway, and Sweden (Borre and Andersen 1997; Holmberg in this volume).

Table 3.4. Confidence in political institutions

	1980–1	1990–1	Change
Austria	62	48	–14
Belgium	50	43	–7
Canada	61	46	–15
Denmark	63	66	3
Finland	72	53	–19
France	57	56	–1
Germany	55	53	–2
Great Britain	64	60	–4
Iceland	62	63	1
Ireland	66	61	–5
Italy	44	41	–3
Japan	46	41	–5
Netherlands	54	54	0
Norway	75	66	–9
Spain	53	45	–8
Sweden	61	54	–7
United States	63	56	–7
AVERAGE	59	53	–6

Note: Table entries are the average percentage expressing confidence in five political institutions: armed forces, legal system, police, parliament, and the civil service. The armed forces item was not available for Iceland and the parliament item was not available for Denmark; the scores in these two nations are based on the remaining items.

Sources: 1981–4 and 1990–3 *World Values Surveys*.

temporary slump in politicians' performance. Rather than a transient phenomenon or merely linked to distrust of incumbents, public scepticism has at least partially generalized to political institutions and thus may be a continuing feature of contemporary democratic politics.

Evaluations of the Regime Performance

How far does the evidence of the public's political disenchantment extend? The next level of political support involves orientations toward the regime performance. There is a relatively long and broad opinion series on evaluations of the functioning of the democratic process.[11] Because these data have been extensively analysed elsewhere (Fuchs *et al.* 1995; Morlino and Tarchi 1996; Clarke *et al.* 1993; Kuechler 1991), we will only summarize the results here. In broad terms, it appears that satisfaction with the functioning of the democratic system has been fairly stable from the early 1970s to the late 1980s,

[11] The specific question asks: *'On the whole, are you very satisfied, fairly satisfied, not very satisfied, or not at all satisfied with the way democracy works (in R's country)?'* Sometimes the question included a prompt referencing the functioning of political parties. Previous research is divided on whether this is a measure of specific or diffuse support (e.g. Fuchs *et al.* 1995). We interpret this item as a measure of specific support because they emphasize the performance of the system.

with a pattern of trendless fluctuations apparent in the early 1990s (see Klingemann Chapter 2 in this volume, Table 2.13).[12]

Unfortunately, there is much less data available on the more important topic of public orientations toward the principles of the democratic process. To the extent that such data are available, they suggest that support for political rights and participatory norms have actually grown over the past generation. For instance, the available long-term data suggest that contemporary publics have become more politically tolerant during the postwar period (Thomassen 1995; McCloskey and Brill 1983).

In addition, there is at least indirect evidence that perceptions of the appropriate role for citizens now emphasizes a more participatory style and a greater willingness to challenge authority. Inglehart's (1990, 1997a) research on post-material value change—with its emphasis on participatory values as a measure of post-materialism—reinforces these points. It would be extremely valuable to expand future data collections to focus on public norms toward how the democratic process should function. It is surprising that we know so little about what citizens expect of the democratic process, and how these expectations have changed over time. Therefore, we shift our attention to support of democratic principles to determine whether the malaise reaches to this level of political orientations.

Support for Democratic Principles

Many of the survey questions analysed so far have measured support for the incumbents or institutions of the democratic process, or could be interpreted in these terms. One might argue that dissatisfaction with politicians is a sign of the vitality of democracy, and an objective reading of politics by the public. If there is a crisis of democracy, this dissatisfaction must have been generalized to the political system itself.

There is an abundance of empirical data on public attitudes toward democracy—the next level of political support. For example, a frequently used opinion survey asked whether democracy is considered the best form of government. Although there is not a long cross-national time-series for this question, the presently high degree of support suggests there has not been a major erosion in these sentiments (Table 3.5).[13] On average, more than three-quarters of the public in advanced industrial democracies feel that democracy is the best form of government. Hans Dieter Klingemann's more extensive analyses of these items in the 1995–7 *World Values Surveys* (in this volume)

---

[12] I see two additional limitations of these data. First, the question wording leads respondents to treat this as an evaluation of the political incumbents. In addition, the *Eurobarometer* series begins only in the mid-1970s (or later). It would be preferable to utilize a measure of democratic performance that was first asked in the 1960s or earlier.

[13] The two questions were as follows: '*Let us consider the idea of democracy, without thinking of existing democracies. In principle, are you for or against the idea of democracy?*' and '*Which of the following opinions about different forms of government is closest to your own? (1) In any case, democracy is the best form of government, whatever the circumstance may be, (2) In certain cases a dictatorship can be positive, (3) For someone like me, it doesn't make any difference whether we have a democracy or a dictatorship.*'

Table 3.5. Support for democracy

Nation	Approve idea of democracy	Democracy as the best form of government
Norway*	—	93
Sweden*	—	93
Denmark	98	93
Greece	99	92
Switzerland*	—	91
United States*	—	88
Japan*	—	88
Netherlands	98	85
Portugal	99	84
Luxemburg	98	83
Australia*	—	83
Germany	96	82
Spain	96	78
France	95	78
Great Britain	93	76
Finland*	—	75
Italy	93	74
Northern Ireland	95	65
Ireland	93	65

Sources: *Eurobarometer* 31a (1989); 1994–7 *World Values Survey* (marked with asterisk).

indicate that these sentiments generally have continued into the 1990s. The two notable exceptions—Ireland and Northern Ireland—may be reflecting the political dissatisfaction that accompanied the violent conflicts in the North. Another question in this survey was less evaluative, tapping public support for the ideal of democracy. Even at the end of the 1980s, before the post-Cold War euphoria for democracy had begun, support for the idea of democracy is nearly universal within Western democracies. Reviewing this evidence, Dieter Fuchs and his colleagues (1995) concluded that these data and other measures of democratic values indicate that democratic legitimacy is widespread.

A relatively long time-series is available for another measure of system support, a question measuring support for social change through revolutionary action.[14] Table 3.6 provides data from 9 nations. These data span the oil shocks and resulting economic crises of the mid-1970s and early 1980s, periods of political violence, the challenges of new social movements, and the miscellaneous political scandals we have described in this paper. Nevertheless, between the early 1970s and the present, support for revolutionary social change represents a mere trace element in each nation. Indeed, support for improving society through gradual reforms is consistently the most preferred response in each nation.

[14] The question wording is as follows: 'On this card are three basic kinds of attitudes concerning the society we live in. Please choose the one which best describes your own opinion: (1) The entire way our society is organized must be radically changed by revolutionary action, (2) Our society must be gradually improved by reforms, and (3) Our present society must be valiantly defended against all subversive forces.'

Table 3.6. Attitudes toward social change (%)

	USA		Great Britain		Germany		France		Belgium		Italy		Netherlands		Ireland		Denmark	
	1981	1990	1976	1990	1970	1990	1970	1990	1970	1990	1970	1990	1970	1990	1976	1990	1976	1990
Change society by revolutionary action	5	6	7	5	2	2	5	4	3	4	7	7	6	2	7	4	4	2
Improve society through reforms	66	67	60	75	70	59	78	70	69	65	73	79	74	70	60	74	51	70
Defend society against subversives	20	11	35	13	20	28	12	20	14	18	10	9	15	23	22	19	38	20
No opinion	9	11	8	8	8	11	5	7	13	14	9	5	5	6	10	3	7	8

In summary, contemporary publics are dissatisfied with the incumbents of office and even with the political institutions of representative democracy, but these feelings of dissatisfaction have apparently not (yet) affected basic support for the political system and the values of the democratic process. If we adopt a sports analogy, can citizens continue to like the game of democratic politics if they have lost confidence in the players and even how the game is now played? How long can this apparent incongruence in political beliefs continue, and how will it be resolved?

Support for the Political Community

Our final analyses of political support examine feelings toward the political community. Identification with the political community is the most fundamental of political identities—to think of oneself as American or British pre-dates specific political identities, such as party or ideological ties. Almond and Verba (1963) described these feelings as 'system affect', a strong emotional attachment to the nation presumably provides a reservoir of diffuse support that can maintain a political system through temporary periods of political stress.

One can imagine that these sentiments have not been immune to the dissatisfactions which have affected other aspects of political support. Expressions of patriotism seem less common, and more anachronistic, than they did a generation ago. Growing emphasis on multiculturalism in many societies has raised questions about the breadth and depth of a common national identity. In Europe, the development of European attachments may be weakening national identities. A decline in national identities would spell a crisis for the nation-state, and not just a crisis of the political system.

One measure of such feelings involves pride in one's nation.[15] Figure 3.1 displays the percentage who feel proud of their nation for a set of advanced industrial democracies.[16] National pride is common in most states. The United States and Ireland display extremely high levels of national pride. Most other publics express their national pride in more moderate tones. Britons express relatively high degrees of national pride; the bifurcated division of the French political culture yields more modest rates of national pride. Germans are especially hesitant in their statements of national pride, which we attribute to the lingering reaction to the nationalist extremism of Third Reich (Dalton 1996; Topf et al. 1989).

Beyond these cross-national variations,[17] it is apparent that national pride

[15] I want to thank David Easton for pointing out that what might be occurring is not the decline of national identities, but the addition of new identities (to regions, Europe, or social collectives) or the nesting of multiple identities that may exist somewhat separate of national loyalties.

[16] The question asked: 'How proud are you to be (nationality)?' The responses were: '(1) very proud, (2) quite proud, (3) not very proud, and (4) not at all proud.' The figure presents the 'proud' and 'very proud' responses.

[17] More interesting are two cases from Eastern Europe in the 1990–1 World Values Survey where the public did not identify with the nation; this raises warning signals for the polity and the system. National pride was relatively low in Czechoslovakia in 1990—within three years the nation had split in two. Similarly, at the time of this survey the Soviet Union was fragmenting and the reformed Russian Republic was born of economic failure and Cold War defeat. Less than two-thirds of Russians expressed pride in their nation in 1990.

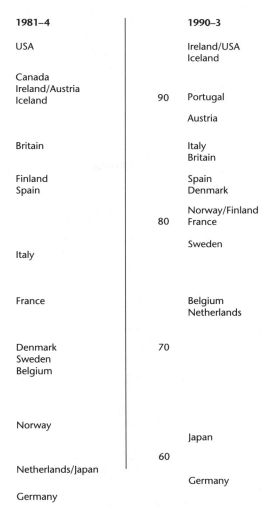

1981–4		1990–3
USA		Ireland/USA Iceland
Canada Ireland/Austria Iceland	90	Portugal
		Austria
Britain		Italy Britain
Finland Spain		Spain Denmark
	80	Norway/Finland France
		Sweden
Italy		
France		Belgium Netherlands
Denmark Sweden Belgium	70	
Norway		
		Japan
Netherlands/Japan	60	
		Germany
Germany		

Fig. 3.1. Feelings of national pride.

Sources: *World Values Surveys* 1981–4 and 1991–3; figure entries are the percentage 'proud' and 'very proud'.

has not followed a systematic trend over the 1980–91 period.[18] Roughly as many nations display a slight increase, as display a slight decrease; all of these changes are also fairly small. Klingemann's more recent data for several nations (in this volume) shows continued patterns of stability. In addition,

---

[18] Inglehart (1990: 411) describes a very large drop in national pride between 1970 and 1980 for a subset of European nations. This trend is not mentioned in Inglehart's most recent analysis of national pride trends (1997: 304–5). Because of the dramatic change, across differences in survey organizations, I am cautious about the 1970–80 comparisons.

when earlier time-series are available for specific nations, they also show a pattern of relative stability over time (Topf *et al.* 1989). In fact, the post-war nation-building process in some Western democracies has led to increasing national attachments over the past generation.[19] However, as one would expect from affective feelings of community attachment, these sentiments generally have proved relatively impervious to change in most advanced industrial democracies.

The Future of Democratic Politics

In their recent study of citizen orientations in European democracies, Fuchs and Klingemann (1995) discounted claims that there have been fundamental changes in the political values of democratic publics in the 1970s and 1980s. They summarize the findings of *Citizens and the State* in fairly sanguine terms: 'The hypotheses we tested are based on the premise that a fundamental change had taken place in the relationship between citizens and the state, provoking a challenge to representative democracy . . . the postulated fundamental change in the citizens' relationship with the state largely did *not* occur' (Fuchs and Klingemann 1995: 429).

Our reassessment and expansion of their empirical analyses yield different results.[20] We find that citizens have grown more distant from political parties, more critical of political institutions, and less positive toward government—this points to fundamental changes in the political orientations of democratic publics over the past generation.

We traced the present boundaries of these sentiments. The decline in political trust is most dramatic for evaluations of politicians and political elites in general. The deference to authority that once was common in many Western democracies has partially been replaced by public scepticism of elites. Feelings of mistrust have gradually broadened to include evaluations of the political regime and political institutions. It is equally important to note, however, that public scepticism has not significantly affected support for democratic principles and the political community. As citizens are criticizing the incumbents of government, they are simultaneously expressing support for the democratic creed.

If we look beyond the empirical data, these findings continue the debate on the vitality of democracy that began in the 1970s (Crozier *et al.* 1975; Huntington 1981). Excessive public demands were supposedly overloading the ability of governments to perform, creating what some analysts felt was a

---

[19] For longitudinal trends in support for the nation or the political community, see: Austria (Ulram 1994: 91); Canada (Clarke *et al.* 1992: 107).

[20] The evidence available to Klingemann and Fuchs indicated declines in party identifications in only 8 of 14 nations (1995: 430); our updated and expanded data documents declines in 18 of 20 nations. Similarly, while they found a 2–2 split for trust in politicians (1995: 430), we uncovered declines in at least 12 of the 14 nations we examined.

crisis of democracy. Some conservatives used the elitist theory of democracy to offer a solution to this crisis. They maintained that if a supportive and quiescent public ensured a smoothly functioning political system, then we must redevelop these traits in contemporary publics. The centrifugal tendencies of democratic politics (and the demands of the public) must be controlled, and political authority must be re-established. Indeed, Huntington (1975, 1981) saw American's commitment to the democratic creed as a weakness of the political culture—rather than a strength, as it should be seen.

An alternative view held that if the government was overloaded, it was because government had not modernized and reformed itself to match the new needs and demands of its citizens (Barber 1984). These researchers noted that the decline in political support had not eroded support for democratic principles, the public was criticizing how these principles were functioning in a system of representative democracy. The solution was to improve the democratic process and democratic institutions, not to accept non-democratic alternatives.

I lean toward the latter interpretation of contemporary democracy (Dalton and Kuechler 1990, chs. 1 and 14). Popular commitment to democratic principles and processes remains strong. Citizens are frustrated with how contemporary democratic systems work—or how they do *not* work. I agree with Klingemann's conclusions (in this volume) that the new sources of dissatisfaction are not among those with anti-system views, but among those who want to risk more democracy. The 'creedal passion' that so worried Huntington is actually a sign of the vitality of democracy, and the force that can generate progressive political reform.

Popular dissatisfaction with present democratic structures is fuelling calls to reform the processes of representative democracy. For example, recent data from the 1996 *British Social Attitudes* survey indicates that the politically dissatisfied are more likely to favour constitutional reforms, such as changes in the role of the House of Lords, judicial protection of human rights, and greater public access to government information (Curtice and Jowell 1997). In addition, political parties in several nations have instituted internal reforms to address the procedural dissatisfactions of their supporters. The recent electoral reforms in Italy, Japan, and New Zealand are additional signs of public dissatisfaction with the electoral process, and attempts to reform democratic institutions. Ironically, however, as one nation moves towards more proportional representation as a solution, another moves in the opposite direction. This makes me sceptical that reforms to political parties and electoral systems are sufficient to address the present malaise. This scepticism is supported by survey evidence showing that public confidence in political parties ranks near the bottom among all political institutions. Widespread declines in political support and growing alienation from various institutions and forms of the democratic process suggest that the sources of dissatisfaction go deeper than can be addressed by electoral reforms. Contemporary publics are also expressing a more fundamental dissatisfaction with the system of representative democracy itself (Klingemann and Fuchs 1995, ch. 14; Dahl 1989). The problem is focused on the institutions and processes of representative democracy, not democratic values and principles. Thus another response to popular dissatisfaction has been a move toward participatory democracy.

The potential for citizen participation is limited by the traditional forms of representative democracy, especially in Western Europe. The opportunities for electoral input are low for most Europeans. The chance to cast a few votes during a multi-year electoral cycle is not a record of citizen input that should be admired. Furthermore, declining vote turnout in advanced industrial societies suggests growing disenchantment with this form of democratic participation. The fundamental structure of contemporary democratic institutions was developed in the nineteenth century; society has changed a good deal since then.

Strengthened commitments to the democratic ideal, and increased skills and resources on the part of contemporary publics, are leading to increased political participation beyond the present forms of representative democracy. For instance, research documents the growth of protest and direct-action methods among Western publics (Barnes and Kaase 1979; Jennings and van Deth 1989). Sidney Verba and his colleagues (1995: 72) similarly show that while Americans' participation in elections has been declining, direct contacting of government officials and work with community groups has been increasing. Participation in new social movements, such as the environmental movement, has also increased substantially over the past generation.

These new participation patterns are creating pressure on governments to develop forms of more direct, participatory democracy (Budge 1996). For example, surveys of the German public and elites indicate that democratic norms are broadening to embrace more participatory forms of democracy (Buerklin 1997b; Fuchs 1996). The use of referendums and initiatives is generally increasing in democratic nations (Butler and Ranney 1994). Younger generations and the better educated are more likely to favour referendums, greater participation by the citizenry, and other forms of direct democracy.

A recent review of the social movement literature describes other ways that institutional reforms can increase direct citizen participation in policy-making (Dalton 1993). In Germany, for example, local citizen action groups have won changes in administrative law to allow for citizen participation in local administrative processes. Italian environmental legislation now grants individuals legal standing in the courts when they seek to protect the environment from the actions of municipalities or government administrative agencies. Similar reforms in the United States provide individual citizens and citizen groups greater access to the political process (Ingram and Smith 1993). These institutional changes are difficult to accomplish and therefore are likely to proceed at a slow pace; but once implemented they restructure the whole process of making policy that extends beyond a single issue or a single-policy agenda.

In summary, the growth of critical citizens is really a challenge.

Democracies need to adapt to present-day politics and the new style of participatory politics. The challenge to democracies is whether they can continue to evolve, to guarantee political right, and to increase the ability of citizens to control their lives.

4

Five Years After the Fall: Trajectories of Support for Democracy in Post-Communist Europe

WILLIAM MISHLER AND RICHARD ROSE

DEMOCRACY thrives on popular support and withers in its absence (Easton 1965). Popular support not only confers legitimacy on democratic regimes but is also vital to their effective performance. A reserve of public confidence in the regime enhances governments' abilities to make decisions and commit resources without resort to coercion or the need to obtain the specific approval of citizens for every decision. As discussed in the Conclusion of the book, when public support is strong, governments, 'are able to make new commitments on the basis of it and, if successful, increase support even more' (Gamson 1968: 45 f.). This can create a virtuous, democratic spiral. Conversely, when support is weak, democratic governments cannot respond effectively to political challenges, losing support in a downward spiral.

Although it is commonplace to observe that support is vital to democracy, it is impossible to identify an absolute level of support sufficient for democracy to flourish. This is because widespread, popular support for the regime is a necessary but not a sufficient condition for democratic stability (see Mishler and Rose 1995a). The vitality of democracy also depends on the severity of social cleavages, levels of political stress, the extent of social capital, the nature of elite attitudes and behaviour and the existence and effective performance of a variety of democratic institutions. Levels of popular support needed to sustain democracy are both relative and contingent. As a consequence, all that can be said about the relationship between levels of support and democratic stability is that stable or increasing levels of support facilitate stable democracy, whereas declining levels of support undermine democracy and threaten its collapse. The trajectory of political support is critical.

The authors appreciate the generosity of the Paul Lazarsfeld Society, Vienna, for permitting use of the data from the *New Democracies Barometer* (*NDB*) I–IV. The *NDB* is sponsored by the Austrian Federal Ministry for Science and Research and the Austrian National Bank. Research support was provided to the authors by the National Science Foundation (SBR–09515079) and by grants from the University of Strathclyde. The authors are solely responsible for analysis and interpretation.

An upward trajectory of public support is even more important to new democracies and those in the process of democratization. Democratizing regimes not only confront greater political stresses, they also lack the institutions and leaders which enable older, established democracies to cope with political challenges. For example, the new democracies of Eastern and Central Europe face a double challenge since the transition to democracy in Eastern and Central Europe has occurred in tandem with the transformation from centrally planned to market economies (cf. Kornai 1992). In the long term, the discipline of the market may increase economic efficiency and enhance performance, but the immediate consequences of market reforms have been widespread economic dislocations which both increase political stress and threaten popular support for the new regimes (Kornai 1992; EBRD 1995).

Whereas support for established democracies is relatively viscous, changing only slowly and incrementally over time, support for new democracies is potentially much more volatile. Contributing to this volatility is the likelihood that support for new regimes depends more heavily on regime performance. An established democracy benefits because citizens are socialized to support the regime from childhood. By contrast, citizens in a new democracy were socialized into a different political order. In the short term, a new regime may benefit from a degree of popular acceptance and approval resulting from the public's rejection of the old regime. In the longer term, however, support for new democracies must be performance based. Support cannot survive indefinitely unless citizens perceive its performance as providing some reasonable measure of individual and collective goods (Hardin 1982; Hirschman 1970; Olson 1965). Thus, whereas established democracies are supported for what they are as well as what they do, new democracies must be supported for what they do and, perhaps, in the short term, for what they are not (cf. Rose 1992). The underlying dynamics of popular support for a new democracy are potentially very different from those of an established democracy.

This chapter assesses the trajectories and dynamics of public support for seven democratizing regimes in Central and Eastern Europe—Bulgaria, the Czech Republic, Slovakia, Hungary, Poland, Romania, and Slovenia—during the first five years following the fall of communism. We begin by examining popular approval of the new regimes in 1991, shortly following the collapse of communism, and track the trajectory of support through 1995. We then develop and test a model of the dynamics underlying these trends, paying particular attention to the extent to which support is contingent on political and economic performance. More generally, we explore whether and to what extent the sources of support change over time as citizens acquire experience with the new regimes.

Reconceptualizing Support for New Democracies

Most models of democracy are based on the experiences of long-established and stable democratic regimes. Stable democracies, however, are rare; undemocratic regimes are the historical norm (see Rose, Mishler and Haerpfer 1998, ch. 3). Even today, the 'median country' in the world is only partly democratic (Freedom House 1996; Bollen 1993; Diamond 1996). Although the 'third wave' of democratization has produced a big increase in the number of countries aspiring to democracy, none of the new regimes have reached an equilibrium in their transition to democracy or qualify as stable democratic regimes. The explosion of new democracies makes particularly apt Dankwart Rustow's (1970) caution that the theories appropriate to explain the genesis of a democracy are not necessarily the same as those explaining the functioning of established, stable democracies. An understanding of support for new democracies requires a reconceptualization of standard democratic models.

In newly democratic countries the survival of the democratic regime is the fundamental concern. In Easton's (1965: 190 ff.) venerable conception, the political regime constitutes the basic framework for governing a country, defining the whole set of relationships between institutions and individuals. Citizens cannot pick and choose among elements of the regime, approving some parts and rejecting others, for example selecting the decisiveness of a dictatorship, the static security of a non-market communist welfare state, and the freedom of a democracy. A regime is holistic, what Ragin (1987) describes as 'an indivisible'.

Within established democracies, support for the democratic regime is rarely an issue. Support for the regime typically is learned unconsciously and without choice during childhood socialization. Citizens grow up in the belief not simply that democracy is the best among alternative regimes but that democracy is the only possible regime for their country. The most fundamental debates in established democracies are not about overthrowing the regime but about modifying its territorial boundaries. Quebec nationalists and Scottish nationalists each seek independence from a multinational state, but both are pledged to maintain democratic regimes when they achieve national independence. Within established democracies with agreed territorial boundaries, political differences may be profound but rarely impinge upon the nature of the regime. Democratic politics are about the articulation and reconciliation of conflicting views of what government should do. The democratic nature of the regime is taken for granted. Citizens can and do distrust the government of the day, oppose its policies, or express dissatisfaction with the performance of particular institutions but they do not promote the overthrow of the regime. Expressions of dissatisfaction are properly interpreted as demands for democratic reform, not as opposition to democratic rule (see, Chapter 7 in this volume).

In newly democratic nations, in contrast, support for the democratic regime is very much in question. By definition citizens have lived under at least two different regimes—an undemocratic predecessor and the new democratizing regime. In Central and Eastern Europe, older citizens have lived under as many as four different regimes including Nazi and communist totalitarianism. They know, as a matter of first-hand experience, that democracy is only one among several alternatives and that government with free elections and political accountability is not the only way their country can be governed. Thus, their support of the new regime is relative; they evaluate the new regime in light of plausible alternatives, including especially the old Communist regime, the alternative they know best.

Choices meaningful to a citizen in a new democracy are historically conditioned. In Britain, democratization involved a series of choices between the status quo and marginal adjustments, for example, expanding the proportion of the adult population eligible to vote. By contrast, in post-communist countries historical alternatives have included a totalitarian, Stalinist regime; a post-totalitarian regime that reduced repression but did not introduce freedom of speech or free elections; and a new democracy. While the alternatives reflect historical conjunctures, they are not path-determined. The introduction of new democratic institutions in countries such as Bulgaria and Romania emphasizes the extent of disjunction between past and present. But for the same reason, there is no assurance that new regimes will evolve into stable democracies supported by the great mass of citizens. At the start of the process, there is a competition—sometimes explicit, other times implicit—for popular support between proponents of democratization and undemocratic alternatives.

How do people evaluate democracy when they have experienced one or more alternatives and know they have a choice among competing regimes? In an established democracy, Dahl poses the choice as between a hypothetical democratic ideal and a realistic if imperfect polyarchy. The optimist sees evidence of a gap as implying a demand for reform, to move the regime still closer to the democratic ideal; the pessimist sees this as threatening something worse. In a new democracy, the choice is very different. It is between an old regime that is at least implicitly regarded as bad by some, and a new regime that has not had time to demonstrate its performance. In so far as any new regime is likely to face more numerous, more challenging and more pervasive difficulties than an established democracy, a new democracy may also make mistakes in a trial-and-error process of learning how to govern with new representative institutions. But it does not follow that dissatisfaction with democracy will lead to a demand for an undemocratic alternative. In a duopolistic situation, a stumbling new democracy may be preferred as the lesser evil. This was the hypothesis advanced by Winston Churchill (1947) in the House of Commons just after the end of World War II:

Many forms of government have been tried and will be tried in this world of sin and woe. No one pretends that democracy is perfect or all wise. Indeed, it has been said that democracy is the worst form of government, except for all those other forms that have been tried from time to time.

The logic of the Churchill hypothesis is realist, not idealist. Whereas an idealist sees democracy as the greatest good, in a duopolistic situation the realist is willing to support democracy as the lesser evil.

Surveying support in a new democracy is fundamentally different than in an established democracy, for it is both necessary and practical to ask people to evaluate both the new and the old regime (cf. Morlino and Montero 1995: 234 ff.). Since the experience of both democratic and undemocratic regimes is recent, there is no risk that asking questions about undemocratic regimes will produce what Philip Converse (1964) called 'non-attitudes', that is, more or less random responses to questions on topics that people have not thought about. Equally important, asking people about their attitudes toward democracy five years after the first free election, will produce a more informed, and perhaps even different response, than asking people what they think of democracy when they have not yet learned at firsthand to separate the symbolic ideal of democracy from the way democracy actually works in post-communist states.

In order to avoid the problem of non-attitudes and to measure support for the new democracies as indivisible and experiential, the *New Democracies Barometer* (NDB) asked citizens in Central and Eastern Europe a very simple question: '*Here is a scale for ranking systems of government; the top, +100, is the best, and the bottom, −100, is the worst. Where would you put: (Show card with scale) (a) the former Communist regime? (b) the present system with free elections and many parties? (c) our system of governing in five years time?'* A useful feature of this question is that it measures support for the current and past regimes on a common metric. It also avoids normatively and emotionally laden words and concepts such as 'democracy' that might bias responses, and it avoids country- and institution-specific references thereby facilitating cross-national comparisons. Importantly, asking people to evaluate the regime, past and present, avoids the confusion that can result when people are asked whether they are satisfied with how democracy is working. The latter conflates ideal and real criteria and provides no information about how people evaluate democracy compared to other possible regimes, which might be even less satisfactory.

Because of the critical importance of support for democracy as against the old regime, the *New Democracies Barometer* of the Paul Lazarsfeld Society, Vienna, has asked this question in every survey undertaken in post-communist countries. The first *NDB* survey was conducted in the autumn of 1991, within a year of the first free post-communist elections. It included: Bulgaria, the still united Czechoslovakia, Hungary, Poland, Romania, and Slovenia. The second wave, *NDB* II, was conducted in the early winter of 1992–3 and included separate Czech and Slovak samples. *NDB* III was conducted in the winter of 1993–4 in the same seven countries and *NDB* IV in the autumn of 1995. A national probability sample of approximately 1,000 adults over the age of 18 was interviewed in each country in each iteration of the *NDB*. All interviews were conducted face-to-face and samples checked to ensure proper representation on the basis of age, sex, education, region, and urban–rural residence. National samples were then weighted (including the *NDB* I half-samples for the Czech and Slovak republics) so that there are equal numbers of cases for each country (1000 per country per year) and 28,000 cases in total (for further details see SWS-Rundschau 1992; Rose and Haerpfer 1996*a*).

Although the seven countries in the survey share the common experience of communism, they are diverse in other respects, including the pace and progress of democratization and of economic reforms. Nevertheless, even though all of the countries may currently fall short of idealist democratic standards, all have at least begun the process of democratization; all have held relatively free elections; and all have experienced at least one peaceful change in party control of government.

Trajectories of Support

For the new democracies in Eastern and Central Europe, the *NDB* baseline is the autumn of 1991, shortly following the collapse of communism and the first free elections. When asked in the winter of 1991 to evaluate the new regimes, most citizens, predictably, were cautious, expressing modest approval (Table 4.1). Across the seven *NDB* countries, an average of 59 per cent gave positive ratings to their new regimes; 28 per cent expressed negative evaluations, and 13 per cent gave the new regime a zero or neutral rating. Nevertheless, the average *level* of support was only very slightly positive (+ 1.4 on a scale ranging from – 10 to + 10).[1]

Initial support for the new regimes varied by country, but the differences were small, suggesting that the shared experience of communism outweighed differences in history and culture in shaping initial reactions to the post-communist regimes. Indeed, majorities supported the new regime in every country except Slovenia and Slovakia. Even in the latter, however, supporters of the new regime outnumbered opponents (by 13 and 14 percentage points, respectively), and the average level of support was slightly positive. Support for the new regime was highest in the Czech Republic and Romania where upwards of 70 per cent of citizens expressed approval. Here, too, however, support was considerably wider than deep; the average level of support was only + 2.6 in the Czech Republic and + 2.2 in Romania.

Although, in absolute terms, initial support for the new regimes appears somewhat tentative and shallow, in relative terms, it is greater than the public's retrospective evaluations of the old Communist regime. When asked in *NDB* I to evaluate the old regime, most citizens expressed disapproval. On

[1] The original scale presented to respondents ranged between – 100 and + 100 with tick marks at 10-point intervals. Because responses were clustered at the tick marks, we collapsed the original scale into a 21-point scale ranging from – 10 to + 10. Similar transformations were performed on the thermometer scales measuring support for the old regime and evaluations (past, present, and future) of the macroeconomy.

Table 4.1. Baseline support for current, communist, and future regimes, 1991

	Bulgaria	Czech Rep.	Hungary	Poland	Romania	Slovenia	Slovakia	NDB
% Supporting current regime	64	71	57	52	69	49	50	59
(Average Support)	(2.6)	(2.6)	(.76)	(.04)	(2.2)	(.36)	(.45)	(1.3)
% Supporting communist regime	30	23	51	34	26	41	44	35
(Average Support)	(−2.4)	(−4.2)	(.39)	(−2.2)	(−3.7)	(−.56)	(−.69)	(−2.0)
% Preferring current vs. old regime:	64	78	51	59	81	50	51	62
(Average difference)	(5.1)	(6.9)	(.35)	(2.2)	(5.8)	(1.0)	(1.1)	(3.3)

NDB = Aggregate seven country result.

Source: Paul Lazarsfeld Society, Vienna, New Democracies Barometer I–IV. For details see Rose and Haerpfer 1992, 1993, 1994, and 1996a.

average only 35 per cent of citizens remembered the communist regime fondly; 55 per cent expressed negative memories, and 10 per cent were neutral. The average level of disapproval was surprisingly benign (– 1.2), however. Overall, support for the old regime largely mirrored support for the new regime; where evaluations of the communist regime were most negative, the initial level of support for the new regime was highest and vice versa. Thus, disapproval of the old regime was highest in the Czech Republic and in Romania and lowest in Hungary where citizens with favourable memories of the old regime outnumbered those disapproving of the old regime by 51 vs. 38 per cent.

At the individual level, an absolute majority of citizens in every country prefer the new democratizing regime to the former communist regime. Consistent with the Churchill hypothesis, however, many people do so by giving a less negative rating to the new regime than the old one. While sceptical about the new regime, this relative open-mindedness compares favourably with their stronger negative ratings of the former communist regime. Thus in Romania, fully 81 per cent of citizens were relatively more favourable (less negative) toward the new regime, and in the Czech Republic the new regime is favoured by 78 per cent. Even in Hungary where the difference in the approval of the new and old regimes is only 6 percentage points in aggregate, 51 per cent of citizens showed a relative preference for the new regime.

Thus, in 1991, shortly after the collapse of communism, there was widespread but relatively shallow support for the new, democratizing regimes everywhere in Central and Eastern Europe. Majorities of citizens everywhere preferred the new regime over the old communist regime, but the differences were precariously thin. Moreover, the economic stresses on the new regimes were severe. Inflation across the seven countries ranged from a low of 34 per cent in Hungary to more than 300 per cent in Bulgaria, and the economies of all the countries were contracting by an average of more than 13 per cent (EBRD 1995). In consequence, renowned Hungarian economist, Janos Kornai (1992 and 1994), predicted 'painful tradeoffs' between macroeconomic stabilization and political stability.

Notwithstanding widespread pessimism about the prospects for democratization and the numerous forecasts of falling support for the new democratic regimes, the *trajectories* of public support in the *NDB* countries have been generally rising (Figure 4.1). Overall, the percentage of citizens expressing positive support for the new regimes has risen slowly but monotonically from 59 per cent in 1991 to 65 per cent in 1995 (*NDB* IV), and the average level of support has increased from + 1.3 to + 1.8—a small but statistically significant gain. In contrast, retrospective evaluations of the former communist regimes rose sharply in the second year of the transition (1992) as the opprobrium initially attached to the old regime apparently began to fade. By 1993, however, retrospective evaluations of the old regime had reversed direction, and have continued to decline modestly since. The combination of rising support for the new regimes and stable to declining support for the former communist

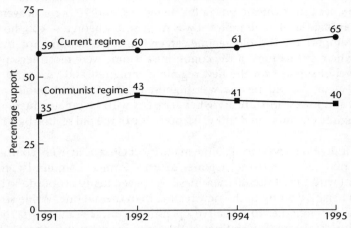

Fig. 4.1. Support for current and communist regimes, 1991–1995.
Source: As for Table 4.1.

regimes means that the ratio of public support for the new regime compared to the principal alternative regime has slowly if steadily increased.

Although in the aggregate there was very high stability in popular support for the new regimes, there were much larger, year-to-year fluctuations and cumulative four-year changes in support within individual countries (Table 4.2). Among the seven countries, the biggest gains in popular support across the period are registered in Poland where the percentage of citizens expressing approval of the new regime increased by 24 percentage points in just four years. Conversely, the largest decline occurs in Romania, where the public's initial euphoria over the fall of Ceausescu has been tempered more recently by the reality of both economic and political disarray. Still, the decline in political support for Romania is only 8 percentage points over four years, a small margin given the high starting point. Together, five of the seven *NDB* countries enjoyed upward trajectories of support across the period with the largest gains occurring in those countries with the lowest initial levels of support. Hungary is a notable exception, having suffered an overall decline of seven percentage points in support since 1991. Hungary is interesting, however, because, after dropping by 12 percentage points in 1992, public support has rebounded and appears to have stabilized since. For the last two years of *NDB* data, popular support for democratization was steady or increasing in all seven *NDB* countries.

Given a lifetime's experience with the old, communist regime and only a few months familiarity with the new regimes, an experiential model of political support predicts that public memories of the communist regime should exhibit greater stability over time than public evaluations of the new, democratizing regime with which citizens are less familiar. In general this appears to

Table 4.2. Trends in support for current and communist regimes, 1991–1995, by country (% supporting regime)

	Bulgaria	Czech Rep.	Hungary	Poland	Romania	Slovenia	Slovakia	NDB
Current regime support								
NDB I: 1991	64	71	57	52	69	49	50	59
NDB II: 1992	55	71	43	56	68	68	58	60
NDB III: 1993	58	78	51	69	60	55	52	61
NDB IV: 1995	66	77	50	76	61	66	61	65
Communist regime support								
NDB I: 1991	30	23	51	34	26	41	44	35
NDB II: 1992	41	29	67	42	35	40	48	43
NDB III: 1993	51	23	58	38	33	32	50	41
NDB IV: 1995	58	24	56	25	29	36	52	40

NDB = Aggregate seven country result.

Source: Paul Lazarsfeld Society, Vienna, *New Democracies Barometer I–IV*. For details see Rose and Haerpfer 1992, 1993, 1994, and 1996a.

be the case, although the differences are small, and there is an interesting twist to the pattern. The twist is that in six of the seven countries in the study, public memories of the old regime *increased* between 1991 and 1992, while in four of these six countries they decrease significantly in the next two surveys. The suspicion, untestable with the data available, is that this pattern reflects the democratizing equivalent of 'buyers' remorse'. In the first year following the collapse of communism, on learning that economic and political transitions take time and require patience, some citizens began to look back, nostalgically, on the familiar old system whose failings they knew how to manage. As more time has passed and as citizens have acquired experience with the new regime and learned how to cope with their new environments as well or better than in the past, then the initial nostalgia for the old regime has fallen. The principal exception to the pattern is Bulgaria where democratization has made the least headway and where nostalgia for the old regime has increased every year, nearly doubling between 1991 and 1995.

The Dynamics of Support

In an analysis of public support for post-communist regimes at the beginning of the transition (Mishler and Rose 1995*a*), we advanced a 'fear and hope' model to explain the initial sources of support. Specifically, we argued that immediately following the collapse of communism, citizens were likely to support the new regime because it represented a break from the rejected communist past and because citizens harboured strong hope that current economic sacrifices would produce real prosperity in the foreseeable future. Although the model performed quite well in explaining variations in individuals' initial support for the new regimes, we concluded with a caution. Observing that political support is inherently dynamic we reasoned as follows:

in social psychological terms . . . fear and hope are variables, not constants. They can change as memories of the Communist system fade or as continuing economic difficulties lead people to lower their economic expectations. If the present regime falters, nostalgia for the past could occur. If perceptions of the current economy and expectations for the future begin to erode, economic hope could turn to despair. (Mishler and Rose 1995*a*: 575)

In the five years since then, both fear and hope have diminished, albeit only modestly. Public attitudes toward the old regime are less negative in 1995 than they were in 1991, and economic optimism has declined as well (Rose and Haerpfer 1996*a*). Neither trend is precipitous, but both are problematic. In a 'fear and hope' model continuation of these trends could seriously erode public support for the new democracies.

There is another dynamic element underlying political support, however. Support can change not only because the numerical values or *levels* of key sources of support vary over time, but also because the relative salience or *impact* of those influences change. For example, if public fears of the old regime persist but the public increasingly dismisses the old regime as irrelevant and discounts its salience to contemporary concerns (i.e. communism was terrible, but there is no chance of its resurrection, so we don't need to worry about it), then, even if the level of public disapproval of the old regime remains unchanged, the reduction in its impact would substantially reduce the positive contribution it makes to the support of the new regime. Moreover, as the impact of fear diminishes, other sources of support would acquire relatively greater salience in causing/explaining subsequent changes in support. Thus, as citizens acquire experience with the new regime, the ways in which they think about and evaluate the regime are likely to change in ways that have important consequences for political support.

In Central and Eastern Europe, the search for potential sources of support for democracy necessarily begins with the legacy of communism. Given its encompassing and authoritarian character, the communist system was a powerful socializing experience for most citizens during their formative years. Most Central and Eastern Europeans spent their entire lives under communism and have good reasons to fear the old regime which subjugated individual interests to those of the Communist Party and the state (cf. Shlapentokh, 1989; and Clarke and Wildavsky, 1990). It is unlikely that the old regime can be restored, but the institution of some other form of authoritarian rule cannot be dismissed.

Although communism provides a common frame of reference for citizens of Central and Eastern Europe, individual experiences under communism varied widely, typically in relation to individuals' positions in the social structure including their education levels, generation, gender, urban vs. rural residence and ethnicity (Finifter and Mickiewicz 1992). In addition, Putnam (1993) emphasizes the importance of citizens' embeddedness in a 'civic community' which he defines as 'dense horizontal networks of association', which also typically are linked to social structure. The implication is that political support is likely to be greater among individuals more deeply involved in civic and political associations including unions, churches, and political parties.

The legacy of communism may be especially important during the early years of transition. In the longer term, however, more contemporary experiences and performance evaluations are likely to assume greater importance. In established democracies, economic performance, including assessments both of individual well-being and of macroeconomic conditions, have been shown to be important determinants of political support (Lewis-Beck 1988; Clarke *et al.* 1993). Economic evaluations should be even more important in post-communist societies not only because the problems connected with the transition to the market are profound, but also because citizens in socialist systems are accustomed to holding government responsible for both macroeconomic conditions and their personal welfare.

Economic conditions, however, are but one basis by which citizens evaluate performance. As Clarke *et al.* (1993) observe with respect to Western Europe, evaluations of political performance influence political support as well. Given the repressive legacy of the past, the effectiveness of government in securing individual liberty and promoting freedom is an important political basis by which citizens might evaluate the performance of the regime. Unlike economic reforms, which are difficult to accomplish, involve tradeoffs between short- and long-term consumption, require massive infusions of money and have relatively long time horizons, reforms expanding individual liberty are relatively inexpensive, involve few tradeoffs and can be accomplished relatively quickly. Liberty requires little more than administrative 'deconstruction' such as closing censorship offices, restraining state police, and allowing independent institutions to operate freely (Rose 1995*b*).

Finally, and consistent with our argument that support is relative and contingent, support for new democracies is likely to be influenced by public assessments of possible alternative regimes (Rose and Mishler 1996). The most obvious alternative, of course, is communism, the immediate predecessor to the current regime. However, a variety of other alternatives are possible as well, including both military rule and rule by a strong man, both of which have precedents in Central and Eastern Europe in the period before communism. Although the possible alternative regimes are diverse, all are fundamentally undemocratic; the adoption of any requires the suspension or elimination of free elections, competitive parties, and an independent parliament.

The logic of this discussion suggests an explanatory model including as influences on political support the legacy of communist rule, individual social-background characteristics, evaluations of both macroeconomic performance and personal financial conditions, the extent of political and personal freedom, and evaluations of alternative regimes. Using multiple measures of these several concepts from the *New Democracies Barometers* I–IV (see Appendices 4A and 4B for details), we estimated separate models of political support for each of the four years under study (Table 4.3). Unstandardized coefficients (b) are reported for all variables; standardized coefficients (BETA) also are reported for statistically significant (p < .001) influences.

Consistent with the 'fear and hope' model of political support, the results indicate that initial support for the new regimes was substantially influenced both by public rejection of the old regime and by public confidence in future economic prosperity. The four regression equations show a consistently good fit explaining between 24 and 29 per cent of the variance in political support. Nevertheless, other factors also were important including the extent of civic community and the public's contemporary economic and political performance evaluations. Of these, contemporary economic performance evaluations are the most important by far. They also are among the most stable over time.

The legacy of communism is measured by three variables: public support for the old regime, public evaluations of the former socialist economy and individual evaluations of their personal living standards under communism

Table 4.3. Models of regime support, 1991–1995

	1991		1992		1993		1995	
	b (se)	BETA	b (se)	BETA	b (se)	BETA	b (se)	BETA
Communist legacy:								
Communist regime support	−.07* (.01)	−.09	−.11* (.01)	−.09	−.09* (.01)	−.11	−.08* (.01)	−.10
Evaluation of communist macroeconomy	.03 (.01)		.00 (.01)		.03 (.01)		−.03 (.01)	
Communist living standards better	−.17* (.04)	−.04	−.10 (.05)		.00 (.04)		−.06 (.04)	
Social structure:								
Education Level	.06 (.03)		.10 (.03)		.08 (.03)		.03 (.03)	
Age cohort	.04 (.03)		.11 (.03)		.04 (.04)		−.04 (.03)	
Gender: Female	−.06 (.09)		−.09 (.09)		−.08 (.10)		−.08 (.09)	
Town size	.02 (.04)		.07 (.04)		.03 (.04)		.12 (.04)	
Party ID	.41* (.10)	.04	.31 (.11)		.40* (.12)	.04	.23 (.10)	
Church attendance	.31* (.04)	.10	.14* (.04)	.04	.12* (.03)	.04	.14* (.04)	.04
Economic performance:								
Evaluation of current macroeconomy	.29* (.01)	.29	.27* (.01)	.27	.28* (.01)	.28	.27* (.01)	.29
Evaluation of future macroeconomy	.19* (.01)	.18	.19* (.01)	.18	.17* (.01)	.17	.15* (.01)	.15
Future living standards better	.29* (.06)	.06	.26* (.06)	.06	.20* (.06)	.04	.10 (.06)	
GDP change	.07* (.01)	.05	−.10* (.05)	−.09	.07* (.03)	.04	.09 (.05)	
log inflation rate	−.01 (.06)		.45* (.05)	.09	−.08 (.07)		.06 (.03)	
Political performance:								
Gastil freedom change	.95* (.09)	.12	.15 (.09)		1.05* (.11)	.13	.89* (.10)	.11
Favour suspension of parliament	−.96* (.14)	−.08	−.94* (.12)	−.08	−1.24* (.13)	−.11	−1.11* (.12)	−.10
R2 adj.	.29		.27		.24		.25	

* P < .001; N = ~ 7000 each year.

Source: Paul Lazarsfeld Society, Vienna, New Democracies Barometer I–IV. For details see Rose and Haerpfer 1992, 1993, 1994, and 1996a.

compared to current standards. Citizens modestly disapproved of the old regime in 1991, held mildly positive views of the socialist economy, but agreed overwhelmingly that their personal financial situations were better under communism. The public's negative attitudes toward the old regime in 1991 provided an initial reserve of positive political support for the new regime.

Moreover, the impact of the old regime is highly stable over time; far from fading with the passage of time, as we surmised that it might, the impact of the
old regime remains undiminished even five years following the collapse of
communism. Specifically, the impact coefficients (b) fluctuate in a very narrow
range (between – .07 and – .11), and the standardized coefficients (BETA) vary
even less (between – .09 and – .11).

In contrast to this pattern, the widespread belief that personal living standards were better under the old regime has a much smaller and unexpectedly
negative effect on support for the new regime (BETA = – .04 vs. – .09). Further,
nostalgia for living standards of the past quickly fades. Its impact on current
support falls by half in the second year and vanishes by year three. Thus the
net positive effects of the communist legacy increase over time, reinforcing
initial support for the new regime.

The impact of economic and political performance evaluations on political
support is even more substantial, however. Three subjective economic variables are examined, including both egocentric and sociotropic evaluations of
the economy (Downs 1957; Kinder and Kiewiet 1979; Fiorina 1981). Also
included are two 'objective' macroeconomic indicators, the year-to-year
change in each country's GDP and the log of its yearly inflation rate.
Interestingly, objective macroeconomic conditions have relatively small and
inconsistent effects on political support. In part, this may be because official
statistics register only a fraction of total economic activity since most people
supplement their incomes by relying on non-monetized resources such as
barter and self-production that are not registered in official statistics. In part,
also, it may be because there is even more variation in support within the
countries in the study than between them.

In contrast, the influence on support of individual economic evaluations is
both strong and enduring. Consistent with voting studies in the United States
and Western Europe (MacKuen, Erickson, and Stimson 1992), citizens in
Central and Eastern Europe weigh future economic performance more heavily
than the past, and they emphasize the performance of the macroeconomy
over their personal financial situations. Indeed, the public's highly optimistic
evaluations of future macroeconomic performance have nearly twice the
impact on initial political support as that of past and future living standards
combined (Beta = .18 vs. 06 + .04).

Nevertheless, the strongest economic effect on political support is registered
by public evaluations of current macroeconomic performance (Beta = .29 in
1992). Indeed, citizens' perceptions of current macroeconomic conditions
dominate all other economic considerations. Moreover, the impact of current
macroeconomic conditions remains remarkably stable over time, whereas the
impact of future macroeconomic evaluations declines slightly over the four
years, and personal financial conditions, both past and future, are discounted
heavily.

Economic performance is critical to generating support for new democracies, but political performance also is important. The third *New Democracies*

Barometer included a battery of questions asking individuals to evaluate the political performance of the new regimes, compared to the past, with regard to providing increased freedom (including speech, press, religion, travel, and association), greater political influence, and increased fairness. Citizens overwhelmingly reported that they enjoy a range of new and highly valued freedoms, although they are less clear about the extent to which they enjoy greater political influence or fairness. Predictably, citizens who credit the new regime with providing greater freedoms express substantially greater political support (Rose, Mishler, and Haerpfer 1998, ch. 7).

Because data on public perceptions of freedom are not available from earlier years, we rely on an aggregate indicator of the extent to which civil liberties and political freedoms have increased in each country since the fall of communism. The indicator, based on the Gastil/Freedom House Index, measures the extent to which civil liberties and political freedoms increased in each of these seven countries between the mid-1980s and 1996 (Gastil 1987: 58 ff.; Freedom House 1996).[2] As expected, support for the new democracies in Eastern and Central Europe increases strongly in direct relationship to the increased freedoms citizens in the several countries have enjoyed since the fall of communism. Although the impact of freedom on political support appears to drop precipitously in *NDB* II (1992/3), this is likely to be a product of the instability inherent in an aggregate measure based on only seven countries. Nevertheless, the impact of freedom is very strong in three of the four years and exerts greater influence on political support than all other factors except the subjective economy.

Finally, the 'Churchill hypothesis', previously advanced, suggests that citizens may support a new regime not only for what that regime has done but also for what it is not. Credence for this view is provided, in part, by the evidence that support for the new regimes increases in direct proportion to citizens' antipathy to the old communist regime. It also is evident in the extent to which individuals reject other plausible alternative regimes. *NDB* III and IV included questions asking about public attitudes toward rule by the army, rule by a strong man and return to communist rule (See Rose and Mishler 1996). Public attitudes toward all three alternative regimes were consistently negative; over two-thirds of the respondents reject all three alternatives. Although these questions were not asked in earlier years, the *NDB* surveys do ask a closely related question, whether individuals approve of the suspension of parliament. About one-quarter of respondents say they would support the suspension of parliament, one of the first steps that would be required to establish

---

[2] The Freedom House index ranks the world's nation-states on a seven-point scale according to their levels of civil liberty and political freedom. In the mid-1980s, before the fall of Communism, the seven *NDB* countries all ranked below the mid-point on the scale. By the mid-1990s, all of the *NDB* countries registered significant gains in freedom. The Czech Republic, Poland, Hungary, and Slovenia, today, rank very near the top of the scale along with such members of the European Union as Britain, France, and Germany. Bulgaria and Slovakia are ranked a bit lower as 'mostly free', and Romania is considered 'partly free'. All seven of the countries continue to fall somewhat short of the very highest standards of freedom in the world, but there is no doubt that all have made enormous progress since the fall of Communism.

an undemocratic regime. Not surprisingly, those who support the suspension of parliament are significantly less likely to support the new regimes. Moreover, this relationship is consistently strong, even increasing slightly over time.

Contrary to the hypothesis that political support for the new regime varies with individuals' positions in the social structure, social background characteristics have little or no effect on popular support for the new regimes. Four background variables are examined: education, age cohort, gender, and town size or urbanization. The coefficients for all four are in the expected direction, but all are small and statistically non-significant. This is not to say that individual experiences, either of communism or of the new regime are undifferentiated. It is to suggest, however, that individual differences in these regards are overwhelmed, at least during the early years of the transition, by the larger societal forces at work.

To measure the impact on support of individuals' embeddedness in a civic community, two indicators are employed, the frequency of church attendance and membership in a political party. Although relatively crude indicators of civic community, church attendance provides the best measure available in *NDB* of an individual's associational activity, and party identification indicates, as much as anything, the extent of an individual's integration into the political system. Importantly, both variables have statistically significant and positive effects on initial political support. The effect of church attendance is relatively large, although the impact of party is marginal. Nevertheless, the impact of both variables diminishes modestly over time.

Durable Trajectories of Political Support

Because political support for new regimes changes in response to both the changing levels and changing impacts of the underlying sources of support, an understanding of the durability and future direction of support requires that trends and dynamics be examined simultaneously. Figure 4.2 focuses on seven key sources of political support for the new regimes in Eastern and Central Europe and charts the combined effect of their changing trends and dynamics—what we call their changing *influence* on support. Specifically, the influence of each variable on support is measured by multiplying the level of that variable in any year (as reported in Appendix 4A) by its impact coefficient (b) in that year's regression equation as reported in Table 4.3. For example, in 1991, the average level of support for the old communist regime was -1.97; the regression coefficient for communist support was $-.07$; therefore, communist Support had a small but positive influence on support in 1991 of $+.14$ (that is, $-1.97 \times -.14$).

The first and most obvious observation from Figure 4.2 is the extent to which political performance dominates all other influences on regime sup-

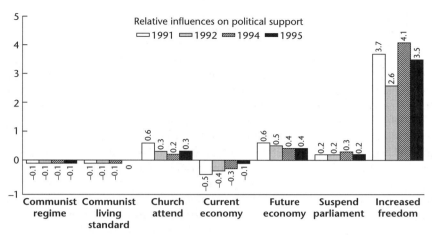

Fig. 4.2. Changing influences on political support, 1991–1995.
Source: As for Table 4.1.

port. Indeed, the aggregate increases in civil liberty and political freedom that have occurred in these countries since the fall of communism have a greater positive influence on popular support for the new democracies than do all other influences combined. Furthermore, the influence of freedom on support has remained consistently high, even increasing slightly over time. Although the level of freedom is a constant, its impact varies substantially—dropping precipitously in the second year of the transition and rebounding afterwards as the public's appreciation of their new freedoms has grown. This is particularly interesting and unexpected because, in the short term, freedom is a constant. Levels of freedom have not changed appreciably in any of the seven *NDB* countries since shortly after the fall of communism. The new regimes in Eastern and Central Europe already provide citizens with a variety of individual liberties and are pledged explicitly to maintain those freedoms under threat of electoral sanction. Moreover, the durability of freedom's impact is unexpected because of the likelihood that citizens would quickly begin to take freedom for granted once it has been established. With the principal institutions of repression already 'deconstructed', the expectation was that the impact of freedom on support would be fully realized from the start, leaving little room for freedom to increase support for democratization in later years. This expectation is wrong, it appears; the appetite for freedom increases with the experience of freedom.

Similarly, opposition to the suspension of parliament also remains consistently significant over time, a sign that the public approves of the new representative assemblies' efforts to carry out their responsibility to criticize governors. However, the actual influence of this variable on regime support is slight and unlikely to increase appreciably in the near future.

The influence of current and future macroeconomic performance on political support for the new democracies of individual evaluations also is consistently significant. While the influence of economic hope is positive, disappointment with current performance is negative. Because these economic influences push in opposite directions, their combined impact on regime support is very limited. Although the influence of both current and future economic evaluations has declined over the early years of the transition, the influence of current economic disappointments has declined somewhat more. As a consequence, the net influence of economic performance on political support has increased steadily, albeit modestly, over the first several years of the transition. The cyclical nature of economic trends, even in established market economies, cautions against the assumption that gains in economic performance can be sustained indefinitely. Nevertheless, the sort of economic recession typically associated with a downturn in the business cycle represents a comparatively minor threat to political support for the new regimes compared to the economic adversity which citizens already have survived. Thus, in the short to middle term, the influence of economic performance is likely to be one of sustaining of public support for the new democracies.

Contrary to the 'early closure' version of political socialization theories, attitudes focused on the communist past have little influence on support for the new democracy because, while public memories remain strong, their statistical impact is small. Net of all other influences, an individual positive about the communist regime is likely to rate the current regime only 0.1 points lower, and individuals who found their living standards better under the old regime are only slightly less likely to support the new regime (Figure 4.2).

We have interpreted church attendance as an indicator of civic community; it registers a small but significant influence on support for the new regimes. There is little indication, however, of significant changes in the level or impact of church attendance on political support over time. As a consequence, the influence of church attendance on regime support is likely to remain small but stable for the foreseeable future. There may be only a rudimentary sense of civic community in the new democracies in Eastern and Central Europe. Still, even the rudiments of a civic community contribute in a small way to the stability of support for the new democracies.

In the five years since the collapse of communism throughout Eastern and Central Europe new regimes committed to civil liberties and free elections have made remarkable progress in gaining the confidence and approval of the public. The prospects for the consolidation of democracy in Central and Eastern Europe have brightened considerably in a surprising short period. The trajectory of support for the new regimes, after fluctuating for the first year or two following the fall of communism has stabilized and, more recently, begun a strongly upward trend, and the underlying dynamics of popular support for the new regimes have changed in ways likely to encourage still higher levels of public support for the foreseeable future.

Among the sources of support for new regimes, political and economic performance have been critical. Improving macroeconomic conditions not only have ameliorated current economic concerns but have also reinforced the public's confidence that current economic reforms will produce long-term benefits. The costs of economic transition have been front-loaded, that is, heaviest at the beginning of the process in the 1990s. But they have been undertaken with the promise that the pains would lead to gains. Thus, even when pain has been most evident, most people remained hopeful about conditions in five years. By 1995, the time of the fourth *NDB* survey, macroeconomic indicators were beginning to register an upturn in all seven of the countries examined here and economic growth rates have been abnormally high by the standards of established market economies (EBRD 1995: 7).

As individuals have gained experience with democracy, their appreciation of newly acquired freedoms also has grown and with it their support for the democratizing regimes. Far from becoming jaded or blasé about the exercise of freedom, citizens' appreciation of freedom has matured and deepened providing a still stronger and more reliable basis of political support in the future.

Of course, the usual caveats apply. The new regimes are still very vulnerable, and the challenges faced are profound. The economies of most of these countries continue to operate at levels somewhat below where they were in the last years of communist rule and the new regimes continue to confront problems of widespread unemployment, growing inequalities of wealth, and ethnic and regional tensions among many other concerns. The most that can be concluded at this point in the transition is that the new regimes have survived the critical early years and have managed to create, in the process, an upward trajectory and positive dynamic of popular support providing the rudiments of a virtuous democratic spiral.

Appendix Table 4A. Means and standard deviations of variables in analysis

	1991 Mean (SD)	1992 Mean (SD)	1993 Mean (SD)	1995 Mean (SD)
Current regime support	1.32 (4.49)	1.34 (4.71)	1.36 (4.68)	1.75 (4.43)
Communist regime support	−1.97 (5.64)	−.85 (5.77)	−1.15 (5.89)	−.87 (5.72)
Evaluation of communist macroeconomy	.07 (5.47)	1.14 (5.31)	1.47 (5.56)	1.21 (5.52)
Communist living standards better	.78 (1.06)	.64 (1.12)	.64 (1.11)	.55 (1.07)
Education level	2.83 (1.56)	3.04 (1.54)	2.90 (1.55)	2.99 (1.56)
Age cohort	3.92 (1.50)	3.87 (1.51)	3.94 (1.42)	3.86 (1.57)
Gender: Female	.53 (.50)	.53 (.50)	.54 (.50)	.52 (.50)
Town size	2.40 (1.23)	2.44 (1.28)	2.33 (1.24)	2.35 (1.19)
Party ID	.32 (.47)	.37 (.48)	.33 (.43)	.37 (.48)
Church attendance	1.91 (1.37)	1.82 (1.38)	1.70 (1.52)	2.01 (1.30)
Evaluation of current macroeconomy	−1.56 (4.56)	−1.40 (4.62)	−1.22 (4.82)	−.55 (4.74)
Evaluation of future macroeconomy	2.87 (4.36)	2.53 (4.56)	2.44 (4.56)	2.74 (4.35)
Future living standards better	.38 (.97)	.32 (1.00)	.31 (.95)	.31 (.87)
GDP change	−12.48 (2.96)	−5.69 (4.43)	−.76 (2.70)	3.11 (1.70)
log inflation rate	4.55 (.98)	4.42 (.99)	4.33 (.94)	4.22 (.93)
Gastil freedom change	3.92 (.56)	3.92 (.56)	3.92 (.56)	3.92 (.56)
Favour suspension of parliament	.24 (.37)	.24 (.41)	.25 (.40)	.21 (.40)

N = ~ 7000 each year.

Source: Paul Lazarsfeld Society, Vienna, *New Democracies Barometer* I–IV. For details see Rose and Haerpfer 1992, 1993, 1994, and 1996a.

Appendix Table 4B. Coding of variables

Current regime support	21-point scale (– 10 to + 10) registering satisfaction/dissatisfaction with the current political system
Communist regime support	21-point scale (– 10 to + 10) registering satisfaction/dissatisfaction with the old communist political system
Evaluation of communist macroeconomy	21 point scale (– 10 to + 10) registering satisfaction/dissatisfaction with socialist economic system before the revolution
Communist living standards better	1 = 'much/somewhat better than current'; 0 = 'much/somewhat worse' or 'same'
Education level	1 = elementary; 2 = secondary; 3 = vocational; 4 = university
Age cohort	1 = 18–29; 2 = 30–39; 3 = 40–49; 4 = 50–59; 5 = 60+
Gender: Female	1 = female; 0 = male
Town size	1 = 1–5,000; 2 = 5001–20,000; 3 = 20,001–100,000; 4 = 100,001+
Party ID	1 = yes; 0 = no
Church attendance	1 = never; 2 = seldom; 3 = several times/yr.; 4 = monthly; 5 = weekly
Evaluation of current macroeconomy	21-point scale (– 10 to + 10) registering satisfaction/dissatisfaction with current economic system
Evaluation of future macroeconomy	21 point scales (–10 to +10) registering satisfaction/dissatisfaction with economic system in five years
Future living standards better	1 = 'much/somewhat better than current'; 0 = 'much/somewhat worse' or 'same'.
GDP change	Per cent yearly change in Gross Domestic Product
log inflation rate	Natural log of yearly inflation rate
Gastil freedom change	Calculated as the difference between the 7-point 1992 Freedom House index of civil and political liberties and the 7-point 1985 index
Favour suspension of parliament	1 = favours suspension of parliament; 0 = opposes suspension

PART II

Testing Theories
with Case-studies

5

Down and Down We Go: Political Trust in Sweden

SÖREN HOLMBERG

INSPIRED by David Easton, research on political support has distinguished between support for different levels of politics. Easton singled out three broad levels: the political community, the political regime and the political authorities (Easton 1965, 1975). As discussed in the Introduction, this book has refined Easton's scheme into a model with five levels: the political community, regime principles, regime performance, regime institutions, and political leaders.

In Scandinavia, as demonstrated by Hans-Dieter Klingemann's analysis of the *World Values Survey*, people remain highly positive towards the political community and democratic principles. In Finland, Norway, and Sweden an overwhelming majority of the public (89 per cent) said they are 'very' or 'quite' proud of their country. On the question about '*willingness to fight for my country*', 92 per cent answered affirmatively among Swedes, 89 per cent among Norwegians, and 84 per cent among Finns. Democracy as a form of government was supported by 93 per cent in Norway and Sweden. Hence, in these countries there is widespread support for the community and for democratic principles. Nevertheless support for the remaining three levels in the model— regime performance, institutions, and politicians—is more problematic in Scandinavia.

The first section of this chapter therefore focuses on how trust in politicians has evolved in Scandinavia, particularly in Sweden, over the last twenty to thirty years. We start at the bottom level since that is where we might expect to find the greatest change over time and where we have access to some of the longest measured time-series in the Scandinavian countries. Subsequent sections analyse support for political institutions and democratic processes. The last section goes on to consider explanations for trends over time.

All the countries under comparison are established, parliamentary, multi-party, unitary, welfare-state democracies—similar to some of the small countries of Northern Europe. Despite considerable similarities in their political and social systems, the Scandinavian countries have evolved differently in important ways.

Trust in Politicians

Trust in politicians is not decreasing in all democracies. Much attention has been paid to the American case where trust in politicians has dropped significantly (Nye *et al*. 1997) but in Northern Europe trust in politicians has been rather stable, and in some cases even increased over the last twenty to thirty years.

In Figure 5.1, Ola Listhaug's (1995) results from the *Beliefs in Government* project on degrees of trust in politicians are updated for Denmark, Norway, Sweden, and the Netherlands, and complemented by results from Iceland and Finland. The survey questions differ across the countries, but most of them are similar in the sense that they are rather crude, cynical statements about politicians, with which respondents are asked to agree or disagree.

Denmark:

- *'In general one may trust our political leaders to make the right decisions for the country.'*
- *'In general politicians care too little about the opinions of the voters.'*

Norway:

- *'Do you think people in government waste a lot of the money we pay in taxes, waste some of it, or they don't waste very much of it?'*
- *'Parties are interested in people's votes but not in their opinions.'*
- *'Those people that are in the Storting and run things don't pay much attention to what ordinary citizens think and believe.'*

Iceland:

- *'Do you think that politicians are in general trustworthy, that many of them are trustworthy, some are trustworthy, few or perhaps none?'*

The Netherlands:

- *'Members of parliament don't care much about the opinions of people like me.'*
- *'Political parties are only interested in my vote and not in my opinion.'*

Sweden:

- *'Those people that are in the Riksdag and run things don't pay much attention to what ordinary people think.'*
- *'The parties are only interested in people's votes not in their opinion.'*

The 'agree' option is usually the distrusting answer, which means that the results—aided by a tendency on the part of respondents to acquiesce —probably exaggerate the degree of political distrust. In our case, since we have computed the percentage of trusting answers, this means that the results in Figure 5.1 probably indicate estimates on the low side.

Trust in politicians has evolved differently in each of the six countries. Over the twenty-year period 1972/4 to 1993/4, where we have comparable data across five of our countries, levels of trust in politicians among eligible voters have increased in Norway and the Netherlands, and stayed about the same in Denmark. In Finland, trust was stable during the 1970s and 1980s, but declined in the 1990s. In Iceland, where we only have data for a shorter period (1983–95), the results have been fairly stable, but with an eventual small downward trend.

The longest Danish and Norwegian time-series on trust in politicians start in 1971 and 1969, respectively (see Figure 5.1). The results for Denmark and Norway indicate somewhat lower trust levels in the 1990s than in the late 1960s and early 1970s, although the downturn is less drastic than in Sweden (Borre and Andersen 1997, Aardal and Valen 1995).

In Sweden the best measures of trust in politicians covering a longer time period are the two Likert-format questions described above. Although marred by the acquiescence problem, they have face validity and, when tested through inter-item analysis and panel analysis, they behave reasonably well.[1] The results demonstrate that Sweden is the only country among the six which, like the USA, shows a long-term and sizeable downturn in the level of public trust in politicians. But in contrast to the American results, the Swedish trust figures continue declining in a steady fashion without any real recovery. In the Swedish data there are no instances of rising levels of trust in politicians, unlike in Denmark and Norway in the late 1970s and early 1980s, or in the USA during Reagan's first term. Trust in politicians has been plummeting more or less constantly for the past thirty years in Sweden. In 1968, 60 per cent of the respondents in the Swedish Election Study said that they did not believe that *'parties are only interested in people's votes not in their opinions'*. Some thirty years later, in 1994, the same trusting answer was given by only 25 per cent of Swedes. Similarly, in 1968, 51 per cent did not agree that *'those people that are in the Riksdag and run things don't pay much attention to what ordinary people think'*. In 1994, the proportion of respondents disagreeing with the negative statement had gone down to 28 per cent. There is no doubt that political trust has decreased drastically among the Swedish public. Why? Hamlet may have been right in his time, when he said: 'There is something rotten in the state of Denmark'. Today, given our results on political trust, Hamlet would have pointed across the straits of Öresund and exclaimed: 'There is something rotten in the state of Sweden'.

---

[1] In the 1994 Election Study, the correlation (r) between the two trust items was .71 and the panel correlations were about .50 for both items in the in-between election panels of 1988–91 and 1991–4. Tested against a self-placement trust question, where respondents were asked to indicate the degree to which they trusted Swedish politicians, the correlations turned out to be .41 for both items. Furthermore, measured over time the self-placement trust question yields the same result as the two Likert items, i.e. trust goes down. The self-placement trust question has been administered in the Swedish Election Studies since the election of 1988 and the per cent trusting answers (*'very large'* and *'rather large'* confidence) has been falling at every election—44 per cent 1988, 38 per cent 1991, 36 per cent 1994, and 32 per cent 1995. The 1995 election was Sweden's first election to the EU Parliament.

Trust in Political Institutions

The strength, and weakness, of our measure of trust in politicians is that they are very broad. It provides a simple, all-inclusive measure, but it is difficult to tell what we are really measuring. The problem becomes apparent when we introduce the concepts of linkage, representation, and institutions. Those concepts are essential since the first order of business for politicians in a

(i)

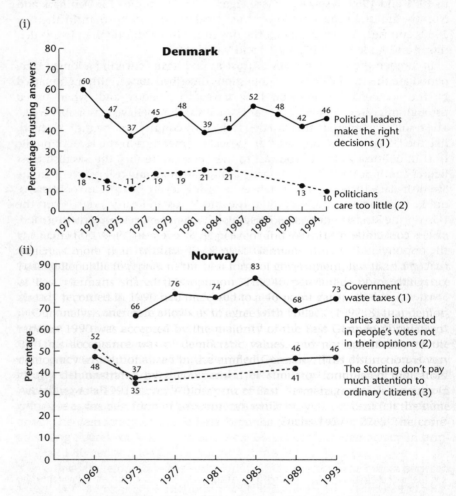

Fig. 5.1. Trust in politicians: Denmark, Norway, Iceland, the Netherlands, Sweden, and Finland.

Sources: The results for Denmark, Norway, Sweden, and the Netherlands are updated from Listhaug and Wiberg (1995). The Finnish and Icelandic data have been supplied by Sami Borg and Olofur Hardarsson, respectively. The updated Danish, Norwegian, and Dutch data were supplied by Ole Borre, Ola Listhaug, and Jacques Thomassen, respectively. 'Don't know' answers have been excluded when the per cent 'trusting' answers were calculated.

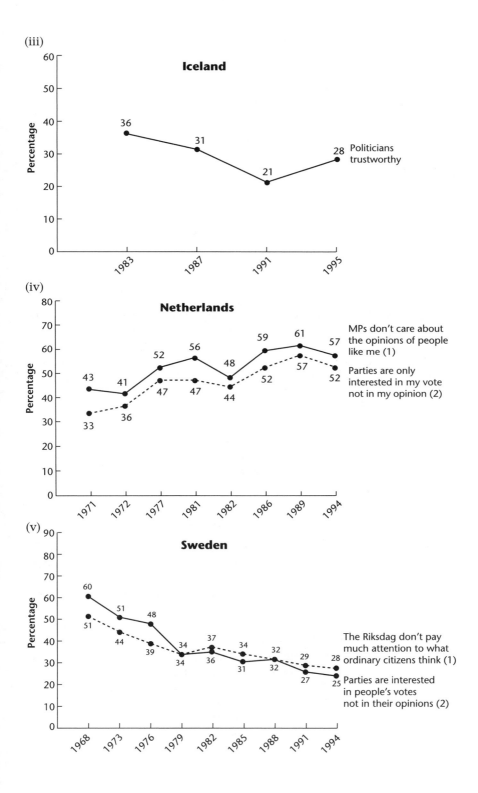

(iii) **Iceland**

36
31
21
28 Politicians
trustworthy

1983 1987 1991 1995

(iv) **Netherlands**

43
41
52
56
48
59
61
57 MPs don't care about
the opinions of people
like me (1)

33
36
47
47
44
52
57
52 Parties are only
interested in my vote
not in my opinion (2)

1971 1972 1977 1981 1982 1986 1989 1994

(v) **Sweden**

60
51
48
34
37
34
32
29
28 The Riksdag don't pay
much attention to what
ordinary citizens think (1)

51
44
39
34
36
31
32
27
25 Parties are interested
in people's votes
not in their opinions (2)

1968 1973 1976 1979 1982 1985 1988 1991 1994

Fig. 5.1. (vi)

representative democracy is to provide linkage between citizens and the state, and to represent constituents. They do that in institutional settings, among which parties and parliament are the most important. Items measuring trust in politicians do not necessarily do a good job of measuring people's assessments and confidence in specified linkage institutions. Bluntly put, it is easier for people to state that they distrust politicians in general than to say that they distrust their own representative or their preferred party. After all linkage and representation should be provided by, first and foremost but not exclusively, the voter's own representative or their chosen party, not by politicians in general. So how does trust in politicians relate to attitudes towards the institutions of representative democracy including parties, elections, the Rikstag, and the Cabinet?

Trust in Politicians and Party Identification

The difference between general trust in politicians and more specific trust in a voter's preferred party is well illustrated in the Swedish case. On the individual level, the association between people's answers to the items on trust in politicians and their strength of party identification is low: in the 1994 Swedish Election Study the correlations were only about .10. This means that many people with strong positive feelings for their chosen party did not trust politicians in general, and vice versa.

Yet as demonstrated in Figure 5.2, there is a much closer fit over time between declining trust in politicians and weakening party identification. Strength of party identification has gone down drastically among Swedes since the 1960s; indeed the decline has been stronger in Sweden over the last thirty years than in most other Western democracies, including the USA (Schmitt and Holmberg 1995). The strength of party identification among Danes and Norwegians has oscillated up and down somewhat since measurements

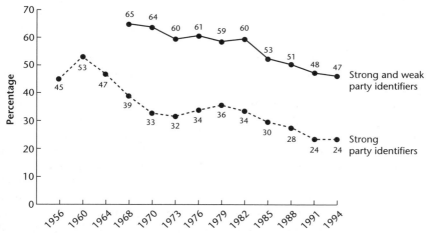

Fig. 5.2. Strength of party identification in Sweden, 1956–1994.

Notes: The question wording was different in the election studies of 1956–64. The party identification measure used since the 1968 Election Study contains four levels: strong identifiers, weak identifiers, leaners, and non-identifiers.

Source: Swedish Election Surveys.

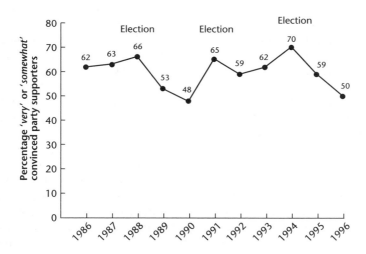

Fig. 5.3. Trends in party support in Sweden, 1986–1996.

Notes: Question (put to respondents stating a party preference): '*Do you regard yourself as a convinced supporter of your party?* with '*Yes, very convinced*', '*Yes, somewhat convinced*', and '*No*' as response alternatives. All respondents are included in the percentage base.

Source: The data comes from the SOM surveys.

started in the mid-1960s (Norway) and the early 1970s (Denmark). The latest results in these countries indicate a decline compared with the first measurements twenty-five years ago. In Denmark, the proportion of party identifiers was 56 per cent in 1971 compared with 49 per cent in 1994. For Norway, the comparable results are 72 per cent party identifiers in 1965 and 59 per cent in 1994 (Schmitt and Holmberg 1995, Borre and Andersen 1997, and Listhaug 1997).

In the early 1960s, about half of respondents in the Swedish Election Studies said they were strong adherents of their preferred party. The comparable result was only 24 per cent in the 1994 Swedish parliamentary election. The total number of party identifiers (strong and weak combined) has diminished from 65 per cent in 1968 to 47 per cent in 1994. All parties, large and small, old and new, have experienced the downward trend, which means that the old rank order between the parties in terms of what proportion of their voters are identified with the party, has stayed the same through the years (Gilljam and Holmberg 1995). The Social Democratic Party enjoys the highest proportion of party identifiers among its supporters (63 per cent in 1994), followed by the Conservatives (53 per cent). At the bottom we find the Liberals and the Greens with 30 per cent and 19 per cent party identifiers, respectively.

The Electoral Cycle

We also need to understand how party attachments develop in between elections. Here we turn to annual surveys comprising about 1,700 Swedish respondents since 1986, conducted by the SOM Institute at Göteborg University (Holmberg and Weibull 1997a). The results in Figure 5.3 show that elections matter for the number of convinced party supporters which increases during election years and decreases when no elections take place. The pattern indicates a distinct electoral cycle. When political parties campaign and try to reach out to people they become more appreciated. This is an important finding which indicates that increased exposure to parties breeds more positive attitudes. This is good news for politicians since it could have been worse: more exposure could have led to more cynicism.

The thesis that political exposure is positively, not negatively, related to political trust and party identification is further substantiated if we look at individual-level data. All kinds of measures of contacts, as measured in the Election Studies, provide the same result: greater contact with parties and politicians is positively correlated with strength of party identification, as well as with trust in politicians. The correlations tend to be modest (about .10), but the point is clear: people in contact with parties or MPs tend to be more appreciative and trusting of them compared to people without any contacts.

Obviously, the causal process behind the correlations could work in two ways. First, people who trust politicians could contact politicians and parties more often than average. Alternatively, political trust could increase as the result of the contacts with parties and politicians. Although our data do not allow us to separate the two processes, the positive correlations are important to note. They strongly suggest that political processes are related to degrees of trust in politicians, implying that if politicians try harder to contact voters they should be able to boost their support.

Furthermore, and equally important, political trust and strength of party identification are also positively related to political interest and political knowledge. Those most politically interested and knowledgeable tend to be most trusting of parties and politicians. The results in Figure 5.4 show that trusting answers were given by half of those showing the highest degrees of interest and knowledge, compared with one quarter of those exhibiting the lowest levels of political interest and knowledge. Again we cannot determine the direction of causality but the association remains significant in itself.

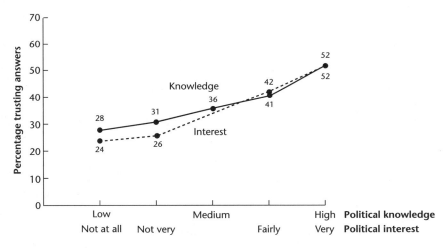

Fig. 5.4. Trust in politicians, knowledge, and interest in Sweden.

Note: The political knowledge variable is constructed from the respondents' answers to a whole series of factual knowledge questions.

Source: Based on data from the 1994 *Swedish Election Study*.

Confidence in Institution

Further proof that exposure to political campaigns can be a positive experience can be found if we look at yearly time-series data on the development of confidence in institutions in Sweden. The SOM Institute has been tracking people's confidence in a broad range of institutions over the last ten years, including the Riksdag and the Cabinet. Like Listhaug and Wiberg (1995) found, in their study of public confidence in institutions in fourteen European countries in the 1980s, there is no general trend of declining trust in all institutions in Sweden. During the period 1986–96, confidence increased for schools, stayed about the same for defence, big business, health care, television, and print media. Nevertheless confidence has declined for trade unions, banks, police, and for political institutions—the Riksdag and the Cabinet (Holmberg and Weibull 1997*d*). Hence, generally, confidence in all public and private institutions does not necessarily move together, like Lipset and Schneider (1983) found in America. Nevertheless confidence in the Riksdag and confidence in the Cabinet follow each other very closely, although it is usually somewhat higher for the Riksdag (see Figure 5.5). And, most importantly, the pattern reveals a very distinct electoral cycle. Like party convictions, confidence in political institutions tends to be higher in election years than in non-election years. This reinforces the finding that democratic elections are a positive experience. They tend to strengthen support for political actors and institutions.

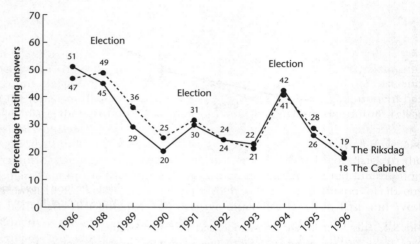

Fig. 5.5. Confidence in the Swedish Riksdag and Cabinet, 1986–1996.

Notes: The years 1988, 1991, and 1994 were parliamentary election years. In 1988, the governing party, the Social Democrats, retained a left majority in the Riksdag, while in 1991 they lost to a non-Socialist coalition. In 1994, the Social Democrats once more regained a left majority in the Riksdag.

Source: The SOM Surveys 1986–96 (Holmberg and Weibull 1997*a*).

On the individual level, there is a strong correlation between confidence in the Riksdag and the Cabinet (r = .75). In a parliamentary democracy like Sweden, where the Cabinet needs majority support on important bills in the Riksdag, we should expect a close fit between how people judge the two institutions. The question, however, is whether the correlation is too high for the good of the Riksdag. In our assessment, it is how people judge the Cabinet that drives the process and influences how the Riksdag is assessed. If we are right, the negative evaluations of the Cabinet and its policies after the elections of 1988, 1991 and 1994 dragged the Riksdag down. In the same way the positive expectations associated with the shifts in government in 1991 (from a Social

Democratic to a non-Socialist Cabinet) and in 1994 (back to a Social Democratic Cabinet) helped lift the confidence figures not only for the Cabinet but for the Riksdag as well.[2]

Satisfaction with the Performance of Democracy

Turning to broader indicators of satisfaction with the performance of democracy, *Eurobarometer* measures show that Swedes are surprisingly critical of the way Swedish democracy works. The *Eurobarometer* standard question here is: *'How satisfied are you with the way democracy works in [Sweden]?'* As discussed earlier in Chapter 2, in the spring 1995 *Eurobarometer*, the proportion of respondents answering that they were 'very' or 'fairly' satisfied with how democracy worked in their own country was 83 per cent in Denmark and 82 per cent in Norway, but only 55 per cent in Sweden.

Moreover, assessments of confidence in the Riksdag and in the Cabinet were strongly related to satisfaction with the performance of Swedish democracy. Responses to the standard *Eurobarometer* question were strongly correlated with confidence in the Cabinet (r = .51) and in the Riksdag (r = .49). Fuchs, Guidorossi, and Svensson (1995) in the *Beliefs in Government* project, argued that the *Eurobarometer* measures 'generalized support for the democratic system'. If so, declining confidence in political institutions could be interpreted as declining support for the democratic system in Sweden. But we doubt whether the *Eurobarometer* question is a valid indicator of generalized support of democratic systems. As argued in earlier chapters, this indicator is strongly influenced by short-term policy evaluations and assessments of Cabinet performance. The measure relates more closely to the performance of the regime than democratic principles. In the Swedish case, by far the strongest correlation with answers to the *Eurobarometer* question concerned judgements about how the Cabinet performs its duty (r = .52 in SOM 1996). Among people who thought the Cabinet did a good job, almost three-quarters (71 per cent) said they were satisfied with the way democracy worked in Sweden. In contrast, among people who thought the Cabinet did a poor job, only 12 per cent declared themselves satisfied with the workings of Swedish democracy. With response differences like this, it is obvious that the *'satisfaction with democracy'* question largely measures how people assess the short-term performance of the ruling government (Holmberg 1997a).

This pattern strongly suggests that the high correlations between confidence in political institutions and satisfaction with how democracy works is spurious and conditioned by how people assess what the Cabinet is doing. The

[2] A strong indication that performance evaluations are important is that confidence in the Riksdag and in the Cabinet are more highly correlated with how people respond to a special question on how the Cabinet performs its duty than to anything else (r = .58 and .73, respectively in the 1996 SOM Survey); and we have checked all possible correlations, totalling more than two hundred. On the other hand, maybe this is to be expected since the SOM question on confidence explicitly asks the respondents to do a kind of job assessment. This is how the question is introduced: *'How much confidence do you have in the way the following institutions do their job?'*

bivariate correlation between the degree of confidence in the Riksdag and the degree of satisfaction with how democracy works was .49 in the 1996 SOM Survey. Controlling for how the respondents evaluated the government's job performance, the correlation (partial r) drops to .28. Moreover, most importantly, the principle of democratic rule is not questioned by the Swedish public. According to the *World Value Survey* (see Klingemann, Chapter 2 this volume), almost all Swedes (93 per cent) approved of democracy as a form of government.

Explaining Trust in Politicians and Regime Institutions

The interrelationship between the trust evaluations on the individual level, as well as the apparent effect of the electoral cycle on people's confidence in the Riksdag and the Cabinet, indicate that political factors having to do with what the government actually does play an important role in increasing or decreasing people's trust in politicians and regime institutions. Put simply, the most plausible hypothesis is that confidence in politicians stems from what people perceive that politicians do. If people like what they see, we expect trust to go up. If they don't like what they see, trust can be expected to fall. Yet we want to know more—about the process that changes levels of trust, about perceptions, about what politicians do (which, among other things, brings economy and welfare policies into the picture), and about people, since individuals have different social backgrounds, cognitive abilities, party identifications and values—all of which could condition political trust. To explore these issues we can examine some of the core hypotheses outlined in the final chapter of the book, *Why People Don't Trust Government* (Nye *et al*. 1997).

Social Inequality and Social Capital

Starting with the hypothesis of rising economic inequality causing increasing cynicism, given a low plausibility rating by Nye *et al*. (1997), it is clear that among Swedes there is no connection between trust in politicians and attitudes towards changing the income distribution (r = .03). People who think income should be distributed more evenly are not less trusting than people who want to preserve the present level of income differences. Furthermore, social groups differ very little in their levels of political trust, although disadvantaged groups such as workers, the unemployed, people with low education, people living in the countryside, and women, tend to have somewhat lower degrees of political trust. Thus, there is probably some support for the hypothesis, but the overall explanatory value remains weak.

The hypothesis that declining social capital/voluntary groups are to blame for low trust receives little plausibility in Sweden. Membership and activities in many voluntary groups have declined in Sweden, as in many other countries, and social capital, defined as trust between people, is correlated with political trust among Swedes. Studies by Rothstein (1997), however, have shown that social trust between people has not declined in Sweden. Vertical trust between elite and mass has decreased, but not horizontal trust between ordinary people. Here Sweden is rather typical of most countries of Western Europe. As Ken Newton shows in Chapter 8 of this volume, while '. . . social trust in the United States is waning, it is high and rising across most of Western Europe'.

Failure of Government Performance?

The hypothesis that low trust is due to weakened government performance depends upon what we mean by 'performance'. If we, for example, look at the areas of employment and welfare, it is obvious, at least for Sweden and most other Western European countries, that government performance has changed drastically. In the 1990s mass unemployment and welfare retrenchments characterize Sweden, whereas in the 1960s Sweden had full employment and an expanding welfare state. If we call this development weakened government performance, this phenomenon could be important for how we assess the hypothesis. On the other hand, it may not be that important, since on the individual level, the connections between political trust and attitudes toward welfare policies are almost non-existent in the SOM Studies, as well as in the Election Studies (correlations around .05). Svallfors (1997) has found the same lack of relationship between political trust and support for welfare state intervention in ISSP data for Sweden as well as for Norway.

Yet if we look instead at policy evaluations (i.e. how people judge the welfare services they get), then more sizeable correlations with political trust arise (around .25 in some cases). People who are critical of the various services they receive tend to be less trusting than people who are satisfied. Thus, from a Swedish perspective, the hypothesis should perhaps be given the plausibility rating of 'mixed' or even 'high'.

An Economic Downturn?

A general economic slowdown has been proposed to explain declining political trust, but evidence for this hypothesis is rated as 'mixed' by Nye *et al*. That is probably a correct assessment for Sweden, too. The relative performance of the Swedish economy has decreased since the mid-1970s. Yet political trust dropped most drastically in Sweden in the late 1960s and early 1970s, when the Swedish economy still was reasonably successful.

In Sweden individual-level assessments of the economic situation, retrospective as well as prospective evaluations, are related to people's level of political trust and confidence in political institutions. The highest correlations run around .25 and apply to the relation between people's confidence in the

Riksdag and their assessment of the development of the Swedish economy. People with a bleak economic outlook have less confidence than people with a positive view. Respondents' assessment of their own economic situation was also related to the level of political confidence, but on a lower level (correlations about .12). Thus, assessments of the development of the national economy are more strongly related to political trust than assessments of what is happening to the respondents' personal economy.

Politics Matters

One political cause of the decline in political trust is identified by Nye *et al.* as 'partisan realignment'. The breakup of the Democratic Party's electoral lock on the South is a very American phenomenon. But viewed more broadly, and taking the polarization of elites into account, there is no doubt that political factors are plausible in the Swedish case as well. Studies of the degree of issue agreement between the public and members of the Riksdag, for example, show that elite polarization has increased in the 1980s and 1990s compared with the 1960s, especially on the important Left–Right dimension. True, the overall level of issue congruence between MPs and voters has improved somewhat since the 1960s, but in a cross-national perspective, issue agreement in Sweden is not especially high. The few available comparative studies show that policy congruence is about the same level in Sweden, Germany, France, and the United States. Among the Nordic countries, Swedish issue agreement is roughly on a par with Denmark and Norway, and lower than in Iceland (Esaiasson and Holmberg 1996; Holmberg 1996, 1997b).

Furthermore, Swedish studies on the dynamic interplay between elite and mass opinion change across time have shown that an elite top-down representation model would be more valid for the Swedish case than a mass-driven model. Simply put, covering the period 1968–94, we have found more cases of opinion change compatible with an elite-driven opinion moulding process than with a mass-driven process (Holmberg 1997c).

Two issues where policy agreement is among the lowest are the issues of Swedish membership of the EU and immigration policy. Members of the Riksdag are more supportive of the EU and of increased immigration than the general public. The issues of EU and immigration, with a very low correlation between them, are also the two issues where attitudes are most highly related to political trust (correlations around .20 in both cases). People who oppose Swedish EU membership and increased immigration tend to have a low trust in politicians. The relationship between anti-EU attitudes and low political trust, and between support of restrictive refugee policies and low political trust, is the same in Norway and Denmark (Aardal and Valen 1995; Borre and Andersen 1997). Ole Borre and Jørgen Goul Andersen talk of '. . . a rather permanent relation between political "homelessness" and the attitude of political distrust' (p. 309). It seems like the lack of opinion representation in these cases has affected people's political trust. As Arthur Miller (1974*a*, *b*) has claimed, discontent with policies enacted in different policy areas breeds distrust.

Evaluations of Party Policies

A slightly different version of Miller's theory has been proposed by Olof Petersson (1977). According to Petersson what matter most is not discontent with policies in general, but frustrations over the policies pursued by the respondents' own party. The results in Table 5.1 give support to Petersson's theory.

Table 5.1. Correlations with levels of political trust

	Perceived distance to own party on the Left–Right scale		Evaluation of own party's policies	
	1985	1994	1985	1994
Left Party (v)	.20	.14	.35	.12
Social Democrats (s)	.16	.02	.25	.11
Center Party (c)	.11	.13	.16	.14
Liberals (fp)	.12	.24	.24	.14
Conservatives (m)	.13	.13	.18	.11
Christian Democrats (kd)	—	.09	—	.02
Greens (mp)	—	.08	—	.14
Average five old parties	.14	.13	.24	.12

Note: The policy evaluation variable is based on open-ended evaluation questions where respondents could indicate which parties they thought had a good or a bad policy on eight (1985) and thirteen (1994) issues. The correlations are average coefficients. Positive correlations mean that persons who perceive a relatively great distance between themselves and their own party on the Left–Right scale, and who have less positive evaluations of their own party's policies, tend to have lower levels of political trust.

Sources: The analysis is based on data from the 1985 and the 1994 Swedish Election Studies.

For all party groups in the Swedish Election Study of 1985, as well as in the Election Study of 1994, people with relatively long subjective distances between themselves and their preferred party on the Left–Right scale, and with less appreciative evaluations of their own party's policies, tend to exhibit lower degrees of generalized political trust. As always, the correlations are not impressive (on average between .12 and .24), but they all support the hypothesis. If people feel let down by their chosen party, the results tend to be a loss of faith in all politicians.

A much discussed theory, at least in Europe, is the 'Home Team' hypothesis. This suggests that political trust is partisan and is affected by which party (or parties) control the government. Generalized trust goes up among people whose preferred party is in the Cabinet and goes down among people whose party is outside the ruling circle. Yet a glance at the results in Figure 5.6, which, across the years 1968–94, show how degrees of generalized political trust have developed among voters for the different parties in Sweden, does not lend any strong support to the 'Home Team' theory.

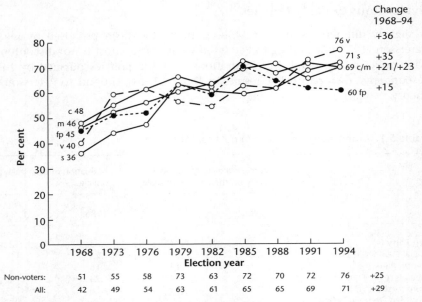

Fig. 5.6. Mistrust of politicians by party vote, 1968–1994.

Notes: The results show the average percentage of respondents answering affirmatively (= distrust) to two negatively phrased trust items (see Figure 5.1). *'Don't know'* answers (on average about 5 per cent for both items through the years) are included in the percentage base. The initials for the parties are as they are used in Sweden: v = Left Party; s = Social Democrats; c = Centre Party; fp = Liberals; and m = Conservatives. The comparable results for the Greens (mp) have been: 1988 67 per cent, 1991 60 per cent, and 1994 75 per cent. The flash right-wing populist party New Democrats (nyd) had 87 per cent in 1991 and 89 per cent in 1994. For the Christian Democrats, the results have been: 70 per cent in 1988, 72 per cent in 1991, and 65 per cent in 1994.

Source: Based on data from the *Swedish Election Studies*.

Distrust in politicians has increased in a parallel fashion for all party groups in Sweden, no matter which party or parties were in the Cabinet. Social Democratic supporters showed increasing distrust levels during the years when their party was in power (in 1968 to 1976 and in 1982 to 1991), as did the non-Socialist voters when their parties formed the Cabinet (in 1976 to 1982 and in 1991 to 1994). Certainly, if we look more closely, some small 'Home Team' effect can be detected. For example, compared to non-Socialist voters, Social Democratic voters were more trusting in the late 1960s when their party held power than in the 1990s when there was a Bourgeois Cabinet.

Furthermore, if we look specifically at the cases where an election has caused a change of government, and compare our trust results in the pre-election and post-election surveys, there is some support for the 'Home Team' hypothesis, although the effect is not particularly strong. In 1991, when the Social Democrats lost the Cabinet to a non-Socialist coalition, the average trust level among Social Democratic sympathizers went down by 2 percentage points between the pre and post surveys, while it increased by 8 percentage points among non-Socialist supporters. In 1994, the Social Democrats regained power and the level of generalized political trust increased by 4 percentage points among the party's supporters between the pre and the post surveys, at the same time as the trust level went down 1 percentage point among the sympathizers of the Bourgeois parties. Evidently, political trust is sensitive to election outcomes and to short-term political changes. Long term, however, the 'Home Team' factor may be less relevant in explaining the secular decline in political trust.

Are the Media To Blame?

As discussed in Chapter 13, many scholars—and politicians—point to the media as one of the culprits behind the declining levels of political trust. And it is difficult to disagree. As Patterson (1993) in the USA and many researchers in Sweden have shown, the media have become more negative in their coverage of politics (Patterson and Donsbach 1997, ch. 13; Westerståhl and Johansson 1985; Asp 1991). At the same time, studies of Swedish party propaganda covering the entire twentieth century find no increase in negative campaigning or inter-party criticism (Esaiasson 1996). The parties slander each other no more in the 1980s or 1990s than they did in the 1950s. In the news, however, politicians are portrayed more negatively today than in the 1950s, especially in broadcast media. Jörgen Westerståhl and Folke Johansson (1985) compare how the media have covered political actors during the years 1912–84 and reveal a small increase in negative reporting toward the end of the period (the 1970s). The increase, however, is limited to broadcast media (radio and TV). Kent Asp (1991), studying political coverage in Swedish radio and TV during the election campaigns 1979, 1982, 1985, and 1988, also found an increase in negative reporting.

A year-round study of the political coverage of the leading Swedish TV-news programme (*Rapport*) covering the period 1979–96 shows the same tendency. News reports dealing with political distrust and political affairs have become more frequent, especially in later years. By contrast, an analysis of the political coverage in three large morning newspapers during the election campaigns of the period 1956–94 does not indicate any increase in negative reporting.[3] Apparently, the increase in negative political reporting is less of a phenomenon in print than in broadcast media.

Looking at individual-level data on the relationship between media exposure and political trust, it is apparent that some connections are present—not

[3] The studies of *Rapport* and of the morning papers have been done by Per Hedberg under the auspices of the *Media Elections Study Program* directed by Kent Asp. *The Media Elections Study Program* works in close co-operation with the *Swedish Election Study Program* at Göteborg University.

strong connections, but all in the expected direction. Exposure to serious media, including public service TV and radio, is correlated with positive trust in politicians, while exposure to commercial TV and radio, as well as to the tabloids, is associated with negative political trust. As always, the correlations are weak (about .10) and they do not prove any causal effect. In theory, the causal order could be the reversed; trusting people tend to seek out serious media. The important point, however, is that a relationship exists. Political trust is either influenced by commercialized media, or commercialized media attract people with a low level of trust—and possibly reinforce their attitudes or, at least, are not instrumental in changing them. Either way, commercialized media are to blame.

Modelling Trust in Politicians

So far we have only discussed the causal factors behind political distrust one by one, and that is of course unsatisfactory. If possible, controls for spurious relationships are useful when dealing with such a complex phenomenon as political distrust, which has not one but multiple possible causes. Ideally, a theoretical model should be specified, with indications of direct and indirect causal links, and tested cross-sectionally on the individual level as well as across time on the aggregate level. That is, however, a daunting task beyond our reach in this chapter.

We will have to be content with the results of a series of multiple regressions involving cross-sectional data from the 1994 Election Study and the 1996 SOM Survey. The fifteen independent variables have been presented earlier in this chapter. They include *demographic* variables (such as gender; age; and education), *economic* variables (economic assessments), *media* exposure variables, and *political* variables (political interest; issue positions on the EU, immigration, and Left–Right; policy and government evaluations; preference for opposition or governing party; and evaluation of the workings of democracy). The dependent variables are defined as trust in politicians (for the Swedish Election Study data) and institutional confidence in the Riksdag (for the SOM data).

The results confirmed that political factors proved most strongly related to trust in politicians and institutions, followed by the economic variables.[4] In contrast, the demographic and media variables had only modest and mostly statistically insignificant effects. Among the political factors, two performance variables clearly were the most important: evaluations of party policies and assessments of the government. Other political variables with lower but significant b-values, included political interest, the 'Home Team' factor, eval-

---

[4] A policy evaluation index, based on the respondents' assessment of their preferred party's policies, had the largest b-value (0.48) in the regression based on the Election Study data (R-squared was equal to .16). In the regression based on SOM data the government assessment variable had the largest b-value (0.40) with R-squared equal to .42. All variables were scored between 1 and 5.

uations of the workings of democracy, and attitudes toward immigration and the EU.

A theoretical analysis of what causes political distrust would preferably be specified as a 'funnel' model, with some more proximate and other more distant causal factors. In such a model, most political factors, especially those having to do with evaluations, would be located fairly close to the dependent variable. In contrast most of the demographic variables, and maybe also the media-exposure variables, would be situated further back in the funnel, indicating that their impact is more distant and indirect.

Given a funnel model of this kind, we would expect—as we found—larger direct effects of the political evaluation variables and smaller effects of, for example, the media variables. Consequently, as in the case of the media factors, nearly non-existent direct effects do not necessarily mean a non-existent causal effect. Indirect and more distant effects could still be relevant, and that is what we think is the case for the media variables.

Conclusions

We can conclude that some level of political distrust, ideally backed by knowledge and informed reasoning, is essential in a democracy. Affective and cynical distrust, unsupported by political knowledge, is more problematic. As we say in Swedish, we need *lagom* distrust—not too much, not too little. And distrust should primarily be based on informed reasoning, not on stereotypes and affective cynicism.

Political distrust, like all complex social and political phenomena has multiple causes. We can conclude that three sets of causes seem most plausible for the drop in political trust among the general public in Sweden over the last thirty years. In increasing order of importance, these include developments in the economy, in the media, and in politics. For all these, we have found individual-level correlations in accordance with expectations, and the timing of the onset of the effects is about right.

The Swedish economy started to decline in the early 1970s, and drastically so in the 1990s. Television entered most homes in the 1960s at about the same time as the media became more critical and negative towards parties and politicians. And politics after the 1960s has become more polarized at the elite level, arguably providing less representation and a larger gap between the performance of parties and the expectations of the people. On the important ideological left-right dimension, for example, the number of people perceiving that they have the same position as their preferred party has declined since the 1970s. In the Swedish Election Study of 1979, 51 per cent of Social Democratic voters located themselves at the same place as their party on the Left–Right scale. In 1994 that number had gone down to only 39 per cent. A more modest decline is also noticeable among Conservative voters: 31 per cent located themselves and their party at the same spot on the Left–Right scale in 1979, while, in 1994, the number had gone down to 28 per cent. Yet without a doubt the most important political explanation has to do with government performance—with people's evaluations of what they get from government and their assessment of what the government does. Government performance, and people's perceptions of that performance, are the central factors. In this sense, political distrust is best explained by politics.

6

The Democratic Culture of Unified Germany

DIETER FUCHS

HOW can a democratic culture develop among people who have lived for decades in an autocratic system? We examine this issue in the unified Germany, which provides a unique case, but for this very reason a particularly instructive one. German unification integrated two communities with a common history until the end of World War II. For a period of 50 years thereafter they lived in two different social systems. A comparative analysis of the political culture of the two parts of Germany thus conforms in almost paradigmatic form to Przeworski and Teune's (1970) 'most similar system design'. We therefore have a quasi-experiment, which permits us to analyse the effects of these different social systems on the political culture of their citizens. Germany can be regarded as a sort of laboratory (Rohrschneider 1994) for a possible European unification encompassing the countries of Western and Eastern Europe.

This chapter starts by outlining the theoretical framework including the concept of political support. We consider various normative models of democracy to understand what type of democracy people in West and East Germany ultimately prefer. We then compare demonstration and socialization theories on the influence of the social structure on political attitudes. On this basis expectations about attitudes towards democracy among the East German population can be formulated. The next section develops the empirical analysis by examining trends in democratic attitudes among Germans. The conclusion summarizes the most important findings and considers their consequences for the prospects of democracy in a unified Germany.

The Theoretical Framework

The Concept of Political Support

Political culture is the subjective dimension of politics constituted by the political attitudes of the citizenry (Verba 1965: 315; Almond 1980: 26). As discussed in the first part of this book, this broad definition can be narrowed down by constructing specific analytical questions. According to Almond (1980), a political system is stable to the extent that its political culture is congruent with its political structure. The model in Figure 6.1 includes all the elements that Almond (1980: 28) assigned to system culture. This includes attitudes towards the political system on the three hierarchically ordered levels of democratic values, institutions and performance. To this must be added the attitude towards the most important incumbents of authority roles, principally the government. Furthermore, the model places these elements in a causal structure which can be tested with survey data (see Fuchs 1998*b*). The model postulates that the values of democracy will influence democratic institutions. This effect can be positive only if the value priorities of the citizens are identical with those embodied in the structure of the system. It is a fundamental assumption of our analysis that, due to socialization in the former German Democratic Republic, East German citizens can be expected to prefer a model of democracy different from that of the unified Germany. This is one reason why the East German population can be expected to have a more sceptical attitude towards the governing institutions of the unified Germany.

Normative Models of Democracy

Ideas about what a democracy is, and how it should look, are not formed by citizens of their own accord. They are instilled by primary and secondary

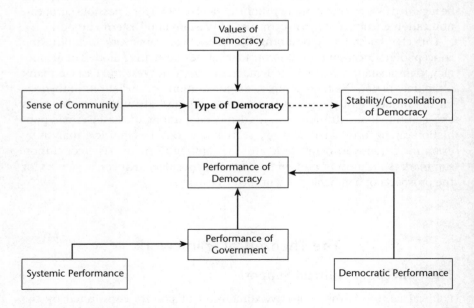

Fig. 6.1. A model of support for democracy.

socialization processes. The socialization agents in their turn reflect a limited number of democracy models (Held 1987). We refer to them as normative models of democracy because they set out certain principles of how a democracy *ought* to be. Such normative expectations are directed at the democratic institutions of one's own country, and if citizens consider them to be fulfilled they evoke convictions of legitimacy in the system.

We restrict our attention to three normative models of democracy: libertarian democracy, liberal democracy, and socialist democracy (see Table 6.1). Other models in the current theoretical debate—communitarian democracy and deliberative democracy—can be left aside in the context of our analysis.

Table 6.1. Normative models of democracy

	Libertarian democracy	Liberal democracy	Socialist democracy
A. Minimal elements of democracy			
1. Constitutional guarantee of liberal basic rights	yes	yes	yes
2. Constitutional guarantee of universal, free, and periodic elections	yes	yes	yes
3. Constitutional guarantee of the rule of law	yes	yes	yes
B. Supplemental elements of a democracy			
4. Constitutional guarantee of social rights	no	no	yes
5. Constitutional guarantee of direct citizen participation	no	no	yes
6. Political realization of social rights	no	yes	yes
Conception of the state	Minimal state	Welfare state	All-embaracing welfare state

Table 6.1 summarizes the models as succinctly as possible (see Fuchs 1997*a* for a more comprehensive discussion), distinguishing between the minimal and supplementary elements of democracy. The minimal elements are those essential conditions that permit a political system to be regarded as a democracy, using the definitions of Bobbio (1987), Sartori (1987), and Dahl (1989). The minimal elements are three constitutional guarantees: concerning liberal rights, the rule of law, and universal, free, and periodic elections. The liberal rights include subjective freedoms and the political rights of participation. The models are distinguished from one another only by the supplementary elements. They include constitutional guarantees relating to social rights and direct citizen participation, and also the political realization of social rights.

Two of the models can be associated relatively easily with prominent representatives of the theoretical discussion: the libertarian model with Nozick (1974) and the liberal model with Rawls (1971, 1993). This is not quite so easy in the case of the socialist model, but the most important supplementary elements of this model are nevertheless relatively clearly identifiable in the literature (Eichler 1973; Euchner 1992; Sik 1992; Held 1987). The two contrasting instances are the libertarian model and the socialist model (see Table 6.1).

In Nozick's (1974) libertarian model the core elements of liberalism, the individual and his freedom, are most rigorously deployed. In Nozick's theory only a minimal State can be justified, since the establishment of a State as such already restricts the freedom of individuals. The notion of the minimal State also implies laying down the rights that individuals have *vis-à-vis* the State. They consist only in the guarantee of so-called negative rights (Taylor 1985) of individuals *vis-à-vis* State authority and in the guarantee of free-market relations between individuals. For all other rights of individuals, the State is not competent. The social inequalities and social insecurity arising in society are externalized by the libertarian State. Since the goals of the individual are attained in the free market, for a rational actor it is quite sufficient to restrict political participation to periodic elections.

In contrast to the libertarian model, the socialist model develops the conception of a paternalist 'nanny' State. The State is responsible for safeguarding against the primary risks of life and for eliminating social inequalities. These social rights are to be constitutionally guaranteed and thus enforceable in the courts. At the political level this means substantial redistribution by the State, in which the citizens are to be directly involved.

Libertarians make a number of objections to the constitutional guarantee of social rights. First, politics is likely to have problems adjusting to the constraints of reality, and the State is likely to be overburdened by the claims made on it. Second, the constitutionalization of social rights can lead to the politicization of the judiciary (Saward 1994: 19). Third, the attempt to realize social rights in material form entails an almost imperative tendency of the State to intervene in autonomous market processes, and at least partially to abolish the functional distinction achieved between the political and economic systems. Fourth, social rights implemented by the State can be in contradiction to individual freedoms. The liberal models seeks to avoid such problems by setting clear priorities.

Rawls's (1971, 1993) version of the liberal model also underlines the importance of social rights. But both in justifying and implementing social rights, it differs from the socialist model in decisive ways. Justification relates directly to the fundamental freedoms. A certain guarantee of social rights or a just distribution of primary goods are first of all to ensure the fair value of individual freedom for all. According to Rawls's theory, in the event of conflict between the freedom of the individual and equality of primary goods, freedom must always win. One of the consequences of this normative weighting is the assignment of the implementation of social rights to the political system actors and overall to the government. They are explicitly not included among Rawls's constitutional essentials.

The constitution of the unified Germany is almost identical with that of the former West Germany. It contains the minimal elements of democracy as enforceable rights. The social aspects are taken into account by a relatively noncommittal precept of social responsibility. At the time it was founded, the former Federal Republic of Germany can be described as a libertarian democracy with the recommendation of a political development towards a welfare state. In the course of its subsequent history, this welfare state was indeed implemented. The actual democracy of the later West German Republic, and hence that of the unified Germany, thus corresponds most closely to the liberal model.[1] What we expect the analysis of public opinion to reveal is that West Germans favour the liberal model whereas East Germans prefer the socialist model.

The Formation of Democratic Attitudes within State-Socialist Systems

According to the paradigm of political culture, a commitment to democratic values, and support for a democratic system, are necessary conditions for the consolidation of the system. We therefore return to the question raised in the introductory chapter: can people have acquired democratic values when they have had no experience of democratic institutions over a long period and have lived in an autocratic system? (Conradt 1997; Rohrschneider 1998) Quite different answers are given to this question. The two opposing positions can be described as the demonstration and the socialization hypotheses.[2]

Weil (1993) has given an incisive account of the demonstration hypothesis, taking unified Germany as his example. He postulates the diffusion of democratic values from the democratic West to the socialist East. The channel of diffusion was primarily mass-media information. To this extent one can speak of system-external learning (Roller 1994). The preconditions for diffusion were the 'demonstration' (Weil 1993) of the superiority of West German society in comparison with the state-socialist system in East Germany. The aspects of the German Democratic Republic felt to be particularly negative in comparison with the Federal Republic were economic deficiencies and various restrictions on freedom. Since the Federal Republic was felt to be the more attractive system, the socialization efforts of the GDR were, according to this theory, fruitless, and a sort of re-socialization in terms of the West German democratic system took place. The demonstration effects produced by the democratic system 'can serve as a functional equivalent for a reservoir of legitimation that otherwise takes years to build up' (Weil 1993: 209). Dalton (1994) largely concurs with this analysis. A number of authors offer similar arguments for other countries of Central and Eastern Europe (Starr 1991; Gibson, Duch, and Tedin 1992; Evans and Whitefield 1995). Shortly after the introduction of democratic institutions, the demonstration hypothesis appeared to find confirmation

[1] In the European discussion, this liberal model would tend to be called social-liberal and the libertarian model would probably be referred to as liberal.

[2] For a differentiated discussion of competing hypotheses on the formation of democratic attitudes already in the state-socialist systems see Rohrschneider (1998).

in surveys carried out in several Central and Eastern European countries. They recorded a remarkably high degree of support among citizens for democracy as an ideal form of government and for democratic values (see Chapter 2). Klingemann and Hofferbert (1994) concluded that there was a challenge to the theory that sees socialization as the core of democratic civic culture.

The socialization hypothesis has a long tradition in political science. It is grounded in the well-established perception that political value orientations are acquired by means of socialization processes, and that the institutional context in which individuals live has a significant impact on this socialization (Almond and Verba 1963; Easton 1965; Parsons 1969; Almond and Powell 1978). Rohrschneider (1994) therefore refers to institutional learning, and Roller (1994) to system-internal learning. The socialization hypothesis has been explicated and affirmed for the state-socialist societies as a whole by Almond (1983) and Eckstein (1988). It was used by McGregor (1991) and by Finifter and Mickiewicz (1992) in studies on specific Central and Eastern European countries. In analyses of the eastern *Länder* in unified Germany, it is represented with varying degrees of explicitness by a range of authors (including Westle 1994; Roller 1994, 1997; Rohrschneider 1994, 1998; Lepsius 1995; Wiesenthal 1996). Lepsius (1995: 27) offers a very peremptory but analytically well-founded view: 'the political culture of a democracy is in strong contrast to the political culture of a dictatorship.' He describes the German Democratic Republic as a 'socialist welfare state with an authority-related, hierarchical decision-making structure' (Lepsius 1995: 24). In this system the State pursues collective interests, which are based firstly on comprehensive social security and secondly in the realization of egalitarian principles of equality. The socialist State is therefore concerned with the realization of substantively defined notions of the common good.

According to the socialization hypotheses, value orientations corresponding to a liberal democracy can develop only to a limited degree in such socialist systems. Some of the constitutive principles of liberal democracy are highly artificial (Lepsius 1995). This is true at least when the thinking and acting of individuals in their everyday life-world is the point of reference. These principles can therefore be acquired only through a combination of socialization efforts and continuous experience with politics within the institutional structure of a liberal democracy. They include an understanding of politics as a permanent conflict of interests with corresponding compromises brought about by rules of procedure. A liberal democracy is therefore precisely *not* concerned with realizing a predetermined common good or notion of justice by means of political decision-making processes. The political rationale of a liberal democracy is purely procedural, not substantive. Acknowledging this procedural rationale includes reacting without resignation if one's own demands are not taken up by the democratic process. Lepsius (1995: 29) cites as a graphic example of the difficulty of coping with such principles the statement by a well-known East German civil rights activist after German unification: 'We demanded justice and we got the rule of law' (Bärbel Bohley).

The constitutive principles of a liberal democracy include limiting the demands of citizens on the State. In contrast to the paternalist 'nanny' state of the GDR, a liberal democracy cannot and should not assume responsibility for all the wishes of the citizens, however justified they may be. The citizenry must recognize that the State cannot be responsible in principle for certain wishes and that under certain conditions of reality it may reject certain demands. What wishes and demands are actually concerned must be determined and negotiated politically, but the principle itself must be acknowledged. Rohrschneider (1998) argues along the same lines when he postulates 'democratic restraint' as an essential requirement of a 'liberal-democratic citizenship'.

Depending on which of the two hypotheses is taken, quite different prognoses on the development of liberal democracy in the countries of Central and Eastern Europe result. According to the socialization hypothesis, the formation of a political culture congruent with the political structure of liberal democracy is a lengthy process with no guarantee for success. According to the demonstration hypothesis, the question of political culture is no longer relevant for further consolidation because there has been an adequate political culture from the outset. If a sceptical attitude among citizens towards their democracy is ascertained after the change of system, it must therefore have to do with current political reality and not with the socialist heritage (Pollack 1997).

Which of the two hypotheses is more appropriate can only be determined empirically. The onus of proof differs for each. The demonstration hypothesis must show why established social research findings have to be revised for the post-socialist systems; especially how such profound pre-socialization could become possible through mass-media communication processes. The socialization hypotheses must show why the democratic systems in the countries of Central and Eastern Europe were supported by the citizens shortly after their introduction, and why these citizens have accepted democratic principles. We consider the socialization hypothesis the more plausible, and in the following analysis we attempt to appraise it.

We assume the simultaneous occurrence of system-internal and system-external learning (Roller 1994). System-external learning is based on a comparison of the two competing systems. The socialist system comes off considerably worse, and this ultimately leads to the collapse of this system in Central and Eastern Europe. Since the measure was the social order of Western countries, and this is characterized by democracy and market economy, initial acceptance of these two characteristics is hardly surprising. Support for personal rights, free elections, and the procedures of the rule of law was equally likely. It is hardly conceivable that reasonable individuals can oppose such principles. On the contrary, such principles are likely to have been an evaluative yardstick in comparing the competing systems. It is not by chance that the data referred to by adherents of the demonstration hypothesis are concerned primarily with such relatively uncontroversial principles. According to our theoretical framework, they are all minimal elements of a democracy (see Table 6.1). It is therefore clear that, shortly after the collapse of the socialist social system, the citizens of Central and Eastern European countries were basically in favour of democracy and of the related minimal principles. Yet two questions remain open. First, the extent to which this acceptance has persisted. It cannot be excluded that this initial advocacy of democracy in their own country was not so much entrenched support (consent) as superficial support (assent), which eroded under the impression of the problems presented by reality (Fuchs and Roller 1998). The second question is whether it is really liberal democracy they have in mind. This is primarily where we have our doubts.

In discussing the socialization hypothesis, we have pointed out that the implications of a liberal democracy become really apparent only through personal experience and that they can be accepted only in a difficult and protracted learning process. Among other things, this involves limiting responsibility for the primary life-risks of citizens and for the inequalities engendered in the economic system. In these two aspects at least, there is a far-reaching contrast to personal experience in state-socialist systems. They provided comprehensive social security and a relatively egalitarian distribution of goods. In most countries social security was underpinned by appropriate constitutional norms. A number of analyses show that, at least in the GDR, these aspects were seen as positive by the population and were considered a clear advantage over West Germany (Bauer 1991; Noelle-Neumann 1991; Rohrschneider 1994; Westle 1994; Roller 1997). These rights acquired in the German Democratic Republic were taken up and stabilized by the socialist model of democracy (see Table 6.1). We have already seen that this is a legitimate model of democracy because it includes the minimal elements of every democracy. This model is no mere ineffectual theoretical construct; in most European countries it is advocated by substantial sections of the political elite. In Germany this has been demonstrated quite clearly by various elite studies (Rohrschneider 1994, 1996; Bürklin 1997a; Welzel 1997). The heritage of socialism thus consists in a preference for a certain normative model of democracy that does not correspond to the implemented liberal democracy. If this analysis is valid, we must assume there to be latent incongruity between the values of democracy and the type of democracy in the countries of Central and Eastern Europe. This latency can become manifest through experience in the new social system and transform the initial assent to the type of democracy into dissent (Fuchs and Roller 1998). How many citizens will undergo this transformation naturally depends on other factors such as the performance of the political actors concerned and international restrictions.

The following empirical analysis keeps to the hierarchical order of the objects of democracy shown in Figure 6.1. It begins with the values of democracy, continues with the type of democracy, and concludes with the performance of democracy.

Empirical Analysis

Commitment to Democratic Values and Principles

Democratic values are seen as the highest level in the hierarchy of the objects of support. They include three kinds of component. First, democracy as a principle, measured by attitudes towards democracy as an ideal form of government. Second, there are other related values, especially freedom and equality. Third, different normative models of democracy are to be assigned to this level. On the basis of the socialization hypothesis, we can formulate certain specific hypotheses about the value level of democracy.

1. *The majority of East and West Germans support democracy as an ideal form of government.*

2. *East Germans favour a socialist model of democracy and West Germans a liberal model.*

3. *Over the period under review, 1990 (i.e. the advent of German unification) to 1997, no systematic changes in these attitudes can be expected.*

Table 6.2. German support for democracy as a form of government (percentage agreeing)

	Democracy is . . .	
	the best form of government (1991)	better than any other form of government (1997)
West Germany	86	88
East Germany	70	81

Sources: Institute for Opinion Research Allensbach(1991); FORSA (1997).

The first hypothesis is confirmed by the distributions shown in Table 6.2. The items are not identical. The indicator used in 1991 refers to the attitude towards democracy as the best form of government. The item used in 1997 asks only whether *democracy is better than any other form of government*. Both items, however, appropriately operationalize the construct of support for democracy as an ideal form of government. The results show that in both parts of Germany, and at both dates, democracy as an ideal form of government was supported by an overwhelming majority of the population. Nevertheless, the difference between East and West Germany is notable. In East Germany, support for democracy as a form of government is significantly lower than in West Germany at both timepoints. This could be because some respondents still favour the system of the German Democratic Republic and associate it not with the concept of democracy but with that of socialism.

Since we have only two recording timepoints for support for democracy as an ideal form of government, and, moreover, the two indicators are not identical, we cannot draw any conclusions here about trends over the period 1990 to 1997. Hypothesis 3 therefore cannot be tested here with these data.

International comparisons reveal the significance of this level of support for democratic values (see also Dalton 1998a: 15). A 1989 *Eurobarometer* study asked about attitudes to democracy as a form of government as opposed to dictatorship. The results show that West Germany is among the countries with the highest rates of support for democratic values (Fuchs, Guidorossi, and Svensson 1995: 349). As the data from the *World Values Surveys* 1994–7 show, little has changed during the 1990s in this favourable ranking (see Chapter 2). The question used in the *World Values Surveys* is: '*Democracy may have problems, but is it better than any other form of government?*' (alternative answers: '*agree strongly, agree, disagree, disagree strongly*'). The rate of agreement in West Germany was 93 per cent and in East Germany 91 per cent. Among the many countries under review, the two parts of Germany rank high in their support for democratic values (see Table 2.7). West Germany, for example, has the same score as Norway, and East Germany ranks with Switzerland, two traditional democracies with a high degree of legitimacy.

The second hypothesis postulates a preference for the socialist model of democracy among East Germans and a preference for the liberal model among West Germans. Indicators for all the relevant factors of these models would be needed for appropriate testing but unfortunately they are not available. We therefore rely upon two indicators that relate systematically to the two models of democracy. The first is the attitude towards socialism and the other the relative priority given to freedom and equality. Current research indicates that the socialism of the German Democratic Republic was abolished with the approval of most of its citizens. But at the same time we assume that these same citizens regard some elements of East German socialism as positive, and even as an advantage over West Germany. The question is therefore how to avoid cognitive dissonance between the unfavourable evaluation of the actual socialism of East Germany and the favourable assessment of some of its characteristics. This can be done by contrasting the idea of socialism with actual socialism. On an ideal level socialism can be considered positive because it contains social and egalitarian values and can also be associated with democratic freedoms. In this view, the idea of socialism was poorly implemented in East Germany. A 1992 survey shows that many East Germans make this distinction. Only 28 per cent of respondents give the failure of socialism as the cause for the collapse of the GDR, whereas 60 per cent attribute it to the incompetence of the politicians (Noelle-Neumann and Köcher 1993: 554). The downfall of socialism in practice was accordingly not the consequence of structural deficiencies of the system but could have been averted by more capable actors.

What East Germans understand by socialism is shown by how they responded when asked what they felt to be a necessary part of socialism

(Noelle-Neumann and Köcher 1993: 552). Social rights were stated to be the most important element. Seventy-three per cent of respondents, for example, considered that the 'right to work' was a necessary element of socialism, and 65 per cent felt the same about the 'right to kindergarten facilities'. Few respondents regarded these two elements as inconsistent with socialism. In Table 6.1 these social rights are described as supplementary elements of democracy, which distinguish the socialist model of democracy from the others. The socialist model also includes the minimal elements of a democracy, and to this extent it is to be considered a legitimate model of democracy. Such elements are also represented in the question battery. No less than 59 per cent of respondents state that 'freedom of expression for citizens' and 'free and secret elections' are necessary elements of socialism. But respondents are in less accord on these two aspects than on social rights. A little over 20 per cent of respondents state that they are *not* consistent with socialism. East Germans thus clearly associate socialism with social rights, and a majority—although not without controversy—with the minimal elements of democracy. For East Germans, the concept of socialism thus largely conserves what is referred to as the socialist model of democracy.

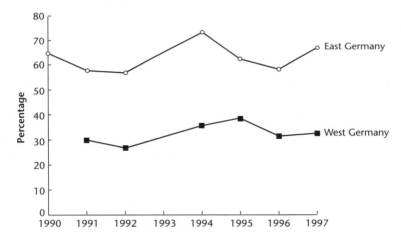

Fig. 6.2. German support for socialism as an idea 1990–1997.

Notes: Question: '*Do you think socialism is a good idea that was badly put into practice?*'
Here: Percentage of positive responses.

Source: Institute for Opinion Research, Allensbach.

Whereas the question on what is understood by socialism is concerned primarily with cognitive orientations, Figure 6.2 shows how socialism is evaluated. It records over time the proportion of respondents in East and West Germany who consider socialism a good idea that was merely badly implemented. This question directly operationalizes the cognitive operation of dissonance avoidance we have noted. According to the data in Figure 6.2, the difference between East and West Germany is substantial over the entire period. Whereas, on average, about two-thirds of East Germans consider socialism to be a good idea, less than a third of West Germans share this opinion. On the premiss that, for East Germans, the idea of socialism is largely associated with the characteristics of the socialist model of democracy, this empirical analysis permits the conclusion that East Germans have a lasting, positive attitude towards this model of democracy. Support for the model is markedly weaker in West Germany. These data are therefore consistent with the second hypothesis but no direct conclusion about the attitude towards the liberal model can be made on this basis.

The time-series in Figure 6.2 show considerable fluctuation, more marked in East Germany than in the West. The attitude towards the idea of socialism is apparently also influenced by situational factors. But the fluctuation reveals no systematic trend in the sense of hypothesis 3.

Freedom and equality are two further values indissolubly linked to democracy, which define it more precisely (Fuchs 1998a). A positive evaluation of democracy implies a positive evaluation of these values. However, the relationship between freedom and equality is not free from contradiction when it comes to institutional and political realization. This raises the question of which of these values should be given priority in the event of conflict. The normative models of democracy provide different answers. Whereas the socialist model prioritizes equality, the liberal model opts for freedom. Rawls (1971, 1993), repeatedly and explicitly stresses that, in the event of conflict, freedom should have *unconditional* priority. The subjective priority given to either freedom or equality therefore provides more direct evidence of citizens' preference for the two models of democracy than was possible in the case of attitudes towards the idea of socialism.

The time-series in Figure 6.3 deal with the proportion of the citizenry that gives priority to freedom over equality. This priority is consistent with the liberal model of democracy and thus with the model closest to the democracy of unified Germany. The difference between East and West Germany is in keeping with the second hypothesis. At all timepoints, significantly greater priority was given to freedom over equality in West Germany than in East Germany, the figure for West Germany being over 50 per cent and for East Germany under 50 per cent at all timepoints.[3]

Hypothesis 3 postulates no systematic changes in values from 1990 to 1997. But the continuous decline in the priority of freedom over equality in East Germany is in conspicuous contradiction to this assumption. Whereas almost 50 per cent of East Germans gave priority to freedom over equality in the year of German unification, by 1997 the figure had dropped to only 20 per cent. Over time, the difference between East and West Germany has thus not dimin-

---

[3] It should be taken into account that undecided respondents were included in the basis for calculating the percentages in Figure 6.4, and that this category varied between 10 and 20 per cent depending on the timepoint.

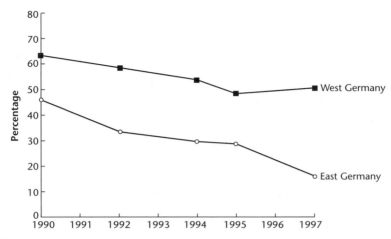

Fig. 6.3. German priority of freedom over equality, 1990–1997.

Notes: Question: '*Ultimately which is probably more important, freedom or the greatest possible equality?*'
Here: Priority of freedom.
Source: Institute for Opinion Research. Allensbach.

ished, indeed it has drastically increased. How is the falsification of the hypothesis to be explained? The explanation is likely to be found in situational factors that took effect only in the unified Germany (Pollack 1997; Walz and Brunner 1997; Pollack, Pickel, and Jacobs 1998). Another factor could be waning memories of the restrictions and material deficits in the German Democratic Republic. For this reason, disappointment with the material situation in the unified Germany, and especially with social security, was able to develop unhindered (Lepsius 1995). This had an impact on the preference for equality, which is a central element of an idealized socialism. Yet the significant difference between East and West in the relative priority of freedom over equality recorded shortly after German unification shows that situational factors were not the only explanation. Moreover, how the situation is defined depends not only on objective factors. It is defined in the light of standards that are acquired in the course of socialization.

If we take the time-series on the attitude towards the idea of socialism and on the priority of freedom over equality together, the empirical evidence suggests that East and West Germans support different models of democracy, and that this preference is attributable at least in some measure to socialization in different social systems. This assumption is confirmed by the following analysis.

Support for Democratic Institutions

On this basis we can assume that the majority of East Germans prefer a socialist model of democracy, and that the majority of West Germans favour a liberal model. If at the same time we assume that a liberal model of democracy is closer to the type of democracy institutionalized in the unified Germany, we must, according to the support for democracy model (see Figure 6.1), assume the effect of the values of democracy on the type of democracy to be different, namely negative in East Germany and positive in West Germany. Just how strong these effects are cannot be specified a priori, but our analysis so far appears to justify the following hypothesis:

4. *In West Germany a majority of citizens, and in East Germany a minority of citizens, support the democratic institutions of the unified Germany.*

Scholars largely agree that in West Germany widespread and firmly established support for democratic institutions developed in the decades following the founding of the former West German State (Conradt 1980, 1991; Baker, Dalton, and Hildebrandt 1981; Gabriel 1987; Fuchs 1989). According to these studies West Germany has clearly proved to be more than a fair-weather democracy, accepted by its citizens only in phases of economic prosperity. Democracy has thus been supported for its own sake, and it is implausible that this should suddenly have changed after German unification. Majority support for the type of democracy of the unified Germany must accordingly already have existed in 1990 and is unlikely to have substantially declined in the period that followed.

Expectations for East Germany are more difficult to formulate. According to the socialization hypothesis we could expect relatively high support for the democracy of the united Germany among East Germany at the beginning of German unity, and a relatively strong decline in this support in the following years. The socialization hypothesis assumes that, shortly after the introduction of democracy to the countries of Central and Eastern Europe, there was only latent incongruity between the normative notions of democracy among citizens and the liberal democracy actually implemented. For this reason the incongruity cannot have had a negative impact on evaluation of the liberal democracy in the countries concerned. The latency is attributable to system-external learning, which had led to a negative assessment of the given social system and to a positive evaluation of the western social order. The comparison between the two social orders was possible primarily only via mass-media communication processes. However, since these processes are indirect in nature, they could supply only limited information and did not provide direct experience. The implications of a liberal democracy can thus become clear only through personal experience with the institutions of the new system of government. Only on the basis of this experience is it more or less probable that the latent incongruity becomes manifest. Just how great this probability is, and what effects such a transformation has on support for the democracy, depends on various factors. One of the most important is the performance of the democracy, which we will examine in the next section.

We consider that the socialization hypothesis, however, needs to be modified in the case of East Germany. In many ways the German Democratic

Republic was much closer to the Western social system than most countries in Central and Eastern Europe. This propinquity was to the society of West Germany. There were three aspects. First, the common historical experience within the borders of a unified nation-state until the end of World War II. Secondly, territorial contiguity. This gave East Germans access to Western television, which they viewed intensively. Thirdly, there were comprehensive family contacts. East Germans must therefore have been relatively well informed about West Germany. They were accordingly also aware of the aspects of this social system that their socialization in the GDR would lead them to regard as particularly detrimental: high unemployment and the comparatively weak social security system (Roller 1997). We therefore assume that East Germans were in certain measure sceptical from the outset about the social system of the Federal Republic. This scepticism does not exclude that they had an overall preference for West Germany over East Germany, and that they were in favour of unification for practical if for no other reasons. Following this argument, we can thus assume that at the time of German unification there was already manifest incongruity between the values of democracy and democratic institutions in the unified Germany for a significant proportion of East Germans. This had the negative impact on support for the type of democracy in East Germany, as we have mentioned. In view of subsequent experience, the initial scepticism tended to stabilize rather than diminish. We can now state a fifth hypothesis:

5. *Already at the time of German unification there was a significant difference between West and East Germans in their support for the type of democracy in the unified Germany. Over time this support declined relatively slightly in West Germany and relatively strongly in East Germany.*

The time-series data in Figure 6.4 record the proportion of respondents who considered that the Federal Republic of Germany provided the best form of government for the period from 1990 to 1997. The empirical findings presented in Figure 6.4 clearly confirm hypotheses 4 and 5. Already in 1990 the extent of support differed markedly in West and East: 81 per cent of West Germans, and 41 per cent of East Germans, support the form of government of the Federal Republic. In considering these figures, it should be remembered that the question about the *best* form of government is probably overstated. Had the question been formulated in more reserved terms, the percentage for East Germany could have been higher. Therefore confirmation of the fourth hypothesis for East Germany could thus be tied to this specific indicator. But it can also be assumed that the situation in 1990 was a special one. The successful unification of Germany certainly had a short-term period effect that somewhat obscured 'true' attitudes towards the democracy of unified Germany. The 41 per cent score in East Germany, and the 81 per cent in West Germany, accordingly represent a situation-specific exaggeration. Nevertheless, the formulation of the question does not affect confirmation of the significant difference between West and East Germany, since the same indicator was used in both cases.

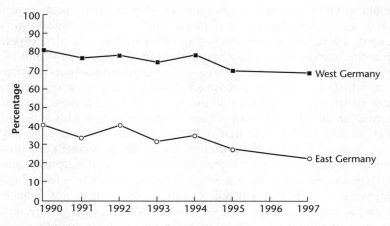

Fig. 6.4. Type of democracy in Germany, 1990–1997.

Notes: Question: *'Do you believe that the democracy we have in the Federal Republic is the best form of government, or is there a better form of government?'*

Here: The democracy we have in the Federal Republic is the best form of government.

Source: Institute for Opinion Research, Allensbach.

This initial support declined in both parts of Germany after 1990. By 1997 the figure for West Germany was 69 per cent and for East Germany 23 per cent. Whereas more than two-thirds of West Germans thus still considered the Federal Republic to represent the best form of government, less than a quarter of East Germans shared this opinion. The 40 percentage point difference already recorded in 1990 had increased to a 46-point gap.

Our analysis therefore allows us to agree with Pollack (1997: 8) that democracy 'in 1990 was accepted by the majority of the East German population'. But this acceptance was of democratic values, and not specifically of the democracy institutionalized in the unified Germany. This distinction is very clearly demonstrated by a comparison of similarly formulated indicators. According to a 1991 survey, 70 per cent of East Germans regard democracy in principle as the best form of government, while only 31 per cent felt the same about the democracy of the Federal Republic (Fuchs 1997*b*: 276). The corresponding figures for West Germany were 86 per cent for democracy in principle and 80 per cent for the democracy of the Federal Republic.

We have therefore shown a substantial difference from the outset between the two parts of Germany in attitudes towards democracy. Attitudes have differed about the idea of socialism, about the priority of freedom over equality, and about the type of democracy instituted in the unified Germany. In all these essential aspects, the political culture of the unified Germany must hence be seen as divided. But East Germans and West Germans also share much in common. In both parts of Germany the preferred form of government is clearly democracy not autocracy. This attitude persists in East

Germany despite disappointment with the government of the unified Germany.

Satisfaction with Democratic Performance

According to the model in Figure 6.1, support for democratic institutions is the most important attitude for the stability and/or consolidation of this democracy. Apart from democratic values, the performance of democracy is assumed to directly influence the formation of this attitude. This means that evaluation of performance can modify the influence of value orientations on the type of democracy. Under certain conditions a lack of positive effect from value orientations can be compensated for by positive performance evaluations. This sort of compensation occurred in the case of the former West Germany (Conradt 1980, 1991; Baker, Dalton, and Hildebrandt 1981; Gabriel 1987; Fuchs 1989). Unlike in East Germany when the country was unified, democracy as a form of government was far from attracting active support among the population when the former Federal Republic was established (Fuchs 1989: 92 ff.). The attitude tended to be one of 'lukewarm' acceptance in the absence of alternatives after the collapse of National Socialism and the lost war. If support for the democracy of the Federal Republic could accordingly not develop 'from the top down', the only alternative was for it to have become established 'from the bottom up'. The so-called *Wirtschaftswunder* or 'economic miracle' that set in in the early 1950s created the necessary conditions. Gradually people transferred the positive assessment of system performance grounded on economic development to the democracy of the Federal Republic, and ultimately to the values associated with this democracy. Another important factor generating support for the democracy of the Federal Republic was certainly the East–West conflict, which manifested itself with particular virulence in the divided Germany. In the course of time, support for the democracy of the Federal Republic became detached from its origins, constituting an autonomous attitude. As such it was able to develop resistance to performance deficiencies, and this was why it did not become a fair-weather democracy. The history of the Federal Republic is thus an almost paradigmatic example of generalization from concrete experience within a democracy to the fundamental attitude towards this democracy.

Empirically we have recorded relatively weak support for the type of German democracy in East Germany. Can we therefore assume that a similar generalization process has occurred there, leading to an increase in support? We will discuss this question on the basis of a further time-series. But first we will again formulate hypotheses. The attitude towards the performance of democracy is based on the extent to which people consider their demands to be met in the reality of the democracy concerned. The demands in question are those that people believe they may legitimately make of the democracy in their country. However, such demands depend on people's own normative standards. And these are not identical in West and East Germany. Although social rights are among the most important political goals of people in both parts of Germany, the guarantee of social rights in East Germany is a demand addressed to democracy itself, whereas in West Germany it is directed only to the incumbent government. This theoretical assumption has also been empirically confirmed by the estimation of a causal model (Fuchs 1998b). But the guarantee of social rights such as job security, security in the event of illness, pension security, etc., always depends on economic development. For the period under review this was marked largely by declining growth rates. The political agenda of the unified Germany therefore tended to address cuts in social spending rather than increases (Roller 1997). Taking the guarantee of social rights as the basis for evaluation, East Germans were therefore hardly able to judge the performance of democracy positively.

On the one hand, economic development is an objective constraint on social policy. On the other, its perception is an independent factor influencing the attitude towards the performance of democracy. This influence may be direct or have an indirect impact via the attitude towards the performance of government. Economic development is the most important dimension of system performance, and, because of the objective course it has taken in the unified Germany, we must assume that the attitude towards system performance will have had a negative impact on the attitude towards the performance of government and/or towards the performance of democracy. This assumption applies in both parts of Germany. Various empirical studies show that this is indeed the case (Walz and Brunner 1997; Pollack, Pickel, and Jacobs 1998).

Having considered the most important factors for the attitude towards the performance of the democracy of the unified Germany, we can state two further hypotheses:

6. *Support for the performance of the democracy of the Federal Republic is significantly higher in West Germany than in East Germany.*

7. *After German unification there was a decline in support for the performance of democracy in East Germany and in West Germany.*

In appraising these hypotheses we take recourse to the indicator of the *Eurobarometer* that asks about *'satisfaction with the functioning of democracy in one's own country'*. As discussed elsewhere in this book, this indicator has provoked considerable criticism that it does not measure what it purports to measure and that it should be used only for pragmatic reasons. We will not take up the discussion again in this context. We merely point out that the value of the indicator can be determined only in relation to a concept of political support and this *Eurobarometer* indicator provides a measure of support for democratic performance.

The results in Figure 6.5 show the percentages of respondents very satisfied or satisfied with the functioning of democracy in the Federal Republic. It is immediately apparent that the significant difference between East and West Germany claimed by the sixth hypothesis exists at all points in time. The seventh hypothesis is also confirmed, but only for West Germany. After the high

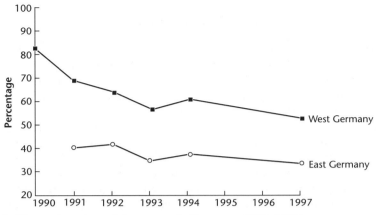

Fig. 6.5. The performance of democracy in Germany, 1990–1997.

Notes: Question: *'All in all, how satisfied are you with the functioning of democracy in the Federal Republic of Germany? (1) Very satisfied, (2) Satisfied, (3) Dissatisfied, (4) Very dissatisfied?'* (1, 2 = satisfaction).

Sources: Eurobarometer (1990–4), FORSA (1997).

rate of satisfaction in 1990, there was a sharp decline in 1991, which continued in weaker form until 1993. Since then satisfaction with the performance of democracy has settled down at a certain level. But at no time has it been below the 50 per cent mark. The strong decline recorded after 1990 is also attributable to the fact that the 1990 figure was the highest recorded in West Germany since 1976 (Fuchs, Guidorossi, and Svensson 1995). This has probably been influenced by the immediately preceding unification of the country.

Unfortunately, there are no figures for East Germany for 1990. Under the impression of German unification, satisfaction with the performance of democracy is likely to have been greater than at other points in time, as has been the case in West Germany. In contrast to West Germany, no unambiguous development since 1991 can be identified, but a slight decline in support seems to have taken place. The seventh hypothesis is thus confirmed only to a very limited degree for East Germany. Situational factors cannot have had the expected impact. Even at an early date, scepticism about the reality of the democracy in the unified Germany was apparently so strong that later experience was unable to change it significantly.

Figure 6.5 shows that no positive generalization from the performance of democracy to the more fundamental attitude towards the type of democracy can yet have taken place in East Germany. This renders plausible the persistently low support for the type of democracy described earlier. Therefore the democracy of the unified Germany is supported by only a minority of East Germans, and support has tended to decline over time. The final section discusses what consequences this could have for the further development of the unified Germany.

Conclusions

According to the paradigm of political culture, congruity of structure and culture is a necessary condition for the stability of the regime, although in many studies congruity remains ill-defined (Kaase 1998). The relevant dimension of political culture is the *support* a democracy receives from its citizens. It still has to be decided to which of the various objects of democracy this support must relate and how strong it must be to satisfy the postulate of congruity.

A liberal democracy lives from permanent disputation about the goals that are to be attained through political processes. Its life-blood is therefore disagreement, *dissensus*, not consensus. However, regulation of this dissensus requires rules of procedure. These rules must be accepted by those involved if they are to fulfil their regulatory function. Consensus at the procedural level is thus a condition for dissensus at the political level. The rules of procedure of a liberal democracy are legally defined by the constitution and embodied in institutions. The specific arrangement of institutions characterizes the type of democracy in a particular country. The support of citizens must primarily relate to this type. It cannot be theoretically determined with any certitude how strong support must be if the stability of democracy is not to be at risk. We therefore propose the following pragmatic solution. If support drops below the 50 per cent mark, hence emanating from only a minority of citizens, the stability of the democracy at issue can be expected to run into problems. The higher the level above the 50 per cent mark that support attains, the more favourable this will be for the stability of the democracy.

If the regulatory structures of a democracy are accepted by its citizens, probably everyday political conflicts can be resolved through the regulatory structures. These assumptions also apply in principle even where there is no consensus among citizens at the value level. However, it is unlikely that adequate support for the regulatory structures of a democracy can develop and persist if the values by which these structures are legitimated are not accepted by the citizenry. Apart from support for the type of democracy, we accordingly consider commitment to the values of democracy as a further specification of the congruity postulate.

Our empirical analysis has revealed a substantial discrepancy between the two parts of Germany at these two levels of democracy. At the level of the values of democracy, the findings indicate that East Germans tend to favour a socialist model of democracy, whereas West Germans prefer a liberal model. And only such a liberal model is consistent with the democracy institutionalized in the unified Germany. For this among other reasons, support for the type of democracy of the unified Germany is relatively high in West Germany and relatively low in East Germany. This difference between West and East therefore relates not to everyday political disputes but to fundamental attitudes towards democracy. The 'inner unity' of the political community of unified Germany is to be still expected (Kaase 1995; Kaase and Bauer-Kaase 1998).

We have assumed socialization in different social systems to be the princi-pal cause of the discrepancies between West Germans and East Germans. Our findings cannot directly and unquestionably confirm this. But it allows much better interpretation of the empirical evidence than competing hypotheses. Rohrschneider (1998) comes to a very similar conclusion in his comprehen-sive analysis. We thus assume that the socialization and experience of East Germans in the German Democratic Republic had a systematic impact on their normative notions of democracy, and produced a sceptical attitude towards the liberal democracy of the unified Germany. These predispositions are again confirmed by negative experience in the unified Germany. Thus in East Germany predispositions shaped by socialization and concrete experience are mutually stabilizing.

Negative experiences may arise for two reasons. First, the deterioration in social security in various areas as a consequence of the economic recession. This deterioration manifested itself in, among other things, increasing unem-ployment and cuts in social benefits. However, we assume that they gain sub-jective relevance only through the application of normative standards that are not derived from these objective facts. According to our analysis, the majority of East Germans regard the guarantee of social rights as a legitimate demand on democracy as a form of government. The growing gap between demand and reality must therefore have an adverse effect on the attitude towards the democracy of the unified Germany. Second, the gap in material conditions between West Germany and East Germany that existed from the outset increased in the course of time. If we may assume that, the point of reference for assessing their material situation for East Germans differs from that of people in other Central and Eastern European countries. The comparison is increasingly not the earlier situation in the German Democratic Republic but the comparison with West Germany, hence relative deprivation is the neces-sary outcome. Such feelings of deprivation can scarcely have a positive impact on the attitude towards a democracy that is still regarded as an import from West Germany. The expectation of many East Germans that a new constitu-tion would be implemented for the unified Germany and that they would be involved in drawing it up, was not fulfilled after unification. Support for the democracy of the unified Germany could therefore not develop through the generalization of positive experience (Gabriel 1997b: 25). All indications on future economic development under the conditions of globalization suggest that conditions are unlikely to improve in the foreseeable future.

Our analysis reveals a political culture in East Germany that is *not* congruent with the democracy of the unified Germany. The low level of sup-port for the type of democracy implies a disposition to change this type struc-turally. The direction in which this disposition points is indicated by the preferences recorded at the value level. The majority of East Germans favour a socialist model of democracy. This contains at least two elements that distin-guish it from the liberal democracy of the unified Germany, namely the con-stitutional guarantee of social rights and the constitutional guarantee of direct participation by the citizens in the political decision-making processes. In a liberal democracy such a disposition of the average citizen will remain latent as long as it is not taken up and mobilized by political elites. As elite studies have shown (Rohrschneider 1994, 1996; Bürklin 1997b; Welzel 1997), in Germany there is substantial potential at the elite level, too, in favour of a socialist model of democracy. It cannot therefore be assumed that the disposition for structural change in the liberal democracy of the unified Germany will necessarily remain latent. It is doubtful whether precisely this direction of structural change can be more effective in the growing economic competition between countries. The agenda is more likely to contain further limitation of citizens' demands on the State and the associated increase in individual responsibility than an expansion of the welfare state. However, a constitutional guarantee of social rights would make a considerable expansion of the welfare state inevitable.

The future development of democracy in the unified Germany will be shaped not only by East Germany but naturally by West Germany as well. The question is therefore what dynamics will arise from the discrepancies between the two parts of the country and how they are to be evaluated from the perspective of the stability of the unified Germany. If only size is taken into account, the pressure to adjust would be exerted by the West on the East, and in the long run the East would adapt to the West. Until this adjustment has taken place, the very positive attitude of West Germans, who constitute a clear majority of the German population, could in certain measure neutralize the sceptical attitude of East Germans. Another argument presents itself if we take account of the welfare state tradition in Germany, which goes back to the Bismarck era in the last century, and which has never suffered interruption (Schmidt 1998). It is still reflected in the high welfare-state demands of citizens in both parts of Germany. The decisive difference between East and West Germany is the addressee of these demands. Whereas social demands in East Germany are addressed to democracy as a form of government, in West Germany the addressee is the current political parties and the incumbent government. In West Germany, social demands are thus merely a political issue and not a systemic one. This is consistent with the liberal model of democracy. But there is no guarantee that this limitation of demands to the everyday political level will continue. The discussion of social rights as legitimate basic rights in a democracy could result in the pressure to adapt coming from East Germany, and could also lead to generalization at the system level in West Germany. It remains to be seen how the dynamics operating between the two parts of Germany actually develop.

We have described East Germans' preference for a socialist model of democracy as a heritage of the state-socialist system of the GDR and explained it in terms of the socialization hypothesis. If this diagnosis is correct, the same should apply for other Central and Eastern European countries. The political elites in these countries thus have to strike a permanent balance between competing demands. On the one hand people expect welfare-state services to be increased, and on the other there are constraints exerted by economic global-ization and international organizations. These international organizations include the European Union, but also economic institutions like the International Monetary Fund. Only the future will show how the political elites of these countries can master the balancing act and what factors make some countries more successful in doing so than others.

7

Tensions Between the Democratic Ideal And Reality: South Korea

RICHARD ROSE, DOH C. SHIN, AND NEIL MUNRO

THE democratic ideal is a paradox: it is desirable yet unattainable. In the words of Robert Dahl (1971: 2), an ideal democracy is a political system that is 'completely or almost completely responsive to all its citizens'. However, he also recognizes that there is an inevitable gap 'between democratic ideals and democratic realities' (Dahl 1997: 74). Dahl has therefore introduced the correlative concept of polyarchy to compare real-world systems of government with the democratic ideal. Countries colloquially described as democratic are, according to Dahl's criteria of polyarchy, regimes that give individuals and institutions many rights and opportunities to influence what government does. While there is inevitably a gap between the ideal and reality, the closer a polyarchy comes to the ideal of democracy, the less the tension between the two. However, regimes vary greatly in the extent to which they are polyarchies—and thus in the extent of tension between the democratic ideal and reality (see e.g. Dahl 1989: 221 ff.; Coppedge and Reinicke 1990).

New democracies are by definition unproven fledgling institutions. A new democracy normally faces great challenges, because of the legacy of the old and now discredited regime. Its leaders will be steeped in practices of undemocratic rule or amateurs in governing because they were in opposition under the old regime. Civil servants will have been trained to treat the populace as subjects with few civil rights, and some may also use office to secure a corrupt side income. In the short run, there are many reasons to expect a new democracy to fall well short of the standards of an ideal democracy, thus creating a substantial gap between democratic ideals and the practice of the new regime.

The greater the gap between democratic ideals and reality, the greater the resulting tension. In this paper we present a model of tension in a new democracy and apply it to the Republic of Korea, drawing on survey data from the 1997 *New Korea Barometer*. Korea is particularly suitable for intensive analysis,

This research was made possible by grants from the Korean Legislative Development Institute and from the British Economic and Social Research R000222308.

since the level of mass education is high and, as subsequent pages show, commitment to democratic ideals is also high. Yet the introduction of free elections in 1987 has produced a succession of presidents whose actions in government have fallen well short of the democratic ideal, leading to convictions on corruption charges. The political fallout of the abuse of power for personal gain was exacerbated in 1997 when the government faced the national humiliation of relying on the biggest International Monetary Fund loan in history to avoid financial collapse.

Tension In A New Democracy

The governance of a democracy is a supply/demand relationship. The public is the source of demands about what governors ought to do and elected officials supply what the voters get. Dahl's ideal of democracy assumes that elected officials are able to provide what the people want. David Easton's (1965: 19 ff.) input/output model of governing recognizes that there can be a greater or lesser gap between what people want and what governors produce. The less the gap, the more a country can be described as a stable democracy. Schumpeter (1952) models democracy as a process in which voters redress disequilibriums between what they demand and what elites supply by voting one team of politicians out of office and putting in a more acceptable alternative.

A polyarchy arrives at a stable equilibrium when there is only a limited gap between how people want to be governed and how the government acts. While there are political debates in a stable polyarchy about what government ought to do, the idea of fundamentally altering major institutions of the regime is not an issue on the political agenda. In a long-established democracy such as Britain, the equilibrium point was reached by an incremental evolutionary process in which tension was never at a high level. By contrast, in historically conflictual political systems such as France and Germany, the tension caused democratic regimes to break down.

In a new democracy the initial relationship between voters and political elites has yet to stabilize. The launch of a new democracy is prima-facie evidence that the majority in the political elite and public opinion support the ideal of democracy. In anticipation of the first competitive election, politicians vie in denouncing the evils of the old regime and proclaiming their commitment to make new institutions work. Voters in the first free election affirm this commitment by supporting parties that promise to do what the people want.

There is no guarantee, however, that the governors of a new democracy will be able to do what the voters want. Free elections offer voters a choice, but economic problems may confront the winner with dilemmas in which any decision can be unpopular as an economic boom cannot be conjured up to pay for everything they have promised, and institutional structures are also likely to be infirm, or even corrupt, as a legacy from the previous regime—a particular problem of governors of new post-communist democracies. Weeks before the 1997 presidential election Korea's governors were forced to seek and accept strict conditions of an IMF loan. Even in non-crisis situations, Rose's (1984) model of party government emphasizes constraints on elected officials from programmes inherited from predecessors, pressures from interest groups and institutions of civil society, and from the international economy.

Nor will tension necessarily be relaxed by political elites agreeing to rely on competitive elections to decide who shall rule, the litmus test of 'consolidation' (see Gunther *et al.* 1995). As Linz and Stepan (1996: 30) caution, 'While we believe that it is a good thing for democracies to be consolidated, consolidation does not necessarily entail a high-quality democracy.' In an incomplete democracy regime competition is replaced by conflicting demands from the public about what ought to be done to complete the process of democratization, and disagreements among elites about whether reforms should be supplied. Old and unpopular elite practices can continue, for a change in regimes does not assure that politicians abandon old habits and civil servants responsible for delivering programmes are too numerous to be replaced wholesale. The consolidation of the new regime is a necessary but insufficient condition for reducing tension, since politicians who abide by the outcome of an election are not necessarily responsive to the electorate, as O'Donnell's (1994) concept of delegative democracy emphasizes.

Tension between democratic ideals and reality is inevitable in a new democracy; in dynamic terms, the tension can lead to any of four very different outcomes. In the extreme, there can be a supply-led pressure to make a new regime approach ideal expectations of citizens. The rapid creation of stable democracies in the Federal Republic of Germany and in Austria after World War II illustrates this process, for both regimes were launched amidst the wreckage of military defeat, yet under the tutelage of allied occupation forces and leadership of pre-totalitarian elites, quickly and unexpectedly created a rule-of-law regime and an economic 'miracle' in place of the political and economic desolation of defeat (Baker *et al.* 1981; Weil 1987).

A demand-side equilibrium is arrived at if popular pressures lead to reform, as elites respond to mass idealism by steadily improving governance to reduce the gap between ideals and reality. In Hirschman's (1970) terms, demands for reform are an expression of voice. In Britain, democratization was the consequence of pressures for reform from those denied the vote; each reform led to incremental change until a complete democracy was established. In new democracies, competitive elections theoretically give voters the opportunity to reward those who deliver reforms and eject from office those who are unresponsive. Italy in the 1990s offers an extreme example of popular demands for reform forcing major changes in representative democracy in a massive attempt to close the gap between Italian ideals and reality.

A democracy is an oligopoly; the supply of political alternatives is inevitably limited, whether choices are as narrow as two candidates in a run-off presidential election or between coalition partners in a multi-party parliamentary system. If a new democracy persistently falls short of popular ideals, this can lead disillusioned citizens to give up on the achievement of their ideals and adjust expectations downwards. Cynicism replaces idealism, venal actions by politicians are accepted matter-of-factly since 'all politicians are on the take' and there is no demand for reform because 'you can't beat the system'. Lowering ideals to the shabby practice of governors creates a low-level equilibrium trap, in which there is stability because there is neither popular demand nor elite will to reform (see Rose *et al.*, 1998: ch. 10). Russia today shows substantial evidence of moving in this direction.

In the extreme, the tension between popular ideals and government practice can result in the breakdown of a new democracy, and its replacement by an undemocratic alternative, as many citizens become so frustrated that they abandon democratic ideals and give elites an opportunity to void the fledging democratic regimes. Evident shortcomings of a new democracy can be seized on by a populist leader to mobilize support at the ballot box, in the streets or both, as Hitler did in a sustained campaign to undermine the Weimar Republic.

Tensions In The New Korean Democracy

Korea is a very old civilization and kingdom (see e.g. Cumings 1997), but it has had a troubled twentieth-century existence. It was under Japanese occupation between 1905 and the end of World War II. In 1948 Korea was divided between the misnamed communist Democratic People's Republic of Korea, and the Republic of Korea, also known as South Korea. North Korea has remained a totalitarian party-state. For nearly four decades after its establishment, the Republic of Korea was governed by a series of dictators, some civilian and some military; all relied on military backing to maintain their power. Changes of government occurred as the result of assassination or coups rather than through free choice at the ballot box. In 1980 the army shot several hundred anti-government demonstrators in the city of Kwangju and dissidents were kept under surveillance and from time to time arrested and jailed by the country's internal security police (cf. Koo 1993; Korean Consortium 1997).

The economy was transformed under the leadership of a 'developmental state' (Leftwich 1995), while democratization was kept off the political agenda. At the beginning of the 1960s, Korea was a poor rural economy, a position similar to that of Japan a decade earlier. General Park Chung Hee, who became ruler in 1961, saw himself as a modernizing dictator analogous to Ataturk or the Meiji rulers of Japan. The state promoted rapid industrialization through state-owned commercial banks, which used soft loans to finance the creation of massive industrial conglomerates, *chaebols*. Fukuyama (1995: 137) describes South Korea's economic boom as linked to having 'the most hyperactive state (with the exception of communist countries)'. Access to credit was the key to control over the economy. Mason (1980: 336) described the logic of the relationship between state and industry thus, 'All Korean businessmen, including the most powerful, have been aware of the need to stay on good terms with the government to assure continuing access to credit and to avoid harassment from the tax officials' (cf. Amsden 1989; Little 1996). The economy was able to prosper because *chaebols* aimed at exports in highly competitive global markets that imposed high standards on Korean manufacturers.

The Republic of Korea started democratization in 1987, when student protests against the imposition of another general as dictator, Roh Tae Woo, led Roh to submit to a competitive election, which he won. The February 1988 constitution institutionalized government by a president elected to a single five-year term. The second presidential election in 1992 was won by Kim Young Sam, who took office as the first popularly elected civilian president in the country's history. In 1997, Kim Dae Jung, a former dissident with trade union support, was elected president. The use of a single ballot without a run-off has made it possible for the victor to be a minority choice, as happened in 1987 when Roh Tae Woo won with 36 per cent of the vote, because his reformist opponents were divided, and in 1997, when Kim Dae Jung won with 40 per cent of the vote thanks to divisions among candidates linked with the previous president.

The achievements of the Korean economy in its undemocratic and democratic periods have been great. From an initial low economic base, Korea has for decades maintained annual rates of economic growth far higher than advanced industrial societies. Between 1985 and 1995 Korea's annual growth rate of 7.7 per cent was four times the average of advanced industrial societies. By 1995 Korea had become an advanced industrial society too, gaining admission to OECD, and its average per capita income was up to the level of Portugal and Greece. Moreover, with 45 million people, the aggregate Gross Domestic Product of Korea had become the eleventh largest in the world, greater than that of the Netherlands or of Sweden and Norway combined.

During the lifetime of the median adult citizen, Korea has undergone a double transformation. For four decades after 1945 the system of government was consistently rated as not free on the Freedom House scale of political and civil liberties. Following the dismantling of repressive institutions and the introduction of free elections the Republic of Korea has earned a place among pluralistic new democracies. Its Freedom House rating is now the equal of that of Greece and Chile, and above that of Argentina, Brazil, the Philippines and such post-communist democracies as Bulgaria, Slovakia, and Russia. However, it is not in the highest category of democratic societies because of continued police harassment of alleged collaborators with North Korea, a degree of media self-censorship, and restrictions on trade unions (Freedom House 1996: 294).

Freely elected presidents have enjoyed a free hand in helping themselves, their friends and *chaebols* to vast wealth, as the rule of law has been violated or distorted for private gain. In its 1997 survey of corruption around the world, Transparency International rates corruption in Korea worse than in Italy, the lowest ranking of European Union countries, or in the Czech Republic, Hungary or Poland, although not nearly so pervasive as in India or Russia. In honest government, it ranks thirty-fourth among fifty-two countries.

The readiness of banks to extend risky loans to *chaebols* with political backers far stronger than their balance sheets led to a financial crisis in autumn 1997. The crisis was not the product of a normal business cycle, nor was it the result of government spending heavily while taxing lightly. It was the outcome of decades of an incestuous relationship between government and business cronies that encouraged borrowing and investment on economically irrational grounds. The upshot was that the International Monetary Fund organized loan guarantees of $55bn. for the Republic of Korea, the largest bailout in IMF history. There were conditions attached, an IMF demand for the restructuring of 'the close collaboration between big business and government' that had fed corruption (Burton 1997). Korea's governors described the events as a 'national humiliation', and the then president, Kim Young Sam, publicly apologized.

The economic crisis of 1997 gave international visibility to the disequilibrium in Korea's democracy; there is a big gap between the standards of an ideal democracy and the practices of political elites who supply governance that not only falls short of these ideals but also echoes the corruption that characterizes most undemocratic regimes.

What Koreans Think About Democracy

While institutional and process indicators can measure the supply of democracy, public opinion data is needed to measure the demand for democracy. Since 1988 Doh Shin has been conducting surveys of mass response to democratization in Korea (cf. Shin 1998). The *New Korea Barometer Survey* (*NKB*) analysed here builds on this work, incorporating also democratization indicators from the *New Democracies Barometer Surveys* conducted by Rose and Haerpfer (1996*b*) and colleagues in post-communist countries.

The *New Korea Barometer* is a representative multi-stage stratified sample survey of the population of the Republic of Korea age 20 and over. The primary sampling units (*ban* or *village*) were randomly selected, with between 6 and 15 respondents in a sampling point. At the household level, the interviewer selected the person whose birthday came next. Face-to-face interviews were conducted by interviewers of Gallup Korea commencing 20 May and concluding 3 June 1997. Interviewing occurred not long after two former Korean presidents had been convicted of treason for their actions as dictators, former President Roh admitted receiving $654m. in corporate donations, and the current president's son had been convicted of taking millions of dollars in bribes.

Flaws in the governance of Korea that suddenly hit the international headlines a few months later were already common knowledge to respondents at the time of interviewing. Of the 2,249 households where an individual name could be selected by the birthday method, 453 individuals were not interviewed because they were either too old, infirm or absent from the household; 604 refused; and 75 interviews were not completed because of the respondent's impatience. A total of 1,117 interviews were satisfactorily completed. Comparison of respondents with census data showed differences were within the expected range of sampling fluctuations (for a full sample report, see Shin and Rose 1997).

To determine the degree of tension between ideal democratic standards and how the Republic of Korea is governed, we must measure an individual's normative commitment to the democratic ideal and his or her cognitive evaluation of the existing system of government. When Koreans were asked how much they personally desired their country to be democratic, replies showed a very high degree of commitment to democracy as an ideal. Half placed themselves at the top two points on the scale, and only 6 per cent placed themselves in the bottom half (Table 7.1). Related questions about attitudes toward free elections, party competition and other democratic processes showed that high endorsement of democracy as an ideal was matched by a positive evaluation of specific democratic institutions. For example, only 16 per cent disagreed with the statement that free elections are the best way of choosing a government, and only 11 per cent said it did not make any difference whether the country had a democratic or an undemocratic government (Shin and Rose 1997: 11 ff.).

Koreans were asked to register how democratic they thought the country's political system actually was today—and replies were much less positive. In all, 30 per cent placed the government closer to dictatorship than to democracy, and the median Korean saw the political system as just democratic, rating it at point 6 on a 10-point scale. Only one Korean in 25 placed the current system at the top two points on the scale. Comparison with related questions showed that this assessment of the political system as a whole was not simply a reaction against the activities of the government of the day. The government of then President Kim Young Sam was far more unpopular; 79 per cent placed the current president in the bottom half of a rating scale, and his mean rating was 3.8.

Together, the replies show tension between how democratic Koreans would like their country to be and what they see their political elites supply in reality. The average Korean gives the ideal of democracy a mean rating of 8.4, compared to a mean rating of 6.2 for the way the country is being governed today. An overwhelming 88 per cent of Koreans gave the democratic ideal a higher rating than the practice of government in Korea today; just over 8 per cent rated them equal, and only 4 per cent thought the practice was better than the ideal. While the average Korean shows a high level of commitment to the democratic ideal, he or she sees the current system of government as lit-

Table 7.1. Korean views of democracy and reality (%)

Scale	Ideal	Real
10 Complete democracy	27	1
9	23	3
8	29	15
7	12	27
6	3	24
5	4	21
4	1	5
3	0	3
2	0	0
1 Complete dictatorship	1	1
MEAN:	8.4	6.2

Ideal: *'Here is a scale ranging from a low of 1 to a high of 10. On this scale, 1 means complete dictatorship and 10 means complete democracy. Where would you place the extent to which you personally desire democracy for our country?'*

Real: *'Where would you place our country at the present time?'*

Source: 1997 *New Korea Barometer Survey*, a nationwide representative sample of 1,117 respondents interviewed between 20 May and 3 June.

tle better than a mild dictatorship, and a long way from being a complete democracy.

Explaining Differences In Ideals And Reality

While there is much commitment to democratic ideals and much scepticism about the practice of Korean democracy, there are substantial differences between Koreans in their placement of both. It follows that the extent to which individuals feel a tension between the democratic ideal and the practice of government in Korea also varies between individuals, with some feeling no tension and others acutely aware of a gap. Three sets of theories offer explanations for these differences.

Macro-sociological theories stress the influence of social structure. Both non-Marxist and Marxist sociologists have stressed class structure as the prime determinant of political outlooks. In an Asian context, it is problematic whether Western definitions of class are more important than other group loyalties. Lipset and Rokkan (1967) have a more differentiated sense of social structure, adding religion, national identity and urban–rural differences, all of which are applicable in contemporary Korea. In addition, 'post-modern' theories of social cleavage give great attention to education; more educated people are believed to be more capable of thinking for themselves whatever their placement in the social structure (Dalton 1996; Inglehart 1997a). This implies that more educated people are likely to be more committed to democratic ideals, more critical and negative about the current practice of democracy, and thus to experience more tension in their views of democratization.

Economic theories of political behaviour provide an alternative explanation for differences in political attitudes. However, the proposition—'It's the economy, stupid'—is capable of many different interpretations. In Korea, phenomenal levels of economic growth under a dictatorship as well as under a popularly elected president have created an environment very different from Western economies, but have made current anxieties about the national economy more striking. We differentiate economic attitudes by reference to the current state of the economy, retrospective comparisons with the past and future expectations (cf. Fiorina 1981; MacKuen *et al.* 1992). Equally important are distinctions between the influence of individual or household microeconomic circumstances and the position of the country as a whole, for national economic growth does not affect every household equally (cf. Kinder and Kiewiet 1981). In so far as the democratic period since 1987 is identified with prosperity, we would expect the more prosperous to be more in favour of the democratic ideal, more in favour of current practice, and thus to feel less tension.

It is logical and parsimonious to theorize that democratic ideals can reflect political attitudes, but this leaves open the specification of political influences. A host of theories hypothesize that popular evaluation of a new democracy depends on the political performance of its leaders, a view fully consistent with the supply–demand hypothesis (cf. Rogowski 1974). But since most Koreans have initially been socialized into an undemocratic regime, the performance that counts most may be the political legacy of the undemocratic regime. The more negative the evaluation of the old regime, the greater the relative favourability of a democratic alternative (cf. Rose *et al.*, 1998). Since democracy is above all about political values, the more an individual is committed to democratic values, or at least to reject undemocratic values, the stronger the likely commitment to democratic ideals.

Support for Democratic Ideals

The *New Korea Barometer* questionnaire includes a great variety of measures of social, economic, and political attitudes; thus, we have multiple indicators to test the variety of theories canvassed above. The appropriate way to do so is by OLS multiple regression analysis (For full details of coding, means and standard deviations of all variables, see Appendix 7A).[1] A multiple regression

---

[1] In preliminary runs, not reported here, we tried more than a dozen additional indicators, but they have been discarded because of consistent statistical insignificance and low theoretical significance. Because commitment to the democratic ideal is positively skewed, we combined the small number of replies in the most extreme bottom categories of the rating to produce a five-point scale with a normal distribution, a mean of 3.47 and a standard deviation of 1.24.

analysis including 28 different political, social and economic influences explains 13.8 per cent of the total variance in commitment to the democratic ideal (Table 7.2).

The regression model includes 13 different measures; the strategy is justified since 7 are statistically significant and they account for most of the explained variance. As Koreans have lived most of their lives under an undemocratic regime, questions about support for undemocratic rule are matter-of-fact rather than hypothetical. The *New Korea Barometer* reminded respondents: '*Our present system of government is not the only one that this country has had, and some people say we would be better off if the country was governed differently*', and

Table 7.2. Influences on endorsement of the democratic ideal

	B	S.E.	Beta
Political influences:			
Rejects army rule	.24	.05	.15**
Rejects strong-man dictator	.14	.05	.09**
Rejects suspension parliament	.13	.05	.07*
Dissatisfied with how democracy works	−.11	.02	−.14**
Trust representative institutions	−.13	.06	−.07*
Patient with democratic government	.10	.05	.06*
Degree of corruption in government	.12	.05	.06*
Central government influences life	−.01	.04	n.s.
Government listens to my views	.02	.05	n.s.
Approves reunification	.09	.05	n.s.
Trusts institutions of authority	.01	.02	n.s.
Rating of dictatorship Chun Doo Whan	.00	.00	n.s.
Rating of President Roh Tae Woo	.00	.00	n.s.
Social structure:			
City size	−.13	.03	−.14**
Identifies Republic Korea	−.22	.08	−.08**
Trust most people	.22	.06	.10**
Christian	.15	.08	n.s.
Age	−.01	.00	n.s
Education	.08	.05	n.s.
Social class	.06	.05	n.s.
Gender: female	.02	.07	n.s.
Economic influences:			
National economy better 10 years ago	−.08	.03	−.08**
National economy satisfactory now	−.11	.08	n.s.
National economy better in future	−.01	.05	n.s.
Household economy situation good now	−.10	.07	n.s.
Household economy better 10 years ago	.04	.04	n.s.
Household economy better in future	−.02	.05	n.s.
Income	.00	.02	n.s.
Adj R^2	.137		

* Significant at <.05.
** Significant at <.01.
n.s.: not significant.

Source: New Korea Barometer Survey, a nationwide representative sample of 1,117 respondents interviewed between 20 May and 3 June 1997. For details of coding of variables, see Appendix 7A.

then invited agreement or disagreement with the following alternatives: *'get-ting rid of Parliament and elections'*; *'the army governing the country'*; and *'having a strong leader decide everything'*. Only 19 per cent favoured the abolition of parliament, 19 per cent said a dictatorship would be better and 15 per cent military rule. Those who rejected each undemocratic alternative are significantly more likely to endorse democratic ideals.

The political performance of the current regime also matters, but in the opposite direction. People who say they are dissatisfied with how democracy now works in Korea are significantly less committed to the democratic ideal. In so far as performance is a consistent influence, then we would also expect people who think government listens to their views or influences their life would be more likely to support the democratic ideal. In fact, this is not the case: neither of these measures is statistically significant.

There is a consensus that government is corrupt. Koreans only differ in the extent to which it is deemed corrupt: 36 per cent say corruption is very high and 49 per cent say it is high; the remaining sixth think it is not so high. Awareness of corruption might be expected to make people disillusioned with democratic ideals, but this is not the case. People who see government as very corrupt are *more* inclined to support the ideal of democracy. This indicates that democratic idealism is associated with high expectations of honesty in government, and an unwillingness to tolerate corruption as normal. Similarly surprising is the fact that the fifth who trust representative institutions of parties and parliament are less likely to be committed to democratic ideals, and those who distrust these institutions are significantly more committed. Here again, we see that idealism encourages an expectation of high standards of performance and thus dissatisfaction with the realities of Korean politics.

The legacy of the past is significant in so far as it encourages political patience. To measure political patience, Koreans were asked whether they thought it would take years for government to deal with problems inherited from the days of undemocratic governance or if the current system should be able to deal with problems right now (cf. Rose 1997*b*). A total of 74 per cent showed patience, saying it would take years to deal with the legacy of the undemocratic past. The more patient people are, the more likely they are to be committed to democratic ideals. Attitudes toward the legacy of the past, as represented by two dictators, Chun Doo Whan and Roh Tae Woo, are not significant.

Reunification with North Korea is a constitutional goal; however, the military mobilization of North Korea has made it appear a distant goal. The 1997 *New Korea Barometer* found that 79 per cent thought reunification desirable, but almost half had significant reservations about the costs of adding 22 million people from a very poor North Korea to 44 million in the Republic. Attitudes toward reunification are not significantly related to commitment to democratic ideals.

The multiplicity of political influences on democratic idealism push in opposite directions. While dissatisfaction with performance encourages disillusionment, idealism is reinforced by values opposing undemocratic alternatives. The important question is whether dissatisfaction with current performance overrides commitment to democratic values. We can answer this by calculating the extent to which a person's democratic idealism would alter, according to its b value in the regression equation, if each significant political influence changed from its mean to its maximum level. For example, the mean for dissatisfaction with democracy is 4.06, and the b value .11. Hence, if a person was totally dissatisfied with Korea as a new democracy, rating it at 1, then net of all other influences this would lower commitment to democratic ideals a third of a point (that is 2.94 × .11). Since the mean for democratic idealism is high, so small a change would still leave a person at the positive end of the scale.

Even after allowing for the negative effect of dissatisfaction with the current performance of democracy, the net effect of political attitudes is to *raise* the level of democratic ideals. Rejection of undemocratic alternatives exactly cancels out the impact of dissatisfaction with how democracy works—and high standards about corruption, representative institutions and political patience boost commitment to the democratic ideal further (Table 7.3).

Table 7.3. Impact of political attitudes on democratic ideals

Mean commitment to democratic ideals on 5-point scale	3.47
Cumulative change in idealism if:	
Strongly against army rule/dictator/suspension of Parliament	3.79
Very patient with new regime	3.89
Corruption seen as very high	3.97
Very distrustful of representative institutions	4.09
Very dissatisfied with how democracy works	3.76
Net change in democratic idealism*	+.29

* Change in idealism is calculated by multiplying the b value by the difference between the mean and maximum values of the independent variables.

Source: B values as reported in Table 7.2; values for each independent variable reported in Appendix 7A.

While some social structure characteristics influence commitment to the democratic ideal, education lacks any significant influence, and the same is true of age (Table 7.2). This is actually encouraging for proponents of democratization, since it shows that support for the ideals of democracy is not just confined to an educated elite or students in the forefront of pro-democracy demonstrations; it is widespread, existing among less educated and older Koreans too. As Przeworski (1991) emphasizes, the more widely democratic values are diffused throughout society, the less risk there is of any social group, whether left-wing students or right-wing peasants, becoming a cohesive obstacle to democratization.

While the population of the Republic of Korea is ethnically homogeneous, the country has strong local and regional loyalties that politicians cultivate in bids for electoral support.[2] Hence, the *New Korea Barometer* offered people a range of identities to select, from a list that included their locality, their region, South Korea or the whole of Korea. It also asked people to select the group that they most identified with, and considered second in importance. National identification is low: only 13 per cent identified first with South Korea and 7 per cent with the historic nation of North and South Korea. When second choices are taken into account, 32 per cent showed some identity with Korea as a nation. The group is 'nationalist' in the undemocratic style of Europeans earlier in the twentieth century, as they are significantly less committed to democratic ideals.[3] In addition, urbanization significantly reduces commitment to the ideals of democracy: people who live in a large city or the capital, Seoul, are less likely to favour democracy. It thus appears that the 'melting-pot' development of a national identity and reduction of local and regional ties by big city life encourages disillusionment with democratic ideals.

Religion offers an alternative focus of individual identity, and in Korea there is a wide choice of religions on offer. The largest group report they have no religion, 29 per cent are Buddhists, and 29 per cent Christians, primarily Protestants. Identification with Christianity is on the margin of significance but has limited effect on endorsement of democratic ideals.

Consistent with Robert Putnam's (1993) views of social capital, Koreans who trust the majority of people are significantly more likely to be committed to democratic ideals. But the evidence does not support Putnam's view that interpersonal trust leads to trust in representative institutions; the opposite is the case. Whereas 77 per cent of Koreans think most people can be trusted somewhat or a lot, only 20 per cent are inclined to trust parties and 22 per cent to trust parliament. Since the minority who do trust representative institutions appear to be less committed to democratic ideals, the significant effects of these two types of trust tend to cancel out.

Household and national economic conditions have surprisingly little influence on commitment to democratic ideals. In the preceding decade, the Korean economy had averaged an annual rate of growth in Gross Domestic Product more than double that of any advanced industrial society. However, in the economic climate of 1997, 50 per cent of Koreans thought the economy had got worse over the past decade. Of the 7 different measures of economic conditions, 6 failed to register any statistical significance, while those who thought the national economy was better ten years ago were less likely to support democratic ideals. Measures of the respondent's household economic situation were consistently insignificant.

---

[2] The absence of anything approaching a stable party system along Western lines made it inappropriate to ask questions about party identification, and uncertainties about candidates in a presidential election more than six months off made it inappropriate to ask about voting behaviour.

[3] Within Asian studies there is a major debate about whether Asian values place a low priority on democracy or are even inimical to it. This debate is remote from the great majority of Koreans; only 1 per cent named Asia as their first identification and 2 per cent gave it as their secondary identification.

Perceptions of Progress to Democracy

The median Korean sees the political regime in which the president is chosen by free election as different from a dictatorship—but not by much. Shin's 1996 *New Korea Barometer Survey* showed that the big difference between the old and new regime is the gain in freedom from the state, in the classic Isaiah Berlin sense (1969). For example, 82 per cent now feel freer to say what they think and 73 per cent feel freer to join any organization of their choice. When the 1997 *New Korea Barometer* asked respondents to place the government today on a 10-point scale, the median score is 6.2, and variations around this median position are substantial.[4]

Using the same variables as for evaluating democratic ideals (Table 7.4), a multiple regression analysis explains 21.1 per cent of the variance in evaluating the new regime's democratic status. Political attitudes are even more important in determining whether Koreans see their new regime as closer to a democracy or a dictatorship—and dissatisfaction with how democracy currently works is by far the strongest influence. The more dissatisfied a Korean is with the current political system, the more likely that person is to regard it as a dictatorship. Furthermore, people who view positively the regime of General Chun Doo Whan, a notorious dictator, are more likely to regard the current system as a 'democracy'. Together, this suggests that those who see the current regime as most democratic do so because they are less likely to be democrats themselves, and those who are most negative about it are so because, by their idealistic standards, the new regime is not democratic enough.

The institutions that people trust also affect their rating of the current regime. The more people trust authoritative state institutions, such as the courts, the police and the military, the more likely they are to see the current regime as democratic. In a complementary fashion, the more people trust representative institutions such as parties and parliament, the more likely they are to see the current system as closer to a dictatorship. In an established democracy, the maintenance of support for the regime arises from a continuing feedback between the demands of citizens and the supply of benefits by government in response to these demands. However, Koreans who are most conscious of the influence of central government on their everyday life are also most likely to see the regime as dictatorial.

Economic circumstances have little effect on whether people perceive the current regime as a democracy; of the 7 economic indicators, 5 are statistically insignificant. Nor is this surprising, given that the political status of the new regime is logically independent of economic conditions. The economic measures that do have a little effect are optimism about the economy in the future and having a satisfactory household income at present. This implies that some Koreans associate a democracy with a regime that will be able to promote

---

[4] To avoid skewness at the extremes, the measure was reduced to a more evenly distributed seven-point scale, with a mean of 4.26 and a standard deviation of 1.36.

Table 7.4. Extent to which democracy is seen as achieved

	B	S.E.	Beta
Political influences:			
Dissatisfied how democracy works	−.29	.02	−.35**
Rating of dictatorship Chun Doo Whan	.004	.001	.14**
Trust institutions of authority	.11	.02	.13**
Trust representative institutions	−.21	.06	−.11**
Central government influences life	−.12	.05	−.07*
Government listens to my views	.09	.05	n.s.
Rating of President Roh Tae Woo	.00	.00	n.s.
Patient with democratic government	.04	.05	n.s.
Rejects army rule	.04	.05	n.s.
Rejects strong man dictator	−.02	.05	n.s.
Rejects suspension parliament	.02	.05	n.s.
Approves reunification	.02	.05	n.s.
Degree of corruption in government	−.09	.06	n.s.
Economic influences:			
National economy better in future	.12	.05	.07*
National economy better 10 years ago	.01	.03	n.s.
National economy now very bad	−.08	.08	n.s.
Household economy situation good now	−.14	.07	−.06*
Household economy better 10 years ago	−.02	.04	n.s.
Household economy better in future	.01	.05	n.s.
Income	.00	.02	n.s.
Adj R²	.212		
Social structure:			
Age	.01	.00	n.s.
Education	.04	.05	n.s.
City size	−.04	.03	n.s.
Identifies Republic Korea	−.11	.08	n.s.
Trust most people	−.02	.06	n.s.
Christian	−.04	.08	n.s.
Gender: female	−.09	.08	n.s.
Social class	−.04	.05	n.s.

  * Significant at <.05.
 ** Significant at <.01.
 n.s.: not significant.

Source: 1997 *New Korea Barometer Survey*, a nationwide representative sample of 1,117 respondents interviewed between 20 May and 3 June. For details of coding of variables, see Appendix 7A.

national economic growth, but, at the same time, those who are better-off are less likely to perceive democracy as having been achieved. The two effects cancel each other out.

No social structure characteristic has a significant influence on the assessment of the current regime. This is true not only of education and age, which were also of no consequence for commitment to democratic ideals, but also of Korean identity, town size, religion, and trust in people, which were significant.

Influences on Tension Between Ideals and Reality

In seven-eighths of the cases in Korea, the tension between what people want and the regime that is supplied arises from the government on offer being less democratic than their aspirations, thus creating tension. In ratings of the democratic ideal and the current regime, there is a gap of 2.15 points on the ten-point scale. A multiple regression analysis, using the same influences as in the preceding analyses, can account for 14.5 per cent of variance in the gap between individual ideals and reality, more than for democratic ideals on its own.

Table 7.5. Accounting for the gap between ideal and achieved democracy

	B	S.E.	Beta
Political influences:			
Dissatisfied how democracy works	.17	.03	.18**
Rating dictatorship Chun Doo Whan	−.003	.001	−.12**
Degree of corruption in govt	.23	.07	.10**
Trust institutions of authority	−.09	.03	−.09**
Rejects army rule	.18	.06	.09**
Rejects strong man dictator	.16	.06	.08**
Rejects suspension parliament	.13	.06	.06*
Rating of President Roh Tae Woo	.00	.00	n.s.
Patient with democratic govt	.07	.06	n.s.
Trust representative institutions	.08	.07	n.s.
Central government influences life	.09	.06	n.s.
Government listens to my views	−.05	.06	n.s.
Supports reunification	.06	.06	n.s.
Economic influences:			
National economy better 10 years ago	−.09	.04	−.07*
National economy satisfactory now	.03	.10	n.s.
National economy better in future	−.12	.06	n.s.
Household economy situation good now	.06	.08	n.s.
Household economy better 10 years ago	.09	.05	n.s.
Household economy better in future	−.01	.06	n.s.
Income	−.02	.02	n.s.
Social structure:			
Age	−.01	.004	−.13**
Trust most people	.23	.08	.09**
Christian	.22	.10	.06*
City size	−.09	.04	−.08*
Identifies Republic Korea	−.13	.10	n.s.
Education	.04	.06	n.s.
Social class	.09	.06	n.s.
Gender: female	.12	.09	n.s.
Adj R²	.143		

* Significant at <.05.
** Significant at <.01.
n.s.: not significant.

Source: 1997 *New Korea Barometer Survey*, a nationwide representative sample of 1,117 respondents interviewed between 20 May and 3 June. For details of coding of variables, see Appendix 7A.

The performance of the current regime influences the tension between ideals and reality. The more dissatisfied people are with the working of democracy and the greater perceived corruption, the bigger the gap between ideals and reality. In other words, the gap is not due to a lack of democratic demand among Koreans but to a failure of elected politicians to supply a high quality democracy. Political values also affect the gap: the more an individual rejects undemocratic alternatives, the higher the commitment to democratic ideals and the less likely an individual is to rate the current regime as very democratic. By contrast, being positive about the dictatorship of General Chun Doo Whan and trusting institutions of authority reduces the gap, showing that those who cannot tell the difference between a dictatorship and a democracy tend to see both past and present Korean regimes as similarly 'democratic' (Table 7.5).

Social structure also contributes to the tension between ideals and reality. Three influences are the same as for commitment to the democratic ideal. Trust in people and being a Christian increase the gap, due to producing an above average level of idealism. The influence of city size is reduced and identification with the Republic of Korea is insignificant. Age has the strongest association; older people are less likely to perceive a gap between democratic ideals and reality. Only 1 of the 7 economic influences shows any statistical significance: the evaluation of the economy ten years ago.

A Political Explanation for a Political Phenomenon

Political scientists differ in their readiness to explain political phenomena by other political phenomena or by economic and social influences. A multiplicity of social, economic, and political measures provides a robust test of alternative types of explanation. The regression analyses confirm the inherently political nature of democracy. The primary influences on commitment to democratic ideals, evaluating the current regime, and the tension between the two are political values and political performance. The legacy of the past, as measured by attitudes toward undemocratic leaders, is also significant.

Social structure is second in importance as an influence on democratic ideals and also influences the tension between ideals and reality, but it has very little influence on whether or not people see the current regime as democratic. A striking feature of Korea is that conventional social structure influences, such as class and education, are consistently insignificant. The social structure influences that matter are those associated with local identities and trust in people, nationalism, and Christianity, which in the Korean context is a departure from Asian values.

Consistently, economic influences show virtually no influence on attitudes to democracy. An economic boom under dictatorship and democracy, at least up to 1997, has dissociated economic conditions from regime change to an extent that has not happened in post-communist countries. People can see that both types of regime are capable of accommodating economic growth—

a point also made by many econometric analyses (see e.g. Helliwell 1994). There are also good theoretical reasons for expecting economic conditions to have less impact on choices between regimes, for fluctuations in economic conditions tend to be marginal, whereas differences between democratic and undemocratic regimes have a pervasive effect on how people live.

Demand-Driven Pressure For Reform

While there is inevitably a gap between the ideal of democracy and the reality of polyarchy, the resolution of tension is problematic. The *New Korea Barometer* shows that two of the four alternative outcomes identified above are not applicable. Koreans have not fallen into a low-level equilibrium trap, lowering their ideals to meet the practice of a corrupt, popularly elected government. Nor have Korean elites raised standards of governance faster than popular demand; if anything, they have lowered standards notwithstanding pressure from popular ideals. Two alternatives remain: repudiating a very imperfect democracy in favour of an undemocratic regime, or keeping up pressure for reform.

The experience of undemocratic rule has turned most Koreans against it. Combining responses to questions about endorsing the abolition of parliament and competing parties, military rule, and a dictatorship shows that 61 per cent of Koreans consistently reject all three alternatives. The proportion doing so in Korea is even higher than in post-communist countries of Central and Eastern Europe (cf. Rose, Mishler and Haerpfer, 1998: ch. 5). Only a tenth of Koreans endorse two or three undemocratic alternatives, and 29 per cent support even one undemocratic alternative. Thus, although Koreans find their new democracy far from ideal, they do not want to close the gap with current practice by rejecting it in favour of another alternative.

Reform is the preferred alternative of Koreans. When the *New Korea Barometer* asked: '*How much do you agree or disagree with the statement that our political system should be made a lot more democratic than what it is now?*' seven out of eight endorsed reform. The chief difference was in the intensity of the demand for reform.

Strongly for more democracy	46%
Somewhat for more democracy	42%
Total wanting more democracy	88%
Somewhat against	8%
Definitely against	2%
Total against more democracy	10%
Don't know, no answer	2%

Dissatisfaction with democracy is a stimulus to resolve the tension between ideal and reality by reforming imperfect institutions, for 89 per cent of those saying they are dissatisfied with democracy say they want a more democratic government, as do 92 per cent of those saying they are satisfied with it.

In a new democracy, political elites have a strategic choice: either they supply democratic institutions that gradually meet the demanding but attainable standards of a polyarchy or they do not reform institutions and offer to supply an undemocratic alternative. Within months of the completion of the 1997 *New Korea Barometer Survey*, financial collapse across East Asia plunged the Republic of Korea into its worst financial crisis in modern history. While there are national precedents for a turn toward undemocratic rule, should Korean elites move that way our evidence shows it would raise to a new height political tension between what the people want and what elites supply. This would encourage Koreans to take to the streets to demonstrate against undemocratic measures and demand that politicians reform themselves and govern more democratically. Otherwise, political costs will be added to the economic costs that the Korean people are now asked to bear because popularly elected political leaders have fallen far short of the standards expected in a stable polyarchy.

Appendix Table 7A. Coding of variables and measures

	Scale/Range		Mean	SD
Dependent variables:				
Extent democracy seen as achieved[1]	1 = least	10 = most	6.25	1.4
Endorsement of the democratic ideal[2]	1 = least	10 = most	8.40	1.4
Gap between ideal and achieved[3]	−9 = surplus	+9 = deficit	2.15	1.8
Independent variables:				
A. Political				
Reject army should rule*	1 = disagree	3 = v.much agree	2.50	.75
Reject strong man dictator*	1 = disagree	3 = v.much agree	2.31	.78
Reject parliament's supension*	1 = disagree	3 = v.much agree	2.23	.74
Dissatisfied with how democracy works*	1 = least	7 = most	4.06	1.65
Trust representative institutions*	1 = v. low trust	3 = trust	1.85	.71
Patience: takes years to solve problems*	1 = v.much agree	3 = disagree	2.01	.74
Degree of corruption in current government*	1 = not bad	3 = very high	2.21	.69
Central government influences my life	1 = none	4 = very much	2.60	.79
Government listens to my views*	1 = never	3 = sometimes	2.05	.71
Support reunification*	1 = disagree	3 = v. much agree	2.26	.78
Trusts institutions of authority	1 = least	8 = most	4.72	1.67
Rating dictatorship of Chun Doo Hwan	−100 = worst	+100 = best	4.33	47.5
Rating of President Roh Tae Woo	−100 = worst	+100 = best	−19.2	41.1
B. Social Structure				
Age in deciles	20	60+	35.7	13.7
Gender: female	1 = yes	0 = no	.51	.50
Formal education*	1 = none	5 = college or higher	3.68	1.17
Self-assessed social class position	1 = upper	5 = lower	3.36	.83
Christian religion	1 = yes	0 = no	.29	.45
Size of community	1 = rural	5 = capital	3.34	1.3
Identifies with Republic of Korea	1 = yes	0 = no	.32	.47
Trust most people*	1 = not trust	3 = trust a lot	1.89	.58
C. Economic				
Income in won/month	1 = <0.5m	9 = >3 million won	5.65	2.24
National economy today*	1 = very bad	0 = quite good	.57	.50
National economy 10 years ago	1 = m.worse	5 = much better	3.28	1.34
National economy in five years	1 = m.worse	5 = much better	3.52	.81
Household economy today*	1 = very bad	3 = satisfactory	2.12	.60
Household economy in 5 years	1 = m.worse	5 = much better	3.69	.78
Household economy 10 years ago	1 = m.worse	5 = much better	2.72	1.08

* Scale collapsed because of skewed distribution.

[1] Collapsed to form a more normal scale from 1–7, as follows: 1–3 = 1; 4 = 2; 5 = 3; 6 = 4; 7 = 5; 8 = 6; 9–10 = 7. Mean: 4.26 SD: 1.36.

[2] Collapsed to form a more normal scale from 1–5, as follows: 1–6 = 1; 7 = 2; 8 = 3; 9 = 4; 10 = 5. Mean: 3.47 SD: 1.24.

[3] Collapsed to form a more normal scale, from −1 to 6, as follows: −1. . .−9 = −1; 0 = 0; 1 = 1; 2 = 2; 3 = 3; 4 = 4; 5 = 5; 6. . .9 = 6 . Mean: 2.19 SD:1.58.

PART III

Explanations of Trends

PART III

Explanation of Trends

8

Social and Political Trust in Established Democracies

KENNETH NEWTON

THE concept of trust is currently on the lips and in the minds of many social scientists. Interest in the concept has expanded rapidly in the last few years and has generated a literature in the social sciences and philosophy (see, for example, Gambetta 1988; Misztal 1996; Bianco 1994; Fukuyama 1995; Warren 1996; Hardin 1996; Sztompka 1996).

One reason for the interest is that trust represents a central concept in social capital theory, which is commanding a good deal of attention. Both social capital and trust are close cousins of the writings on civil society and communitarianism, and all are developing along rather similar lines. Moreover, the concepts of social capital and trust are, in some ways, modern social science equivalents of the classical idea of fraternity, and in the late 1990s social scientists have rediscovered the importance of fraternity, or something like it, as a necessary condition of democracy. For much of the past twenty or thirty years, politics and political science have tended to ignore fraternity, concentrating instead on liberty and equality. Indeed, in the Reaganite and Thatcherite ethos of the 1980s, political discussion often focused exclusively on liberty and overlooked or ignored completely both fraternity and equality. More than this, discussion of liberty tended to circle around a peculiarly narrow view of the concept as if it were related only to economic and market freedom.

The late 1990s have reacted against this view of the world, recognizing that citizens are more than the sum of their shopping. Such things as economic growth, social integration, political stability, and government efficiency may well depend upon underlying values, norms, and attitudes, and social conditions which create the capacity to trust and co-operate (see, for example, Inglehart 1990: 23–4, 34–8; Inglehart 1997a: 172–4; Inglehart and Abramson 1994). Without these underlying values and social capacities, society could barely function, and then only with great friction and inefficiency. In the

I would like to thank the Wissenschaftszentrum Berlin fur Sozialforschung where I spent a wonderful sabbatical year, 1996–7, during which this paper was written. I would especially like to thank Andreas Dams of WZB and Paul Whiteley of Sheffield University for help with computing.

1980s political scientists 'brought the state back in'; now they are busy 'bringing fraternity back in', except they call it social capital, or trust, or sociability, or the capacity to co-operate and reciprocate. Trust is a handy empirical way of approaching this clutch of concepts, because it narrows them down and makes them amenable to survey investigation. Yet the nature, origins and consequences of trust, and its relationship with associated concepts are unclear. An important part of contemporary social sciences may be to try to sort out the causes and the consequences of trust, and its implications for social, political and economic life.

This chapter will deal with three main topics.

- The *nature and origins of social trust* and its importance in society.
- *Trends in social trust* in Western societies.
- The *relations between social and political trust*, and their implications for theories of politics and society.

In terms of the main concepts and measures of this volume, as outlined in the Introduction, social trust is a feature of the most basic level of community, while political trust refers primarily to attitudes about political institutions and leaders. The general assumption seems to be that social and political trust are closely linked, perhaps different sides of the same coin. Social trust is regarded as a strong determinant of, or influence upon, political support of various kinds, including support for the political community, confidence in institutions, and trust in political leaders. As a result it is believed that the accumulation of social capital, in the form of social trust, will also result in the accumulation of political capital. This chapter will present theory and evidence questioning these assumptions.

Social Trust

The Nature of Social Trust

> Those who liked one another so well as to joyn into Society, cannot but be supposed to have some Acquaintance and Friendship together, and some Trust one in another.
>
> (John Locke, *Two Treatises on Government*, 1690)

A's trust in B is based on A's belief that B will not knowingly or willingly do him/her harm. Trust involves the belief that others will, so far as they can, look after our interests, that they will not take advantage or harm us. Therefore, trust involves personal vulnerability caused by uncertainty about the future behaviour of others; we cannot be sure, but we believe that they will be benign, or at least not malign, and act accordingly in a way which may possibly put us at risk (Baier 1986: 235). We are often forced to take this risk because it is the best or only way of smoothing out difficulties with the unknown future (Bates 1988). If we can trust others then life is easier, social transactions more efficient, and co-operation more likely (Parry 1976; Coleman 1990: 91; Putnam 1993: 170–1; Sztompka 1996: 43). Trust is built upon imperfect knowledge; the more we know about others the more we may trust (or distrust) them, but we cannot be certain of our judgement, or it would not involve trust. In other words, trust involves a leap of faith. Sometimes this faith is rooted in religious teaching and sometimes in secular ideas, but always it involves personal risk, the unknown, and judgement about the motives and behaviour of others.

Trust does not involve rational calculation of a tit-for-tat nature in which one good turn is repaid with another of equal value. Rather it is based upon an assumption that good turns will be repaid at some time in the future, perhaps even by unknown people (Sahlins 1972). In this way trust and generalized reciprocity are similar, and both are different from instrumental and rational calculation. Nevertheless trust is not blind; it involves the accumulation and updating of experience and the modification of trust or distrust according to events (Hardin 1992).

We can put it the other way round and treat trust as a way of reducing risk and uncertainty. In an increasingly risky and unknown world, trust opens up possibilities for action by providing the basis for risk reduction (Luhmann 1979: 40). Without trust in those upon whom we depend, daily life would be much more difficult, if not actually impossible, for everyone but the lawyers, who would make a lot of money. For the rest of us life would be like the British summer—nasty, brutish, and short. There are social types who are trust-averse and they are called paranoids; for the rest of us trust helps to make the world go round.

The Origins of Social Trust

> Among the laws that rule human societies there is one which seems to be more precise and clear than all the others. If men are to remain civilized or become so, the art of associating together must grow and improve in the same ratio in which the equality of conditions is increased.
>
> (de Tocqueville 1956: ii. 118)

According to de Tocqueville social trust in nineteenth-century America was bred, if not actually born, in civic associations, community organizations, and voluntary clubs, and above all in political associations. The state did not and could not create trust; rather, the democratic state, with its freedom of political association, was built upon trust. The idea is taken up as a central theme in the social capital theory of Putnam (1993, 1995a, b) who focuses less upon political associations than on non-political ones such as the choirs and bird-watching associations of Italy, and the community associations and voluntary organizations of the United States. Particularly important are those voluntary activities which bridge different groups and cut across social divisions. Closed groups which do not bridge social cleavages may create trust internally among their own members, but distrust externally with other groups and wider society. Organizations which cut across social cleavages may help to teach tolerance and understanding, and thereby create the 'habits of the heart' (Bellah *et al.* 1985) associated with trust, reciprocity and co-operation.

Two observations can be made about the de Tocqueville/Putnam model of social capital as rooted in community groups, voluntary associations, and intermediary organizations. First, there is, indeed, a huge number and great diversity of such organizations in all Western societies, and they cater for almost every conceivable sort of interest and activity known to humankind (Newton 1976: 31–88). At the same time they account for a relatively small proportion of the time of most citizens. A large minority of people in most Western societies do not belong to any voluntary organization, and most of the rest do not spend much time with them. Only a highly active but small stage-army of community leaders and organizers (the 'joiners') give a significant proportion of their adult life and emotional commitment to voluntary associations.

By most measures the Netherlands has one of the highest levels of voluntary membership and activity in the Western world, but members and volunteers spend an average of between four and five hours a week with their organizations (Dekker and de Hart 1996: Table 12). This amounts to around 8 per cent of their leisure time. In the Republic of Ireland two-thirds of volunteers give less than ten hours a month to the activity (Ruddle and O'Connor 1995: 93). In ten Western and Eastern European countries the average is around ten hours a week (Gaskin and Smith 1995: 31).

For the great majority who participate in associational life, other institutions are likely to have a much more important role in generating sociability: for the young it is school and the family; for adults, work and neighbourhood. Coleman (1988: 109–16) emphasizes school and the family; Putnam (1995*b*: 667) suggests that education has a strong connection with both trust and association membership; Verba *et al.* (1995: 320, 514) find the workplace and education important. School, family, work, and neighbourhood are likely to have a far greater significance in the origins of trust, reciprocity, and co-operation than the limited and sporadic involvement of most people in voluntary organizations (see also Levi 1996: 48). It is not surprising, therefore, that recent American research finds much higher levels of social participation than trust (Broder 1997).

Nor is it a surprise that *World Values* data show no statistically significant relationships between voluntary activity and social trust in four countries, and only a weak relationship in three others (Table 8.1). Only in Italy is the statistical association strong, and even here it is weaker than four other measures dealing with satisfaction with life, morality, national pride, and social and economic status. The voluntary organization variable in these regressions is the strongest available, dealing not merely with members but with the most deeply involved activists who do unpaid voluntary work. If activists do not show much evidence of higher levels of trust there is little reason to believe that ordinary members will, but then one of the unresolved mysteries of the voluntary activity literature is that it fails to find much difference in attitudes and activity between activists and ordinary members (van Deth 1996; Decker and van den Broek 1996).

Table 8.1. Social trust in five Western countries: The role of voluntary activism

	USA	France	UK	Italy	W. Germany	Spain	Neths.
Satisfaction with life	.23	.17	.15	.18	.27	.17	.19
	(6.5)	(4.6)	(5.0)	(4.8)	(7.3)	(4.5)	(3.7)
Morality index	−.10	−.13		−.17	−.13	−.16	
	(3.0)	(3.6)		(4.5)	(3.5)	(4.3)	
Voluntary activity	.07	.07		.10			
	(2.0)	(1.9)		(2.6)			
National pride	.11	.15	.10	.20	.11		
	(3.2)	(4.5)	(3.2)	(5.2)	(3.3)		
SES	.14	.09	.06	.18		.15	
	(4.40)	(2.7)	(1.9)	(5.0)		(4.2)	
Age	.15		.06			.10	
	(5.44)		(1.9)			(2.7)	
Gender			.07	.06			
			(2.4)	(1.8)			
Left–Right		−.12		.13			
		(3.2)		(4.6)			
Religiosity	.07	.10		.08		.10	.10
	(2.1)	(2.8)		(2.0)		(2.9)	(2.9)
Income		.14				.10	.14
		(4.6)				(2.7)	(2.4)
Education	.12	.19	.14	.12	.12	.11	.15
	(4.0)	(6.7)	(4.3)	(4.38)	(4.8)	(2.8)	(2.41)
R2	.17	.12	.09	.17	.15	.04	.07
F ratio	17.7	12.3	11.2	14.5	15.6	10.2	11.1
(n)	1,839	1,002	1,484	2,010	2,201	1,017	1,510

Note: Table reports standardized Beta coefficients significant at 5 per cent or greater (t statistics in parentheses).
Source: *World Values Survey*, 1990.

In the USA, Brehm and Rahn (1997) find a significant path from civic engagement to interpersonal trust but equally strong or stronger ones from education, confidence in government, life satisfaction, and ethnicity. Together with Table 8.1, this indicates that association membership is not unimportant for the generation of social trust, but less important than some other social and political factors.

The second comment on de Tocqueville is that the world has changed dramatically since his time. He assumed that the democratic state was built upon trust, not that the state generates trust. This was no doubt right for the caretaker state of nineteenth-century America, but government is vastly larger and more powerful now, and has a far broader and deeper impact on its citizens. It sets many of the conditions of modern life, including the social and political framework and institutions within which trust might be sustained. The changes from de Tocqueville's small-town America to large-scale modern society can be illustrated with two simplified ideal-types of society and the social trust to be found in them: communal and modern society. These are presented in Appendix 8A in a highly simplified form. De Tocqueville's America fits neither the communal nor modern type, being located somewhere in between, but the models are useful to analyse changes in the nature and origins of social trust since his time.

In communal society, trust is built upon intense and constant interaction with a relatively small number of people, many of them family. Trustworthy codes of conduct are reinforced by a common religion with simple moral codes enforced by powerful social sanctions that are difficult to avoid or escape because communal society is closed. That is, communal society generates a particularly durable and strong form of trust—thick trust (Williams 1988), or particularized trust (Yamigichi and Yamigichi 1994).

Modern society, however, is large, open, multicultural and either secular or with a weak or mixed religious basis. Codes of conduct are weaker and more varied, and the effectiveness of social sanctions reduced by the scale and openness of society, the frequency of intermittent relations, and constant interaction with strangers. Social and geographical mobility is greater, individualism stronger, and relations more frequently based on the amorality of market relations. If social trust is built upon common interests and constant contact, then the heterogeneity of modern society undermines trust.

At the same time, modern society also increasingly produces situations of risk in which trust is essential: we are forced to trust other drivers, the hygiene of restaurants, the pilots and ground-crews of planes, doctors, dentists, drug manufacturers, teachers, lawyers, car mechanics, lift-maintenance engineers, bank managers, food and drink manufacturers, bridge-builders, high-rise architects, hotel safety officers, to say nothing of others in a dark street on the way home at night. On the one hand, the social foundations of personal trust are undermined by many developments in modern society; on the other, modern life also requires more trust (Eisenstadt 1995: 312–14). How, then, is social trust sustained?

Part of the answer may be that the nature of trust and its origins is changing. In communal society, and to a certain extent in de Tocqueville's America, trust took the thick form. In modern society it is thinner and more abstract in nature, and based upon a loose but extensive array of secondary relations. Society is held together by the strength of its multiplicity of weak ties (Granovetter 1972), so that to look for a high incidence of thick, Tocqevillean trust in modern society is to look for disappointment. In this case we would expect social trust not to decline so much as to change both its origins and nature in the contemporary world. Does the evidence support this?

Is Social Trust Declining?

Survey evidence about social trust in Western societies show a mixed pattern. We can judge this from *Eurobarometer* and *World Values* data shown in Tables 8.2 and 8.3. The *Eurobarometer Survey* suggest that levels of trust are fairly high in Western Europe, in the sense that only one score shows more distrust than trust (Italy in 1976). The other figures are consistently above levels of distrust, some of them substantially higher. There is no evidence of a general decline. On the contrary, nine of the EU twelve show higher levels of trust at the end of the series than at the beginning. Only three nations (West Germany, Greece, and Luxembourg) are lower in 1993 than 1976, and even here the figures do not dip into distrust. The figures suggest fluctuations in trust, rather than long-term decline.

Table 8.2. Western European trust in people of your own country

Country	1976	1980	1986	1990	1993
Belgians	3.26	3.26	3.12	3.55	3.34
Danes	3.08	3.20	3.25	3.13	3.55
West Germans	3.56	3.54	3.31	3.02	3.50
Greeks		3.29	3.04	2.53	3.22
Spanish			3.24	2.72	3.28
French	3.05	3.13	3.03	3.14	3.19
Irish	3.18	3.05	3.04	2.87	3.43
Italians	2.44	2.71	2.76	2.55	2.82
Luxemburgers	3.43	3.53	3.37	3.52	3.32
Dutch	3.17	3.20	3.08	3.12	3.36
Portuguese			3.04	2.57	3.32
British	3.19	3.35	3.07	2.85	3.31
EC 9	3.15	3.22	3.11	3.08	3.31

Notes: The question asked is: 'Now I would like to ask you how much trust you have in people from [your own coun-try]. Please tell me whether you have a lot of trust in them (4), some trust (3), not very much trust (2), or no trust at all (1).' The scores above were calculated by weighting each response 4,3,2,1, respectively, and dividing the total by the number of responses, excluding the 'don't knows'. Earlier years have been recalculated to make them consis-tent with later years. The mid-point on the scale is 2.50 which indicates neither trust nor distrust. Scores above 2.50 show more trust than distrust. Scores below 2.50 show more distrust than trust.

Sources: Eurobarometers 25, 33, 39, 1976–93.

The same general conclusion emerges from *World Values* and *Civic Culture* data (Table 8.3) which show trust generally increasing across twenty-one nations. Between 1981 and 1990, fourteen of the figure increase, four fall, and three remain the same. Over a longer time period (1959–96, or 1981–96) the figures fluctuate quite a lot, but clear evidence of decline is restricted to the United States, and even here there seems to be fluctuation rather than consis-tent, long-term decline. In contrast to national studies in the USA, the *World Values Survey* also shows an increase in social trust in the USA, 1981–90. A sep-arate time-series shows social trust rising in Japan from 26 per cent in 1978 to 31 per cent in 1983 and 38 per cent in 1993 (Sakamoto 1995), although it is

Table 8.3. Interpersonal trust (percentages)

Country	1959	1981	1990	1996
Belgium		29	34	
Great Britain	56	43	44	
Canada		49	53	
Denmark		53	58	
Finland		57	63	49
France		25	23	
West Germany	24	32	44	42
Hungary		34	25	
Iceland		40	44	
Ireland		41	47	
Italy	7	27	35	
Japan		42	42	42
Mexico	31	18	34	
Netherlands		45	54	
Northern Ireland		44	44	
Norway		62	65	65
South Africa		29	28	
Spain		35	34	30
Sweden		57	66	60
USA	58	41	51	36
USSR/Russia		35	38	

Notes: The question asked is: 'Generally speaking would you say that most people can be trusted or that you can't be too careful in dealing with people?' Entries are percentages saying 'most people can be trusted'. 'Don't knows' are excluded (Civic Culture figures have been recalculated to make them consistent with World Values data).

Source: 1959, Civic Culture; 1981, 1990, 1996 World Values.

difficult to know how to interpret figures for a culture which expresses so little, but acts with so much, trust. A long time-series for West Germany shows a strong and consistent upward trend in social trust from 1948 to 1994 (Table 8.4). The figures are in clear contrast to the trend in the USA (see also Conradt 1980: 253–6).

International Personal Trust

By international personal trust is meant the extent to which the citizens of different nations trust each other (as opposed to the extent to which their governments trust each other, or citizens of one country trust the government of another). If there is any merit in the argument that modern society is shifting from thick, personal trust, towards thin, abstract or impersonal trust, we would expect signs of increasing trust between the citizens of different nations. According to the *Eurobarometer Surveys* this is indeed the case (Table 8.5). Trust between citizens of the nine EU member states increased in every case between 1976 and 1993. The increases were not large—although on a four-point scale, many are not trivial either—but they are consistent across all nations in the survey.

Table 8.4. Personal trust in West Germany and the USA, 1948–1996 (percentages saying 'most people can be trusted')

Year	W. Germany	USA (1)	(2)	Year	W. Germany	USA (1)	(2)
1948	9			1979	30		
1953	13			1980		47	
1957	19			1981	29	41	
1960		58		1983	37	39	37
1964	28	54*		1984		49	48
1966		54*		1985	35		
1967	26			1986	38	39	37
1968		56*		1987	42	40	44
1969	23			1988	39	41	39
1972	32	47*	46	1989	38	41	41
1973	27		46	1990	37	40	38
1974		47*		1991	35	40	38
1975			39	1992	42	45*	
1976	39	53	44	1993	45	38	36 (3)
1978	35	41	39	1994	35	37	34 (3)

* National Election Studies. Both the NES and the GCC ask the same question.

Sources: West Germany: Cusack, 1997; USA: (1) Uslaner and Putnam 1996, (2) General Social Surveys. Both the NES and GSS in the USA ask the same question (see previous table).

The second part of Table 8.5 shows that Western European trust in Americans, Chinese, and Russians is also inching up over time. At this point it is clear that something about the responses to the trust question has changed; to say I trust my family and that I trust the Chinese mean different things. It is possible that expressions of international trust are just another example of random, 'door-step opinion', but in that case what explains the uniformity across time and space that is anything but random? It is more likely that respondents have something in mind when they express trust in the Chinese, but not the same thing as their trust in family. Perhaps they locate trust on a continuum ranging from personal, thick trust for the family, to thin trust in the Chinese; they would risk much more in the family, and less with the Chinese, but nevertheless, are prepared to invest more trust in the Chinese in so far as relations with them are distant and very limited.

The puzzle is what explains these rising levels of international trust. It can scarcely be international travel, as one *Eurobarometer* report suggests, because this involves relatively few people, and sporadic and shallow contacts. Nor can holiday or business connections explain the slight increase in trust of EC 9 citizens in the Chinese, or the somewhat larger increase in the Russians. For that matter, it is doubtful whether international trust cannot be explained in terms of personal contacts at all. A more plausible hypothesis is that the increasing safety of the international world (no democracy has yet gone to war with

Table 8.5.
(a) Personal trust among citizens of different member states of the EC 9, 1976–1993

	1976	1993
Danes	2.93	3.08
Dutch	2.96	3.08
Luxemburgers	2.94	3.02
Belgians	2.91	3.13
West Germans	2.63	2.83
Irish	2.33	2.85
French	2.29	2.85
British	2.33	2.89
Italians	2.20	2.57

(b) Personal trust between citizens of the EC 9 and citizens of non-member states, 1976–1993

	1976	1980	1990	1993
Americans	2.78			2.88
Chinese	2.15		2.18	
Japanese		2.63		2.60
Russians	1.90			2.27

Note: For the calculation of trust scores see Table 8.2.

Sources: *Eurobarometer*, 25, June 1986, Table 8, *Eurobarometer*, 33, June 1986, Tables 15, and 16; and *Eurobarometer*, 39, June 1993, Table 57.
Question: *'I would like to ask you a question about how much trust you have in people from various countries. Please tell me whether you have a lot of trust, some trust, not very much trust, or no trust at all.'*

another) and the absence of major wars since 1945 has contributed to a greater international trust.

Political Trust

> . . . the grounds for trusting rulers are to be found in the sanctions that punish breaches of trust.
>
> (John Locke, *Two Treatises on Government*, 1690)

> The aim of every political constitution is, or ought to be, first to obtain for rulers men who possess most wisdom to discern, and most virtue to pursue, the common good of society; and in the next place, to take the most effectual precautions for keeping them virtuous whilst they continue to hold the public trust.
>
> (James Madison, *The Federalist Papers*, No. 57)

The first and most obvious difference between social and political trust is that the former is built more often upon personal knowledge of others, whereas trust in political leaders is not. For most of us it is built upon second-hand sources, especially the mass media. Personal trust belongs to the private sphere; political trust belongs to the public political sphere, where there are more unknowns, greater risks, and less predictability. For these reasons, political trust is usually of a thinner kind than social trust, and it may be getting thinner under the influences and pressures of modern political life.

The argument can be illustrated by comparing modern society, not with primitive society—which is rarely democratic—but with early democracy at the turn of the century. Comparisons are drawn in Appendix 8B, which like Appendix 8A, suggests changes in the basis and nature of political trust in the twentieth century. Whereas political trust was once based on social identities and ideological loyalties, and reinforced by personal ties and similarities (see Bianco 1994), it now seems to be more pragmatic, instrumental, and dependent upon second-hand political information and performance. Politicians are less likely to be trusted because they are 'one of us' (Catholic, black, southerner, farmer, worker, gentleman), but because of their policy record and personal performance and appearance.

Political trust, like social trust, is also more dependent on formal sanctions in the shape of rules and regulations about the conduct of politicians. Most Western countries are developing more powerful mechanisms for controlling the public and private behaviour of politicians—laws, codes of conduct, review bodies, commissions, committees of enquiry, legal procedures. In addition the media may also be more critical and probing. As a result, we are less inclined to trust our politicians because of common social and ideological identities, but because they are increasingly unable to avoid the price of being untrustworthy. To this extent the observations of Locke and Madison may be more apposite than ever before.

The Relationship Between Social and Political Trust

Much writing tends to assume that trust is all of a piece, that social trust and political trust are different sides of the same coin, and that social trust created by voluntary organizations and a strong civil society tends to create or strongly reinforce political trust. Conversely, the assumption often seems to be that confidence and trust in political institutions and officials is built on the basis of a strong civil society, well-developed organizations and associations in the community, and high levels of trust between citizens. The point emphasized here, however, is that social and political trust are not necessarily related, and may not be closely related at all in any given place or at any given time. The point has been made before (Wright 1976: 104–10; Craig 1993: 27; Orren 1997) and is supported here by comparative data, although since few comparative surveys ask questions about both social and political trust there is not a great deal of evidence. The *World Values Survey* asks about social trust in both 1981 and 1990, but unfortunately it does not ask about political trust in 1981. To complicate matters further, in 1990 it asks the question in only a few of the forty-three countries in the survey. However, in the countries for which we have *World Values* data, trust in people, family, government, and countrymen do not intercorrelate strongly (Table 8.6). The figures shown in the table are all statistically significant, but this is because the numbers of observations (between 13,802 and 52,408) are very large. The substantive significance of the correlations is negligible in all but one case, that between trust in family and in countrymen. The correlations between trust in people and trust in government (–.03) and between trust in family and trust in government (0.05) are substantively so small that they may be safely ignored. These figures suggest there is no general syndrome of trust, a conclusion strongly supported by figures for twelve nations separately (Kaase 1997: 14).

Table 8.6. Correlations between measures of trust

Trust in:	People	Government	Family
Government	–.03		
Family	–.06	.05	
Countrymen	–.16	.14	.30

Note: All significant at .001 level.

Source: Computed from *World Values Survey*, 1990.

The reason seems to be that social and political trust are related to different sets of social, economic, and political variables. A quick inspection of a few figures from the *World Values Survey* of 1990 shows this. Table 8.7, for example, presents simple cross-tabulations of social and political trust scores in twelve nations for a handful of standard variables. Among other things the figures suggest that age, education, and income are often related to variations in social and political trust, but the relationships vary from country to country. For example, in Turkey the better educated are more trusting politically but less socially, whereas in Lithuania it is the other way round, while in India education seems to make rather little difference to either social or political trust. In short, patterns of social and political trust vary from one social group to another in different countries in a way which makes it difficult to generalize about trust as a general concept.

Who Trusts?

On closer inspection, however, there are patterns of social and political trust, although they vary independently of one another. The evidence of Table 8.1 suggests that social trust tends to be high among those who hold a central position in society, that is among the well-educated, high income, high socio-economic status males, and social majorities. Those who are satisfied with life are trusting, and they are satisfied with life because their income, education, status, and social position give them good cause to be so. Is it surprising that the successful in society are blessed with a benign view of their fellow citizens? Conversely, the losers—the minorities, blacks, unemployed, working class, poor, poorly educated, low socio-economic status, low income—take a dimmer view of the world and its inhabitants. The point is confirmed by the figures in Table 8.7 which generally show that the largest differences in social trust occur between different age, education, and income groups.

In contrast, political trust is often rather randomly distributed throughout social groups and types, at least in Germany (Gabriel 1997b), the USA (Abramson 1983: 52; Putnam 1995b: Orren 1997: Table 4.1; Lawrence 1997: 19–21) and Britain (Newton 1997b. See also Table 2.11 in this volume). But not quite randomly. Political distrust quite often correlates strongly with political variables. In Table 8.8 the largest differences in political trust often appear under the Left–Right column, although whether it is the Left or Right which is more distrustful varies from one country to another. In Turkey and Spain, the Left is politically more distrustful than the Right, but in Chile, Czechoslovakia, Mexico, Canada, and the USA it is the other way round. This is probably because it is identification with the governing party or parties which is important, rather than Left–Right as such. Those whose party is in power will probably express more political trust, than those who identify with the opposition parties.

The point is made more clearly in Table 8.8 which shows that trust in British government and public officials is not strongly associated with standard social variables such as income, gender, employment status, or (often) education. Rather it is closely and consistently associated with the Left–Right variable (see also Curtice and Jowell 1995: 148). In other words, those who identified with the Conservative government in Britain in 1996 consistently expressed substantially higher levels of political trust in government and other public officials, than those who identified with the opposition parties. The single exception concerns trust in local government councillors, where party identification is not merely insignificant, but in contrast to its strength in the other six equations, the beta coefficient is zero. Of course it is. Local government is controlled by different parties, so Conservatives in Labour areas are inclined to distrust their councillors, and vice versa. Over the whole country they cancel each other out, and in 1996 did so exactly.

The British pattern is consistent with German data showing a strong association between citizen trust in local politics and satisfaction with local government performance in both East and West Germany (Cusack 1997: 38). It is also supported for the USA by King's (1997) finding that partisanship is related to political distrust. And last, it is supported by comparative data (see Norris in this volume) which shows that those who vote for winning parties are more satisfied with government than those who vote for losing parties, especially

Table 8.7. Differences in political and social trust scores between selected social and political groups, 1990

	Female	Older	Well-educated	High income	Political right
India					
Political	−5	−2	−1	−12	8
Social	−3	2	5	3	8
Nigeria					
Political	0	21	−10	3	−3
Social	−2	4	2	−4	7
Turkey					
Political	3	13	−15	−2	29
Social	0	1	12	0	−10
Chile					
Political	−9	4	3	3	−23
Social	−1	−4	9	10	−6
Czech.					
Political	−3	8	9	−1	22
Social	−3	−9	8	3	−2
Lithuania					
Political	−4	1	7	4	n.a.
Social	−4	−7	16	10	n.a.
Mexico					
Political	3	4	−6	−1	22
Social	4	0	−1	−8	−1
Latvia					
Political	6	2	−14	−50	n.a.
Social	−2	21	4	16	n.a.
Estonia					
Political	1	−3	−2	−14	n.a.
Social	−6	7	7	27	n.a.
Spain					
Political	−2	14	−11	−5	−14
Social	−4	−1	17	24	−8
Canada					
Political	2	1	5	2	10
Social	1	10	16	17	−2
USA					
Political	5	−6	0	18	11
Social	7	−14	22	10	−14

Note: Entries are based on percentages of people who say they '*trust government almost always/most of the time*', and '*most people can be trusted*'. The figures are the percentage differences between females and males, the older (50 and over) and the younger (16–29), those with higher and lower educational qualifications, those with higher and lower incomes, and those on the political left and right. A positive figure shows higher levels of trust among the former than the latter for each variable, and a negative figure shows lower levels of trust. In other words, the first figure in the table show that women are 5 per cent less trusting politically than men in India.

Source: M. Basanez *et al.* 1989, Tables 94, 289.

persistent losers. As a result, systems with coalition governments (though not highly fragmented ones) generally show higher levels of support for the political system, than single party systems.

The general conclusion seems to be that political distrust is not caused so much by social or economic factors, but by political ones, especially the record

Table 8.8. Regressions of social, economic, and media variables on six measures of trust in public officials in Britain, 1996

	Government	Politicians	Civil servants	Councillors	Police	Judges	Trust factor
Income	.03	.03	.06	−.02	−.02	.00	.02
	(0.76)	(0.73)	(1.51)	(0.38)	(0.54)	(0.23)	(0.47)
Education	.01	.09*	.07	.10*	.13***	.09**	.13***
	(−0.22)	(2.28)	(1.85)	(2.50)	(3.34)	(2.44)	(3.22)
Government ID	.15***	.19***	.16***	.00	.11***	.17***	.21***
	(4.7)	(5.88)	(4.68)	(0.80)	(3.37)	(5.28)	(6.08)
Unemployment	−.07	−.06	−.02	−.01	.01	.06	−.03
	(2.28)	(1.93)	(0.71)	(0.28)	(0.24)	(1.68)	(0.84)
Gender	−.01	.06	.06	.06	.067*	−.08**	−.06
	(0.36)	(1.84)	(1.91)	(1.88)	(2.03)	(2.54)	(1.73)
Newspapers	.10**	.10**	.13***	.06	.01	.10**	.12***
	(2.92)	(2.90)	(3.59)	(1.65)	(0.34)	(2.99)	(3.30)
TV total hours	−.05	−.03	−.05	.01	−.02	.04	−.04
	(1.36)	(0.10)	(1.49)	(0.36)	(0.44)	(1.18)	(1.12)
TV News	−.09**	−.00	.01	.03	−.06	−.02	−.02
	(2.70)	(0.10)	(0.18)	(0.83)	(1.75)	(0.74)	(0.69)
R2	.05***	.06***	.05***	.02**	.04***	.08***	.07***
F ratio	6.43	7.70	5.80	2.70	4.78	9.90	9.30

Notes: Entries are standardized regression coefficients, t-ratios in brackets. *** = significant at .001; ** = significant at .01; * = significant at .05. Variables are entered simultaneously in the regression equations. n = 861.
Dependent variables:
Trust—Responses for each trust question are scored from 1–4.
Trust factor—A composite of scores on all six questions; range from 0–24.
Independent Variables:
Income—Respondents' earnings are scored in groups from 0–6.
Education – Education is scored from 1 (no qualifications) to 5 (degree or equivalent).
Government ID—Identifiers with the government party (Conservative) are scored 1, all other party identifiers are scored 0.
Unemployment—Unemployed seeking work are scored 1, employed 0.
Newspapers—Irregular paper readers and regular tabloid readers are scored 0, regular broadsheet readers 1.
TV total hours—Total number of hours of TV during the week (range 0–98).
TV News—Number of days TV news is watched during the week (range 0–7).
Source: British Social Attitudes 1996.

and colour of the party in power. The Right is more likely to express political distrust when the Left is in power, and vice versa. The importance of the Left–Right (or government–opposition) dimension in Table 8.8 supports other conclusions about the significance of political variables, especially Left–Right variation, in explaining political attitudes in Western Europe (Kaase and Newton 1995: 92–5). It also reinforces the argument that political trust cannot be reduced to, or explained in terms of, social factors, such as membership of voluntary organizations, community involvement, or social trust.

Nor is political trust necessarily a variation or product of social trust. Indeed, the link between social and political trust, and between the two of them and patterns of social and political behaviour seem to be rather weak, and contingent upon a set of other factors, as an examination of some of the relevant literature suggests.

- Whiteley and Seyd (1997: 21) find a weak and statistically insignificant relationship between voluntary political and non-political activism among Conservative Party members in Britain.

- Montero *et al.* (1997) find a statistically significant and positive but rather modest association between interpersonal trust and both conventional and unconventional political participation in Spain. The strength of the association is heavily outweighed by other variables (internal efficacy, ideological moderation, the impact of government policies, education, and gender). The relationship between membership of voluntary organizations and social trust in Spain is similarly significant, positive, and modest (Torcal and Montero 1996, Table 10).

- Across Western Europe as a whole, Dekker *et al.* (1996) and Kaase (1997: 17) find a rather weak relationship between social trust and both conventional and protest political behaviour, and between participation in voluntary organizations and political activity.

- In the USA (Uslaner, undated) social trust was not significantly associated with voting turnout in 1964, and only weakly associated with it in 1992. It was more strongly related to social behaviour (working on community problems, making charitable contributions, and volunteering) than political behaviour (voting and giving campaign contributions).

- In Britain, the USA, and Canada personal trust has a stronger connection with moral codes about interpersonal behaviour (buying stolen goods, joyriding, keeping found money, lying in one's own interests) than in dealings with public bodies (cheating on taxes, avoiding public transport fares, claiming unentitled benefits) (Uslaner 1996).

- In Flanders, Billiet and Cambre (1996) find that political trust is associated with membership of political organizations, but not social organizations.

- Brehm and Rahn (1997) find a significant relationship between interpersonal trust and confidence in American political institutions, but a much stronger relationship running from institutions to trust. This is consistent with the idea that the ability of government to maintain confidence in political institutions may help to sustain personal trust—the top-down relationship again (see also Levi 1996; Tarrow 1996; Foley and Edwards 1996; Warren 1996; and Newton 1997*b*).

- Low levels of personal trust seem to be characteristic of authoritarian and totalitarian systems (Kolankiewicz 1994, Sztompka 1996). In this case the causal relationship clearly runs from political systems and institutions to individual attitudes and behaviour, rather than vice versa.

The general conclusion seems to be that political trust often has a weak and contingent relationship with social trust and such things as involvement in voluntary and community work. It seems to be related less to social and economic factors than top political ones, especially the record and colour of the party in power. The Right is more likely to express political distrust when the Left is in power, and vice versa. It also seems that political trust cannot be reduced to, or be explained in terms of, social factors such as membership of voluntary associations or community involvement. Nor can political trust be treated as a variation on the theme of social trust. In political science the term 'trust' must always be qualified by the terms 'social' or 'political'.

Conclusions

More than enough has been said to highlight the need to be careful with the survey data and cautious with the conclusions. Not only do different surveys sometimes fail to agree with each other, but there is a lack of data, especially of time-series figures for the early post-war years in most countries. Nevertheless, the *Eurobarometer* and *World Values* studies present a good deal of evidence from the early 1970s that personal trust in Western Europe is rising, even international personal trust in Western Europe and beyond. In this respect the USA seems to be an exception to the general Western pattern of a long-term rise in social trust within and between Western societies. The increase is not steady, for there are examples of declines followed by rises, but it is consistent across most of the countries for which we have comparable, time-series data.

In a world in which the social basis for trust seems to be weakening by greater risk, anonymity, and impersonal relationships, how can we explain rising levels of social trust? Part of the answer may be that the basis of trust is shifting from primordial face-to-face social contacts which are strong and intensive to a greater variety of looser social relations. This, in turn, suggests that the nature of social trust may be shifting from personal, particular, or thick trust, to a more impersonal, general, or thin trust of an abstract nature.

The evidence suggests that while membership of voluntary associations has some importance for the creation of social trust, their influence is generally weak, though not trivial. Social trust is most strongly expressed, not by members of voluntary organizations, or even by their most active members, but by the winners in society, in so far as it correlates most strongly with education, satisfaction with life, income, class, and race. For that matter social trust is the prerogative of the winners in the world. Inglehart (1990: 37; 1997a: 174) finds high levels in many wealthy countries, and low ones in the poor.

There is not a close or consistent association between social and political trust, between social trust and political behaviour, or between activity in voluntary associations and political attitudes of trust and confidence. The links, where they exist, tend to be weak and contingent. Assumptions that social and political trust go together, move in harmony, or are somehow causally related do not seem justified. In other words, social capital is not necessarily translated into political capital and political capital seems not to be dependent on social capital. There is, however, some evidence that political capital may help to sustain social capital, and that political institutions and leadership may have important consequences for social capital—the top-down relationship. Conversely, there is no strong or widespread evidence to suggest that a decline of political capital is the result of a decline in social capital. On the contrary, social capital in the form of social trust has maintained itself, if not actually increased, in Sweden and in Britain in recent decades, but in both countries there has been a sharp loss of political trust. This suggests that the relations between social and political trust should be treated as a matter of empirical investigation, and the word 'trust' should always be qualified with the word 'social' or 'political'.

If social trust is most strongly related to social variables, political trust seems to be the product of political factors. The evidence suggests that while political trust is fairly randomly distributed across different social groups, it is strongly associated with political differences, especially with Left–Right groups, and those who identify with the government and with the opposition. The implication of the political interpretation of political distrust is that trends in political trust and distrust may well be halted or reversed as left- or right-wing governments come and go, or as those voting for a winning party at one time, find themselves on the losing side at another, or as a bad government record is replaced by a good one. While social capital is not easily or quickly accumulated, political capital may show greater fluctuation, as democratic governments come and go, losers become winners, and government performance improves or worsens.

In this sense the analogy of the fish 'rotting from the head' may be misleading where political trust is concerned, because it assumes that the fish is dead in the first place. If the fish is suffering from an illness or deficiency then it may recover. At any rate, the lack of an immediate or direct relationship in society between the community level of social trust, and the regime and authority level of political trust suggests that there is no necessary tendency for loss of trust at one level to spread to another. Similarly, there is plenty of evidence in this chapter to show that trends in social and political trust can be reversed. The rot does not necessarily spread; it can be cured.

Appendix Table 8A. Social trust in communal and modern society

COMMUNAL SOCIETY	MODERN SOCIETY
Almost entirely primary face-to-face relations	Mainly secondary relations
Small numbers of people	Large numbers of people
Strong and extensive family and kinship networks	Weak and limited family and kinship networks
Few, constant, intensive, and repeated interactions with others	Many, sporadic, and low-intensity relationships

COMMUNAL SOCIETY	MODERN SOCIETY
Simple, dangerous life	Complex, less dangerous life
Little geographical and social mobility	High rates of geographical mobility
Socially homogeneous	Socially heterogeneous
Tightly integrated on a personal level	Loosely integrated on a personal level
Personal	Impersonal
Closed	Open
Fusion of public and private spheres	Separation of public and private spheres, with a different basis and type of trust in each
Religious, with strong religious and moral codes	Secular, with mixed and culturally different moral codes
Personal, particular; or thick trust	Personal, particular; or thick trust in the private sphere. Impersonal, generalized, or thin trust in the public sphere
Powerful personal and social sanctions against those who betray trust	Weak personal and social sanctions in the public sphere, but strong institutional, legal and administrative sanctions
Limited government with a narrow scope	All-encompassing government with broad scope pervasiveness, which sets the framework for social trust

Appendix Table 8B. Political trust in early modern and contemporary democracies

EARLY DEMOCRACIES	CONTEMPORARY DEMOCRACIES
Party politics based upon religion, class, or region with trust between different elites and citizens based upon religion, class ties, and loyalties	Catch-all parties with weaker social ties, and trust based less upon social, religious, class, or regional loyalties
Ideological politics	Pragmatic politics
Relatively small populations per elected representative	Relatively large populations per elected representative
Narrower scope of government. Lower taxes. Fewer services. Fewer grounds for distrust	Broader scope of government. Higher taxes. More services. More grounds for distrust
Greater deference towards political elites	Less deference
Collective and group politics	More individualism
Lower rates of political activity	Higher rates of activity
Lower democratic standards and expectations	Higher democratic standards and expectations
A greater separation of the personal and public lives of politicians	Fusion of personal and public lives. Higher standards expected of politicians
More conservative, less critical news media	Less conservative, more critical news media
Comparatively low levels of political trust at the beginning of democratic government	A decline in political trust after the unusual conditions of the long boom, 1950–75
Great reliance on social, economic, and ideological ties to underpin trust	Greater reliance on formal rules of conduct and formal sanctions to underpin trust

9

The Economic Performance of Governments

IAN MCALLISTER

ONE major conclusion of this book is that there are few consistent trends in popular support for the political community but there is high and perhaps even growing support for democratic values and declining support for regime institutions and political leaders. An earlier chapter by Hans-Dieter Klingemann has traced these patterns with respect to democracy world-wide, while Russell Dalton, William Mishler and Richard Rose have confirmed the existence of these patterns in particular regions of the world. This chapter focuses specifically on the role of public policy in shaping popular support for democratic institutions among OECD countries. The data are aggregate indicators across 24 of the 29 member countries of the OECD in 1997, as well as individual-level data from the same 24 countries based on the 1990–1 *World Values Survey*.[1]

The role of public policy in shaping electoral outcomes—most particularly with regards to government economic performance—has long been a major preoccupation of political science. Aside from the voter attributes of party identification or social group membership, economic management has traditionally been viewed as the single most important factor that can deliver electoral success or failure. By contrast, studies focusing on the role of the economy in shaping confidence in democratic institutions are comparatively rare (but cf. Clarke, Dutt, and Kornberg, 1993; Finke, Muller, and Seligson 1987), and almost no attention has been devoted to the impact of the broader policy outputs of government. Most studies which examine confidence have focused on aggregate over-time trends, usually concentrating on democracy as a value and tracing changes among particular social, political, and national groups (Listhaug and Wiberg 1995; Fuchs, Guidorossi, and Svensson 1995; Miller and Listhaug 1990).

Yet if economic performance has a major impact on electoral outcomes, as we know, then it should also have some influence on popular confidence in demo-

[1] The 1990–1 *World Values Survey* was co-ordinated by Ronald Inglehart and the data supplied by the ESRC Archive at the University of Essex. The survey is used in preference to other surveys (such as the International Social Survey Program) because of its wide coverage of the OECD countries.

cratic institutions. Equally, social policy outputs may have some influence in shaping confidence. The impact of public policy on institutional confidence is likely to be greatest where there is widespread economic dissatisfaction for a prolonged period of time, as was the case in many of the advanced democracies following the Arab oil embargo in 1973. The embargo initiated a prolonged period of 'stagflation' that most governments were unable to quell until the early 1980s, and which had significant consequences for government support (Weatherford 1984). It should also be apparent in newly democratic societies, where civil society is underdeveloped and where many citizens fail to make a clear distinction between democratic governments and the democratic institutions of the state. Many Central and Eastern European countries have experienced severe economic dislocation, just at the time when they are endeavouring to generate popular support for their embryonic democracies.

Explaining Institutional Confidence

One explanation why government policy outputs in general, and the economy in particular, has received relatively little attention in studies of institutional confidence is the view, originating in the earliest empirical studies of democracy, that popular support for democratic norms has its origins in political culture. A more recent view identifies economic performance as the mainspring for how citizens evaluate their governments and, in turn, for how they rate their democratic institutions. Many studies have demonstrated the pivotal role of popular economic expectations in deciding the fate of incumbent governments in established democracies (Lewis-Beck 1988; Fiorina 1981). Governments that are perceived as delivering wealth and prosperity to their voters are more likely to be re-elected, while those that are perceived as depressing economic conditions through their policies are likely to be replaced. In general, it is collective rather than individual judgements that have most weight in the popular economic calculus, and those judgements are usually (though not exclusively) retrospective rather than prospective.[2]

In evaluating the influence of economic conditions on political behaviour, there is a crucial distinction between economic perception and economic reality. Considerable evidence suggests that voters believe that it is a central responsibility of government to deliver high levels of economic performance. Since economic performance is judged by collective (sociotropic) rather than individual (egocentric) criteria, popular perceptions about the economy are shaped principally by the mass media and through an assessment of national economic conditions, and less by individual economic circumstances. Since these perceptions are mainly collective, they relate directly to governments and also, to some degree, to political institutions. But the linkages remain

---

[2] In both cases, however, there are significant cross-national variations in how electorates weigh these various factors in making their vote decision (Lewis-Beck 1988).

unclear, as do the specific circumstances in which economic performance and expectations will impact on the direction and strength of citizen beliefs about democratic institutions.

The conventional way in which citizens deal with an economic performance deficit in a democratic polity is to assign responsibility for the problem to the government of the day and to vote them out of office. The economic performance hypothesis is predicated on the assumption that citizens distinguish between the role of the government and the role of the political system. This is more likely to occur in the established democracies, where citizens make a clear distinction between the operation of the system as a whole, and the activities of particular party governments. In the newer democracies, which often do not enjoy widespread popular support, or where support is unevenly distributed across social groups, such distinctions are more likely to be blurred since the 'reservoir of good will' that allows citizens to accept performance deficits does not exist. However, a more generalized loss of confidence is possible in an established democracy where the economic performance deficit is more intense and sustained (Fuchs, Guidorossi, and Svensson 1995: 327). The policy hypothesis we will explore therefore identifies a performance deficit as the explanation for institutional confidence, through changes in macro and micro socio-economic circumstances that affect popular perceptions of collective socio-economic conditions.

There are, of course, a range of difficulties in evaluating and measuring the policy performance of governments (Bok 1997; Klingemann, Hofferbert, and Budge 1994). Public opinion may be used as the main measure evaluating policy performance, but opinions often change for reasons unrelated to policy. Moreover, popular satisfaction with government policy is mediated by expectations, which also vary according to external criteria: a major policy success when expectations are high will have less impact than a more modest success, delivered when popular expectations are low. One alternative is to evaluate the *outcomes* of specific policies, aggregated across several major areas, such as health, welfare, or education. This approach, too, has significant disadvantages, most notably changes in external conditions which may affect programme performance, as well as the inability to make evaluative judgements (Bok 1997). For these reasons two sources of data are used in the chapter, aggregate-level indicators of policy performance across the OECD countries, and individual-level public opinion data from the 1990–1 *World Values Survey*. These two perspectives enable a more informed judgement to be made of the impact of public policy on institutional confidence.

Evidence for Trends in Institutional Confidence

'Support' and 'confidence' in democratic institutions are used interchangeably since they convey a broad meaning concerning the links between popular beliefs about government and representative institutions. As discussed in the Introduction, the concept of support for democratic institutions can be defined in various ways (for a review, see Fuchs, Guidorossi, and Svensson 1995; Kornberg and Clarke 1992). Narrowly defined, the object of support can mean the political system itself, encompassing parliaments and the bureaucracy. A broader definition might take in the institutions that preserve public order, namely the legal system, police, and armed forces. More broadly still, the concept of democratic institutions could encompass the core institutions of civil society, such as the educational system, the mass media, the trade unions and major companies.[3] The narrower definition based on parliaments and the bureaucracy is used here for two reasons. First, it is less ambiguous, particularly where cross-national analyses are concerned. Secondly, in newly democratic societies, the democratic institutions are associated most directly with representative government, and much less so with the general institutions of civil society which are often underdeveloped.[4]

Arriving at an appropriate list of democracies to include in the analysis presents several difficulties. First, many of the democracies currently in existence have very different levels of socio-economic development. India, for example, has been a democracy since 1949, yet it ranks close to, or at the bottom of, any measure of economic development. Secondly, some of the current democracies only recently achieved that status, which raises technical difficulties in matching the survey results with the time at which the country became a competitive democracy. A third problem concerns the items included in the 1990–1 *World Values Survey*. Although the survey contains a wide range of questions and covers over 40 countries,[5] not all of the items were asked in every country. To arrive at a suitable list of countries for analysis it was decided to take the 29 countries which were OECD members in 1997, and for whom adequate data were available in the *World Values Survey*; this results in the list of 24 countries shown in Table 9.1.

The two items used in the survey to measure institutional confidence relate to confidence in parliament and the civil service. Table 9.1 shows considerable variation in levels of confidence across the 24 countries, with Poland registering a mean value of 6.6 for confidence in parliament (on a 0–10 scale) to 3.7 for Mexico. In most countries parliament is rated at a similar level to the civil service. The main exceptions are countries where there is stronger confidence in the civil service than in the parliament: this occurs in the United States, South Korea, and Hungary. The average correlation between the two items is 0.53, ranging from a low of 0.39 in Korea to a high of 0.80 in Japan. There is,

---

[3] All of these items were included in the 1990–1 *World Values Survey*. An additional item was included which asked about trust in the political system, but this item was included in only a small proportion of the countries; this is used in the final section of the paper.

[4] Listhaug and Wiberg (1995: 306) show that across most Western European countries there is a clear distinction in how citizens view representative state institutions (parliament, bureaucracy) and how they view coercive state institutions (police, armed forces).

[5] In total the survey included 43 separately identified countries, although East and West Germany were sampled separately, as was Moscow and Russia as a whole, and Northern Ireland and mainland Britain.

192   Explanations of Trends

then, a wide range of variation in popular support for democratic institutions across the 24 countries under examination.

Much of the literature on confidence in democratic institutions assumes that there has been a decline; the assumption is that the challenges to representative democracy have been sufficiently severe both in their frequency and intensity to erode popular institutional confidence. Fortunately, we can provide a partial test of this hypothesis since the first round of the *World Values Survey*, conducted among a more limited range of countries in 1981, also asked about confidence in institutions. Although there are only two time-points, 1980 and 1991, the results are clear. Trends across the 19 OECD countries for which over-time data exist show that, overall, popular confidence in democratic institutions has registered a modest decline, from a mean of 4.8 in 1981, to 4.5 in 1990–1. This provides further confirmation of the analysis presented earlier by Dalton (Chapter 3).

Table 9.1. Confidence in political institutions

Rank	Country	Confidence (0–10)			
		Parliament	Civil Service	(r)	(N)
1.	Poland	6.6	6.7	(.73)	(938)
2.	Turkey	5.5	5.2	(.52)	(1,030)
3.	Norway	5.3	4.6	(.44)	(1,239)
4.	Iceland	5.1	4.8	(.43)	(702)
5.	Ireland	5.1	5.4	(.53)	(180)
6.	Germany	5.0	4.4	(.51)	(3,075)
7.	Netherlands	4.9	4.7	(.45)	(522)
8.	Britain	4.8	4.8	(.44)	(2,805)
9.	Sweden	4.8	4.6	(.64)	(1,047)
10.	United States	4.7	5.6	(.46)	(2.010)
11.	Denmark	4.6	5.0	(.47)	(155)
12.	France	4.5	4.6	(.43)	(2,806)
13.	Austria	4.5	4.6	(.62)	(1,460)
14.	Czechoslovakia	4.5	4.0	(.45)	(1,396)
15.	Belgium	4.4	4.4	(.46)	(307)
16.	Canada	4.4	4.9	(.48)	(1,729)
17.	Hungary	4.2	4.8	(.57)	(999)
18.	Finland	4.1	4.2	(.53)	(588)
19.	Spain	4.1	4.0	(.54)	(2,224)
20.	Japan	4.0	4.2	(.80)	(2,193)
21.	South Korea	3.9	5.5	(.39)	(1,251)
22.	Portugal	3.9	4.0	(.63)	(478)
23.	Italy	3.8	3.3	(.60)	(2,307)
24.	Mexico	3.7	3.3	(.62)	(1,531)
	MEAN	4.5	4.6		(32,847)

Note: The question was: '*Please look at this card and tell me, for each item listed, how much confidence you have in them, is it a great deal, quite a lot, not very much or none at all?*' Scaled from 0 (low) to 10 (high).

Source: 1990–1 *World Values Survey*.

In the G7 countries, however, Figure 9.1 shows that there has been a change in only two countries—the USA and France—while institutional confidence in the remaining five countries has remained stable. The results for the G7 countries tend to emphasize the Fuchs, Guidorossi, and Svensson (1995) conclusion that confidence has remained remarkably unchanged in the established democracies, despite a variety of challenges.[6]

The decline in the US is confirmed by other trend studies which have shown a consistent weakening in confidence in Congress throughout the 1970s and early 1980s (Lipset and Schneider 1987). Some suggest that the mainsprings of this decline were the widespread opposition to the Vietnam War and the Watergate crisis in the late 1960s and early 1970s, both of which had major effects on political trust (Abramson 1983; Nye *et al.* 1997). Nevertheless, the results demonstrate the wide variation in institutional confidence that exists across the G7 countries. Although there has been a decline in the USA, it is still almost 50 per cent higher than trust in Italy, the lowest among the G7 countries. The Italian results underline the consequences of widespread political corruption and the accompanying loss of confidence in the political class. These survey results date from 1990; the 1994 Italian elections caused a major upheaval in the party system, reflecting the low standing of democratic institutions.

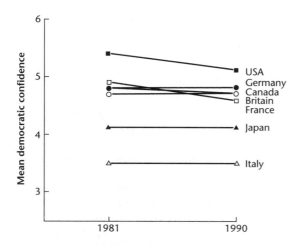

Fig. 9.1. Trends in institutional confidence in the G7 countries, 1981–1990.
Sources: 1981 and 1990–1 *World Values Surveys*.

---

[6] Fuchs, Guidorossi, and Svensson (1995: 351) show that eight countries have stable levels of confidence (Denmark, Norway, Germany, France, Britain, Ireland, Spain, and Belgium), while five have increasing confidence (Luxemburg, Portugal, Netherlands, Northern Ireland, and Italy) and one declining confidence (Greece).

The overall downward trend in institutional confidence across the 19 countries included in the over-time analysis is largely explained by significant declines in five countries: confidence declined in Hungary from 7.2 in 1980 to 4.5 in 1990; South Korea, from 6.9 to 4.7; Finland, from 5.3 to 4.1; Norway, from 5.9 to 5.0; and Spain, from 4.7 to 4.0. Several countries showed a much more modest increase in institutional confidence, although the only one of significance is Iceland, where confidence increased from 4.4 to 4.9 over the period. In most of these countries special factors may help explain the decline. In Hungary, the transition to democracy has caused particular strains, especially in regard to economic conditions. In South Korea, uncertainty over the intentions of the communist North, widespread corruption within the political elite, and martial law between 1979 and 1981, all served to undermine popular confidence in democratic institutions (Rose, Shin, and Munro, Chapter 7 this volume).

The Role of Democratic Experience

Do broad patterns exist in support for democratic institutions across the 24 OECD countries? While it is obviously possible to construct a simple classification based on the level of institutional confidence that exists, this would group countries with high levels of confidence, such as Poland and Turkey, together with countries such as Norway and Iceland, which have clearly different experiences with democratic institutions. A more fruitful approach is to relate the level of confidence in democratic institutions to the length of time that these institutions have remained in existence. Studies of democratic stability suggest that the longer a democracy persists, the greater the probability that it will attract widespread popular support and, as a consequence, be seen as legitimate by its citizens and act more effectively in coping with crises (Powell 1982; Dahl 1989). If we relate the period of time during which each of the 24 countries has been a representative democracy to levels of popular confidence in democratic institutions, four distinct groups of countries can be identified.

The largest group of countries is those in which levels of confidence are high, democracy is well established, and there have been few, if any, threats to the operation of the democratic system. These countries include Britain, the United States, and France, as well as Ireland and the Scandinavian countries. The second largest group is those countries at the other end of the spectrum, where democracy is a more recent innovation and confidence is lower. Some of these countries are the new democracies of Central and Eastern Europe, such as Hungary; countries where democracy emerged in the later post-war years out of dictatorship, such as Portugal and Spain; and countries where there have been periodic challenges to democracy, such as Mexico and South Korea.

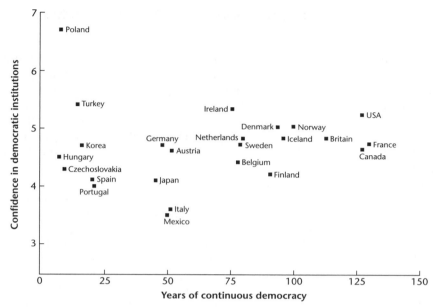

Fig. 9.2. Institutional confidence and democratic experience,1990.

Note: A year of continuous democracy is the period that has elapsed since the introduction of universal manhood suffrage, disregarding the periods of wartime occupation by a foreign power.

Source: 1990–1 *World Values Survey*.

The remaining two groups of countries are comparatively small. Divided countries have well-established democracies, but their citizens exhibit low popular confidence; the two countries in this category, Belgium and Canada, have both experienced major regional and ethnic challenges to their legitimacy, and this explains the relative lack of popular confidence in their democratic institutions. The remaining three countries, Poland, Turkey, and Germany,[7] have high popular confidence in democratic institutions, but are less well-established democracies. The first two countries have strong religious elements in their societies, which have had periodic political involvement, and this would seem to have bolstered confidence in political institutions. In the case of Germany, where there is modest confidence coupled with a comparatively newly established democracy, national pride has been associated with the institutions of civil society, rather than with political institutions (Conradt 1980).

[7] Because the 1990–1 survey was conducted just after reunification, 'Germany' relates to West Germany, rather than the reunified nation.

Policy Outputs and Confidence: A Macro Analysis

Studies of the political economy of vote choice suggest that macroeconomic conditions have a major impact on election outcomes, particularly if those conditions are channelled through the mass media so that they influence collective (sociotropic) rather than individual (egocentric) perceptions of economic performance (Kinder and Kieweit 1981; Lewis-Beck 1988). However, there is also a demonstrated link between egocentric economic evaluations and emotional reactions towards the government that is viewed as responsible for a performance deficit (Conover, Feldman, and Knight 1986). We would therefore expect that a range of macroeconomic factors might influence confidence in democratic institutions.

Among the macroeconomic factors that may be of importance, the amount of wealth produced by the society could influence institutional confidence, with greater wealth generating reduced confidence support since governments will be unable to satisfy the rising expectations that emerge. Unemployment and inflation have both been identified as factors in weakening support for incumbent governments (Monroe 1984). We might expect, then, that high levels of unemployment and inflation would undermine support for the democratic system as a whole. This link could come about directly, by eroding the spending power and savings of citizens, or indirectly, by presenting a visible measure of economic underperformance which could harm the system's credibility in the eyes of the electorate.[8] Unfortunately, the strong relationship between GDP and inflation among our 24 OECD countries precludes us testing the inflation hypothesis, but we can test the impact of unemployment.[9]

In addition to economic conditions, policy outputs also include social programmes, two of the most prominent of which are health and education. The ability of advanced societies to sustain high levels of health care for their populations is often seen as a primary indicator of social and economic well-being. Equally, the ability of governments to deliver increasingly well-educated entrants to the labour force is viewed as crucial to economic growth, as well as being central to more diffuse goals such as the successful operation of the political system via a sophisticated and knowledgeable electorate. We would hypothesize, therefore, that increased life expectancy and higher levels of human capital within a society would result in stronger support for democratic confidence. Finally, the accessibility of mass communications should reduce democratic confidence, because the watchdog role of journalists and predominant news values focus on the shortcomings not successes of public policy.[10]

---

[8] The other major indicator of economic performance which could influence democratic confidence is unemployment; this is examined in the next section using individual-level survey data.

[9] The correlation between inflation over the previous decade and GDP across the 24 countries is r = .84.

[10] The data come from the United Nations World Development Program, *Human Development Report* (New York: Oxford University Press, various years), and the *World Development Report* (New York: Oxford University Press, various years).

These hypotheses are tested in Table 9.2 which predicts confidence in democratic institutions from a range of social and economic variables across the 24 democracies. In addition, the model controls for the period of time that the country has been a democracy. The results suggest that macroeconomic conditions have a major impact, mainly via GDP (which is measured as a ratio).[11] Higher levels of GDP result in lower levels of confidence, net of other things. This tends to support the hypothesis that more affluent countries may have populations which have higher expectations of their democratic institutions than countries that have a lower GDP. Increased levels of unemployment undermine popular confidence, although not significantly.

Table 9.2. Policy outputs, mass media consumption, and institutional confidence

	Mean	b	Beta	(t value)
Health:				
Life expectancy (yrs)	74.6	−.01	−.06	−0.27, p = .79
Human capital:				
Schooling (yrs)	9.4	.18	.67	2.24, p = .04
Tertiary graduates (%)	13.6	.02	.21	0.81, p = .43
Economic conditions:				
Adjusted GDP (ratio)	100.0	−.17	−.95	−4.90, p = .00
Unemployment (%)	7.9	−.01	−.06	−0.40, p = .70
Mass media:				
Daily newspapers (copies per 100 people)	28.5	−.01	−.22	−1.15, p = .27
Televisions (per 100 people)	42.0	−.01	−.18	−.73, p = .48
Democratic experience:				
Continuous democracy (yrs)	63.8	.01	.17	0.64, p = .53
Constant		20.9		
Adj. R-squared		.60		
(N)		(24)		

Note: OLS regression results shows partial and standardized regression coefficient predicting support for democratic institutions among 24 OECD countries. The dependent variable is scored from 0–10 and was extracted from the 1990–1 *World Values Survey*.

Among the social policy outputs, life expectancy has no significant effect on confidence. The increasing availability of human capital in society does increase confidence, but only through primary and secondary schooling, not via tertiary education. This supports other findings which show that democratic values and support are enhanced more by increased civic education during the teenage years, and not by university study: while tertiary education does produce a more politically sophisticated and aware electorate, it has few consequences with regard to support for the system as a whole (Neumann 1986). As we hypothesized, popular access to mass communications reduces democratic confidence, more so via daily newspapers than television, although the former just fails to reach statistical significance.

[11] The ratio sets the mean GDP across the 24 nations in $US to 100, and calculates the GDP of each country accordingly.

We can conclude, then, that there is a major role for macroeconomic conditions in shaping confidence in democratic institutions, and a lesser role for social conditions. But these economic conditions influence institutional confidence indirectly, through the aggregate wealth that the society accumulates, rather than more directly, through the effects of unemployment. This endorses the finding of Clarke, Dutt, and Kornberg (1993) who concluded that while unemployment was a significant predictor of satisfaction with democracy in Western Europe, its net impact was comparatively modest. The results are, of course, based on a strictly limited sample of 24 countries; moreover, while the model controls for the period of time that the country has been democratic, it does not take into account the wide variety of other factors which may influence democratic confidence. For that reason, the next section conducts a parallel individual level analysis, using the 1990–1 *World Values Survey*.

Policy Outputs and Confidence: A Micro Analysis

The previous section showed the importance of macroeconomic conditions in shaping confidence in democratic institutions. In this section, the analyses move to the individual level in order to examine the micro social and economic factors that may prove to be important in this equation. In particular, we need to know the relative importance of objective economic factors, such as the material wealth that the person has, measured against subjective economic factors, such as their own feelings of economic satisfaction. The relative effects of these economic factors must also be estimated once other things have been taken into account, notably the human capital that they possess and their country of residence.

It is obviously impractical to analyse each country separately—and, in any event, we are more interested in identifying any underlying commonalities that may exist between the countries rather than country-specific effects. Two separate analyses are conducted, one for the group of ten countries that were earlier categorized as established, and one for the group of nine countries that were categorized as unstable.[12] The independent variables form four groups. First, there are three variables reflecting economic position and satisfaction, the major focus of the analysis. These are composed of three measures of objective economic position—whether the respondent is a labour-force participant or unemployed, and total household income before tax—and one measure of economic satisfaction.[13] Popular expectations of government are

---

[12] For reasons of space, analyses of the two countries in the hybrid category and the three in the divided category are not shown here.

[13] Labour-force participant and unemployed are both dummy variables. Household income was measured on a 1–10 scale, and has been standardized here to a ratio, where the mean household income in the country in question is taken as 1 and individual incomes are scored accordingly. Economic satisfaction was based on the question: 'How satisfied are you with the financial situation of your household?' and scored from a low of 1 to a high of 10.

Table 9.3. Micro social and economic factors and institutional confidence

	Established democracies		Newer democracies	
	b	Beta	b	Beta
Economic position:				
Labour-force participant	−.36	−.08	−.31	−.06
Household income	−.08[ns]	−.02[ns]	−.02[ns]	−.01[ns]
Unemployed	−.08[ns]	−.01[ns]	.26[ns]	.02[ns]
Economic satisfaction	.08	.10	.12	.13
Economic collectivist	.14	.08	.10	.05
Health:				
Self-assessed health	.04[ns]	.02[ns]	.04[ns]	.02[ns]
Human capital:				
Schooling	.02[ns]	.02[ns]	−.07	−.09
University educated	.12[ns]	.02[ns]	−.20[ns]	−.03[ns]
Country (France/Italy):				
Norway/Portugal	.49	.07	.52	.05
Ireland/Japan	.75	.04	1.1	.18
Netherlands/Spain	.08[ns]	.01[ns]	.67	.10
Britain/Mexico	.36	.07	.23[ns]	.03[ns]
Sweden/Finland	.26	.03	.91	.09
United States/Hungary	.60	.10	1.4	.18
Denmark/Czechoslovakia	.15[ns]	.01[ns]	1.1	.18
Austria	.11[ns]	.02[ns]	—	—
Constant	3.5		2.9	
Adj R-squared	.04		.05	
(N)	(9,343)		(8,202)	

[ns] = not statistically significant at $p<.01$, two-tailed.

Note: OLS regression results shown partial and standardized regression coefficients predicting confidence in democratic institutions, which is scored from a low of 0 to a high of 10. See text for details of variables and scoring.

Source: 1990–1 *World Values Survey*.

based on a question about whether the respondent preferred an individualist or a collectivist approach to economic management.[14]

The remaining three groups of independent variables in Table 9.3 reflect the influence of social factors. Health is measured by self-assessed personal health, a highly subjective indicator but nevertheless some measure of the state of the respondent's health. As in the aggregate analysis, human capital is measured by years of primary and secondary schooling, and by whether or not the person possessed tertiary education. Finally, the countries are measured by dummy variables, with France (in the case of the established countries) and Italy (in the case of the newer countries) forming the reference category.

[14] The question was: '*We are more likely to have a healthy economy if the government allows more freedom for individuals to do as they wish*', where the respondents were asked whether they agreed completely, agreed somewhat, neither agreed nor disagreed, disagreed somewhat or disagreed completely with the statement.

By any standards, the roots of democratic confidence in the social structure of the two groups of OECD countries are weak. Table 9.3 shows that for both groups, the models predict only 4 and 5 per cent of the total variance, respectively, even when inter-country variances are taken into account. Disregarding for the moment these inter-country differences, the strongest and most consistent predictor of confidence is economic satisfaction, with greater satisfaction producing stronger support for democratic institutions. However, it is notable that economic satisfaction has a greater impact on confidence in the newer democracies (with a partial coefficient of .12) than it does in the established ones (coefficient .08). In contrast to subjective feelings concerning economic conditions, objective economic position has relatively little effect on confidence. In both countries those outside the labour force are likely to exhibit higher levels of confidence compared to those who are in the labour force, while the total household income has no significant effect for either group. In line with studies of economic voting, the political consequences of egocentric economic evaluations are weaker than their sociotropic counterparts. However, since the *World Values Survey* did not include any economic evaluations other than the economic satisfaction question used here, it proved impossible to examine this further.

Among the other factors included in the models, support for economic collectivism has a consistent influence in predicting confidence across the two groups of countries, providing some support for the government expectations hypothesis. Health is unimportant, as is human capital, with the partial expectation of schooling, among the newer democracies. Finally, there are important variations between the countries in each of the two models, but also in the patterns between the two models themselves. Judged against the excluded country (France for the first group, Italy for the second), there are significant variations among the established countries. However, these never exceed three-quarters of a point on the 0–10 scale used to measure democratic confidence. By contrast, the inter-country variations in the second group are nearly twice as large: for example, the mean level of democratic confidence in Hungary is 1.4 points higher than Italy, even after all of the variables in the model are taken into account.[15]

Although the models in Table 9.3 have comparatively weak predictive power, as has been shown in other analyses (Listhaug and Wiberg 1995), the results do permit us to make some broad conclusions about the importance of economic position and expectations in shaping democratic institutional confidence in the established and newer groups of democracies. First, subjective evaluations of the person's economic position are consistently important, more so in the newer democracies than in the established ones. This undoubtedly reflects the economic instability that has occurred in the newer countries, and their comparative inexperience with democracy. Second, there is little to

---

[15] This is emphasized by the variances explained by the models with and without the country dummies. In the first model, the addition of the country dummies increases the variance explained from 2.7 to 3.6 per cent; in the second model, from 1.4 to 4.6 per cent.

suggest that the person's economic position in the society—judged by wealth or employment status—has any impact. This is particularly notable in the case of unemployment, which, like inflation, directly threatens a person's social and economic well-being. Whatever its potential to cause personal economic disruption, it has little impact on institutional confidence, as other studies have shown (Clarke, Nutt, and Kornberg 1993).

Discussion and Conclusions

Popular confidence in democratic institutions is at the heart of representative government. Widespread confidence reduces the potential for radical change to the system, but it also encourages a constructive desire for social reform. Perhaps most importantly of all, it builds a reservoir of support which can be expended during periods of crisis when democratic institutions are placed under stress. To date, most studies have examined the origins of democratic confidence in the political culture of the country concerned, or in the norms and values of mass opinion, slowly accumulated over several generations. By contrast, this chapter has examined the political economy of popular confidence in democratic institutions, by focusing on the macro and micro social and economic conditions of the country.

The results show that institutional confidence is strongly related to the period of time that democratic institutions have been in existence. This supports the argument that confidence is formed cumulatively within the mass electorate; but it also supports the argument, often found in democratic theory, that democratic confidence is predicated on the frequency of free, competitive, national elections. In terms of the political economy theories, the macro analysis showed that national GDP was negatively related to institutional confidence, providing support for the economic expectation hypothesis, which predicted that the electorates of the established democracies had higher expectations of their systems than those in new democracies. The survey analysis found a modest yet consistent effect for economic satisfaction, but little or none for objective economic position.

In general, then, the conclusion is that *economic conditions* are more important than *social ones*, but together their impact is negligible when compared to such factors as *political culture* or *historical circumstance*. This confirms the conclusion of Clarke, Nutt, and Kornberg (1993: 1015; see also Kornberg and Clarke 1992) that 'the political economy of public orientations toward polity and society in contemporary Western democracies is real but limited'. It also supports the argument that deep-rooted cultural values shape popular views of political and social arrangements although, as others have pointed out (see, for example, Miller and Borrelli 1991; Miller and Listhaug 1990), there are dangers in using country variables as proxies for broadly-based cultural values.

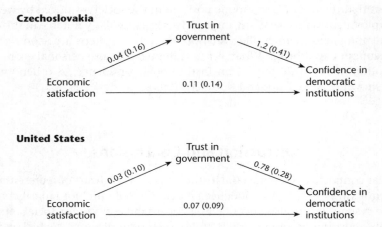

Fig. 9.3. Economic satisfaction, political trust, and institutional confidence, Czecho-slovakia and the United States.

Notes: Figures are partial regression coefficients and (in parentheses) standardized regression coef-ficients. The models also control for (but do not show) the full range of independent variables in Table 9.3.

Source: 1990–1 *World Values Survey*.

Why do policy outputs in general, and economic performance and expec-tations in particular, play such a minor role in shaping confidence in democ-ratic institutions, particularly in view of the important impact that they enjoy in shaping electoral outcomes? Although there is a modest role for economic satisfaction in predicting confidence, the cultural values of the country redi-rect feelings about personal and collective economic conditions towards the incumbent government, rather than towards the system as a whole. This is, in effect, the reservoir of support that the established democracies can rely on to provide them with a buffer between the political system and citizen demands during times of economic stress. Such a reservoir of support should be greater within the established democracies than in the newer ones, since they have had more time and opportunity to accumulate popular goodwill. More specif-ically, we would expect the link between economic beliefs and democratic confidence to be weaker in the established democracies than in the newer ones, and for the impact to be mediated via beliefs about the government.

Although it is impossible to test this hypothesis across the range of OECD countries examined here, the *World Values Survey* did include a question about trust in government which was asked in just five countries; of those five, we can compare the impact of economic satisfaction and political trust on demo-cratic confidence in two: the United States, and one of the new democracies, Czechoslovakia (Figure 9.3). The results show that the direct effect of eco-nomic satisfaction in shaping confidence is significantly higher in Czechoslovakia than it is in the United States, as we would expect. In the absence of a fully developed civil society and without a reservoir of goodwill towards democratic institutions, citizens are more likely to blame economic difficulties on the institutions of the state than they are in an established democracy such as the United States. It is also notable than in Czechoslovakia there is a much stronger link between trust in the government and democratic confidence than in the United States.

The political economy of confidence of democratic institutions is therefore strictly limited: political circumstances are much more important. This conclusion underlies the gradual transformation that has taken place in the established democracies, where the frequency of national elections has slowly generated a reservoir of popular support for democratic institutions, with citizens drawing a clear distinction between the institutions of the state on the one hand, and the party and leaders elected to conduct public policy on the other. In parallel with this accumulation of democratic skill, political oppositions gradually come to be viewed as legitimate, and operate within clearly limited parameters (Weil 1989). The challenge in the twenty-first century will be to see whether the political economy of confidence in democratic institutions has the same limited role in the newer democracies of Central and Eastern Europe as it has in the established ones.

10

Political Performance and Institutional Trust

ARTHUR MILLER AND OLA LISTHAUG

A S previous chapters have demonstrated, low and declining citizen respect for government institutions and political leaders is characteristic of contemporary industrialized societies. Empirical evidence dating back to the early 1970s reveals a trend toward growing distrust of government institutions in a number of countries (for previous reviews see, for example, Miller and Listhaug 1990; Miller and Borrelli 1991; Dalton 1996; Norton 1997; Nye *et al.* 1997).

While the trend toward distrust is evident, the explanations for, and interpretations of, this phenomenon have proved far more controversial (see, for example, the early Miller/Citrin exchange, 1974). This lack of definitive explanation derives partly from the complexity of the task and partly from a dearth of systematic evidence available for operationalizing plausible explanations. Any long-term social development is bound to have several causes, and the factors stressed at one point in time may not be the same as those that are important later.

Nevertheless, one explanation that has appeared frequently in the literature is public dissatisfaction with government performance. Miller (1974*a*) argued that when citizens' expectations of government performance went unfulfilled over the course of successive administrations, growing distrust of government institutions would result. He also demonstrated empirically that when governments pursued centrist policies, citizens of both the extreme left and right became distrustful at a faster rate than citizens of a moderate ideological persuasion. Others contended that in the post-war period, citizens were making increasing demands on government; demands that the government simply could not meet, hence government overload, an emerging 'crisis of the state' and growing citizen discontent with government (Crozier, Huntington, and Watanuki 1975; Sundquist 1980; Huntington 1981; Lipset and Schneider

We wish to thank Peggy Swails for her secretarial assistance, Darcie Carsner, Tom Klobucar, Julie Meyers, and Chia-Hsing Lu for research assistance and Stephanie Holstad for producing the graphs contained in the chapter.

1987). Weatherford (1992) also argues that public evaluations of government performance constitute one major dimension of the broader concept of regime legitimacy. Lockerbie (1993) and Anderson and Guillory (1997) likewise conclude that dissatisfaction with how governments manage the economy in Western societies was correlated with perceptions of how well democracy functioned in these countries. In short, a significant body of previous literature has investigated the hypothesis that dissatisfaction with government performance leads to increased distrust of government institutions and a loss of regime legitimacy in the eyes of the citizenry.

Despite this, the resolution of the hypothesis is far from definitive. Previous research suffers from certain limitation. Much focuses only on the United States; hence it is not clear to what extent the findings can be generalized to other countries. Studies often use a limited time period or one single point in time. On occasion there is some confounding of the dependent and independent variables; that is, what conceptually may be better treated as a measure of perceived government performance is occasionally used as a measure of support for the political regime. For example, satisfaction with the way democracy works, the dependent variable used by Lockerbie, was intended to measure political alienation but on face value might be construed as a measure of performance, a point that Lockerbie (1993: 282) himself acknowledges. The specific item in the *Eurobarometers* is a question asking: '*On the whole, are you very satisfied, fairly satisfied, not very satisfied, or not at all satisfied with the way democracy works in your country?*' As discussed earlier in the book, some respondents may have taken this to be a question about how well the government is currently performing rather than thinking about the extent to which they support political institutions or even democratic principles.

What conceptually and operationally constitutes a measure of government performance is open to discussion. For example, some suggest that *direct* performance matters, so that what is important is the ability or inability of government to meet the demands of the modern citizenry (Crozier *et al.* 1975; Sundquist 1980). In this view the failure of government performance, by some objective standards, brings about declining public support or trust in government. Others argue that citizen *expectations* are the critical factor. Government may be performing better today than ever before, but that performance may still fall far short of citizen expectations. Of course 'expectations' are also quite complex. Do we mean expectations with respect to the past? The future? With respect to some ideal of what is fair? Or with respect to what certain groups in society are perceived to obtain by way of government outputs?

This chapter explores these questions. We first examine the *direct* link between government performance, as measured by objective indicators of inflation, unemployment, or government deficits, and support for government in many countries. Next we examine the role that *expectations* play in translating evaluations of the government's performance into political distrust in three countries where we have long-term time-series data—the United States, Norway, and Sweden. We go on to explore how ethical expectations about government standards influence trust in politicians. The conclusion draws some general lessons from these results.

Various survey data[1] are employed in the analysis including the 1990–1 *World Values Survey*, the Norwegian, Swedish, and United States Election Studies, and the Iowa Social Science Institute (ISSI) surveys in the United States, Russia, Ukraine, and Lithuania. Finally, some data from the International Monetary Fund (IMF) and OECD are used to measure inflation, unemployment, and government deficits.

Cross-National Comparisons of the Government Performance and Institutional Confidence

The basic thesis we will explore is that failure of government performance may erode confidence in government institutions. The effect may not be immediate, but it could be expected to occur if policy performance deteriorated or remained low over successive administrations. For example, if government was responsible for providing public services such as medical care, unemployment insurance, or pension benefits, and some or all of these services deteriorated or failed to meet public demands, a growing discontent with government might result. If services were not improved over time, the public might begin to question the institutional arrangements that exist to deal with the problems.

The hypothesized direct relationship between government performance and trust in government is, conceptually, rather straightforward. Yet measuring government performance, particularly from a cross-national, comparative perspective is anything but straightforward. Countries with governments that turn in a better performance should also exhibit relatively higher levels of diffuse public support than countries with poorly performing governments. The challenge to test this hypothesis empirically is finding measures of government performance that are meaningful, reliable, and comparable across countries. Measuring how effectively the government delivers certain public services raises problems in the comparative framework, as some services may be more critical to assessing the performance of some governments than others. The delivery of health-care services, for example, could be significant when evaluating government performance in countries with a national health-care system but potentially unimportant in nations with privately insured health care.

There are at least three alternative measures which can be employed to assess economic performance. First we could use indicators of *economic growth*, measured by GDP. As demonstrated in the previous chapter by Ian McAllister,

[1] All the survey data-sets used in this report are available through major data archives such as the University of Michigan, Inter-University Consortium for Political and Social Research, or the National Data Archives of Norway and Sweden.

in OECD countries macro-level indicators of GDP[2] are related to institutional confidence, as measured in the 1990–1 *World Values Survey*. Yet the aggregated economic measures used by McAllister may reflect the relative wealth or economic prosperity enjoyed by each country more than government performance per se.

An alternative measure of government performance utilizes *short-term changes* in the *inflation* and *unemployment* rates. This measure reflects the psychological notion that people focus more on how well things have been going recently rather than thinking about how things have gone over a long period of time.

Lipset and Schneider (1983: 62–5) found a very strong correlation between institutional confidence and recent change in inflation and unemployment in the United States. Accordingly we re-examined this relationship for a wider range of countries. We used an index of institutional confidence that combined the confidence in parliament and civil service items in the 1990–1 *World Values Survey*. To measure economic performance we used standardized data on absolute levels of unemployment and inflation, and changes in these levels during the preceding year, provided by the OECD. The results demonstrated weak but insignificant correlations between institutional confidence and these economic indicators. While country differences in longer-term economic conditions may be related to the level of confidence in government cross-nationally (as demonstrated by McAllister), it seems that institutional confidence is not influenced by either recent economic conditions or recent change in those conditions, as measured by current year inflation and unemployment rates compared with the previous year.

How can we account, however, for the difference between our findings and those of Lipset and Schneider (1987)? First, Lipset and Schneider examined only the United States, whereas the *World Values Surveys* contain complete data on roughly 24 countries. Secondly, the Lipset and Schneider confidence measures focused on confidence in the *leaders* of various institutions (such as the executive branch, Congress, and the Supreme Court) rather than the institutions per se. Finally, many people in various cultures may not blame the government for short-term economic changes. They may blame their employer, themselves, or even general global economic conditions rather than holding the government responsible; thereby weakening any relationship between economic conditions and evaluations of government performance.[3]

---

[2] GDP is measured as the sum of all final expenditures: exports of goods and services, government consumption and investment, private gross fixed capital formation, increase/decrease in stocks, private consumption, and imports of goods and services. The budgetary surplus/deficit figures cover consolidated central government (beginning in 1972 (USA), 1971 (Norway), and 1970 (Sweden)) and exclude social-security funds.

[3] We refer here only to the retrospective evaluations. Some researchers (e.g. Lockerbie 1993) suggest using the prospective evaluations as well, that is, the question asking how the economic conditions will be in one year compared to the current situation. The argument against using the prospective items is that they are projections and therefore are subject to influence from any current dissatisfaction the respondent feels. Such measures should only be used when reciprocal links can be built into the equation, or as controls in a panel analysis as is done somewhat later in this report.

Table 10.1. Change in political trust by change in economic expectations

	Norway 1985–9		United States 1972–6	
Change in expectations	Personal finances	National economy	Personal finances	National economy
Better to Worse	−.57	−.63	−.36	−.48
Better/Same to Worse	−.33	−.56	−.37	−.32
No Change	−.30	−.26	−.22	−.28
Worse/Same to Same/Better	−.39	+.03	−.25	−.23
Worse to Better	+.31	−.10	+.20	−.02
TOTAL SAMPLE	−.35	−.35	−.27	−.27
(n)	(655)	(605)	(534)	(536)

Notes: The first response under 'Change in Expectations' refers to what the respondent expected the economy to do in the future when asked in the first panel survey while the second response indicates the retrospective evaluation given at the later interview. For example, the 'Better' in the first row indicates that when a Norwegian respondent was interviewed in 1985 they said they expected the economic situation to get better in the future and when they were interviewed in 1989 they said the situation had gotten worse.

The Table entries are the extent to which the mean level of trust in government changed between the two waves of the panel for the designated subgroup. The entry for the Total Sample shows the change in the mean trust for all the panel respondents taken together.

Sources: National Election Studies for Norway and United States.

While no measure is entirely flawless, the *government deficit* as a percentage of GDP may provide a more direct measure of government performance that is comparable across countries. Some might suggest that GDP per capita would function equally well as a measure of government performance. But this suggestion rests on the assumption that citizens expect their government to manage the economy in a Keynesian fashion that protects against economic downturns. Unlike GDP, however, the deficit measure reflects directly on how the government is handling its budget, and it does not depend on assumed expectations about the role of the government in the economy. A government running a deficit may experience difficulty delivering services, at least in the long run. Granted, governments can boost their short-run popularity by running a deficit, as Ronald Reagan did very successfully in the United States during the 1980s. Eventually, however, this deficit led to considerable political conflict and discontent. Although a lag effect may occur, it seems reasonable to hypothesize that countries with greater deficits will experience relatively lower confidence in government and that, across time, public support will also reflect longer-term trends in government deficits.

The 1990–1 *World Values Survey* again provides evidence for testing this hypothesis in a comparative context, as shown in Figure 10.1. The two-dimensional array of countries is anchored at the positive end by Norway and Chile, countries that enjoyed a small budget surplus and high confidence in government. Italy, on the other hand, had the distinction of anchoring the negative end with very low citizen confidence in government and a budget

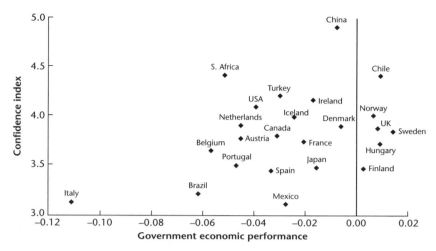

Fig. 10.1. Institutional confidence and government economic performance.

Notes: The Institutional Confidence Index is calculated by adding confidence in parliamentary values and confidence in civil service values, then subtracting 1. The index range is from 1 to 7 where high values indicate high confidence and low values indicate low confidence in the government. The government performance measure is the government deficit or surplus as a percentage of the GDP. Negative values indicate a deficit while positive numbers indicate a surplus.

Sources: The survey data measuring confidence in the government are from the 1990 *World Values Survey*. The government performance data are from the *International Financial Statistics Yearbook* published by the International Monetary Fund, Washington, 1996.

deficit that equalled 11 per cent of GDP. The correlation of .41 between confidence and government performance for these 24 countries is significant at the .03 level, a reasonably strong relationship given the small number of cases. Of course, this correlation does not constitute causality, but it does provide some evidence in support of the hypothesis.

The strong correlation reflected in Figure 10.1 also remains virtually unchanged when controlling in a multivariate regression for simple GPD, current inflation, and unemployment rates, as well as recent changes (current year compared to previous year) in unemployment and inflation. In short, the relationship between institutional confidence and government deficit does not appear to be simply a direct reflection of current economic conditions. It may be the case, however, that the performance measure is indirectly reflecting changing economic conditions. That is, economic problems may put pressure on the government budget, which then fluctuates with respect to the economy. In short, it may be simple economic change that influences political confidence, not general government performance as hypothesized. Unfortunately, it is statistically difficult to control for potentially confounding or spurious economic effects at the macro level with so few countries for cases.

Moving to the micro level of the combined surveys for the countries, how-ever, allows us to introduce some controls for personal economic conditions, as well as assessments of the macro economy. In this analysis, all the respon-dents in a country are given the same value for government performance in their country (the value of the budget deficit displayed in Figure 10.1). Government performance, therefore, can only be expected to explain across-country variance in confidence, not individual variation in confidence within a single country. Other relevant variables can then be introduced to determine if the relationship between institutional confidence and government perfor-mance (measured by the level of budget deficit) is eliminated statistically after controlling for these other factors.

As expected the micro-level relationship is weaker than the macro-level. Nevertheless, the micro-level .28 correlation is significant at the .001 level for the roughly 28,000 valid cases in the combined *World Values Survey*.

Unfortunately, the *World Values Survey* is limited in the type of control vari-ables available. Ideally one should control on variables that reflect the impact of economic factors. The studies do contain a couple of questions asking about whether the health of the economic system needed changing. Presumably anyone feeling the brunt of an economic downturn should be more pes-simistic about the health of the economy and more supportive of change in the economic system. Likewise, some demographic variables such as age, edu-cation, income, and employment status can be used as indirect measures of susceptibility to the hardships of an economic recession. While the demo-graphic and attitudinal variables available in the *World Values Survey* are not ideal, they constitute a reasonable set of controls.

Yet, even after applying these controls in a multivariate regression predict-ing institutional confidence, the government performance measure remains significant (T = 8.5, p = .001) and contributes (Beta = .15) to the overall expla-nation of confidence (adjusted R squared = .11). Because of the limitations of the *World Values* data these are not definitive results, but the findings support the hypothesized effect of government performance on confidence even after controlling for some measures of sensitivity to economic conditions at the individual level. In short, the results suggest that the government deficit mea-sure is reflecting an evaluation of political performance, not just economic conditions or effects.

The Dynamics of Political Trust and Government Performance

So far our tests of the performance hypothesis have been static and cross-national. We have not yet considered the potential impact of changes in performance on trends in support for political actors within a country. Presumably, as government performance deteriorates over a period of time we should expect a decline in their support. Unfortunately little available empirical evidence is suited to testing the performance hypothesis across time. Most survey data are either limited by dearth of relevant measures or a very short time-series. Fortunately, in a few advanced industrialized countries—Norway, Sweden, and the United States—the national election studies provide comparable measures of trust in politicians over a period of about three decades (see Chapters by Dalton and by Holmberg in this volume for a discussion of these items).

As Figure 10.2 illustrates, even a cursory visual examination of these time-series data confirms a dynamic relationship: the simple time-series correlation between trust in politicians and performance, without considering lags or any more sophisticated modelling, for all three countries combined is .47 (p = .01). Yet it is evident from Figure 10.2 that the correspondence in trends is stronger for Sweden (r = .55) and the United States (.41) than for Norway (.24). The lower correlation for Norway, however, may not accurately reflect the overall correspondence between the general trend in trust and performance. When the entire period between 1968 and 1993 is considered, we can conclude that despite some noticeable ups and downs, trust in Norway has generally remained relatively high and fairly flat compared with the trends for Sweden and the United States (see Figure 10.2). One could come to exactly the same conclusion when taking a broader view of the government deficit measure for Norway.

In summary, comparative data from the *World Values Survey*, and time-series data from Norway, Sweden, and the United States, suggest that failed government performance directly contributes to declining public support for government institutions and for politicians even after controlling for economic conditions. This finding helps to explain some of the cross-national differences in levels of political support, as well as the dynamics underlying longer-term trends. Yet if government performance is linked with support for political institutions, this link must occur through the public's evaluations of that performance. Public evaluations, however, involve a number of complexities. What one person judges as an excellent performance another may regard as relatively poor. It is to an examination of these complexities of public judgements that we now turn.

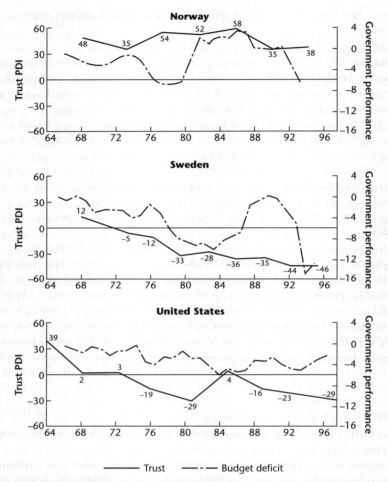

Fig. 10.2. Trust in politicians and government performance across time.

Sources: Budget Deficit information from IMF. Trust data from National Election Studies.

Expectations Concerning Standards of Government Performance

Previous research has argued that citizens utilize various criteria when evaluating government performance (see Tyler, Rasinski, and McGraw 1985). One criterion may be the absolute level of outputs or the benefits received from government. Yet other standards may be more relative, such as current benefits as compared with past benefits. Or, citizens may compare the level of outputs they receive from government with what they think the average citizen receives. Presumably if a citizen feels that the benefits they get from government are low, or below what they think the average citizen receives, they will be less supportive of government than someone who thinks they obtain many benefits from government. Citizens may also invoke ethical principles of fairness or distributive justice when evaluating the allocation of government benefits and outcomes (for a review of social justice research, see Jennings 1991). An early study by Gurr (1970) argued that violations of a sense of deservedness in a society might stimulate political discontent and rebellion.

Much dissatisfaction fuelling the demand for democracy in Eastern Europe and the Soviet Union appeared to arise from feelings of unjust outcomes. As Jennings (1991) points out, these perceptions of unfair allocations were especially visible in the outrage citizens expressed toward the party and government *apparatchiks* who often lived exceedingly well while the masses were asked to tolerate a standard of living clearly below that enjoyed by the average citizen in Western countries. Even in relatively affluent societies, however, citizens may feel that they deserve more from government than they get. Katz *et al.* (1975), for example, found that trust in government was influenced by how individuals felt about the absolute level of outcomes, and the fairness of outcomes received when making demands on government bureaucrats. For the most part, previous comparisons of distributive justice have focused on individuals, that is, whether a citizen feels unjustly deprived compared with perceptions of what other individuals receive. However, groups[4] could also form the focus of this comparison, regardless of whether the person drawing the comparison was a member of the group. For example, an individual may feel that some group is deprived of government benefits that they rightfully deserve, such as full protection of civil rights for gays. They may also feel that some groups, such as the rich, are undeservedly advantaged by government decisions. In both these cases, the perception of unfair treatment of these groups may lead to discontent with government. Likewise, Tyler, Rasinski, and McGraw (1985) have suggested that perceptions of procedural injustice may influence citizen trust in government. Citizens may judge the fairness of government outcomes not only by considering the level and relative distribution of those outcomes, but also by assessing the fairness of the procedures used to reach the decisions that allocate the benefits. Tyler *et al.* (1991) argue that perceptions of procedural injustice actually have a greater impact on distrust of government than comparisons involving either the perceived absolute level of government benefits they receive or their feelings of how fair or unfair they think these benefits are.

While these studies raise important theoretical issues, little empirical evidence exists for testing the impact of perceived fairness on diffuse political support. Even Tyler *et al.* (1985) used only a sample of college students and a

[4] The groups referred to included: people on welfare, rich people, blacks, gays, political refugees, and Hispanics. The index simply counted the number of these groups that the respondent said received 'too many' benefits from government. The distribution on the index was as follows: 0 = 8 per cent, 1 = 18 per cent, 2 = 23 per cent, 3 = 22 per cent, 4 or more groups = 29 per cent.

very small sample (n = 300) of Chicago residents to test their hypothesis that judgements regarding procedural justice had a stronger effect on political trust than did evaluations of distributive justice.

A survey by the Iowa Social Science Institute (ISSI) including 2,100 respondents from the Midwest region does, however, provides some evidence that partially confirms the Tyler *et al*. (1991) contention. The ISSI survey, conducted in the fall of 1994, contained questions asking respondents about the absolute level of benefits they received from government; whether these benefits were more, less, or the same as they had received in the past; whether this was a fair amount of benefits; whether or not government procedures were fair; how their current personal financial situation, and the condition of the national economy compared with the past year; as well as trust in politicians and standard demographic controls such as age, education, and income. A multivariate analysis incorporating these variables demonstrates that the strongest correlate (Beta = .26) of trust in politicians was indeed perceptions of procedural justice. Yet, while this correlation is significant, the distribution of responses largely fail to explain the overall distribution of trust. Roughly two-thirds of Midwesterners felt that the federal government always or sometimes considers all views when making decisions. Similarly, 65 per cent said that the government always or sometimes uses fair procedures when making decisions. Yet, only 17 per cent of the respondents felt that they could always or most of the time trust the government in Washington to do what is right. Clearly perceptions of procedural injustice are important to a broader understanding of trust in politicians, but alone they do not fully explain this phenomenon.

All of the other substantive variables (disregarding control variables) in the multivariate equation based on the ISSI data were statistically significant except the measure asking the respondent to compare their current level of benefits with those received in the past. Out of the remaining variables, the feeling that certain groups in society were getting more benefits from government than they deserved was the strongest predictor (Beta = .17). The larger the number of groups that a respondent thought were getting more than they deserved from government, the more distrusting the respondent. A similar question was also asked in the 1989 Norwegian[5] election studies and it likewise proved to be the strongest predictor (Beta = .18) of trust in that particular analysis.[6] These studies suggest that perceptions of how many government benefits various groups in society receive may be more important to a sense of fairness than judgements regarding the fairness of one's own benefits.

---

[5] The group-measure in the Norwegian study also used six groups, but the groups were more mainstream than the ones used in the ISSI index. The groups used in the Norwegian study were: the unemployed, students, single parents, elderly, refugees, and the handicapped. Not surprisingly, fewer groups were mentioned in the Norwegian study as receiving too many government benefits. The distribution for the group-measure was: 0 = 59 per cent, 1 = 34 per cent, 2 = 5 per cent, 3 or more = 2 per cent.

[6] In the ISSI multivariate analysis, the Beta coefficient for the perceived fairness of the respondent's own benefits was only .04. Even the perceived absolute level of benefits received was more strongly related with trust (Beta = .09).

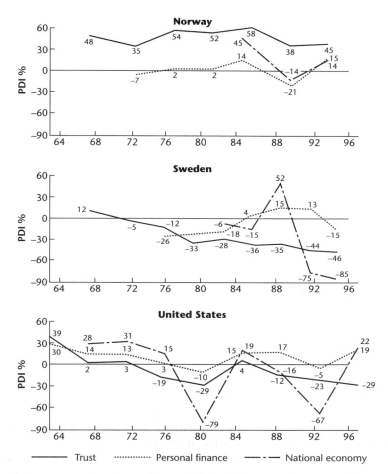

Fig. 10.3. Trust in politicians and economic evaluations over time.
Source: National Election Studies.

While these results are limited by the dearth of comparable data across time and across countries, they are none the less suggestive. Clearly the perceived fairness of government performance ought to consider group-related criteria as well as individual concerns about fairness. Perhaps even more important is a suggestion that arises from the impact of the procedural justice considerations. Government performance need not be judged simply from the perspective of economic or material outcomes. Public evaluations of government processes may also be very important when judging the trustworthiness of government. It may very well be that the public employs certain moral and ethical standards when evaluating government performance. If government performance falls below these standards over some period of time, we can expect diffuse support for political institutions to decline.

Citizens may indeed have some ideal notion of democracy in mind against which they evaluate government performance (see Chapter 7). Even citizens in the newly emerging democracies of Russia, Ukraine, and Lithuania have expectations that their governments will function democratically (see Miller, Hesli, and Reisinger 1997 for an analysis of what democracy means to the citizens and leaders in these newly independent states). Those who perceive the government as operating in a way that does not fit with their notions of what a democracy is like are much less trusting of government than those who perceive government as functioning democratically.

Conclusions

Based on the evidence presented here, it appears that citizen distrust of government is associated with high expectations. Given that economic performance is critical to overall public support of government, it may be that some citizens expect more from the government in managing the level of social well-being than is realistic. If this is the case, one remedy emphasizes the need to lower public expectations. Yet, the evidence presented here also suggests that government performance is not simply gauged by material standards or economic conditions. Citizens also expect the government to follow procedures that are unbiased, and to produce outcomes that neither advantage nor disadvantage particular groups unfairly. Additionally, citizens expect political leaders to operate in an honest, competent, and efficient manner. Surely in a democracy those expectations should not be reduced. Moreover, we should not be surprised if public confidence in government falls when these norms are perceived to be continuously violated by numerous public officials. In this case the solution to the problem of political discontent is reform of government, not reform of public expectations.

11

Institutional Explanations
for Political Support

PIPPA NORRIS

SINCE the early 1960s an extensive literature has documented public support for political regimes in Western nations, and more recently in emerging democracies. As demonstrated in the first part of this book, there are substantial cross-national variations in regime support. In some democracies cynicism about government institutions seems to be endemic, widespread and deep-rooted, such as in Japan and Italy, while in contrast people seem consistently more positive towards the regime in some other nations (see Chapters 2 and 3). Why are there these major differences between countries? We can identify at least three separate schools of thought seeking to explain this phenomenon, focusing on the role of cultural values, government performance, and political institutions.

Theories of Cultural Values

Following in the footsteps of Almond and Verba (1963), one strand of research has emphasized how cross-national differences towards the regime are related to deep-rooted social and political values in each country. The imprint of founding ideas may persist in the chromosomes of each culture and leave its mark on the dominant public philosophy towards government. Theories of post-materialism, and more recently post-modernization, provide the most comprehensive account of political culture (see Chapter 12), suggesting that a deep-rooted process of value change is gradually transforming citizens' relationship towards government (Inglehart 1977, 1990, 1997a; Abramson and Inglehart 1995). In this view, core values transmitted through the socialization process are shaped by family, friends and formative experiences in early youth. These accounts are most powerful when explaining persistent and long-term differences between nations, secular trends over time, and diffuse support such as feelings of national identity. Nevertheless the focus on the socialization process means we have to turn elsewhere when accounting for short-term fluctuations in attitudes towards the regime, such as a sudden drop in approval of Congress.

Theories of Government Performance

Alternatively, as discussed in the preceding two chapters, theories of political economy commonly focus on how system support relates to public evaluations of government performance, particularly concerning the economy. This perspective notes that confidence in government and trust in political leaders are not stable phenomena. Fluctuations in support, it is suggested, reflect the public's overall evaluation of the performance of political leaders and, more generally, the ability of the administration to handle the economy. Where successive governments have succeeded in meeting public expectations of peace and prosperity, and more generally fulfilling their campaign promises, it is believed that this generates diffuse support towards the political regime in general. A series of studies have focused on the relationship between aggregate levels of economic growth, unemployment, or inflation, as well as individual-level retrospective and prospective evaluations of the economy, and confidence in governance in North America and Western Europe (Clarke, Dutt, and Kornberg 1993; Kornberg and Clarke 1992; Weatherford 1984, 1991, 1992; Anderson 1995; Weil 1989).

If 'performance' is defined fairly narrowly as purely economic, for example growth in per capita GNP, then this perspective seems to provide a poor fit, prima facie, for trends in many countries. Both Italy and Japan have experienced rapid economic growth in the post-war era, for example, although political cynicism seems pervasive and widespread in both these countries (Pharr 1997; Morlino and Tarchi 1996). Moreover American confidence in government declined throughout the 1960s despite a relatively prosperous economy during this period (Lawrence 1997). In Chapter 9 of this volume McAllister concluded that, at the individual level, attitudes towards economic performance played only a minor role in shaping confidence in democratic institutions. This theory becomes more convincing if non-economic aspects of government performance are included in the equation, including critical events, for example in the United States the events of Watergate and the failure of foreign policy in Vietnam, but then it becomes harder to define any independent and objective measure of 'performance' (Bok 1997). In Chapter 10 of this volume Miller and Listhaug argue that we need to broaden our evidence to include citizens' perceptions of the fairness of policy outcomes, as well as their expectations of government, although this is difficult to do with the available sources of comparative survey data. Moreover, if performance accounts are correct, then we need to explain why the records of some governments seem *consistently* more successful than others.

Institutional Theories of Political Support

In contrast, one of the most plausible, and yet neglected, explanatory frameworks, examined in this chapter, seeks to understand the attitudes of citizens towards the political system within their broader constitutional context. In this regard, we return to the idea, first suggested by David Easton, that diffuse institutional support relates to our accumulated experience:

> Members do not come to identify with basic political objects only because they have learned to do so . . . from others—a critical aspect of socialization processes. If they did, diffuse support would have entirely the appearance of a non-rational phenomenon. Rather, on the basis of their own experiences, members may also adjudge the worth of supporting these objects for their own sake. Such attachment may be a product of spill-over effects from evaluations of a series of outputs and of performance over a long period of time. Even though the orientations derive from responses to particular outputs initially, they become in time disassociated from performance. They become transformed into generalised attitudes towards the authorities or other political objects. (Easton 1975)

But what experience counts in this regard? The argument in this chapter is that the pattern of winners and losers from the political system is structured by the constitutional arrangements, meaning the core institutions of state and the rules of the game, both written and unwritten. Some citizens win, some lose. Some parties are mobilized into power, some are mobilized out. Over a long period of time this accumulated experience can be expected to shape our general orientations towards the political regime. At the simplest level, if we feel that the rules of the game allow the party we endorse to be elected to power, we are more likely to feel that representative institutions are responsive to our needs so that we can trust the political system. If we feel that the party we prefer persistently loses, over successive elections, we are more likely to feel that our voice is excluded from the decision-making process, producing dissatisfaction with political institutions. Over time, where constitutional arrangements succeed in channelling popular demands into government outcomes, then we would expect this to be reflected in diffuse support for the political process. Weatherford (1992) suggests, in this respect the methodological challenge for empirical researchers is to ground individual-level findings in macro-level theories about the polity.

What evidence is there that institutions matter for political support? Since political structures are a relatively stable phenomena, usually characterized by incremental evolution, the most appropriate evidence concerns cross-national comparisons which maximize the variance in structural arrangements, for example a wide variety of electoral systems. In contrast, comparisons over-time are less appropriate, unless we monitor institutional confidence 'before' and 'after' major constitutional reforms within nations, such as changes to the electoral systems in Italy, Japan, and New Zealand. An extensive literature has explored the consequences of alternative constitutional designs, for example, the influence of presidentialism or parliamentarianism on executive stability (Powell 1982; Lijphart 1992; Linz 1990), and the impact of majoritarian or proportional electoral systems on the representation of political minorities, party fragmentation, and voter participation (Lijphart 1994a; Sartori 1994; Norris 1997b), as well as the process of constitutional change (Banting and Simeon 1985; Bogdanor 1988; Lijphart and Waisman 1996). The 'new institutionalism' school emphasizes the importance of understanding political attitudes within their structural context. Yet few studies have looked systematically at the relationship between constitutional arrangements and public support for the political system.

The most thorough recent analysis was conducted by Anderson and Guillory (1997), who compared satisfaction with democracy among consensual and majoritarian political systems in Western Europe. The study hypothesized that: (1) system support is consistently influenced by whether people are among the winners or losers in electoral contests, defined by whether the party they endorsed was returned to government; and (2) that this process is mediated by the type of democracy. Following Lijphart (1984), nations were classified into *majoritarian* (Westminster) or *consensual* (consociational) democracies (see Figure 11.1). Theories of responsible party government stress that majoritarian systems empower the winners to impose their preferences over the losers. Accountability and effective government are valued more highly by these systems than representation of all viewpoints. Anderson and Guillory found that in majoritarian democracies, winners who supported the governing party consistently expressed far higher satisfaction with democracy than losers. In contrast, consensual democracies place a higher value on the inclusion of all political minorities in decision-making, giving less emphasis to accountability and the rotation of parties in power. Anderson and Guillory found that these systems produced a narrower gap in democratic satisfaction between winners and losers. Cross-national differences in system support could therefore be explained as the product of the *type* of democracy and the *distribution* of winners and losers in each country. Majoritarian system with few winners could be expected to be characterized by low aggregate levels of political support, while consensual democracies with many winners could be expected to display high satisfaction with democracy. It should be noted that this theory only takes account of the proportion of winners and losers (their distribution), not how much they win or lose (their strength).

Anderson and Guillory provided valuable theoretical insights and an innovative research design linking individual characteristics and macro-level contexts. This approach needs to be expanded, however, since the study suffers from certain limitations. First, the use of *'satisfaction with democracy'* as the indicator of system support is open to challenge, since as previous authors in this book have noted, this measure is ambiguous. Responses may be reporting instrumental satisfaction with the performance of government, or they may be expressing more general approval of the *idea* of democracy. Secondly, by focusing only on European Union member states the study was necessarily restricted to a limited range of established parliamentary democracies and we need to widen the scope of the comparison, for example to presidential systems. The broader the institutional variance, the more confidence we can have in the results. Moreover, the analysis is of limited value for issues of constitutional design in emerging and transitional democracies, since it is not clear what specific institutions within majoritarian or consensual systems influ-

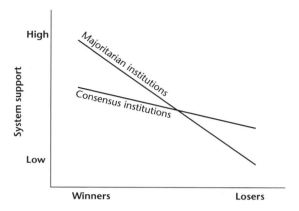

Fig. 11.1. Model of system support.

enced levels of public support: whether the electoral system played the most important role, for example, or whether the division of executive and legislative powers was also significant. Equally important, recent work has thrown doubt on Lijphart's classification of democracies into the consociational and majoritarian categories. Comparisons have found that in practice there is as much institutional variation within, as between, these ideal-types (Lane and Ersson 1996; McRae 1997).

For all these reasons we therefore need to extend this approach by comparing a wider range of institutional arrangements and a broader span of established and newer democracies. The logic of our research design in exploring these issues, following Anderson and Guillory, is to test whether consensual institutions which maximize the number of 'winners' produce higher levels of institutional confidence than winner-take-all majoritarian arrangements. This chapter compares how institutional confidence varies according to the overall levels of political rights and civil liberties in each country, as a summary indicator of the level of democratization, and then who 'wins' and 'loses' within each system. We will then compare the most important constitutional arrangements which vary between nations including the executive–legislative relationship, party systems, electoral systems, and federal or unitary states.

The Research Design

Our research design requires comparison among a broad range of political systems. We therefore draw on the *World Values Surveys* which tapped public opinion in 24 nations in 1981–4 and 43 nations in 1990–1. We also re-analyse some of the data from the *World Values Survey* 1995–7 provided by Hans-Dieter Klingemann in Chapter 2. To analyse confidence in parliament we also draw on the *Latinobarometer* covering 17 nations in 1996 and the *Eurobarometer* in 1996 (Europinion 9) covering 17 states.[1] For our multivariate analysis for a consistent comparative universe we focus on 25 major democracies, defined as countries with a population of 3 million or more, and with a Gastil Political Rights score of 4 or less at the time of the survey, based on the Freedom House monitor (McColm 1991). This included in total 41,791 respondents living in the Americas (the United States, Canada, Mexico, Brazil, and Chile), Central and Eastern Europe (Hungary and Czechoslovakia), Asia (Japan and India), Scandinavia (Denmark, Norway, Sweden, and Finland), and Western Europe (France, Britain, West Germany, Italy, Netherlands, Belgium, Spain, Ireland, Switzerland, Portugal, Austria, and Turkey). This universe included a wide array of political systems—including presidential and parliamentary executives, federal and unitary states, and significant variations in party and electoral systems—as well as established and newer democracies, and developed and developing economies. We excluded countries where the voting intention question was not asked in the *World Values Survey*[2] and also non-democracies at the time of the survey (rated between 4.5 to 7 in the Freedom House scale), such as China, Romania, and Nigeria.[3]

Measure of Institutional Confidence

The dependent variables for analysis concern confidence in parliament and then combined confidence in five major political and civic institutions, including parliament, the civil service, the legal system, the police, and the army. These items do not refer directly to the government, particular parties in office, or political authorities, but rather to broad attitudes towards the major institutions of state, which makes them suitable measures for our purposes. Given the range of political systems under comparison, these items are also more suitable than more value-laden questions relating to 'satisfaction with democracy'. Responses to these five items were highly inter-correlated, forming a reliable scale (Cronbach's Alpha = .75), suggesting that they reflected a general orientation towards political institutions rather than specific attitudes towards each one. The combined Institutional Confidence Scale ranged from 6 to 24 points.

Winner and Losers

Based on our earlier arguments, we can develop some testable propositions. First, we would expect that (*H1*) 'winners' would have higher confidence in

---

[1] Information about the parties in government came from the *Political Data Handbook* 2nd Edition edited by Jan-Erik Lane, David McKay and Kenneth Newton (Oxford: Oxford University Press 1997).

[2] Including Argentina, Lithuania, Latvia, Estonia, China, and Russia.

[3] It was anticipated that reactions towards the political system monitored through surveys might carry very different connotations to citizens in authoritarian regimes.

governing institutions than 'losers'. This is what Holmberg (Chapter 5) refers to as the 'Home Team' hypothesis. The 'winners' and 'losers' within each country were defined according to the voting intentions of respondents, and whether they supported a party which formed part of the government.

Political Rights and Civil Liberties

Within democracies we would expect *(H2)* the existence of widespread political rights and civil liberties should be associated with higher levels of public confidence in the regime. We can examine this using the Gastil Index published by Freedom House which monitors countries world-wide on an annual basis(McColm 1991). We used the monitor for the year prior to the survey in each country. Political rights are measured using a seven-point scale including such items as whether elections are free and fair, whether people have the right to organize competing parties, and whether minority groups have reasonable participation in the decision-making process. Civil liberties are gauged in a similar way monitoring, for example, whether there is a free and independent media, whether there is protection from political terror, and whether there is freedom of religion. The mean combined score for political rights and civil liberties was used in the analysis.

Presidential vs. Parliamentary Systems

Within democracies there is a major distinction between parliamentary and presidential systems. The merits of these systems have been widely debated (Lijphart 1992). Linz (1990) claims that presidentialism with a weak legislature has the advantages of executive stability, greater popular control, and more limited government, but the disadvantages of executive–legislative deadlock, temporal rigidity and winner-take-all government. Parliamentarianism is claimed to reverse the pros and cons. Therefore our hypothesis, based on Linz's arguments and our prior assumptions, would be to expect that *(H3)* parliamentary systems, where all parties continue to have a stake in the policy-making process, should generate greater system support than winner-take-all presidential systems. Democracies can be categorized based on Lijphart's (1992) three-fold definition: (1)In presidential systems the head of government has a fixed term of office, in parliamentary systems the head of government is dependent upon the confidence of the legislature; (2) presidents are elected (directly or by electoral college) whereas prime ministers are selected by the legislature; and (3) presidents have one-person, non-collegial executives whereas parliamentary systems have collective executives. Most Western European democracies, as well as countries which were former British colonies, are parliamentary systems. In contrast, many nations influenced by the United States adopted presidentialism, including the Spanish and Portuguese colonies in Latin America, the Philippines, and South Korea.

World-wide there are around 55 parliamentary and 78 presidential executives, plus 12 semi-presidential (or dual) executives (Derbyshire and Derbyshire 1996). The democracies under comparison in this chapter fall roughly equally into the parliamentary and presidential categories, based on the criteria of direct election to the executive, although some semi-presidential systems like France and Finland are more difficult to classify (LeDuc *et al*. 1996: 283–4).

Party Systems

Parties remain the most important mediating institutions between citizens and the state, the focus of many previous studies of system support. The existence of minor 'protest parties', especially those on the right, has been found to act as a channel for disaffected voters (Miller and Listhaug 1990), although Weil (1989) found that party fragmentation or polarization was associated with lower levels of democratic support overall. De-alignment among the American electorate, combined with greater ideological polarization among the Republicans and Democrats in Congress, may have weakened the linkages between voters and their representatives in the United States (Nye *et al*. 1997).

To analyse this more systematically we need to compare party systems, meaning the durable structure of party competition in government and in the electorate. In a classic study, Sartori (1976) classified systems by two principle dimensions: the strength of parties, conventionally measured by votes in the electorate and seats in parliament, and the position of parties across the ideological spectrum. This yielded four principal types of party system: *predominant one-party* systems where one party consistently wins a majority of parliamentary seats; *two-party* systems, characterized by few parties and a small ideological distance; *moderate pluralism* characterized by multi-parties and a small ideological distance; and *polarized pluralism* characterized by extreme multi-partyism and a large ideological distance. To compare a diverse range of polities we need to count the number of parties, although the practical problem is how to measure those of unequal size, particularly very small ones. This chapter uses the Laakso and Taagpera index to estimate the 'effective' number of parties in parliament (ENPP) (Laakso and Taagepera 1979; Lijphart 1994*a*), based on seat shares in the lower house (Leduc *et al*. 1996, Table 1.4).

Building on Powell's (1989) argument, we would predict that in countries with predominant one-party government and fragmented oppositions it is extremely difficult for citizens to use elections as an opportunity to 'kick the rascals out', if dissatisfied with the performance of officeholders. This pattern certainly seems to fit some of the anecdotal evidence about Japan and Italy, both countries which have experienced considerable economic growth yet with predominant one-party systems throughout most of the post-war period. The net effect may have been to make successive governments unaccountable and unresponsive to public opinion, producing disillusionment with the political system in general. Fragmented party systems are characterized by ideological polarization, weak and unstable coalition governments, and bidding war, whereas systems with a few broadly based and centrist parties are better placed to aggregate interests into broad social and ideological coalitions. In contrast, we expect two-party and moderate multi-party systems to function more effectively as a mechanism for translating electoral choices into government policy. On this basis we hypothesize that (*H4*) countries with two-party and moderate multi-party systems should have the highest levels of institutional support.

Federal vs. Unitary States

Democracies can also be classified into unitary and federal states. In unitary systems the state is one and indivisible, meaning that the central government exercises authority over the population directly, whereas in federal systems the central government shares authority with other states within its own territory. Lane and Ersson's comparison classifies most countries within the new Europe as unitary, with the exceptions of Germany, Switzerland, Austria, and Belgium, with perhaps a semi-federal model with decentralized regions in Spain and Italy (Lane and Ersson 1996). Other federal states within our comparison include India, Brazil, Mexico, and Canada, and the United States. World-wide only 24 out of 192 states have a federal structure (Derbyshire and Derbyshire 1996), although many more have adopted some form of regional decentralization. Federal states are common in deeply divided societies, characterized by a historical legacy of strong ethnic and/or religious cleavages, and also in countries with a large land mass, like Canada, Australia, and Brazil. In terms of confidence in government, advocates like Elazar argue that federalism manages to accommodate simultaneously the needs of different regions, and different groups in the electorate, whereas unitary states allow less flexibility and produce more losers from the system (Elazar 1997). In the light of this thesis, based on our previous assumptions, we would expect that (*H5*) federal systems should produce higher levels of institutional support than unitary states.

Electoral Systems

The electoral system can also be expected to play a major role linking citizens and the state. Ever since the seminal early studies (Duverger 1969; Rae 1971), a flourishing literature has classified the main types of electoral systems and sought to analyse their consequences (Lijphart 1994*a*; Lijphart and Grofman 1984; LeDuc *et al.* 1996; Bogdanor and Butler 1983; Taagepera and Shugart 1989; Farrell 1997; Cox 1997; Norris 1997*b*; IDEA 1997). Systems vary according to district magnitude, ballot structures, effective thresholds, malapportionment, assembly size, and open/closed lists, but the most important variations concern electoral formula which determine how votes are counted to allocate seats. There are four main types: *majoritarian* formulas (including plurality, second ballot, and alternative voting systems); *semi-proportional* systems (such as the single transferable vote, the cumulative vote, and the limited vote); *proportional representation* (including open and closed party lists using largest remainders and highest averages formula); and, *mixed* systems (like the Additional Member System combining majoritarian and proportional elements). We will therefore compare electoral formula used for the lower house of the national legislature in each country (LeDuc *et al.* 1996, Table 1.2). We can also measure the degree of proportionality of electoral systems as an alternative indicator of electoral system effects. Based on our assumptions, we would expect that (*H6*) majoritarian systems should produce less institutional support than proportional systems. Mixed and semi-proportional systems could be expected to fall somewhere between these poles. To summarize, the core propositions tested within this chapter are listed in Table 11.1.

Table 11.1. Summary of core hypotheses

Hypotheses	Positive support	Negative support
Support for party in government	Winners	Losers
Level of democratization	Extensive political rights and civil liberties	Restricted political rights and civil liberties
Executive	Parliamentary	Presidential
Party system	Moderate multi-party	Other
State structure	Federal	Unitary
Electoral system	Proportional	Majoritarian

Ordinary least-squared regression models were used to examine the *direct* effects of constitutional arrangements on institutional confidence including the impact backing 'winning' and 'losing' parties in the system, levels of political rights and civil liberties, types of executives, party systems, federalism, and electoral systems, as already defined. To compare the relative explanatory power of institutional factors with alternative theories we subsequently develop models which control for (1) differences in political culture, using the standard (four-item) measure of post-materialism; (2) differences in economic development, as measured by per capita GNP in 1990; and, (3) the usual social background variables (age, income, education, and gender) which have often been found to be associated with variations in political attitudes.

Cross-national Variations in Institutional Confidence

First, we can examine the distribution of institutional confidence at macro level among different democracies. Looking first at public support for parliaments—the main institution linking citizens and the state in representative democracies—the evidence from different surveys in the mid-1990s presented in Table 11.2 demonstrates the proportion who said that they had 'a great deal' or 'a lot' of confidence in parliament. Two themes emerge from the results. First, there were substantial cross-national variations in responses ranging from countries like Norway, South Africa, and the Netherlands, where half or more of citizens expressed confidence in parliament, down to countries such as Venezuela, Panama, and Columbia where less than a fifth of all people expressed support. The second theme was the remarkably low level of confidence displayed in most newer democracies, especially in the Americas and Eastern Europe, as well as in established democracies like Italy, West Germany, and Finland. As shown earlier (Table 2.11), where we have evidence of change from the early to the mid-1990s, the *World Values Surveys* monitored declining confidence in parliament in 15 out of the 22 countries, often by substantial amounts.

Nor is this pattern confined to legislatures. As shown in Figure 11.2, we can compare the results of the combined scale of Institutional Confidence, including the mean level of confidence in parliament, the civil service, the legal system, the police, and the army, as monitored by the *World Values Survey* in the early 1990s. As expected we confirmed considerable cross-national variations in support, with citizens in Mexico, Italy, and Czechoslovakia (which was going through a significant upheaval at the time of the survey) displaying least confidence in their political institutions. Japan also displayed widespread lack of confidence, confirming other observations (Pharr 1997), as did Spain and Portugal, both newer democracies which had been through the transition process during the 1970s. At the other end of the spectrum, citizens proved most confident of their regime institutions in many Anglo-American democracies, including India, Ireland, Britain, the United States, and Canada. Confidence in Congress may have declined over time within America (Hibbing and Theiss-Morse 1995), but even so, compared with many other nations, institutional support in the United States remains relatively high. Citizens were also relatively positive about their institutions in Norway and Denmark, as noted earlier by Holmberg (Chapter 5).

To analyse trends over time we can compare institutional confidence in seventeen countries included in both the 1981–4 and 1990–3 *World Values Surveys*. With only two points of comparison, we cannot monitor secular trends, since both measurements could be at a particular point in a cycle, but we can measure the direction of differences over time. The results are quite striking and consistent: institutional support declined slightly in every country under comparison although usually by only a modest amount. France, the Netherlands, and West Germany remained fairly stable, while countries characterized by relatively low support, including Japan, Italy, and Mexico, drifted only marginally downwards. Only Finland, Argentina, and South Korea fell by more than one point during this period, and the shifts over time were rarely sufficient to change the rank order of countries on the scale. Given the overall stability of institutional arrangements, and their performance, this pattern was to be expected. This analysis further confirms some of the trends already observed elsewhere in this volume (see in particular Chapters 2, 3, and 9).

Table 11.2. Confidence in parliament, mid-1990s

Country	Global regions					
	Western Europe	Eastern Europe	Pacific Rim	Africa	North & Central America	South America
Norway	69					
South Africa				60		
Netherlands**	53					
Ireland**	50					
Turkey	48					
France**	48					
Sweden	45					
Estonia		44				
Britain**	44					
Chile*						43
Belgium**	42					
Denmark**	42					
Paraguay*						42
Nicaragua*					39	
Uruguay*						38
Canada					37	
Nigeria				37		
Spain	37					
Finland	33					
Peru*						33
Guatemala*					32	
El Salvador*					31	
Italy**	31					
Australia			30			
Belarus		30				
United States					30	
West Germany	29					
Ecuador*					27	
Japan			27			
Honduras*					26	
Lithuania		26				
Argentina*						25
Latvia		25				
Slovenia		25				
Russia		23				
Mexico*					22	
Bolivia*						21
Costa Rica*					20	
Brazil*						19
Venezuela*						19
East Germany		17				
Panama*					16	
Colombia*						15

Note: Unless marked otherwise, cells show percentage of respondents indicating 'a great deal' or 'a lot' of confidence in parliament.

Source: *Latinobarometer* 1996; **Eurobarometer* 1996; Table 2.11.

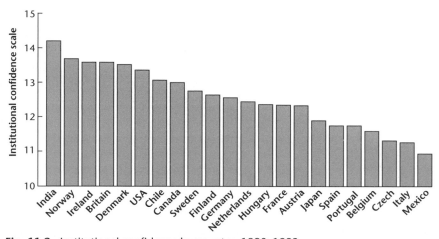

Fig. 11.2. Institutional confidence by country, 1990–1993.
Source: World Values Surveys 1990–3.

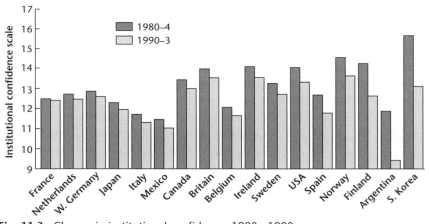

Fig. 11.3. Change in institutional confidence, 1980s–1990s.
Source: World Values Surveys.

To see how this pattern relates to our first main hypothesis we can compare institutional support in 1990–3 among the winners and losers within each nation. As shown in Figure 11.4 there is a clear and consistent pattern: winners who backed the party or parties in government consistently displayed greater confidence in political institutions in every country except one (France). This nicely replicates and confirms the earlier findings of Anderson and Guillory (1997) who compared democratic satisfaction in the *Eurobarometer* in a more limited range of countries. Moreover the gap between winners and losers was particularly marked in three countries which at the

230   **Explanations of Trends**

time of the second survey (1990–3) had been characterized by long periods of one-party predominant government and fragmented oppositions (Pempel 1990), notably Mexico (the PRI), Japan (the LDP), and Italy (the Christian Democrats). In such systems, the losers have been consistently excluded from power over successive elections, and we might expect them to lack faith in political institutions. More recent reforms in these systems might have proved unable to disturb the accumulated experience of successive generations.

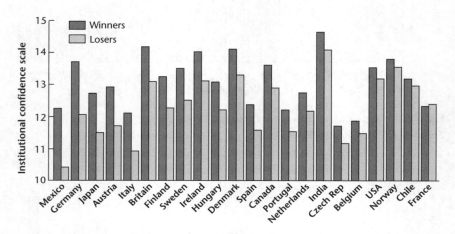

Fig. 11.4. Institutional confidence: winners and losers.
Source: World Values Surveys 1990–3.

We can compare the relationship between public evaluations of the performance of democracy in their own country, using data provided by Hans-Dieter Klingemann in Table 2.10, against the Freedom House combined rating of the actual level of political rights and civil liberties (with a reversed scale ranging from low (1) to high (7)) in each country in the mid-1990s. The results, in Figure 11.5, show a pattern which produces a moderately strong correlation (r = .21). Citizens in countries classified as low on the Freedom House rating of political rights and civil liberties, such as Russia, Mexico, and the Ukraine, tend to give poor marks to the performance of democracy in their country. On the other hand, those countries which are regarded as fully democratic by the Freedom House index tend to show far higher evaluations of democracy in their country. Yet there are some exceptions, for example citizens in Italy, Hungary, and Chile, all countries rated as highly democratic by Freedom House, give relatively low evaluations of the performance of democracy in their countries. On the other hand, the performance of democracy in Albania, which continues to have many problems of human rights, is rated relatively positively by its citizens. There may also be a 'ceiling' effect in the Freedom House grading schema: among established democracies rated highly (grade 7)

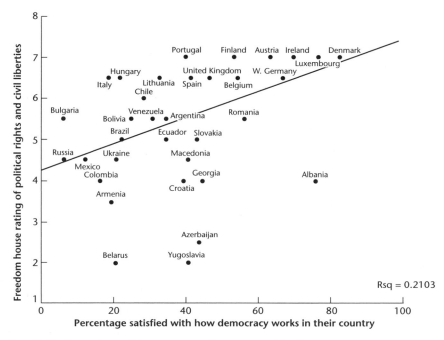

Fig. 11.5. Evaluations of democratic performance, mid-1990s.
Sources: Klingemann, Ch. 2 this vol., Table 2.10; Freedom House 1997.

by the Freedom House index, there is a wide spectrum of public satisfaction with democratic performance between countries like Denmark and Portugal. Nevertheless despite these outliers this overall pattern tends to suggest that there is a link between independent evaluations of political rights and civil liberties and public assessments. If so, lack of trust in the political system is not simply an affective attitude, or the product of early socialization, or the result of the ability of governments to deliver peace and prosperity. Instead support for the political system among citizens seems to reflect, quite accurately, independent judgements of the actual performance of regimes in terms of the level of democratization. If political systems are characterized by extensive political rights and civil liberties, then this is associated with more positive evaluations by citizens. In contrast, where governments do not deserve trust, then it is indeed often absent.

To analyse this pattern at the individual level we can use ordinary least-squared regression analysis in a multivariate model, with the institutional confidence scale as the dependent variable in 25 major democracies. We first entered the indicators of political rights and civil liberties, and whether respondents were winners and losers from the system. We then added in the main institutional variables and the controls in terms of post-material values, levels of economic development, and the social background of respondents.

The results in Table 11.2 confirm the first two hypotheses. Whether respondents were classified as winners (who endorsed the governing party or parties) or losers (who backed one of the opposition parties) was significantly related to their level of institutional confidence. Moreover, the level of democratization also proved important (H2): citizens express more confidence in countries where, according to the Freedom House classification, there are widespread opportunities for civic participation and protection of human rights. We might expect that the level of democratization might prove even more significant in a wider range of political systems, if we compared democratic and authoritarian regimes, and this is worth exploring further in future research.

Table 11.3. Models of institutional confidence

	Beta	Sig.	Coding
Political system:			
Level of democratization	.10	**	Combined mean political rights and civil liberties (1 = low 7 = high) (Freedom House index)
Win/Lose	.11	**	Endorses governing party (1)/Not(0)
Executive	.02	*	Parliamentary (1); or presidential (0)
Federalism	−.06	**	Federal (1); or unitary dtate (0)
Party system	.10	**	ENPP recoded into two-party and moderate multi-party (1); other (0)
Electoral system	−.15	**	Majoritarian (0); Mixed (0.5); or PR (1)
Cultural and economic factors:			
Post-materialism	.12	**	Postmaterialist (1) Mixed (2) Materialist(3)
Economic development	.09	**	Per capita GNP 1990
Social background:			
Age	.12	**	Years old
Gender	−.02	**	Male (1); Female (0)
Socioeconomic status	−.02	*	Respondent's occupational scale
Education	.07	**	Age completed education (1–10 scale)
Adjusted R2	.09		

Note: The figures represent standardized beta OLS regression coefficients with institutional confidence as the dependent variable.
Source: *World Values Survey* 1990–3 in 25 democracies (N. = 38,828).

All the institutional variables proved significant but not necessarily in the direction predicted by our hypotheses 3–6. The clearest confirmation was found for (H4): countries with two-party and moderate multi-party systems had the highest levels of institutional confidence. As argued earlier, this suggests that parties are important institutions linking citizens and the state, and both fragmented party systems and predominant one-party systems produce governments which may be regarded as unaccountable and unresponsive to public opinion. Moreover, institutional confidence did prove to be slightly higher in parliamentary than in presidential systems, as predicted in (H3), although the difference was extremely modest.

Yet contrary to our hypothesis 5, institutional confidence proved to be greater in unitary than federal states. We can speculate that this may be a problem of operationalization, if federalism is a poor indicator of decentralization per se (Lane and Ersson 1996). Interpreted in this light, this suggests that we may need better indicators of the devolution to regional and local governments before we can examine whether a broader distribution of powers produces greater system satisfaction. An alternative interpretation is that unitary states may increase public confidence through producing accountability and responsible party government. These arguments cannot be explored further here but they deserve further investigation in future research.

Moreover, contrary to (H6), confidence was also greater in countries with majoritarian rather than proportional electoral systems. This comparison of a broader range of countries therefore challenges Anderson and Guillory's (1997) thesis that consociational democracies generate higher system support than majoritarian systems. Our findings indicate that institutional confidence is most likely to be highest in parliamentary democracies characterized by plurality electoral systems, two-party or moderate multi-party systems, and unitary states.

Lastly, we found that these relationships were confirmed even after controlling for differences in levels of economic development and post-material values. In terms of the social background of respondents, older respondents expressed more confidence in the system, as previous studies have commonly found, education was also related to institutional confidence, while the influence of socioeconomic status and gender proved very modest. Therefore using a different data-set and different measures of system support, the results replicate one of the main theoretical principle of Anderson and Guillory (1997): winners express more confidence in the system than losers. Nevertheless by comparing a wider range of countries than previous studies we found that majoritarian institutions tended to produce greater institutional confidence than consociational arrangements. Based on this analysis the core thesis—that institutions have the capacity to influence attitudes towards the regime—does seem a plausible proposition worthy of further exploration.

Conclusions and Implications

The study started from the premiss that regime support reflects the general constitutional arrangements which structure behaviour and attitudes towards governance into stable and predictable patterns. We found that *citizens who live in democracies with a strong tradition of civil liberties expressed considerable confidence in their political system.* In contrast, people are more sceptical about government, for good reason, in states which lack such conditions, for example where there is widespread electoral corruption and intimidation, where opposition publications are censored or banned, and where rights to protest are suppressed. This finding may seem obvious, but, perhaps surprisingly, it has rarely been examined systematically in comparative studies, perhaps because these have usually focused on Western democracies where such rights are taken for granted.

Secondly, we found that *evaluations of the political regime reflect our experience of whether we are winners or losers over successive elections*, defined by whether the party we endorse is returned to government. Democratic institutions represent intermediary mechanisms linking public preferences with the performance of the state. In this regard institutions are not neutral. Instead the arrangements—whether for majoritarian or proportional electoral systems, federal or unitary states, and presidential or parliamentary executives—consistently rule some groups into, and some groups out of, the decision-making process (Powell 1989). We confirmed that people who voted for the governing party or parties are more likely to believe that the political system is responsive to their needs. In contrast, losers in elections are less satisfied with the way democracy works. Cynicism is highest in countries which produce many persistent losers over successive elections, for example, systems governed by one-party predominant parties facing a fragmented opposition. Lastly, we can conclude that *institutional arrangements are significantly related to political support*: majoritarian electoral systems and moderate multi-party systems, in particular, tend to generate slightly higher levels of institutional confidence than alternative arrangements.

The implications of these findings may be significant for at least two distinct reasons. First, theoretically this question throws light on the general issue of whether institutions matter (Weaver and Rockman 1993). One of the basic assumptions of 'new institutionalism' is that individual behaviour is constrained and channelled by its rule-based institutional context. If so, the research traditions seeking to explain system support based on long-standing cultural values, or the political economy of government performance, need to be supplemented by taking account of the mediating influence of political institutions.

Equally importantly, if institutional confidence is systematically and consistently related to institutional design this may have significant implications for public policy. The constitutional order and the basic rules of the game, like electoral systems, are usually regarded as fairly stable features of the political landscape. Yet the wave of constitution-building following the explosion of new democracies during the 'third wave', combined with new pressures on institutional reform in many established democracies, has encouraged greater interest in the choices involved in 'constitutional engineering' (Sartori 1994) and 'institutional design' (Lijphart and Waisman 1996). Constitutional debates—whether about electoral systems, devolution or executive–legislative relations—have risen on the policy agenda to become first-order issues in countries as diverse as South Africa, New Zealand, Russia, Canada, Mexico, Italy, Japan, and the United Kingdom (Laponce and Saint-Jacques 1997). If institutional arrangements influence political support, as we found, this may have important consequences for constitutional debates. The challenge for further research is to consider these issues in terms of the democratization process and to monitor how institutional confidence varies within countries which change their constitutional arrangements, like New Zealand, Italy, and Japan. Some nations seem to have managed the successful transitions towards consolidated democracies, including South Africa, the Czech Republic, and Argentina, generating a reservoir of support among the public to tide the political regime through good times and bad, but in contrast other fledgling democracies like Nigeria have reverted back towards authoritarian rule. If institutional designs can strengthen public support for the regime this may provide significant lessons for the process of democratization.

12

Postmodernization Erodes Respect for Authority, but Increases Support for Democracy

RONALD INGLEHART

THE post-modern phase of development leads to declining respect for authority among the publics of advanced industrial societies—but at the same time, it gives rise to growing support for democracy. This phenomenon has contributed to declining trust in government in the United States and other advanced industrial societies. Governing has become more difficult than it used to be: the tendency to idealize authority that characterized societies of scarcity has given way to the more critical and demanding publics of post-modern societies. Authority figures and hierarchical institutions are subjected to more searching scrutiny than they once were. But does this mean that people are losing confidence in democratic values? The analysis presented here indicates that the answer is an unequivocal 'No'. On the contrary, the same publics that are becoming increasingly critical of hierarchical authority, are also becoming increasingly resistant to authoritarian government, more interested in political life, and more apt to play an active role in politics. Although hierarchical political parties are losing control over their electorates, and elite-directed forms of participation such as voting are stagnant or declining, elite-challenging forms of participation are becoming more widespread, as Inglehart (1997a) has demonstrated. And though they tend to distrust political authority and big government, the publics of advanced industrial societies value democracy more, not less, than the publics of economically less secure societies. In the terms used elsewhere in this book, respect for the political leaders is generally declining in advanced industrial societies; but support for democratic principles is rising. These changes do not undermine democracy; they tend to make it more secure.

But these changes *do* make life more difficult for the governing elites. During the past forty years, a massive decline in trust in politicians has taken place among the US public. This phenomenon has given rise to a good deal of scholarly discussion (for an early view, see Miller 1974a; for more recent ones, see Craig 1993, and Nye *et al.* 1997). But there is sharp disagreement about *why* it has occurred. Has the public become fed up with the waste and ineffectiveness of big government? Has the public's sense of entitlement grown to the point where it outstrips anything government can realistically do, as Samuelson (1995) argues? Or are today's politicians more corrupt than ever before? While there is little evidence that today's public officials are less competent than previous ones, there are some indications that the growth of government has reached natural limits and people are less likely to see government as the solution to their problems. But this chapter argues that the decline of trust in political leaders has roots that go beyond these factors. It reflects a pervasive decline in deference to authority that is taking place throughout advanced industrial society.

Modernization, Postmodernization and Cultural Change

Why is deference to authority declining throughout advanced industrial society? In a recent book (Inglehart 1997*a*) I tested the hypothesis that economic development leads to specific, functionally related changes in mass values and belief systems. This revised version of modernization theory argues that once a society has embarked on industrialization, a whole syndrome of related changes, from social mobilization to diminishing differences in gender roles, are likely to occur. Though any simple, iron-law version of modernization theory has long since been refuted, we do endorse the idea that some scenarios of social change are far more probable than others.

Furthermore, modernization is not linear. In advanced industrial societies, the prevailing direction of development has changed in the last quarter-century and the change of direction is so fundamental that it seems appropriate to describe it as 'postmodernization', rather than 'modernization'. Modernization was facilitated by the emergence of a worldview of materialistic rationality. The rise of advanced industrial society leads to a second fundamental shift in basic values—a shift from the instrumental rationality that characterized industrial society, toward increasing emphasis on individual self-expression.

For Weber, the key to Modernization was the shift from a religion-oriented world-view to a rational-legal world-view. Key components of Modernization were:

- Secularization: The rise of the scientific worldview was one factor that led to the decline of the sacred/pre-rational elements of religious faith. Religious orientations were central in most pre-industrial societies. In the uncertain world of subsistence agriculture, the need for absolute standards and faith in an infallible higher power, filled a major psychological need. One of the key functions of religion was to provide a sense of certainty in an insecure environment. Physical as well as economic insecurity intensifies this need: the old saying that 'there are no atheists in foxholes' reflects the fact that physical danger leads to a need for belief in a higher power. More recently, the rise of a sense of security among mass publics of advanced welfare states has become an equally important factor in the decline of traditional religious orientations.

- Bureaucratization: This reflects the rise of 'rational' organizations, based on rules designed to move efficiently toward explicit goals, with recruitment based on impersonal goal-oriented achievement standards. During the first phase of industrialization, it seemed (to Marxists and non-Marxists alike) that the direction of social evolution was toward the increasing subordination of the individual to a 'leviathan' state having superhuman powers. The state would become an omnipotent and benevolent entity, replacing God in a secular world. And for most of the nineteenth and twentieth centuries, the dominant trend (the wave of the future, as it was sometimes called) was a shift from societal authority toward state authority, manifested in the apparently inexorable growth of the economic, political, and social role of government.

The Postmodern Shift

The socialist 'leviathan' state *was* the logical culmination of the modernization process, but it did not turn out to be the wave of the future. Instead, the expansion of the bureaucratic state eventually approached a set of natural limits, and change began to move in a new direction. Figure 12.1 illustrates what happened. From the Industrial Revolution until well into the second half of the twentieth century, industrial society underwent modernization. This process transformed political and cultural systems from traditional regimes legitimated by religious belief systems, to rational-legal states legitimated by their claim to maximize the welfare of their people through scientific expertise. It was a transfer of authority from family and religious institutions, to political institutions.

Within the last few decades, a major deflection in the direction of change has occurred that might be called the 'Postmodern shift'. Its origins are rooted in the economic miracles that occurred first in Western Europe and North America, and later in East Asia and now in Southeast Asia. Coupled with the safety net of the modern welfare state, this has produced unprecedentedly high levels of economic security, giving rise to a cultural feedback that is having a major impact on both the economic and political systems of advanced industrial societies. This new trajectory shifts authority away from *both* religion and the state to the individual, with an increasing focus on individual concerns such as friends and leisure. Postmodernization de-emphasizes *all* kinds of authority, whether religious or secular, allowing much wider range for individual autonomy in the pursuit of individual subjective well-being.

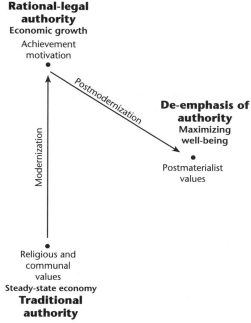

Fig. 12.1. The shift from Modernization to Postmodernization: changing emphasis on key aspects of life.

Source: Inglehart 1997a: 75.

The findings from the *World Values Surveys* indicate that in global perspective, a wide range of seemingly diverse orientations go together in coherent patterns. For example, certain societies place relatively heavy emphasis on religion—and the people of these societies also show high levels of national pride, and prefer to have relatively large families, and would like to see more respect for authority; furthermore, the peoples of these societies tend to rank relatively low on achievement motivation and political interest, oppose divorce, and have a number of other distinctive cultural orientations. The people of other societies consistently fall toward the opposite end of the spectrum on all of these orientations, giving rise to a dimension that reflects traditional vs. secular-rational orientations. This dimension reflects cross-national variation linked with varying degrees of modernization.

In the Postmodernization phase of development, emphasis shifts from maximizing economic gains to maximizing subjective well-being. This gives rise to another major dimension of cross-cultural variation, on which a wide range of orientations are structured. Postmaterialist values are a central element in this broader Postmodern syndrome. Societies with large numbers of Postmaterialists are characterized by relatively high levels of subjective well-being. Their publics emphasize tolerance and imagination as important qualities to teach a child, rather than hard work. They emphasize careers for women more and the role of mother less, than societies located near the left-hand pole. The people of societies emphasizing well-being values tend to have relatively little faith that scientific advances will help, rather than harm, humanity, and they tend to doubt that more emphasis on technology would be a good thing. Conversely, the people of these societies have relatively high levels of support for the ecology movement. The fact that societies with high levels of security tend to de-emphasize economic growth, science, and technology, is a major departure from the basic thrust of Modernization: this dimension reflects change in a Postmodern direction.

Both modernization and postmodernization are linked with economic development. We find coherent differences between the belief systems of rich and poor countries: though the process of modernization is not quite as automatic or linear as Marx claimed, economic development clearly *is* linked with major changes in world-views.

One of the most basic of these cultural changes is a shift in orientations toward authority. As Figure 12.1 indicates, we find that:

- Modernization brings a shift from traditional-religious authority, toward rational-bureaucratic authority and the rise of the modern state; and that

- Post-modernization brings a shift away from *both* traditional and state authority.

If economic development is indeed conducive to declining respect for authority, it should show up in cross-sectional comparisons: the publics of rich societies should be less likely to emphasize authority than those of poorer ones. Inglehart (1997a) tested this proposition, finding that it was true. The idea that '*More respect for authority would be a good thing*' is part of a coherent world-view that is much less likely to be found in rich societies than in poor ones. The data from the third wave of the *World Values Surveys* enable us to test this finding in a considerably larger number of societies than have ever before been available. As Figure 12.2 demonstrates (using the latest available data from a total of 57 societies), the finding is confirmed strongly. The correlation between the percentage who feel that '*more respect for authority would be a good thing*' and the society's per capita GNP is −.62, significant at the .0000 level. This suggests that as economic development takes place, respect for authority tends to decline.

It is not a matter of simple economic determinism, however. The five Nordic societies (all relatively rich, and characterized by the most Postmodern values of any group of countries in the world) all rank low on this variable. But the four Confucian societies also tend to rank low on this variable, despite the fact that Japan is rich, while Taiwan and South Korea are much less so, and China is somewhat relatively poor. Nevertheless, the overall correlation with economic development is strong and highly significant.

With modernization, people increasingly looked to the state, rather than to a Supreme Being, to provide security. During the past several decades in

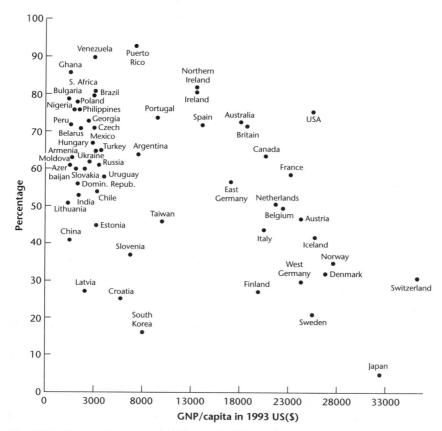

Fig. 12.2. Support for authoritarian values, by level of economic development. (r = −.62 p < .000).

Note: Percentage of respondents wanting '*more respect for authority*' by level of economic development.

Sources: World Values Surveys 1981–96.

advanced industrial society, peace, prosperity and the welfare state have produced an unprecedented sense of security that one will survive. This has diminished the need for the strong authority that religion and the centralized nation-state provided. Insecurity is conducive to xenophobia, a need for strong decisive leaders and deference to authority. Accordingly, the Great Depression gave rise to xenophobic and authoritarian politics in many societies around the world. A sense of security concerning one's survival has the opposite effect: people with Postmodern values are relatively tolerant of out-groups and may even regard exotic things and cultural diversity as stimulating and interesting, instead of finding them threatening. They seek out foreign restaurants and spend large amounts of money on travel to exotic places. The

Postmodern world-view emphasizes self-expression, rather than deference to authority. It is linked with declining acceptance of rigid religious norms concerning sex and reproduction, and a diminishing need for absolute rules. It also reflects a growing rejection of bureaucratic authority.

The Authoritarian Reflex and the Postmodern Shift

Some observers have interpreted the decline of trust in government as a sign of general alienation. Pointing to declining rates of voter turnout, they argue that the American public has become disenchanted with the entire system and withdrawn from politics completely. The empirical evidence contradicts this interpretation. Though voter turnout has stagnated (largely because of weakening political party loyalties), Western publics have *not* become apathetic: quite the contrary, in the last two decades, they have become markedly more likely to engage in elite-challenging forms of political participation. Furthermore, the erosion of trust does not apply to all institutions: it is specifically a withdrawal of confidence from authoritarian institutions. During the same period that trust in political authority was fading, environmental protection movements rose from obscurity to attain remarkably high levels of public confidence. In the 1990–1 *World Values Survey*, fully 93 per cent of these publics approved of the environmentalist movement—with 59 per cent approving 'strongly'. But support for certain types of institutions is sharply differentiated according to whether one has Materialist or Postmaterialist values, with Materialist being much more likely to support authoritarian institutions; and with the emergence of Postmaterialist values, authoritarian institutions suffered a decline in mass confidence throughout advanced industrial society.

Declining trust in government seems to be part of a broader erosion of respect for authority that is linked with the processes of modernization and postmodernization. Rapid change leads to severe insecurity, giving rise to an Authoritarian Reflex that may bring fundamentalist or xenophobic reactions or adulation of strong leaders. As we have argued, insecurity leads to a need for strong authority figures to protect one from threatening forces, and breeds an intolerance of cultural change, and of different ethnic groups.

Conversely, conditions of prosperity and security are conducive to greater emphasis on individual autonomy and diminishing deference to authority. Until recently, existential insecurity was a usual part of the human condition. Only recently have societies emerged in which most of the population does *not* have any fear of starvation (which is still a very real concern for much of humanity). Both pre-modern agrarian society and modern industrial society were shaped by survival values. The Postmodern shift has brought a broad de-emphasis on all forms of authority.

A major aspect of the Postmodern shift is a shift away from *both* religious and bureaucratic authority, bringing declining emphasis on all kinds of authority.

Deference to authority has high costs: the individual's personal goals must be subordinated to those of a broader entity. Under conditions of insecurity, people are more than willing to do so. Under threat of invasion, internal disorder or existential insecurity, people eagerly seek strong authority figures who can protect them. Conversely, the shift toward well-being values is linked with declining emphasis on political, religious and economic authority.

Declining Confidence in Hierarchical Institutions

Modern industrial society was made possible by two key institutions: the mass production assembly line and bureaucracy. These institutions made it possible to process huge numbers of products and huge numbers of people, using centrally controlled standardized routines. They were highly effective, but they sharply reduced individual autonomy. These hierarchical, centrally controlled institutions are becoming less acceptable in Postmodern society.

The rise of Postmodern values is bringing a move away from acceptance of both traditional authority and state authority. It reflects a declining emphasis on authority in general—regardless of whether it is legitimated by societal or state formulae. This leads to declining confidence in hierarchical institutions. For the past several years, political leaders throughout the industrialized world have been experiencing some of the lowest levels of support ever recorded. This is not simply because they are less competent than previous leaders. It reflects a systematic decline in deference to authority, and a shift of focus toward individual concerns.

Declining confidence in leaders and authoritarian institutions is not worldwide. We do not necessarily find it in developing nations. But declining respect for authority *is* pervasive throughout advanced industrial societies.

This phenomenon is not a decline of trust in *all* institutions. It is specifically linked with the emergence of Postmaterialist values and Postmodern values more generally. In virtually all advanced industrial societies, Postmaterialists are less likely to consider more respect for authority desirable, than are Materialists in the same society.

The decline in respect for authority seems to be taking place through a process of intergenerational change. As Figure 12.3 demonstrates, throughout advanced industrial society, the young are less likely than the old to feel that more respect for authority would be a good thing. The results from 18 societies having 1993 per capita incomes over $15,000 are generally similar, and for the sake of conciseness are combined into one category of 'advanced industrial societies' in this figure (these societies are: Austria, Belgium, Canada, Denmark, Finland, France, German Democratic Republic, Federal Republic of Germany, Iceland, Italy, Japan, the Netherlands, Norway, Spain, Sweden, Switzerland, the United Kingdom, and the United States). Throughout these societies, the older respondents are much more likely to say that '*more respect*

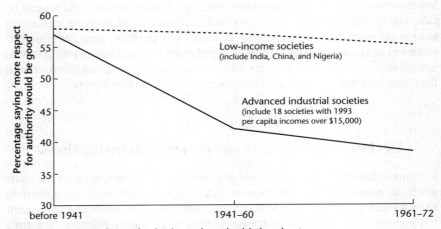

Fig. 12.3. Support for authoritarian values, by birth cohort.

Note: Percentage saying '*more respect for authority would be a good thing*', by birth cohort.

Source: 1990 *World Values Survey*.

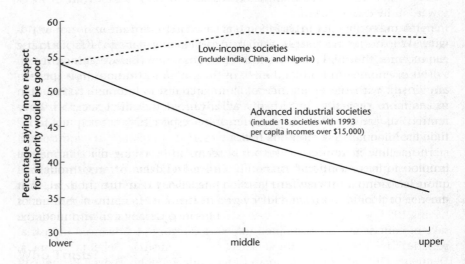

Fig. 12.4. Support for authoritarian values, by educational level.

Note: Percentage saying '*more respect for authority would be a good thing*', by educational level.

Source: 1990 *World Values Survey*.

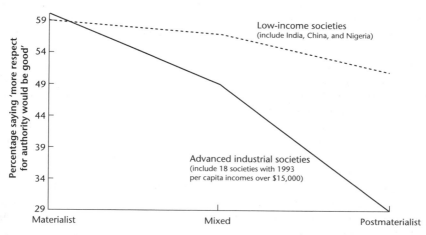

Fig. 12.5. Support for authoritarian values, by value type.

Note: *Percentage saying 'more respect for authority would be a good thing', by value type.*

Source: 1990 *World Values Survey.*

for authority would be a good thing' than are younger respondents. Weighting each country equally, we find a mean 19 percentage point gap between the attitudes of those over 50 and those under 30 years of age.[1]

We do *not* find significant age-related differences in the three low-income societies included in the *World Values Surveys*, India, China and Nigeria. In these societies, the young remain about as likely as the old to favour more respect for authority. In China, there is a modest tendency for the young to differ from the old, but in India and Nigeria, there is no difference whatever between the attitudes of old and young concerning respect for authority. The tendency for the old to place more emphasis on respect for authority is not something inherent in the human life-cycle; it reflects specific historic changes in specific societies.

If, as our theory implies, a shift toward less emphasis on respect for authority is linked with the rising levels of security, then we would expect to find less emphasis on authority among the more educated, since they tend to come from the economically more secure strata. As Figure 12.4 demonstrates, this is indeed the case—in advanced industrial societies, but *not* in low-income societies. Indeed, in low-income societies, the more educated place slightly *more* emphasis on respect for authority than do the less educated. Apparently, the intergenerational shift away from respect for authority is not inherently linked with education. In all three low-income societies, the most educated group is more likely to say that '*more respect for authority would be a good thing*'

---

[1] For the detailed country by country results, see Basanez, Inglehart, and Moreno (1998, Table 268).

than is the less educated group. This might be interpreted as a straightforward consequence of self-interest: the more educated tend to be the ones in authority. But this pattern applies only to low-income societies. Throughout advanced industrial society, the more educated are *less* likely to favour more respect for authority.

Theoretically, Materialist/Postmaterialist values are an even more direct indicator than is education, of the degree to which one experienced existential security during one's formative years. And as Figure 12.5 demonstrates, Materialist/Postmaterialist values are even more strongly linked with attitudes toward authority than are age or education. Since Postmaterialists are rare in the low-income societies and the few Postmaterialists present there have weakly crystallized values, the impact of Postmaterialism is mainly found in advanced industrial societies—but it is powerful there. Across the 18 advanced industrial societies examined here, we find a mean difference of 31 percentage points in attitudes toward authority (as compared with a spread of 19 points linked with birth cohort and, again, 19 points linked with education).

These findings have clear implications for social change. It has been demonstrated that Postmaterialist values have become increasingly widespread in advanced industrial societies; consequently we would expect to find growing acceptance of the entire broad range of post-modern orientations that are closely correlated with these values. Postmaterialists have less trust in *certain* institutions: as Inglehart (1997a) demonstrated, they show lower levels of confidence in their society's most hierarchical and authoritarian institutions—in particular, the armed forces, the police, and the church.

The hierarchical and authoritarian nature of the military and police is self-evident: they are based on unquestioning obedience of subordinates to superiors, and differences in rank are blatantly explicit: one can identify another person's rank at a glance. Though it deals with spiritual rather than secular power, the hierarchical nature of traditional churches is equally clear (indeed, the word 'hierarchy' itself, originally referred to the priesthood). Traditional religious institutions are anything but democratic. They explicitly require obedience to higher authority. Crucial decisions are decided by those in authority, not by discussion among equals or by majority vote.

As younger, more Postmaterialist cohorts have replaced older ones in the adult population, confidence in the most hierarchical institutions—the military, the police and the church—has declined over time in most advanced industrial societies .[2]

But Postmaterialism is not a form of paranoia. On the contrary, throughout advanced industrial society (but not necessarily in low-income societies,

---

[2] In the USA, confidence in the armed forces shows a deviant trend: the earliest time point at which it was measured in US surveys was during an abnormally low level during the Vietnam era; consequently, in the USA the long-term trend from the 1970s to the present is dominated by recovery from that extremely low level. But in most other advanced industrial societies, trust in the armed forces is clearly linked with materialist values and shows the same downward trend that we find in connection with attitudes toward the police and the church. And even in the USA, the *World Values Surveys* show a downward trend from 1981 to 1997.

where Postmaterialists are few), Postmaterialists have relatively *high* levels of trust in people in general. In the USA in 1990, for example, 43 per cent of the Materialists said that '*most people can be trusted*', while 63 per cent of the Postmaterialists did so. Furthermore, Postmaterialists show relatively *high* levels of confidence in non-hierarchical, non-authoritarian institutions such as the environmentalist movement and the women's movement. And they generally show as much or more trust in labour unions and the European Union as do Materialists.

Orientations toward various other institutions shows no consistent linkage with Materialist/Postmaterialist values: the relationship is situation-specific. In the USA, the Nordic countries, and the Netherlands, Postmaterialists have more trust in the educational system than do Materialists; but in the newer democracies and in authoritarian countries, Postmaterialists see the educational system as dominated by hierarchical authority, and have less trust in it than do Materialists. A similar pattern holds true of trust in parliament.

Predicted and Observed Changes in Norms Concerning Authority

Let us examine some actual changes that were predicted and observed in the three waves of the *World Values Surveys*. In the 1981 survey, we found a substantial correlation between attitudes toward authority and Materialist/Postmaterialist values across nearly all of the 21 countries for which we have data. Materialists tend to support the proposition that '*more respect for authority would be a good thing*', while Postmaterialists tend to reject it. Consequently, we predicted a gradual shift toward the values of the Postmaterialists—that is, toward less emphasis on respect for authority.

Table 12.1 tests this prediction. It shows that from 1981 to 1997, emphasis on more respect for authority became less widespread in 28 of the 36 countries for which we have time-series data. The absolute levels of support for authority, and the size of the changes from 1981 to 1997, vary a good deal from country to country.

Our prediction that this shift toward declining respect for authority would occur, is based on a simple population replacement model: as the younger, more Postmaterialist birth cohorts replace the older, more Materialist cohorts in the adult population, we should observe a shift toward the Postmodern orientation. Moreover, since the size of the respective cohorts is known from demographic data, and since we have survey data on the attitudes of the various birth cohorts, we can also estimate the *size* of the attitudinal shift that population replacement should produce over a 10-year period. We do this by simply removing the oldest 10-year cohort from our sample and replacing it with a new 10-year cohort at the youngest end. In creating this new cohort, we assume that it will have values similar to those of the youngest cohort in

Table 12.1. Respect for authority, 1981–1997

Country	1981	1990	1996	Change
Slovenia	—	66	37	−29
Chile	—	80	54	−26
W. Germany	45	30	23	−23
Italy	63	44	—	−19
E. Germany	—	57	39	−18
Switzerland	—	46	31	−15
Lithuania	—	53	38	−15
Canada	77	64	—	−13
Nigeria	—	91	79	−12
Hungary	72	61	—	−11
USA	85	77	76	−9
Sweden	30	22	21	−9
Russia	—	70	62	−8
Iceland	50	42	—	−8
Belgium	57	50	—	−7
Norway	37	32	31	−6
Spain	77	68	72	−5
N.Ireland	87	82	—	−5
Netherlands	54	51	—	−3
Mexico	68	65	65	−3
Belarus	—	71	68	−3
Japan	7	6	5	−2
Great Britain	74	72	—	−2
Finland	29	26	27	−2
France	60	59	—	−1
Turkey	—	65	65	0
Ireland	80	81	—	+1
Brazil	—	81	83	+2
Argentina	61	69	64	+3
Australia	68	—	73	+5
Denmark	29	35	—	+6
S. Korea	10	14	16	+6
S. Africa	66	88	80	+14
China	—	21	41	+20

Sources: *World Values Surveys* carried out in 1981–3, 1990–3, and 1995–7.

the sample—a conservative assumption, since younger cohorts usually show *more* Postmodern values than older ones (for a more detailed discussion of how to estimate the effects of population replacement on mass attitudes, see Abramson and Inglehart 1995).

When we perform this calculation it indicates that, for most of these countries, we would expect to find a decline of only four or five points in the percentage favouring more respect for authority. This is a small shift. If we found it in only one case, it would be an unimpressive finding: a difference between samples of this size is statistically significant at only about the .05 level. But if we observed several such consecutive shifts over 30 or 40 years, the finding would be highly significant, both statistically and substantively: over that time it could convert a 60 : 40 division of attitudes into a 40 : 60 split.

The same principle applies to a pattern of cross-cultural findings. Such a finding from only one country would hardly be worth mentioning. But if data from three or four countries all showed shifts of this size in the predicted direction, it would be highly significant. And when we find that the predicted shifts in values or attitudes generally hold true across a score of societies, the probability of its being a random event dwindles to the vanishing point.

With attitudes toward authority, our theory predicts a shift of only 4 or 5 percentage points per country during this 9-year period. This is modest. In the short run, the impact of current economic or political events (or even sampling error) could easily swamp it in a given society. Thus, it would be astonishing if our predictions *did* hold up in every case. They don't: we find that in some countries, attitudes concerning authority moved in the predicted direction, while in others they didn't. Moreover, some countries show shifts in the predicted direction which are too *large* to be due to population replacement alone: in these cases, situation-specific factors must be adding to the results of population replacement, exaggerating the shift.

We can predict only one component of what is shaping mass attitudes, but we know that a number of factors are relevant. Consequently, we cannot predict precisely what will happen in every country. Nevertheless, because we *do* have information about one component of the process, our predictive power across many societies should be considerably better than random. And since there is a good chance that in the long run, situation-specific factors or period effects will cancel each other out, in the long run, over many countries, our predictions should point in the right direction.

In the present case, the predicted shift toward less emphasis on respect for authority is actually observed in 28 out of the 36 countries in which any change occurred (with one country showing no change). In other words, we find the predicted change in 78 per cent of the cases. Though well short of 100 per cent accuracy, this is far better than random prediction. Across the 37 societies for which we have time-series data, we observe a mean decline of 5.7 points in emphasis on respect for authority. We will not attempt to identify the various nation-specific effects that were *also* at work, but it is clear that the population-replacement mechanism was not the only factor involved here. For example, in Nigeria, national elections were held in 1993 that were expected to bring a long-awaited transition to democratic government. But the elections were nullified after the fact and a widely resented and increasingly repressive military government seized power. This authoritarian abuse of power almost certainly contributed to the substantial decline in respect for authority that was observed in Nigeria from 1990 to 1996. Our theory did not predict this event. It was due to factors outside our model. Nevertheless, the values of most publics *did* move in the predicted direction.

The evidence indicates that respect for authority actually *is* declining in most advanced industrial societies. We suspect that this has contributed to the erosion of institutional authority. Performance still counts. But the tendency to idealize national leaders has been growing weaker; and their performance is being evaluated with a more critical eye.

Postmaterialists evaluate politics by more demanding standards than do Materialists. Though they live in the same political systems as Materialists, and are more able to make these systems respond to their preferences (being more articulate and politically more active), they do not register higher levels of satisfaction with politics. The rise of Postmaterialist values is one symptom of a broader Postmodern shift that is transforming the standards by which the publics of advanced industrial societies evaluate governmental performance. It brings new, more demanding standards to the evaluation of political life; and confronts political leaders with more active, articulate citizens. The position of elites has become more difficult in advanced industrial society. Mass publics are becoming increasingly critical of their political leaders, and increasingly likely to engage in elite-challenging activities.

This leads to a paradoxical finding: even though they are better-off in almost every respect, the publics of prosperous, stable, and democratic advanced industrial societies do *not* show higher levels of satisfaction with their political systems than do the publics of poor, authoritarian countries. Quite the contrary, astonishing as it may seem, the publics of rich democracies show *less* confidence in their leaders and political institutions than do their counterparts in developing countries. In the short run, economic development tends to bring rising levels of political satisfaction; in the long run, however, it leads to the emergence of new and more demanding standards by which governmental performance is evaluated—and to lower levels of respect and confidence in their authorities.

The Erosion of Confidence In Hierarchical Institutions

Let us now examine the shifts that took place in political values from 1981 to 1997, testing our deliberately over-simplified prediction: that all orientations linked with Postmaterialist values should become more widespread. We find that pervasive changes are taking place in political, as well as social values. There is evidence of a long-term shift in which the publics of advanced industrial societies are becoming more likely to act in autonomous, elite-challenging fashion. These changes make mass publics less respectful of elites and more likely to challenge them. Confidence in established political and societal institutions is declining; but the participant potential of most publics is rising. Thus, we find two related trends: the erosion of institutional authority; and the rise of citizen intervention in politics.

These processes have both alarming and encouraging implications. On one hand, established institutions that have shaped industrial society for generations seem to be losing their authority over the average citizen. Public confidence is declining, not only in key governmental institutions such as parliament, police, civil service, and armed forces; but also in political parties, churches, educational systems, and the press. We even find a weakening sense of attachment to that most basic of all Western institutions, the nation-state itself.

When evidence of such changes emerged in given countries in the past, it was usually attributed to the fact that the specific government then in office was less effective, and instilled less confidence, than the previous government. This undoubtedly *is* part of the explanation: incompetent and corrupt governments tend to evoke less confidence than competent, honest ones. But we believe that a long-term component is also involved here, in addition to fluctuations linked with specific office-holders.

It has often been observed that in time of national danger the public tends to seek the security of strong leaders and strong institutions. Thus, during the traumatic insecurity of the Great Depression, a wave of upheavals took place in newly established democracies, from Italy to Germany to Hungary to Spain, which led to the rise of authoritarian leaders such as Mussolini, Hitler, Horthy, and Franco. Even in the United States, with its deep-rooted democratic tradition, the American people rallied behind Franklin Roosevelt, who exercised exceptionally sweeping powers, and was elected for an unprecedented four terms.

Long-enduring security paves the way for the reverse phenomenon: the public gradually sees less need for the discipline and self-denial demanded by strong governments. A Postmaterialist emphasis on self-expression and self-realization becomes increasingly central.

There are potential dangers in this evolution. Societal institutions could become too atrophied to cope with a national emergency if one arose. But there are positive aspects as well. In the long run it seems to produce a declining sense of nationalism. More immediately, it is conducive to democratization. For the erosion of state authority has been accompanied by a rising potential for citizen intervention in politics. Partly this is due to a shift in values, with a weakening emphasis on the goals of economic and physical security that favour strong authority; but another factor that favours rising citizen intervention is the long-term rise in educational levels and in mass political skills that have characterized all industrial societies. In the long run, industrialized societies of both East and West must cope with long-term changes that are making their publics less amenable to doing as they are told, and more adept at telling their governments what to do.

Declining Confidence in Hierarchical Institutions

Evidence from the 1981, 1990 and 1996 surveys demonstrates the claims we have just laid out. Across nearly all of our societies, Materialists place more confidence in their country's most hierarchical institutions—the armed forces, police, and church—than do Postmaterialists.

These findings are consistent with our argument that a sense of insecurity tends to motivate support for strong institutions and for strong authority in particular. Having experienced a relatively high sense of economic and physical security throughout their formative years, Postmaterialists feel less need for strong authority than do Materialists. Moreover, Postmaterialists place relatively strong emphasis on self-expression—a value that inherently conflicts with the structure of hierarchical bureaucratic organizations.

The value-related differences point to the possibility of a shift over time, toward the outlook of the younger and more Postmaterialist respondents. Do we find it? The answer is 'Yes'. In most countries, we find lower levels of confidence in government institutions in 1997 than those that existed in 1981.

Our respondents were asked how much confidence they had in a dozen national institutions. Postmaterialists show lower levels of confidence in most established institutions than do Materialists, and in three cases, the correla-

Table 12.2. Confidence in the armed forces, 1981–1997

Country	1981	1990	1996	Change
S. Korea	55	31	18	−37
Nigeria	—	41	20	−21
Spain	24	8	8	−16
Canada	19	11	—	−13
Italy	18	7	—	−11
Norway	17	11	10	−7
Australia	22	—	15	−7
Great Britain	38	32	—	−6
Ireland	26	21	—	−5
Russia	—	33	28	−5
W. Germany	10	6	6	−4
Iceland	8	4	—	−4
Latvia	—	6	2	−4
USA	36	29	33	−3
France	15	12	—	−3
Belgium	8	5	—	−3
Mexico	21	9	18	−3
S. Africa	21	24	18	−3
Netherlands	5	3	—	−2
Brazil	—	32	31	−1
Denmark	9	9	—	0
Sweden	7	7	7	0
Slovenia	—	9	9	0
Japan	6	3	7	+1
N. Ireland	33	35	—	+2
E. Germany	—	1	3	+2
Estonia	—	4	6	+2
Argentina	3	9	6	+3
Chile	—	16	19	+3
Belarus	—	22	29	+7
Finland	20	13	27	+7
Turkey	—	59	67	+8

Sources: World Values Surveys carried out in 1981–3, 1990–3, and 1995–7.

Table 12.3. Confidence in the Police, 1981–1997

Country	1981	1990	1996	Change
S. Korea	29	10	7	−22
Great Britain	40	24	—	−16
Nigeria	—	30	15	−15
Norway	30	20	16	−14
USA	27	21	16	−11
Australia	27	—	18	−9
Spain	19	10	11	−8
W. Germany	16	12	10	−6
Canada	30	24	—	−6
Italy	18	12	—	−6
Mexico	12	7	6	−6
N. Ireland	37	33	—	−4
Brazil	—	13	10	−3
France	12	9	—	−3
Belgium	10	7	—	−3
E. Germany	—	6	4	−2
Slovenia	—	11	9	−2
Russia	—	8	6	−2
Sweden	16	13	15	−1
Japan	15	11	14	−1
Lithuania	—	2	1	−1
Latvia	—	3	2	−1
Argentina	4	5	4	0
Finland	24	10	24	0
Denmark	28	29	—	+1
Turkey	—	30	31	+1
Ireland	32	36	—	+2
Belarus	—	5	9	+4
Estonia	—	2	6	+4
Iceland	8	19	—	+11
S. Africa	19	25	31	+12

Sources: World Values Surveys carried out in 1981–3, 1990–3, and 1995–7.

tions were high enough to meet our criterion of 'reasonably strong': Postmaterialist values are especially strongly linked with *low* levels of confidence in their country's police, armed forces, and church. Consequently, we predicted that confidence in these institutions will decline.

Confidence in the country's armed forces shows a similar pattern (see Table 12.2). It declined in 20 of the 29 countries that registered change.

As Table 12.3 demonstrates, from 1981 to 1997, confidence in the given society's police declined in 23 of the 29 countries in which any change was registered. Among the societies in which it rose by more than 2 points, three of the four societies had experienced regime changes.

Confidence in one's country's church also moved on the predicted trajectory, falling in 23 of the 33 cases where changes occurred, as Table 12.4 demonstrates. Here again, in four of the five countries where it rose by more than two points, the nation had undergone a regime change.

Table 12.4. Confidence in the church, 1981–1997

Country	1981	1990	1996	Change
Nigeria	—	82	65	−17
E. Germany	—	18	3	−15
W. Germany	19	12	5	−14
S. Korea	24	21	13	−11
Australia	21	—	12	−9
Belgium	22	14	—	−8
Spain	25	24	17	−8
Canada	30	24	—	−6
Norway	16	11	10	−6
U.S.A.	45	46	40	−5
Mexico	48	46	43	−5
France	17	12	—	−5
Great Britain	20	16	—	−4
Netherlands	10	7	—	−3
Japan	5	3	2	−3
Iceland	22	19	—	−3
Slovenia	—	14	12	−2
Italy	28	27	—	−1
Sweden	7	7	6	−1
Russia	—	24	24	0
Ireland	38	39	—	+1
Argentina	22	26	23	+1
Finland	11	8	12	+1
Lithuania	—	15	16	+1
Latvia	—	17	18	+1
N. Ireland	45	47	—	+2
Estonia	—	12	15	+3
Denmark	8	11	—	+3
Hungary	16	22	—	+6
Belarus	—	22	33	+11
S. Africa	48	59	60	+12

Sources: World Values Surveys carried out in 1981–3, 1990–3, and 1995–7.

Summing up the predicted and observed changes examined in Tables 12.1 through 12.4, we find that the predicted shift away from emphasis on respect for authority was observed in 78 per cent of the cases for which we have time-series data; declining confidence in the police was observed in 79 per cent of the available cases; declining confidence in the armed forces was observed in 69 per cent of the cases; and declining confidence in the church was observed in 67 per cent of the cases for which we have data. Across the 127 cases for which we have time-series data at two or more points, the predicted trend is observed 73 per cent of the time when any change occurred.

The old standards for evaluating elites no longer apply. A record that once would have ensured re-election, is now insufficient. Thus in 1952, more than seven years after he had led allied forces to victory in World War II, a grateful nation elected Dwight Eisenhower President by a landslide margin. By contrast, in 1992, shortly after the Cold War had come to a sudden and (from an

American perspective) astonishingly successful conclusion; and immediately after a swift and (from an American perspective) almost bloodless victory in the Gulf War; and with an economy that was in the second year of the longest sustained expansion in post-war history, George Bush failed to win re-election. This was not just a failure of charisma on Bush's part. For within two years, his successor had become widely distrusted and his party had lost control of both houses of Congress. This happened though the economic indicators were doing even better than they were under Bush. It has become clear that the standard economic indicators no longer explain as much as they once did, in the realm of political behaviour. Postmodern publics evaluate their leaders by different, and more demanding, standards than were those applied through-out most of the modern era.

We find one striking exception to the decline of mass confidence in estab-lished institutions: during the period 1981–90, confidence in 'major corpora-tions' did not decline. Though it started from relatively low levels in 1981, confidence in corporations showed a rising trend in most societies. This may have been linked with the collapse of state-socialist economies, which made private enterprise look good by contrast. And in a sense, it is a logical reaction to the pronounced decline of trust in government: if the state is coming to be seen as the problem, rather than the solution, it becomes all the more impor-tant to have a strong countervailing force to offset the power of the state.

In keeping with this interpretation, we find that the publics of more devel-oped societies show *less* support for a state-run economy than those of low-income societies. It seems clear that one of the most pervasive defining tendencies of the modernization era—the tendency to look to the state, as the solution to all problems—has reached its limits.

The bottom-line question is, 'Do these trends tend to undermine support for democratic institutions?'

The answer is 'No'. They undermine support for hierarchical authority. This makes governance more difficult. But the Postmodern shift constitutes a move away from a deference to authority that can, under conditions of insecurity, give rise to authoritarian government. The third wave of the *World Values Surveys* contains a number of items designed to measure support for democra-tic institutions, including the following question: *'I'm going to describe various types of political systems and ask what you think of each as a way of governing this country. For each one, would you say it is a very good, fairly good, fairly bad, or very bad way of governing this country?'* . . . *'Having a strong leader who does not have to bother with parliament and elections'*. Figure 12.6 shows the percentage in each country who clearly rejected this alternative, describing it as *'very bad'*. The societies are also arrayed according to the proportion of Postmaterialists in their public (with 'Postmaterialists' defined here as those who gave high pri-ority to at least three of the five Postmaterialist goals in the twelve-item bat-tery).

There is a great deal of cross-national variation in response to this question. In the Western region of Germany (the former Bundesrepublik), fully 70 per

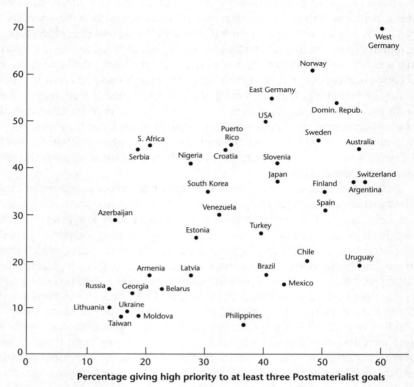

Fig. 12.6. Support for strong leadership.

Note: Percentage of people saying '*having a strong leader who does not have to bother with parliament and elections*' is a '*very bad*' system, by percentage 'postmaterialist'.

Source: World Values Surveys 1981–96.

cent of the public reject government by a strong leader, ruling without parliament or elections, as a 'very bad' system. In Russia, only 12 per cent do so, and in Lithuania, Ukraine, Moldova, Taiwan, and the Philippines, less than 10 per cent do so.

But we find a clear overall pattern. The publics of the most Postmaterialist societies (which, as we have seen, show relatively low levels of respect for authority) also tend to reject authoritarian government most strongly. The overall correlation is .60, significant at the .0000 level.

The Postmodernization phase of development leads to declining respect for authority among the publics of advanced industrial society—but it also gives rise to growing support for democracy.

13

Conclusions: The Growth of Critical Citizens and its Consequences

PIPPA NORRIS

THE first part of this book has clearly demonstrated the increased tensions between democratic values, which seem to have triumphed across the globe, and yet the erosion of confidence in the institutions of representative democracy. As Lipset and Schneider note (1987), it is often difficult to establish the precise impact of the decline in institutional confidence in any quantifiable way. Some effects are direct and behavioural. Others are more inferential and intangible. In this concluding chapter we can consider certain common claims.

- It is widely believed that growing cynicism about government may deter conventional participation: discouraging electoral turnout, political activism, and civic engagement.

- Moreover alienation with the regime is commonly expected to effect protest politics: fostering unconventional activism, support for anti-state extremist movements, and even occasional incidents of urban terrorism.

- A deep reservoir of public trust is generally thought to encourage voluntary compliance with the law, enhancing the ability of governments to pass and implement effective legislation and raise revenues, without the need for coercion.

- Lastly, theorists suggest that growing tensions between ideal and reality will undermine the stability of regimes, increasing the pressures for political reform in established democracies and hindering the consolidation process in newer democracies.

This chapter will critically examine support for and against these claims, and then consider the implications for strengthening transitional, consolidating, and established democracies.

The Consequences for Conventional Political Participation

It is commonly assumed that eroding faith in government has discouraged conventional political participation. During the post-war era the decline in the number of American voters at the polls is well established: turnout as a proportion of the voting age population during presidential elections peaked in 1960 at 65.4 per cent before falling to 48.8 per cent in 1996, its lowest level in seven decades (Gans 1997; Teixeira 1992). Studies are divided about the comparative pattern. Topf (1995: 41) noted no general decline in turnout in Western Europe during the post-war era although Dalton (1996: 45) found a modest slide in a broader comparison of 21 advanced industrialized democracies, where turnout fell from an average of 82 per cent in the 1950s and 1960s down to 76 per cent in the mid-1990s. The most comprehensive world-wide review confirmed a relatively modest dip in turnout from 1945–97 in established democracies (around 6 per cent on average during the last quarter-century), although the study monitored a substantial increase in voter participation in all other states world-wide (IDEA 1997).

Following Verba and Nie (1972), political participation has generally been understood as a multi-dimensional phenomenon, with different costs and benefits associated with alternative types of activities. The most comprehensive study of political participation in the United States, by Verba, Schlozman, and Brady, (1995: 71) reported that the drop in voting turnout has not been accompanied by a general decrease in political activism, indeed Americans have become more engaged in contributing money towards campaigns and in contacting officials. Putnam (1995a, b, 1996) has presented the most extensive evidence for growing civic disengagement in the United States, in activities as diverse as community meetings, social networks, and associational membership. This interpretation of the American data has aroused considerable debate (Ladd 1996; Norris 1996; Smith 1997). One plausible view is that channels of political participation may be evolving rather than declining, if people are becoming more active in new ways. Compared with earlier decades, by the end of the century American citizens may not be joining the Elks or striking in trade unions or demonstrating about civil rights, any more than they are hula-hooping or watching sputnik or going to discos. But they may be engaging in civic life by recycling garbage, mobilizing on the internet, and volunteering at women's shelters or AIDS hospices. Putnam and Yonish (1998) indicate that newer forms of civic engagement may be developing in America. Changing patterns of civic engagement can be found in many Western democracies where new social movements are challenging the political order (Dalton and Kuechler 1990; McAdam, McCarthy, and Zaid 1996).

The comparative picture remains complex to interpret. While the thesis about the decline of social capital in America has aroused considerable debate it remains difficult to know how far this pattern is evident in other post-industrial societies. Britain, for example, has experienced a significant resurgence of group membership and civic engagement in recent decades (Hall 1997). Studies in Western Europe report no clear cross-national decline in party membership (Widfeldt 1995; Katz and Mair 1994), nor in associational membership (Aarts 1995). Comparative data suggests that the overall pattern of political participation is one of trendless fluctuations, or mixed indicators, in many established democracies, rather than a clear secular decline across all forms of activity.

In terms of explanations, ever since *The Civic Culture* political cynicism has been regarded as one plausible reason depressing activism. Since the rising tide of political cynicism in the United States occurred during roughly the same period as the fall in turnout these factors are commonly linked by popular commentators. Nevertheless systematic analysis has failed to establish a causal connection at individual-level between feelings of political trust and electoral turnout in the United States (Citrin 1974; Citrin and Green 1986; Abramson 1983; Teixeira 1992) or in Britain, Germany, and France (Dalton 1996). Indeed, contrary to the conventional wisdom, the most thorough study of participation in Britain, (Parry, Moyser, and Day 1992), found that the most cynical were actually more politically engaged than the average citizen across a range of activities including voting. Much commentary assumes that if people don't have confidence in the core institutions of representative democracy, such as parliaments or the legal system, they will be reluctant to participate in the democratic process, producing apathy. But it is equally plausible to assume that alienation with representative democracy could mobilize citizens, if people are stimulated to express their disaffection, throw out office-holders, and seek institutional redress (Citrin and Green 1986).

Moreover the weight given to cultural factors remains a matter of debate. The extensive literature comparing levels of electoral turnout has usually focused on the *micro* conditions influencing individual citizens, including their political attitudes (such as efficacy, interest, and trust) and their background characteristics (notably age, gender, education, and social status) (Almond and Verba 1963; Verba and Nie 1972; Verba, Nie, and Kim 1978; Verba *et al.* 1995; Topf 1995). In contrast another body of work has emphasized the *macro* conditions of participation set by the political system, such as registration laws, voting facilities, and the salience of elections (Jackson 1987; IDEA 1997*a*). The last strand of the literature has emphasized the '*intermediary*' conditions set by mobilizing agencies like parties, interest groups, and the media (Powell 1982; Fox Piven and Cloward 1988; Rosenstone and Hansen 1993).

Evidence for the relationship between conventional political participation and confidence in representative government can be analysed by drawing on data from 44 countries including established democracies, semi-democracies, and non-democracies included in the *World Values Study* 1995–7. Since conventional participation is understood as a multi-dimensional phenomenon it is gauged here by four indicators: frequent engagement in political *discussion*;

active membership in a *political party*; active membership in *traditional economic associations* (trade unions and professional organizations); and active membership in *voluntary organizations* (such as church, environmental, and charitable groups) (for details see Appendix 13A).

To measure institutional confidence this chapter uses a similar index to that already developed in Chapter 11, based on summing confidence in five political institutions: parliament, the civil service, the legal system, parties, and the government. Responses to these items were strongly inter-correlated and formed a reliable scale (Cronbach's Alpha = 0.75). Controls were introduced into the models based on the literature on patterns of participation. At individual-level we controlled for background factors commonly associated with activism including the age, gender, education, and socioeconomic status of respondents, and other political attitudes including political interest, social trust, and Left–Right self-placement (see Appendix 13A). At national-level we controlled for the level of economic development of a country (based on per capita GNP) and the country's mean rating in 1996 on the Freedom House index of civil liberties and political rights. The models were run with the activism scales as the dependent variables, using ordinary least-squared regression analysis. The aim was not to develop a comprehensive explanation of political participation, for example by including a range of attitudinal factors like political efficacy in causal models, but rather to isolate the consequences of institutional confidence on activism with a limited range of controls.

Table 13.1. Models of conventional participation and civic engagement

	Political discussion		Party activism		Economic associations		Voluntary organizations	
	Beta	Sig.	Beta	Sig.	Beta	Sig.	Beta	Sig.
Political attitudes								
Institutional Confidence	−.02	**	.07	**	.07	**	.09	**
Social trust	.02	**	.05	**	.09	**	.09	**
Political interest	.49	**	.20	**	.07	**	.06	**
Left–Right self-placement	−.02	**	.04	**	−.02	**	.03	**
Social background								
Gender	.07	**	.04	**	.06	**	.01	
Age	.05	**	.03	**	−.02	**	−.06	**
Education	.09	**	.04	**	.09	**	.05	**
Socioeconomic status	−.03	**	−.02	*	−.06	**	−.10	**
National context								
Level of democratization	−.03	**	.06	**	.01		.10	**
Level of economic development	.03	**	−.11	**	−.006		−.08	**
Adjusted R2	.29		.07		.05		.06	

** = sig. p>.01. N. 64,975 in 44 nations.

Note: The figures represent standardized Beta coefficients in ordinary least squared regression models.

Source: *World Values Survey* 1995–7.

The result of comparing activism across these dimensions (Table 13.1) shows that institutional confidence was significantly related to conventional participation, even after controlling for social background, other political attitudes and national context, although the effect usually proved very weak. Those with confidence in government institutions proved more likely to be active members of political parties, economic associations, and voluntary organizations. More trusting citizens, however, were slightly less likely to engage in political discussions. There were familiar patterns with the control variables. Political interest consistently proved a strong predictor of conventional participation, while greater social trust also proved significant. As expected women proved slightly less active than men across all dimensions of conventional politics except for voluntary associations, where there was no gender gap. In the expected pattern the better educated and those of higher socioeconomic status were far more likely to be politically engaged. Age was not strongly related to participation except that the young proved less active in voluntary associations, confirming the Putnam thesis (1995*a*, *b*), yet more engaged in political discussion. Greater participation in parties and voluntary associations was related to higher levels of democratization and yet also to less-developed societies.

Greater confidence in the core institutions of representative democracy—such as parliament, the civil service, and the legal system—is therefore associated with more active involvement in conventional forms of political participation and civic engagement. Yet the effects should not be exaggerated since the overall impact of institutional confidence on conventional activism remains relatively weak. From a public policy perspective, the findings suggest that it may be more important to generate attitudes like political interest rather than trust. The results suggest that we should be cautious about oversimple accounts blaming declining institutional trust alone for any major erosion in political participation and civic engagement.

The Impact on Protest Politics

Another common claim concerns the impact of declining confidence in government on protest politics (Gamson 1968; Gurr 1971; Muller 1979; Muller, Jukam, and Seligson 1982; Cheles *et al.* 1995). It is widely believed that political cynicism fuels protest activity ranging from peaceful demonstrations like the Million Man March, through non-violent direct action such as British blockades preventing the import of French trucks of calves, to incidents of urban terrorism like the Oklahoma bombing, yet the behavioural consequences remain unclear. Evidence within this book and elsewhere indicates that many American voters are unhappy with Congress, hold politicians in low esteem, and don't vote. But still outside the beltway there is no serious popular debate demanding radical constitutional changes, in marked contrast to active reform movements in Canada, Italy, or Britain, let alone any ground-swell of public mass demonstrations, civic disobedience, or revolutionary action. Even recent mass demonstrations in America, like the Million Man March, seem designed to focus attention on individual responsibility more than demands for government intervention.

At the most extreme, a widespread lack of trust in the political system in the mainstream culture may foster a public climate which facilitates the growth of anti-state movements and occasional outbreaks of urban terrorism among the minority—whether the bombing of abortion clinics in America, threats of bio-logical terrorism in Japan, radical assassinations of public figures in the Basque region, violent racist incidents in France and Germany, heated ethnic/religious conflict in Kashmir, or splinter terrorist groups sabotaging the peace process in Northern Ireland and Israel/Palestine. It is hard to establish the conditions which foster the beliefs and values of extreme anti-state groups, since insulated minority sub-cultures like neo-Fascist and anti-Semitic groups can flourish even in the most tolerant and deeply-rooted democratic societies (Cheles *et al.* 1995; Taras and Ganguly 1998). Nevertheless we suspect a significant connec-tion between mainstream and minority cultures in the long term.

The most extensive evidence concerning protest activism was collected by the five-nation 1973–6 Political Action Study (Barnes and Kaase 1979; Jennings and van Deth 1989). This examined the factors associated with protest potential, measured by willingness to engage in a series of activities such as refusing to pay taxes and willingness to occupy buildings or block traf-fic. Farah *et al.* (1979) found no significant association between protest poten-tial and beliefs in the responsiveness of the political system (system efficacy). In the follow-up study, Thomassen confirmed that protest potential was unre-lated to support for the political regime in the Netherlands and West Germany (Thomassen 1990). More recently, however, Dalton found that dissatisfaction with the democratic process was related to protest potential, albeit weakly, in the USA, Britain, Germany, and France (Dalton 1996: 80). It is difficult to com-pare the results of previous studies since each employs slightly different mea-sures of system support. There are also problems of interpreting the evidence since the standard battery of questions available to measure protest potential has proved a poor indicator of what activities people actually perform (Jennings *et al.* 1989). Responses can best be understood as what citizens think they ought to do, rather than what they actually will do (Topf 1995). In addi-tion some of the items termed 'unconventional' in the 1960s have now become mainstream, like signing petitions.

Bearing these qualifications in mind we can re-examine the evidence draw-ing on the 1995–7 *World Values Study* to analyse the association between protest potential and the Index of Institutional Confidence used earlier. 'Protest potential' is measured using the standard five-item scale, as follows:

'Now I'd like you to look at this card. I'm going to read out some different forms of political action that people can take, and I'd like you to tell me, for each one, whether

you have actually done any of these things (2), whether you might do it (1) or would never, under any circumstances, do it (0) . . .

- *Signing a petition*
- *Joining in boycotts*
- *Attending lawful demonstrations*
- *Joining unofficial strikes*
- *Occupying buildings or factories.'*

These items formed a reliable uni-dimensional scale (Cronbach's Alpha = 0.78) ranging in protest potential from low (0) to high (10).

Table 13.2. Models of protest potential and law compliance

	Protest potential		Willingness to obey law	
	Beta	Sig.	Beta	Sig.
Political attitudes				
Institutional confidence	−.03	**	.07	**
Social trust	.11	**	.02	**
Political interest	.29	**	.03	**
Left-Right self-placement	−.12	**	.004	
Social background				
Gender	.04	**	−.08	**
Age	−.18	**	.22	**
Education	.10	**	.03	**
Socioeconomic status	−.03	**	−.007	
National context				
Level of democratization	.15	**	.21	**
Level of economic development	.00		−.16	**
Adjusted R2	.20		.09	

** = sig. p>.01 N.64,975 in 44 nations.

Note: The figures represent standardized Beta coefficients in ordinary least squared regression models.

Source: World Values Survey 1995–7.

The result of the OLS regression analysis in Table 13.2 shows a very modest relationship in the expected direction between institutional confidence and protest potential: the most cynical were slightly more prone to sympathize with protest politics. But, although this relationship proved statistically significant, it was also weaker than nearly all the other control variables. The strongest predictors of protest potential were political interest and age, with young people far more likely to approve of these newer forms of direct activism, followed by (respectively) level of democratization, Left–Right self-placement, social trust, and education. We can conclude that trust in government is significantly related to protest potential but the association remains very weak.

The Effects on Voluntary Compliance with the Law

Systems support has also been thought to be associated with the willingness of citizens to obey the law and pay taxes without the penalty of coercion, thereby facilitating effective government (Easton 1965). We expect citizens who support the regime will be more likely to believe that the laws are legitimate and should be followed voluntarily. This, even more than political participation, has proved a critical issue for many new democracies since many incomplete or semi-democracies, such as Russia, Colombia, and Mexico, are characterized by widespread tax avoidance, rampant crime and corruption, and ineffective law enforcement (Transparency International 1997).

We can examine whether confidence in democratic institutions is related to voluntary compliance with the law by drawing on a battery of questions tapping attitudes in the *World Values Survey* 1995–7.

'Please tell me for each of the following statements whether you think it can always be justified (0), never be justified (2), or something in between (1), using this card . .

.

- *Claiming government benefits to which you are not entitled*
- *Avoiding a fare on public transport*
- *Cheating on tax if you have the chance*
- *Buying something you knew was stolen*
- *Someone accepting a bribe in the course of their duties.'*

Factor analysis revealed that these loaded onto a single dimension which formed an internally consistent law-compliance scale (Cronbach's Alpha = .78) ranging from low (0) to high (10).

If we compare the results across all countries, in Table 13.2, the results show that trust in government institutions was positively associated with willingness to obey the law voluntarily. The results proved significant, and in the expected direction, although other control factors proved better predictors of compliance, notably the levels of economic development and democratization of the society. What this suggests from a policy perspective is that the legitimacy of regime institutions is one contributing factor which helps promote voluntary compliance with the law, and therefore an effective public policy-making process, but strengthening human rights and civil liberties in transitional democracies may be even more important.

The Consequences for Regime Stability

The systemic consequences of growing political cynicism may be expected to prove even more serious for regime stability, particularly in newer democracies. Theories have long emphasized that growing tensions between culture and structure may be expected to lead to regime instability (Almond and Verba 1963). Yet systematic evidence for this relationship is complex and difficult to interpret. Here we can consider three claims.

1. Contrary to popular perceptions, the growth of democratization world-wide stabilized in the 1990s, rather than steadily expanding in linear fashion.

2. Many countries have benefited from the tide of growing political rights and civil liberties since the early 1980s, but some regimes have experienced reverse waves of democratization.

3. Growing tensions between ideals and reality, and increased disenchantment with the institutions of representative democracy, may add to the pressures for political reform, which may ultimately strengthen democratic systems, or alternatively may undermine support for the fledgling structures of democracy in newer regimes.

The first claim is easiest to establish. The process of democratization surged during the late 1980s but then subsequently stagnated. The world-wide growth of democracies over time has been monitored most consistently by the Freedom House index. This uses seven-point scales of political rights and civil liberties to classify states into democracies ('free'), semi-democracies ('partly-free') and non-democracies ('not free') (Karatnycky 1997). According to this index, world-wide the proportion of democracies rose from 34 per cent in 1983 to 41 per cent in 1997 (see Figure 13.1). By 1997, out of 194 states around the world (excluding independent territories), 81 countries could be classified as democratic. But this leaves 60 countries as incomplete or semi-democracies, and another 53 undemocratic states including major nations such as China, Indonesia, and Nigeria. Undoubtedly the overall news has been positive: since 1983, twenty more countries have joined the ranks of consolidated democracies. Yet the trend over time is a period-specific stepped-shift in democratization, not a steady secular rise. The dramatic gains occurred following the end of the Cold War and the proportion of democratic states world-wide then stabilized. Moreover some regions, notably the Middle East, seem to have largely resisted the pressures for democratic reform.

We can also demonstrate that despite progress the process of democratization has experienced some significant setbacks in recent years and historically previous waves of democracy have commonly been followed by major reversals (Huntington 1991). In Latin America during the mid-1980s scholars stressed the precariousness and uncertainty of the transition from authoritarian rule (O'Donnell, Schmitter, and Whitehead 1986). In the early years after the fall of the Berlin Wall some predicted the return of authoritarian rule or anarchy in Central Europe, particularly following appeals to extreme nationalism in Russia and the Ukraine. So far these predictions have proved unduly alarmist in this region, but the process of democratic transition has been

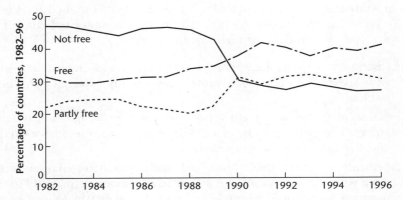

Fig. 13.1. The growth of democracies, percentage of countries, 1982–1996.
Source: Freedom House Index.

highly uncertain and fragile elsewhere, notably throughout Africa. In Algeria, the Gambia, and Nigeria human rights have been undermined by military-backed executives who have persecuted minorities, banned opposition forces, and crippled elections through intimidation and violence. Between 1983 and 1997, although the overall tide flowed towards greater democracy, a dozen countries experienced significant erosions of political rights and civil liberties (by more than one grade in the Freedom House index), with particularly sharp deteriorations in Nigeria, Sudan, and the Dominican Republic (see Figure 13.2). Despite progress during the 1990s, many incomplete or semi-democracies continue to face serious problems in the consolidation process.

Yet it is more difficult to establish the consequences of the growth of critical citizens for regime stability, and to relate changes in public opinion with the democratization process. While we strongly suspect that a supportive political culture is necessary for democratic consolidation, the exact weight given to system support remains a matter of debate. On the one hand, ever since Lipset's (1959) classic study, the consolidation literature has stressed that countries may revert to authoritarian rule, or never progress beyond being incomplete or semi-democratic states, unless they build reservoirs of popular support for democratic institutions to tide the political system over bad times as well as good (Almond and Verba 1963; Linz and Stepan 1978; Lipset 1993; Diamond, Linz and Lipset 1995; Linz and Stepan 1996: 3–15; Diamond *et al.* 1997). Widespread adherence to democratic values and norms is thought to bolster institutions like free elections and competitive parties so that they become 'the only game in town'. Democratic institutions are believed vulnerable to breakdown in times of crisis unless rooted in shared norms of political trust, tolerance, respect for human rights, willingness to compromise, moderation, and belief in democratic legitimacy.

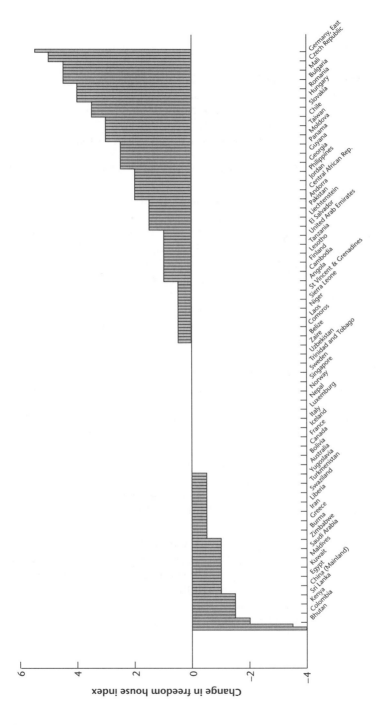

Fig. 13.2. Change in levels of democratization, 1983–1997.

Yet on the other hand the importance of political culture has been challenged by elitist theories which suggest that democratic processes can become consolidated in Central and Eastern European nations, with the commitment of political leaders, even if the public remains lukewarm or indifferent. Both Robert Dahl (1971) and Dankwart Rustow (1970) argued that stable democracies are likely to be developed where the expansion of political competition among elites preceded mass participation. Arend Lijphart (1977) has suggested that consociational democracies function through elite accommodation and a shared commitment among leaders to the values of bargaining, moderation, and compromise, even if the mass society is deeply polarized and fragmented. In similar vein others have pointed out that democracies continue to survive even in societies like Italy and Japan which are characterized by rampant and persistent cynicism about government, deep mistrust of political leaders, and widespread discontent with political institutions (Budge and Newton 1997). Pursuing a slightly different line of reasoning, Rose and Mischler have demonstrated that citizens of Central and Eastern European countries remain sceptical of democracy as an ideal, and critical of the workings of democratic institutions in practice, but nevertheless they prefer the new regimes to the old (see Mishler and Rose, Chapter 4 this volume; Rose *et al.* 1998). Cultural factors may therefore prove less important for consolidation than other conditions such as the role of political institutions, economic development, political leadership, civic society, the social structure, and the international environment.

This is an important debate, requiring complex sources of evidence, and we cannot hope to do more than highlight these arguments here. But, despite the elitist arguments, we have a nagging concern that where regimes are not widely believed to be legitimate then public opinion will not act as an effective deterrent against anti-democratic forces. If fledgling democratic structures are threatened by leadership coups, extremist nationalist parties, or more commonly by a gradual erosion of civil liberties and human rights, then a disillusioned public will not function as a check on authoritarianism. If the public has little faith in existing channels of representative democracy, they will not mobilize to defend the Russian Duma, the Mexican Camara de Diputados, or the Panamanian Asemblean Legislativa. In such circumstances, it becomes more likely that these institutions may fold against external forces. If these institutions do not deserve public support, because of widespread corruption, venality, or inefficiency, then this may prove a positive boost for reform movements. But at the same time, even if the public does not actively desire a return to the old regimes, the danger remains that citizens may not stand as a bulwark to defend fledgling democratic institutions, for all their flaws, against authoritarian forces.

Discussion and Summary

The evidence presented in this volume suggests that we have seen the growth of more critical citizens, who value democracy as an ideal yet who remain dissatisfied with the performance of their political system, and particularly the core institutions of representative government. The cross-national pattern of critical citizens is illustrated most clearly in Figure 13.3, which compares evaluations of the current regime against support for democratic values (see Appendix 13A for details of the items used). By the mid-1990s this volume demonstrates that citizens in most countries showed widespread support for democracy as an ideal, *'better than any other form of government'*. This pattern was evident among citizens in established democracies such as Norway and West Germany, as well as for newer democracies like South Africa, and even authoritarian regimes like Nigeria. Yet at the same time citizens in many

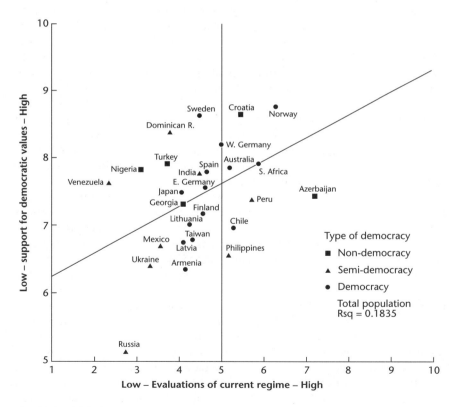

Fig. 13.3. Critical citizens, 1995–1997.
Source: *World Values Surveys* 1995–7.

countries showed fairly negative evaluations of the performance of their current political system.

The growth of critical citizens is open to different interpretations, as discussed by contributors within this volume, and we cannot hope to settle this debate here. On the one hand, the effect of growing tensions between democratic ideals and the perceived performance of democratic institutions may have destabilizing effects on the body politic, which may slow the consolidation process in newer democracies. On the other hand, these trends in public opinion can be expected to prove healthy if they fuel pressure for major institutional reforms designed to strengthen representative and direct democracy. In America, concern about growing cynicism has spurred the rise of diverse movements like civic journalism seeking to rekindle public engagement in community life, as well as the term-limits movement and pressures on campaign finance reform (Craig 1993). During the last decade, partly in response to perceived problems of public trust, Italy, New Zealand, and Japan have adopted radical reforms to their electoral systems for parliament while Israel introduced direct elections for the executive (Norris 1995). The UK opted for a sweeping and radical set of constitutional initiatives including devolution for Scotland and Wales, electoral reform, reform of the Lords, an elected mayor for London, a new settlement in Northern Ireland, stronger regulations of political finance, a Freedom of Information Act, and the adoption of a written Bill of Rights. In Canada and Italy constitutional debates about regional devolution or independence have proved deeply divisive and remain unresolved. In many established political systems, therefore, constitutional settlements which seemed frozen appear to suddenly break and reform, in a model of punctuated equilibrium. It is far too early to say whether these types of reforms will prove effective in re-establishing confidence in the core institutions of representative government, or whether secular trends will continue on a downwards path. For those who continue to believe in the conventional channels of representative democracy, the solution lies in designing more effective institutional reforms. For those committed to more direct decision-making, the solution to more critical citizens lies in expanding the opportunities for participation via these channels.

Although we have demonstrated that there are genuine causes for concern about the issue of public trust in government, nevertheless the evidence in this volume suggests that the sky is not falling down for democracy. In the 1970s crisis theories suggested that even established political systems like Germany and Britain might not be able to survive the new pressures and new demands on the state caused by exuberant democracy (Crozier, Huntington, and Watanuki 1975). By the end of the twentieth century we know that these doubts were exaggerated and the jeremiads put to rest. The state proved capable of evolving and adapting to new demands. We can conclude that the growth of more critical citizens has increased the pressures for constitutional reforms in many older democracies, and in many newer democracies the consolidation process has often proved hazardous and fraught. These are the major challenges facing democratic states as we enter the twenty-first century.

Appendix Table 13A. Measures, questions, and coding of variables

Measure	Question	Coding
Institutional confidence	*I am going to name a number of organizations. For each one, could you tell me how much confidence you have in them: is it a great deal of confidence (3), quite a lot of confidence (2), not very much confidence (1), or none at all (0)?* *The legal system* *The government in (your capital)* *Political parties* *Parliament* *The civil service*	Standardized 0–100-point scale constructed by summing responses to each institution.
Social trust	*Generally speaking, would you say that most people can be trusted (1) or that you can't be too careful in dealing with people (0). DK (0).*	0/1 scale.
Political interest	*How interested would you say you are in politics? very interested (4), somewhat interested (3), not very interested (2) or not at all interested (1). DK(0).*	Scale from low interest (1) to high (4).
Protest potential	See pp. 262–3.	Scale from low (0) to high (10).
Voluntary compliance with the law	See p. 264.	Scale from low compliance (0) to high (12).
Party activism	*Now I am going to read off a list of voluntary organizations; for each one, could you tell me whether you are an active member (2), an inactive member (1), or not a member of that type of organization (0)?* *Political party*	Scale from low (0) to high (2).
Economic association activism	*See item on party activism.* *Labour union* *Professional association*	Summed scale from low (0) to high (4).
Voluntary organization activism	*See item on party activism.* *Church or religious organization* *Sport or recreational organization* *Art, music, or educational organization* *Environmental organization* *Charitable organization* *Any other voluntary organization.*	Summed scale from low (0) to high (12).
Left–Right self-placement	*In political matters, people talk of the left and the right. How would you place your views on this scale, generally speaking?*	Scale from Left (1) to Right (10).
Political discussion	*When you get together with your friends, would you say that you discuss political matters frequently (3), occasionally (2) or never (1)?*	Scale from low (1) to high (3).
Gender		Male (1) Female (0).

Measure	Question	Coding
Age		Number of years old (18–95).
Education	*What is the highest educational level that you have attained?*	Scale from no formal education (1) to university-level education with degree (9).
Socioeconomic status	*In which profession/occupation do you, or did you, work?*	11-point standard occupational scale from 1 (professional and managerial) to 11 (unskilled working class).
Level of democratization	Combined rating on political rights and civil liberties of each country by Freedom House, 1997.	Reversed scale from 1 (low) to 7 (high).
Level of economic development	Real GNP per capita (PPP$) from Freedom House/UN Human Development Report (1996).	PPP$
Evaluations of current regime	*People have different views about the system for governing this country. Here's a scale for rating how well things are going: 1 means very bad and 10 means very good.* *Where on this scale would you put the political system today?*	Scale from 1 (low evaluation) to 10 (high evaluation).
Support for democratic values	*I'm going to describe various types of political system and ask you what you think about each as a way of governing the country. For each one, would you say that it is a very good (4), fairly good (3), fairly bad (2), or very bad (1) way of governing the country?* *Having a democratic political system.* *I'm going to read off some things that people sometimes say about a democratic political system. Could you please tell me if you agree strongly (4), agree (3), disagree (2) or disagree strongly (1).* *Democracy may have its problems but it's better than any other form of government.*	Responses scaled from 1 (low support for democratic values) to 10 (high support).

Source: World Values Survey 1995–7.

BIBLIOGRAPHY

Aardal, Bernt and Henry Valen (1995), *Konflikt og Opinion*. Oslo: NKS-forlaget.

Aarts, Kees (1995), 'Intermediate Organizations and Interest Representation', in Hans-Dieter Klingemann and Dieter Fuchs (eds.), *Citizens and the State*. Oxford: Oxford University Press.

Abramson, Paul R. (1983), *Political Attitudes in America: Formation and Change*. San Francisco: W. H. Freeman.

—— and Ronald Inglehart (1995), *Value Change in Global Perspective*. Ann Arbor: University of Michigan Press.

Almond, Gabriel A. (1980), 'The Intellectual History of the Civic Culture Concept', in Gabriel A. Almond and Sidney Verba (eds.), *The Civic Culture Revisited*. Boston: Little, Brown and Company, 1–36.

—— (1983), 'Communism and Political Culture Theory', *Comparative Politics*, 15: 127–38.

—— (1993), 'Forward: The Return to Political Culture', in Larry Diamond (ed.), *Political Culture and Democracy in Developing Countries*. Boulder, Colo.: Lynne Reinner, pp. ix–xii.

—— and G. Bingham Powell (1978), *Comparative Politics: System, Process, and Policy*. Boston: Little, Brown and Company.

—— and Sidney Verba (1963), *The Civic Culture: Political Attitudes and Democracy in Five Nations*. Princeton: Princeton University Press.

Amsden, Alice (1989), *Asia's Next Giant: South Korea and Late Industrialization*. New York: Oxford University Press.

Anderson, Christopher (1995), *Blaming the Government: Citizens and the Economy in Five European Democracies*. New York: M. E. Sharpe.

—— and Christine A. Guillory (1997), 'Political Institutions and Satisfaction With Democracy', *American Political Science Review*, 91/1: 66–81.

Anderson, Perry, and Patrick Camiller (1994), *Mapping the West European Left*. London: Verso.

Asp, Kent (1991), 'Medierna bäddar för politikerförakt', *Dagens Nyheter* (Sept.), 23.

Avishai, Bernard (1990), *A New Israel: Democracy in Crisis 1973–1988*. New York: Tickner and Fields.

Baier, Alan (1986), 'Trust and Anti-Trust', *Ethics*, 96: 231–60.

Baker, Kendall, Russell Dalton, and Kai Hildebrandt (1981), *Germany Transformed: Political Culture and the New Politics*. Cambridge, Mass.: Harvard University Press.

Banting, Keith and Richard Simeon (1985), *The Politics of Constitutional Change in Industrial Nations*. London: Macmillan.

Barber, Benjamin (1984), *Strong Democracy*. Berkeley: University of California Press.

Barnes, Samuel, and Max Kaase (1979), *Political Action: Mass Participation in Five Western Democracies*. Beverly Hills: Sage.

Basanez, Miguel, Ronald Inglehart and Alejandro Moreno (1998), *Human Values and Beliefs: A Cross-Cultural Sourcebook*. Ann Arbor: University of Michigan Press.

Bates, Robert H. (1990), 'Contra Contractarianism: Some Reflections on the New Institutionalism', *Politics and Society*, 16 (June–Sept.), 387–401.

Bauer, Petra (1991), 'Politische Orientierungen im Übergang. Eine Analyse politischer Einstellungen der Bürger in West- und Ostdeutschland 1990/1991', *Kölner Zeitschrift für Soziologie und Sozialpsychologie*, 43: 433–53.

Beetham, David (1994), *Defining and Measuring Democracy*. London: Sage.

Bellah, Robert, Richard Madsen, William M. Sullivan, Ann Swindler, and Steven M. Tipton (1985), *Habits of the Heart: Individualism and Commitment in American Life*. Berkeley and Los Angeles: University of California Press.

Berlin, Isaiah (1969), 'On Liberty', in *Four Essays on Liberty*. Oxford: Oxford University Press.

Bianco, William T. (1994), *Trust: Representatives and Constituents*. Ann Arbor: University of Michigan Press.

Billiet, Jaak B. and Bart Cambre (1990), 'Social Capital, Active Membership in Voluntary Associations and Some Aspects of Political Participation: A Case-Study', unpub.

Birch, Anthony H. (1984), 'Overload, Ungovernability and Delegitimation: The Theories and the British Case', *British Journal of Political Science*, 14: 135–60.

Blendon, Robert, John M. Benson, Richard Morin, Drew E. Altman, Mollyann Brodie, Mario Brossard, and Matt James (1997), 'Changing Attitudes in America', in Joseph Nye, Philip Zelikow, and David King (eds.), *Why People Don't Trust Government*. Cambridge, Mass.: Harvard University Press.

Bobbio, Norberto (1987), *The Future of Democracy. A Defence of the Rules of the Game*. Minneapolis: University of Minnesota Press.

Bogdanor, Vernon (1988), *Constitutions in Democratic Politics*. Aldershot: Gower.

—— and David Butler (1983), *Democracy and Elections: Electoral Systems and Their Political Consequences*. New York: Cambridge University Press.

Bok, Derek (1997), 'Measuring the Performance of Government', in Nye, Zelikow, and King (eds.), *Why People Don't Trust Government*. Cambridge, Mass.: Harvard University Press.

Bollen, Kenneth (1993), 'Liberal Democracy: Validity and Method Factors in Cross-National Measures', *American Sociological Review*, 54: 612–21.

Booth, John A. and Mitchell A. Seligson (1994), 'Paths to Democracy and the Political Culture of Costa Rica, Mexico and Nicaragua', in Diamond (ed.), *Political Culture and Democracy in Developing Countries*.

Borg, Sami and Risto Sänkiaho (1995), *The Finnish Voter*. Helsinki: Finnish Political Science Association.

Borre, Ole and Jørgen Goul Andersen (1997), *Voting and Political Attitudes in Denmark*. Aarhus: Aarhus University Press.

Brace, Paul and Barbara Hinckley (1992), *Follow the Leader*. New York: Basic Books.

Brehm, John and Wendy Rahn (1997), 'Individual-level evidence for the causes and consequences of social capital', *American Journal of Political Science*, 41/3: 999–1023.

Brittan, Samuel (1975), 'The Economic Contradictions of Democracy', *British Journal of Political Science*, 5: 129–59.

Budge, Ian (1996), *The New Challenge of Direct Democracy*. Oxford: Polity Press.

—— and Kenneth Newton (1997), *The Politics of the New Europe*. Harlow: Addison Wesley Longman.

Bürklin, Wilhelm P. (1997a), 'Einstellungen und Wertorientierungen ost- und westdeutscher Eliten 1995. Gesellschaftliches Zusammenwachsen durch Integration der Elite?', in Oscar W. Gabriel (ed.), *Politische Orientierungen und Verhaltensweisen im vereinigten Deutschland*. Opladen: Leske & Budrich: 235–61.

—— (1997b), *Eliten in Deutschland*. Opladen: Leske & Budrich.

Burton, John (1997), 'Korean Inc. May Turn to the Market System', *Financial Times*, 4 Dec.

Butler, David and Austin Ranney (1994) (eds.), *Referendums Around the World: The Growing Use of Democracy?* Washington: American Enterprise Institute.

Cappella, Joseph N. and Kathleen H. Jamieson (1997), *Spiral of Cynicism*. New York: Oxford University Press.

Castles, Francis G., Rolf Gerritsen, and Jack Vowles (1996) (eds.), *The Great Experiment: Labour Parties and Public Policy Transformation in Australia and New Zealand*. Sydney: Allen and Unwin.

Cheles, Luciano, Ronnie Ferguson, and Michalina Vaughan (1995), *The Far Right in Western and Eastern Europe*. New York: Longman.

Churchill, Winston (1947), House of Commons. *Hansard*, 11 Nov., col. 206.

Citrin, Jack (1974), 'Comment: The Political Relevance of Trust in Government', *American Political Science Review*, 68: 973–88.

—— and Donald Green (1986), 'Presidential Leadership and Trust in Government', *British Journal of Political Science*, 16: 431–53.

Clark, John and Aaron Wildavsky (1990), *The Moral Collapse of Communism: Poland as a Cautionary Tale*. San Francisco: ICS Press.

Clarke, Harold D. and Allan Kornberg (1989), 'Public Reactions to Economic Performance and Political Support in Contemporary Liberal Democracies', in Harold Clarke *et al.* (eds.), *Economic Decline and Political Change: Canada, Great Britain, the United States*. Pittsburgh. University of Pittsburgh Press.

—— and Marianne Stewart (1995), 'Economic Evaluations, Prime Ministerial Approval and Governing Party Support: Rival Models Considered', *British Journal of Political Science*, 25/2: 145–70.

—— Nitish Dutt, and Allan Kornberg (1993), 'The Political Economy of Attitudes Toward Polity and Society in Western European Democracies', *Journal of Politics*, 55/4: 998–1021.

—— Euel W. Elliott, William Mishler, Marianne C. Stewart, Paul F. Whiteley, and Gary Zuk (1992), *Controversies in Political Economy*. Boulder, Colo.: Westview Press.

Coleman, James S. (1988), 'Social Capital in the Creation of Human Capital', *American Journal of Sociology*, 94: 95–120.

—— (1990), *Foundations of Social Theory*. Cambridge, Mass.: Belknap.

Conover, Pamela Johnston, Stanley Feldman, and Kathleen Knight (1986), 'Judging Inflation and Unemployment: The Origins of Retrospective Evaluations', *Journal of Politics*, 48: 565–88.

Conradt, David P. (1980), 'The Changing German Political Culture', in Almond and Verba (eds.), *The Civic Culture Revisited*.

—— (1991), 'From Output Orientation to Regime Support: Changing German Political Culture', in Ursula Hoffmann-Lange (ed.), *Social and Political Structures in West Germany: From Authoritarianism to Postindustrial Democracy*. Boulder, Colo.: Westview: 127–42.

—— (1997), 'Political Culture in Unified Germany: Will the Bonn Republic Survive and Thrive in Berlin?', presented at the *German Studies Association*, 25–8 Sept., Washington.

Converse, Phillip E. (1964), 'The Nature of Belief Systems in Mass Publics', in David E. Apter (ed.), *Ideology and Discontent*. New York: Free Press.

Cooper, Barry, Allan Kornberg, and William Mishler (1988), *The Resurgence of Conservatism in Anglo-American Democracies*. Durham, NC: Duke University Press.

Coppedge, Michael and Wolfgang Reinicke (1990), 'Measuring Polyarchy', *Studies in Comparative International Development*, 25: 51–72.

Cox, Gary W. (1997), *Making Votes Count*. New York: Cambridge University Press.

Craig, Stephen C. (1993), *The Malevolent Leaders: Popular Discontent in America*. Boulder, Colo.: Westview Press.

—— and Michael A. Maggiotto (1981), 'Political Discontent and Political Action', *Journal of Politics*, 43: 514–22.

Crewe, Ivor and D. T. Denver (1985), *Electoral Change in Western Democracies: Patterns and Sources of Electoral Volatility*. New York: St. Martin's Press.

Crozier, Michel, Samuel P. Huntington, and Joji Watanuki (1975), *The Crisis of Democracy: Report on the Governability of Democracies to the Trilateral Commission*. New York: New York University Press.

Cumings, Bruce (1997), *Korea's Place in the Sun*. New York: W. W. Norton.

Curtice, John and Roger Jowell (1995), 'The Sceptical Electorate', in Roger Jowell *et al.* (eds.), *British Social Attitudes: The 12th Report*. Aldershot: Ashgate, 140–72.

—— —— (1997), 'Trust in the Political System', in Jowell *et al.* (eds.), *British Social Attitudes*.

Cusack, Thomas R. (1997), 'On the Road to Weimar? The Political Economy of Popular Satisfaction with Government and Regime Performance', *Germany Discussion Paper FS I 97–303*. Berlin: Wissenschaftszentrum Berlin für Sozialforschung (WZB).

Dahl, Robert A. (1971), *Polyarchy: Participation and Opposition*. New Haven: Yale University Press.

—— (1989), *Democracy and its Critics*. New Haven: Yale University Press.

——(1997), 'A Brief Intellectual Biography', in Hans Daulder (ed.), *Comparative European Politics: The Story of a Professor*. London: Pinter.

Dalton, Russell J. (1993), 'Citizens, Protest and Democracy,' special issue of *Annals of Political and Social Sciences* (July).

—— (1994), 'Communists and Democrats. Democratic Attitudes in the Two Germanys', *British Journal of Political Science*, 24: 469–93.

—— (1996), *Citizen Politics: Public Opinion and Political Parties in Advanced Western Democracies*. Chatham, NJ: Chatham House.

—— (1997), 'Citizens and Democracy: Political Support in Advanced Industrial Democracies', presented at the *Workshop on Confidence in Democratic Institutions: America in Comparative Perspective*, 25–7 August, Washington.

—— (1998a), 'Political Support in Advanced Industrial Democracies', *University of California, Irvine, Research Monograph Series No. 16*.

—— (1998b), 'Parties without Partisans: The Decline of Party Identification among Democratic Publics', presented at the Annual Meeting of the Midwest Political Science Association, Chicago.

—— and Manfred Kuechler (1990) (eds.), *Challenging the Political Order: New Social and Political Movements in Western Democracies*. New York: Oxford University Press.

—— Scott C. Flanagan, Paul A. Beck, and James E. Alt (1984), *Electoral Change in Advanced Industrial Democracies: Realignment or Dealignment?* Princeton: Princeton University Press.

Davis, James A. (1997), 'System Cynicism in Twenty Contemporary Nations', presented at the *Workshop on Confidence in Democratic Institutions: America in Comparative Perspective*, 25–7 August, Washington.

de Tocqueville, Alexis (1956), *Democracy in America*. New York: Anchor Books.

Dekker, P. and J. de Hart (1996), 'Civic Engagement in the Netherlands', paper presented to the *Conference on Social Capital and Democracy*, Milan, Oct.

—— R. Koopmans, and A. van den Broek (1995), 'Citizen Participation in Civil Societies', presented to the 18th Annual Scientific meeting of the International Society of Political Psychology, Washington, July.

—— —— —— (1996), 'Voluntary Associations, Social Movements and Individual Political Behaviour in Western Europe: A Macro–Micro Puzzle', Presented to the *ECPR Joint Sessions of Workshops*, Oslo, March–April.

Delacourt, Susan (1993), *United We Fall: The Crisis of Democracy in Canada*. Toronto: Viking.

Derbyshire, J. D. and Ian Derbyshire (1996), *Political Systems of the World*. New York: St. Martin's Press.

Diamond, Larry (1994), *Political Culture and Democracy in Developing Countries*. Boulder, Colo.: Lynne Reinner.

—— (1996), 'Is the Third Wave Over?' *Journal of Democracy*, 7/3: 20–7.

—— Juan J. Linz, and Seymour M. Lipset (1995), *Politics in Developing Countries: Comparing Experiences With Democracy*, 2nd edn. Boulder, Colo.: Lynne Reinner.

—— Marc F. Plattner, and Yun-han T. H. Chu (1997), *Consolidating the Third Wave Democracies*. Baltimore: Johns Hopkins University Press.

Dionne, Jr., E. J. (1991), *Why Americans Hate Politics*. New York: Simon and Schuster.

Downs, Anthony (1957), *An Economic Theory of Democracy*. New York: Harper & Row.

Duch, Raymond M. (1993), 'Tolerating Economic Reform: Popular Support for Transition to a Free Market in the Former Soviet Union', *American Political Science Review*, 87/3: 590–608.

Duverger, Maurice (1969), *Partis Politiques*, 3rd edn. trans. Barbara and Robert North. London: Methuen.

Easton, David (1965*a*), *A Framework for Political Analysis*. Englewood Cliffs, NJ: Prentice-Hall.

—— (1965*b*), *A Systems Analysis of Political Life*. New York: Wiley.

—— (1975), 'A Reassessment of the Concept of Political Support', *British Journal of Political Science*, 5: 435–57.

—— and Jack Dennis (1969), *Children in the Political System: Origins of Political Legitimacy*. New York: McGraw Hill.

EBRD (European Bank for Reconstruction and Development) (1995), *Transition Report Update*. London: EBRD.

—— (1996), *Transition Report Update*. London: EBRD.

Eckstein, Harry (1988), 'A Culturalist Theory of Political Change', *American Political Science Review*, 82: 789–804.

Eichler, Willi (1973), *Zur Einführung in den demokratischen Sozialismus*. Bonn: Verlag Neue Gesellschaft.

Eisenstadt, Schmuel N. (1995), *Power, Trust, and Meaning: Essays in Sociological Theory and Analysis*. Chicago: University of Chicago Press.

Ekiert, Grzegorz (1991), 'Democratization Processes in East Central Europe: A Theoretical Reconsideration', *British Journal of Political Science*, 21: 285–313.

Elazar, Daniel J. (1997), 'Contrasting Unitary and Federal Systems', *International Political Science Review*, 18/3: 237–51.

Esaiasson, Peter (1996), 'Käbblar Politikerna? Om skryt, attacker och bortförklaringar i partiernas valbudskap', in Bo Rothstein and Bo Särlvik (eds.), *Vetenskapen om politik*, Festskrift till professor emeritus Jörgen Westerståhl. Department of Political Science, Göteborg University.

—— and Sören Holmberg (1996), *Representation from Above: Members of Parliament and Representative Democracy in Sweden*. Aldershot: Dartmouth.

Ester, Peter, Loek Halman, and Ruud deMoor (1993), *The Individualizing Society*. Tilburg: Tilburg University Press.

Euchner, W. (1992), 'Die Herausbildung des Konzepts "Demokratischer Sozialismus"', in H. Münkler (ed.), *Die Chancen der Freiheit*. München/Zürich: Piper, 47–80.

Evans, Geoffrey and Stephen Whitefield (1995), 'The Politics and Economics of Democratic Commitment: Support for Democracy in Transition Societies', *British Journal of Political Science*, 25/4: 485–513.

Fallows, James (1996), *Breaking the News: How the Media Undermine American Democracy*. New York: Pantheon.

Falter, Jürgen and Hans Rattinger (1997), 'Die deutschen Parteien im Urteil der öffentlichen Meinung 1977–1994', in Oscar Gabriel, Oskar Niedermayer, and Richard Stöss (eds.), *Parteiendemokratie in Deutschland*. Bonn: Bundeszentrale für politische Bildung.

Farah, Barbara G., Samuel H. Barnes, and Felix Heunis (1979), 'Political Dissatisfaction', in S. H. Barnes and M. Kaase (eds.), *Political Action: Mass Participation in Five Western Democracies*. Beverly Hills: Sage.

Farrell, David (1997), *Comparing Electoral Systems*. London: Prentice-Hall.

Finifter, Ada W. (1996), 'Attitudes Toward Individual Responsibility and Political Reform in the Former Soviet Union: Replication and Analysis of Recent Findings', *American Political Science Review*, 90: 138–52.

—— and Ellen Mickiewicz (1992), 'Redefining the Political System of the USSR: Mass Support for Political Change', *American Political Science Review*, 86/4: 857–74.

Finke, Steven E., Edward N. Muller, and Mitchell A. Seligson (1987), 'Economic Crisis, Incumbent Performance and Regime Support', *British Journal of Political Science*, 19: 329–51.

Fiorina, Morris P. (1981), *Retrospective Voting in American National Elections*. New Haven: Yale University Press.

Foley, Michael W. and Robert Edwards (1996), 'The Paradox of Civil Society', *Journal of Democracy*, 7/3: 38–52.

—— —— (1997), 'Escape From Politics?: Social Theory and the Social Capital Debate', *American Behavioral Scientist*, 40/5: 550–61.

Fox Piven, Frances (1992), *Labour Parties in Post-industrial Societies*. Oxford: Oxford University Press.

—— and Richard Cloward (1988), *Why Americans Don't Vote*. New York: Pantheon.

Franklin, Mark, Tom Mackie, and Henry Valen (1992), *Electoral Change: Responses to Evolving Social and Attitudinal Structures in Western Countries*. New York: Cambridge University Press.

Freedom House (1996), *Freedom in the World: The Annual Survey of Political Rights and Civil Liberties, 1995–1996*. New York: Freedom House.

Friedman, Edward (1994), 'Democratization: Generalizing the East Asia Experience', in E. Friedman (ed.), *The Politics of Democratization*. Boulder,Colo.: Westview Press.

Fuchs, Dieter (1989), *Die Unterstützung des politischen Systems der Bundesrepublik Deutschland*. Opladen: Westdeutscher Verlag.

—— (1993), 'Trends of Political Support in the Federal Republic of Germany', in Dirk Berg-Schlosser and Ralf Rytlewski (eds.), *Political Culture in Germany*. London: Macmillan, 232–68.

—— (1995), 'Support for the Democratic System', in Klingemann and Fuchs (eds.), *Citizens and the State*.

—— (1996), 'Wohin geht der Wandel der demokratischen Institutionen in Deutschland?', research paper of the Wissenschaftszentrum Berlin.

—— (1997a), 'Welche Demokratie wollen die Deutschen? Einstellungen zur Demokratie im vereinigten Deutschland', in Oscar W. Gabriel (ed.), *Politische Orientierungen und Verhaltensweisen im vereinigten Deutschland*. Opladen: Leske & Budrich, 81–113.

—— (1997b), 'Wohin geht der Wandel der demokratischen Institutionen in Deutschland? Die Entwicklung der Demokratievorstellungen der Deutschen seit ihrer Vereinigung', in Gerhard Göhler (ed.), *Institutionenwandel, Leviathan Sonderheft*, xix. 1996: 253–84.

—— (1998a), 'Kriterien demokratischer Performanz in Liberalen Demokratien', in Michael Th. Greven (ed.), *Demokratie: eine Kultur des Westens?* Opladen: Leske & Budrich.

—— (1998b), 'A Causal Model of Support for Democracy in Unified Germany', unpub. MS.

—— and Hans-Dieter Klingemann (1995), 'Citizens and the State: A Relationship Transformed', in Klingemann and Fuchs (eds.), *Citizens and the State*.

—— and Edeltraud Roller (1998), 'Cultural Conditions of the Transformation to Liberal Democracies in Central and Eastern Europe', in Laszlo Bruzst, János Simon, and Samuel H. Barnes (eds.), *Post-Communist Publics*. Budapest: Ungarische Akademie der Wissenschaften.

—— Giovanna Guidorossi, and Palle Svensson (1995), 'Support for the Democratic System', in Klingemann and Fuchs (eds.), *Citizens and the State*.

Fukuyama, Francis (1991), *The End of History and the Last Man*. New York: Free Press.

—— (1992), *The End of History and the Last Man*. New York: Maxwell-Macmillan.

—— (1995), *Trust: The Social Virtues and the Creation of Prosperity*. New York: Free Press.

Gabriel, Oscar W. (1987), 'Demokratiezufriedenheit und demokratische Einstellungen in der Bundesrepublik Deutschland', in *Aus Politik und Zeitgeschichte. Beilage zur Wochenzeitung Das Parlament B22/87*, 32–45.

—— (1989), 'Systemakzeptanz und Wirtschaftslage in der Bundesrepublik Deutschland', in Jürgen W. Falter, Hans Rattinger, and Klaus G. Troitzsch (eds.), *Wahlen und Politische Einstellungen in der Bundesrepublik Deutschland*. Frankfurt am Main: Verlag Peter Lang, 196–252.

—— (1997a), 'The Confidence Crisis in Germany', University of Stuttgart, unpub.

—— (1997b), 'Politische Orientierungen und Verhaltensweisen im Transitionsprozeß', in Oscar W. Gabriel (ed.), *Politische Orientierungen und Verhaltensweisen im vereinigten Deutschland*. Opladen: Leske & Budrich, 9–33.

Gambetta, Diego (1988) (ed.), *Trust: Making and Breaking Co-operative Relations*. Oxford: Blackwell.

Gamson, William (1968), *Power and Discontent*. Homewood: Dorsey Press.

Gans, Curtis (1997), 'It's Bruce Who Got the Turnout Story Wrong', *Public Perspective*, 8/6: 44–8.

Gaskin, Katherine and Justin D. Smith (1995), *A New Civic Europe? A Study of the Extent and Role of Volunteering*. London: The Volunteer Centre.

Gastil, Raymond D. (1987), *Freedom in the World: Political Rights and Civil Liberties*. New York: Greenwood Press.

Gibson, James L. (1993), 'Perceived Political Freedom in the Soviet Union', *Journal of Politics*, 55/4: 936–74.

—— (1994), 'The Structure of Democratic and Economic Commitments in Russia and Ukraine', presented at the XVI World Congress of the International Political Science Association, Berlin.

—— (1996), 'The Paradox of Political Tolerance in Processes of Democratisation', *Politikon: South African Journal of Political Studies*, 23: 5–21.

Gibson, James L. (1997), 'Support for the Rule of Law in the Emerging South African Democracy', *International Social Science Journal*, 152: 209–24.

—— Raymond M. Duch, and Kent L. Tedin (1992), 'Democratic Values and the Transformation of the Soviet Union', *Journal of Politics*, 54/2: 329–71.

Gilljam, Mikael and Sören Holmberg (1995), *Väljarnas val*. Stockholm: Norstedts.

Granovetter, Mark (1972), 'The Strength of Weak Ties', *American Journal of Sociology*, 78: 1360–80.

Greeley, Andrew (1997), 'Coleman Revisited: Religious Structures as a Source of Social Capital', *American Behavioral Scientist*, 40/5: 587–94.

Gunther, Richard, P. Nikiforos Diamandouros, and Hans-Jürgen Puhle (1995) (eds.), *The Politics of Democratic Consolidation: Southern Europe in Comparative Perspective*. Baltimore: Johns Hopkins University Press.

Gurr, Ted (1971), *Why Men Rebel*. Princeton: Princeton University Press.

Hadenius, Axel (1994), 'The Duration of Democracy', in David Beetham (ed.), *Defining and Measuring Democracy*. London: Sage.

—— (1997) (ed.), *Democracy's Victory and Crisis*. Cambridge: Cambridge University Press.

Hall, Peter A. (1997), 'Social Capital in Britain', *Vertelsmann Stifung Workshop on Social Capital*, Berlin (June).

Hardarson, Olafur Th. (1995), *Parties and Voters in Iceland*. Reykjavik: Social Science Research Institute–University Press, University of Iceland.

Hardin, Russell (1982), *Collective Action*. Baltimore: Johns Hopkins University Press.

—— (1992), 'The Street Level Epistemology of Trust', *Analyse & Kritik*, 14: 152–76.

—— (1996), 'Trustworthiness', *Ethics,* 107: 26–42

Harmel, Robert and John D. Robertson (1986), 'Government Stability and Regime Support: A Cross-National Analysis', *Journal of Politics*, 48: 1029–40.

Hart, Roderick (1994), *Seducing America*. New York: Oxford University Press.

Hayward, Jack (1995), *The Crisis of Representation in Europe*. London: Frank Cass.

—— (1996), *Elitism, Populism, and European Politics*. Oxford: Clarendon Press.

Held, David (1987), *Models of Democracy*. Stanford: Stanford University Press.

Helliwell, John F. (1994), 'Empirical Linkages between Democracy and Economic Growth', *British Journal of Political Science*, 24/2: 225–48.

Hibbing, John R. and Elizabeth Theiss-Morse (1995), *Congress As Public Enemy*. New York: Cambridge University Press.

Hirschman, Albert O. (1970), *Exit, Voice and Loyalty*. Cambridge, Mass.: Harvard University Press.

Holmberg, Sören (1996), 'Policy Congruence Compared', in Warren Miller *et al.*, *Political Representation in Western Democracies*. Ann Arbor: University of Michigan Press.

—— (1997*a*), 'Svenska folket är si så där nöjda med hur demokratin fungerar i Sverige', in Sören Holmberg and Lennart Weibull (eds.), *Ett missnöjt folk*. Göteborg: Som Institute, Göteborg University.

—— (1997*b*), 'Issue Agreement', in Peter Esaiasson and Knut Heidar (eds.), *Beyond Congress and Westminster. The Nordic Experience*.

—— (1997*c*), 'Dynamic Opinion Representation', *Scandinavian Political Studies*, 20: 265–83.

—— and Lennart Weibull (1997*a*) (eds.). *Trends in Swedish Opinion*. Göteborg: SOM Institute, Göteborg University.

—— (1997*d*), 'Förtroendets fall', in Sören Holmberg and Lennart Weibull (eds.), *Ett missnöjt folk*. Göteborg: SOM Institute, Göteborg University.

Hoover, Kenneth and Raymond Plant (1989), *Conservative Capitalism in Britain and the United States*. London: Routledge.

Huntington, Samuel P. (1975), 'The Democratic Distemper', *Public Interest*, 41: 9–38.

—— (1981), *American Politics: The Promise of Disharmony*. Cambridge, Mass.: Harvard University Press.

—— (1991), *The Third Wave: Democratization in the Late Twentieth Century*. Norman: University of Oklahoma Press.

IDEA (1997*a*), *Voter Turnout From 1945 to 1997: A Global Report*. 2nd edn. Stockholm: International Institute for Democracy and Electoral Assistance.

—— (1997*b*), *The International IDEA Handbook of Electoral System Design*. Stockholm: International Institute for Democracy and Electoral Assistance.

Inglehart, Ronald (1977), *The Silent Revolution: Changing Values and Political Styles Among Western Publics*. Princeton: Princeton University Press.

—— (1990), *Culture Shift in Advanced Industrial Society*. Princeton: Princeton University Press.

—— (1997*a*). *Modernization and Postmodernization: Cultural, Economic and Political Change in 43 Societies*. Princeton: Princeton University Press.

—— (1997*b*), 'The Erosion of Institutional Authority and Post-materialist Values', in Joseph S. Nye, Philip D. Zelikow, and David C. King (eds.), *Why People Don't Trust Government*. Cambridge, Mass.: Harvard University Press.

—— and Paul Abramson (1994), 'Economic security and value change', *American Political Science Review*, 88: 336–54.

Ingram, Helen and Steven Smith (1993) (eds.), *Public Policy for Democracy*. Washington: Brookings Institution.

Iyengar, Shanto (1991), *Is Anyone Responsible? : How Television Frames Political Issues*. Chicago: University of Chicago Press.

Jennings, M. Kent (1991), 'Thinking About Social Injustice', *Political Psychology*, 12: 187–204.

—— and Jan van Deth (1989), *Continuities in Political Action*. Berlin: de Gruyter.

Jowell, Roger and Richard Topf (1988), 'Trust in the establishment', in R. Jowell, S. Witherspoon, and L. Brook (eds.), *British Social Attitudes: The 5th Report*. Brookfield, Vt.: Gower Publishing.

Kaase, Max (1995), 'Die Deutschen auf dem Weg zur inneren Einheit? Eine Längsschnittanalyse von Selbst-und Fremdwahrnehmungen bei West-und Ostdeutschen', in Hedwig Rudolph (ed.), *Geplanter Wandel, ungeplante Wirkungen*. Berlin: Sigma: 160–81.

—— 'Trust and Participation in Contemporary Democracies', unpub.

—— (1998), 'Die Bundesrepublik. Prognosen und Diagnosen der Demokratieentwicklung in der rückblickenden Bewertung', in Jürgen Friedrichs, M. Rainer Lepsius, and Karl-Ulrich Mayer (eds.), *Diagnosefähigkeit der Soziologie. 38. Sonderheft der Kölner Zeitschrift für Soziologie und Sozialpsychologie*. Opladen/Wiesbaden: Westdeutscher Verlag.

—— and Kenneth Newton (1995), *Beliefs in Government*. New York: Oxford University Press.

—— and Petra Bauer-Kaase (1998), 'Deutsche Vereinigung und innere Einheit 1990–1997', in Heiner Meulemann (ed.), *Werte und nationale Identität im vereinigten Deutschland: Erklärungsansätze der Umfrageforschung*. Opladen: Leske & Budrich.

Karatnycky, Adrian (1997), 'Freedom on the March', *Freedom Review*, 28/1: 5–27.

Katz, D., B. A. Gutek, R. Kahn, and E. Barton (1975), *Bureaucratic Encounters*. Ann Arbor: Institute for Social Research.

Katz, Richard S. and Peter Mair (1994), *How Parties Organize: Change and Adaptation in Party Organizations in Western Democracies*. Thousand Oaks: Sage Publications.

Kinder, Donald and D. Roderick Kiewiet (1979), 'Economic Discontent and Political Behavior: The Role of Personal Grievances and Collective Economic Judgements in Congressional Voting', *American Journal of Political Science*, 23: 281–325.

—— —— (1981), 'Sociotropic Politics: the American Case', *British Journal of Political Science*, 11: 129–61.

—— and W. R. Mebane (1983), 'Politics and Economics in Everyday Life', in K. B. Monroe (ed.), *The Political Process and Economic Change*. New York: Agathon Press.

King, Anthony (1975), 'Overload: Problems of Governing in the 1970s', *Political Studies*, 23: 284–96.

King, David C. (1997), 'The Polarization of American Political Parties and Mistrust of Government', in Nye, Zelikow, and King (eds.), *Why Americans Mistrust Government*.

Kitschelt, Herbert (1994), *The Transformation of European Social Democracy*. Cambridge: Cambridge University Press.

Klingemann, Hans-Dieter and Richard I. Hofferbert (1994), 'Germany: A New "Wall in the Mind"?' *Journal of Democracy*, 5: 30–44.

—— and Dieter Fuchs (1995) (eds.), *Citizens and the State*. Oxford: Oxford University Press.

—— Richard I. Hofferbert, and Ian Budge (1994), *Parties, Policies, and Democracy*. Boulder, Colo.: Westview Press.

Koechler, Hans (1987), *The Crisis of Representative Democracy*. New York: P. Lang.

Kohli, Atul (1990), *Democracy and Discontent: India's Growing Crisis of Governability*. New York: Cambridge University Press.

Kolankiewicz, G. (1994), 'Elites in Search of a Political Formula', *Daedalus* (Summer), 143–57.

Koo, H. (1993) (ed.), *State and Society in Contemporary Korea*. Ithaca, NY: Cornell University Press.

Koole, Ruud and Peter Mair (1991), *European Journal of Political Research, Political Data Yearbook*, 21/4. Dordrecht: Kluwer.

Korean Consortium of Academic Associations (1997), *The June Mass Uprising and Korean Society after Ten Years*. Seoul: Dangdae.

Kornai, Janos (1992), *The Socialist Economy*. Princeton: Princeton University Press.

—— (1994), 'Painful Tradeoffs in Postsocialism', *Transition*, 5/5: 5–6.

Kornberg, Allan and Harold D. Clarke (1992), *Citizens and Community: Political Support in a Representative Democracy*. Cambridge: Cambridge University Press.

Krieger, Joel (1986), *Reagan, Thatcher and the Politics of Decline*. Oxford: Polity Press.

Kuechler, Manfred (1991), 'The Dynamics of Mass Political Support in Western Europe', in Karlheinz Reif and Ronald Inglehart (eds.), *Eurobarometer*. London: Macmillan.

Laakso, Markuu and Rein Taagepera (1979), ' "Effective" Number of Parties: A Measure With Application to West Europe', *Comparative Political Studies*, 12: 3–27.

Ladd, Everette C .(1996), 'The Date Just Don't Show Erosion of America's Social Capital', *Public Perspective*, 7/4.

Lagos, Marta (1997), 'Notes on Democratic Perceptions in Latin America: Evidence from the Latinobarometro', paper presented at the *Workshop on Confidence in Democratic Institutions: America in Comparative Perspective*, 25–7 Aug. 1997, Washington.

Lane, Jan-Erik and Svante O. Ersson (1996), *European Politics*. London: Sage.

—— David McKay, and Kenneth Newton (1997) (eds.), *Political Data Handbook*. 2nd edn. Oxford: Oxford University Press.

Laponce, Jean and Bernard Saint-Jacques (1997), 'Contrasting Political Institutions', *International Political Science Review*, 18/3.

Lawrence, R. Z. (1997), 'Is it Really the Economy, Stupid?', in Nye, Zelikow, and King (eds.), *Why People Don't Trust Government.*

LeDuc, Lawrence (1995), 'The Canadian Voter', in Robert Krause and R. Wagenberg (eds.), *Introductory Readings in Canadian Government and Politics*, 2nd edn. Toronto: Coop Clark.

—— Richard G. Niemi, and Pippa Norris (1996), *Comparing Democracies: Elections and Voting in Global Perspectives.* Thousand Oaks: Sage Publications.

Leftwich, Adrian (1995), 'Bringing Politics Back In: Towards a Model of the Developmental State', *Journal of Development Studies*, 31: 400–27.

Lepsius, M. Rainer (1995), 'Das Legat zweier Diktaturen für die demokratische Kultur im vereinigten Deutschland', in E. Holtmann and H. Sahner (eds.), *Aufhebung der Bipolarität—Veränderungen im Osten, Rückwirkungen im Westen.* Opladen: Leske & Budrich: 25–39.

Levi, Margaret (1996), 'Social and Unsocial Capital: A Review Essay of Robert Putnam's *Making Democracy Work*', *Politics and Society*, 24/1: 45–55.

Lewis-Beck, Michael (1988), *Economics and Elections: The Major Western Democracies.* Ann Arbor: University of Michigan Press.

Lijphart, Arend (1977), *Democracy in Plural Societies: A Comparative Exploration.* New Haven: Yale University Press.

—— (1984), *Democracies: Patterns of Majoritarian and Consensus Government in Twenty-One Countries.* New Haven: Yale University Press.

—— (1992) (ed.), *Parliamentary Versus Presidential Government.* Oxford: Oxford University Press.

—— (1994a), 'Democracies: Forms, Performance and Constitutional Engineering', *European Journal of Political Research*, 25: 1–17.

—— (1994b), *Electoral Systems and Party Systems: A Study of Twenty-Seven Democracies, 1945–1990.* New York: Oxford University Press.

—— and Bernard Grofman (1984), *Choosing an Electoral System: Issues and Alternatives.* New York: Praeger.

—— and Carlos H. Waisman (1996), *Institutional Design in New Democracies: Eastern Europe and Latin America.* Boulder, Colo.: Westview Press.

Linz, Juan J. (1990), 'The Perils of Presidentialism', *Journal of Democracy*, 1/1.

—— and Alfred C. Stepan (1978), *The Breakdown of Democratic Regimes.* Baltimore: Johns Hopkins University Press.

—— —— (1996), *Problems of Democratic Transition and Consolidation: Southern Europe, South America and Post-Communist Europe.* Baltimore: Johns Hopkins University Press.

Lipset, Seymour M. (1959), 'Some Social Requisites of Democracy, Economic Development and Political Legitimacy', *American Political Science Review*, 53: 69–105.

—— (1981), *Political Man.* Baltimore: Johns Hopkins University Press.

—— (1990), *Continental Divide: The Values and Institutions of the United States and Canada.* New York: Routledge.

—— (1993), 'A Comparative Analysis of the Social Requisites of Democracy', *International Social Science Journal*, 136/2: 155–75.

—— (1994), 'The Social Requisites of Democracy Revisited', *American Sociological Review*, 59: 1–22.

—— (1996), *American Exceptionalism: A Double-Edged Sword.* New York: W. W. Norton.

—— and Stein Rokkan (1967) (eds.), *Party Systems and Voter Alignments.* New York: Free Press.

Lipset, Seymour M. and William C. Schneider (1983), *The Confidence Gap: Business, Labor, and Government in the Public Mind*. New York: Free Press.

—— —— (1987), *The Confidence Gap: Business, Labor, and Government in the Public Mind*, rev. edn. Baltimore: Johns Hopkins University Press.

Listhaug, Ola (1995), 'The Dynamics of Trust in Politicians', in Klingemann and Fuchs (eds.), *Citizens and the State*.

—— (1997), 'Confidence in Political Institutions: Norway 1982–1996', paper prepared for a research seminar on *Confidence in Governance*, John F. Kennedy School of Government, Harvard University, November.

—— and Matti Wiberg (1995), 'Confidence in Political and Private Institutions', in Klingemann and Fuchs (eds.), *Citizens and the State*. Oxford: Oxford University Press.

Little, I. M. D. (1996), *Picking Winners: The East Asian Experience*. London: Social Market Foundation, Occasional Paper No. 13.

Lockerbie, B. (1993), 'Economic Dissatisfaction and Political Alienation in Western Europe', *European Journal of Political Research*, 23: 281–93.

Longchamp, Claude (1991), 'Politische-kultureller Wandel in der Schweiz', in Fritz Plasser and Peter Ulram (eds.), *Staatsbürger oder Untertanen?* Frankfurt: Lang.

Luhmann, Niklas (1979), *Trust and Power*. New York: Wiley.

Lull, James and Stephen Hinerman (1997) (eds.), *Media Scandals*. Cambridge: Polity Press.

McAdam, Doug, John D. McCarthy, and Mayer N. Zald (1996), *Comparative Perspectives on Social Movements*. Cambridge: Cambridge University Press.

McAllister, Ian (1992), *Political Behaviour*. Melbourne: Longman Cheshire.

McClosky, Herbert and Laid Brill (1983), *Dimensions of Tolerance: What Americans Believe About Civil Liberties*. New York: Russell Sage Foundation.

—— and John Zaller (1994), *The American Ethos: Public Attitudes Towards Capitalism and Democracy*. Cambridge, Mass.: Harvard University Press.

McColm, R. B. (1991), 'The Survey 1991', *Freedom Review*, 22/1.

McGregor, James P. (1991), 'Value Structures in a Developed Socialist System: The Case of Czechoslovakia', *Comparative Politics*, 23: 181–99.

MacKuen, Michael B., Robert S. Erickson, and James A. Stimson (1992), 'Peasants or Bankers? The American Electorate and the U.S. Economy', *American Political Science Review*, 86: 597–611.

McQuaid, Kim (1989), *The Anxious Years: America In the Vietnam–Watergate Era*. New York: Basic Books.

McRae, Kenneth D. (1997), 'Contrasting Styles of Democratic Decision-Making: Adversarial Versus Consensual Politics', *International Political Science Review*, 18/3.

Maier, Charles S. (1994), 'Democracy and Its Discontents', *Foreign Affairs*, 73/4: 48–65.

Mair, Peter (1997), *Party System Change*. Oxford: Oxford University Press.

Marshall, T. H. (1965), *Class, Citizenship and Social Development*. Garden City, NY: Doubleday.

Mason, Edward S. (1980), *The Economic and Social Modernization of the Republic of Korea*. Cambridge, Mass.: Harvard University Press.

Miller, Arthur H. (1974*a*), 'Political Issues and Trust in Government, 1964–1970', *American Political Science Review*, 68: 951–72.

—— (1974*b*), 'Rejoinder to "Comment" by Jack Citrin: Political Discontent or Ritualism?', *American Political Science Review*, 68: 989–1001.

—— and Ola Listhaug (1990), 'Political Parties and Confidence in Government: A Comparison of Norway, Sweden and the United States', *British Journal of Political Science*, 29: 357–86.

—— and Stephen A. Borrelli (1991), 'Confidence in Government During the 1980s', *American Politics Quarterly*, 19/2: 147–73.

—— and Bruce E. Gronbeck (1994), *Presidential Campaigns and American Self Images.* Boulder, Colo.: Westview Press.

—— Vicki L. Hesli, and William M. Reisinger (1996), 'Understanding Political Change in Post-Soviet Sociaties', *American Political Science Review*, 90/1: 153–66.

—— —— —— (1997), 'Conceptions of Democracy Among Mass and Elite in Post-Soviet Societies', *British Journal of Political Science*, 27/2: 157–90.

Miller, Stephen D. and David O. Sears (1985), 'Stability and Change in Social Tolerance: A Test of the Persistence Hypothesis', *American Journal of Political Science*, 30: 214–36.

Miller, William L., Stephen White, and Paul Heywood (1998), *Values and Political Change in Postcommunist Europe.* New York: St. Martin's Press.

Mishler, William, and Richard Rose (1994), 'Support for Parliaments and Regimes in the Transition Toward Democracy', *Legislative Studies Quarterly*, 19: 5–32.

—— —— (1995*a*), 'Trajectories of Fear and Hope: Support for Democracy in Post-Communist Europe', *Comparative Political Studies*, 28: 553–81.

—— —— (1995*b*), 'Trust, Distrust and Skepticism: Popular Evaluations of Civil and Political Institutions in Post-Communist Societies', *Journal of Politics*, 59/2: 418–51.

—— —— (1997), 'Five Years After the Fall: The Trajectory and Dynamics of Support for Democracy in Post-Communist Europe', paper presented at the *Workshop on Confidence in Democratic Institutions: America in Comparative Perspective*, 25–7 Aug., Washington.

Misztal, Barbara A. (1996), *Trust in Modern Societies.* Oxford: Blackwell.

Monroe, James A. (1990), *The Democratic Wish.* New York: Basic Books.

Monroe, Kristen (1984), *Presidential Popularity and the Economy.* New York: Praeger.

Montero, Jose R., Richard Gunter, and Mariano Torcal (1997), 'Democracy in Spain: Between discontent and crisis of confidence', unpub.

Morlino, Leonardo, and Jose R. Montero (1995), 'Legitimacy and Democracy in Southern Europe', in R. Gunter, N. Diamandorous, and Hans-Jurgen Puhle (eds.), *The Politics of Democratic Consolidation: Southern Europe in Comparative Perspective.* Baltimore: Johns Hopkins University Press.

—— and Marco Tarchi (1996), 'The Dissatisfied Society: The Roots of Political Change in Italy', *European Journal of Political Research*, 30/1: 41–63.

Muller, Edward N. (1979), *Aggressive Political Participation*, Princeton: Princeton University Press.

—— and Thomas O. Jukam (1977), 'On the Meaning of Political Support', *American Political Science Review*, 71: 1561–95.

—— Thomas O. Jukam, and Mitchell A. Seligson (1982), 'Diffuse Political Support and Anti-system Political Behavior', *American Journal of Political Science*, 26/3: 240–64.

Neuman, W. R. (1986), *The Paradox of Mass Politics.* Cambridge, Mass.: Harvard University Press.

Newton, Kenneth (1976), *Second City Politics: Democratic Processes, and Decision-making in Birmingham.* Oxford: Oxford University Press.

—— (1997*a*), 'Politics and the News Media: Mobilization or Videomalaise?', in R. Jowell *et al.* (eds.), *British Social Attitudes: the 14th Report*, 1997/8 vol. 14. Aldershot: Ashgate.

—— (1997*b*), 'Social Capital and Democracy', *American Behavioral Scientist*, 40/5: 575–86.

Noelle-Neumann, Elisabeth (1991), 'The German Revolution: The Historic Experiment of the Division and Unification of a Nation as Reflected in Survey Research Findings', *International Journal of Public Opinion Research*, 3: 238–59.
—— and Renate Köcher (1993), *Allensbacher Jahrbuch der Demoskopie 1984–1992*. Munich: K. G. Saur.
—— —— (1997), *Allensbacher Jahrbuch der Demoskopie 1993–1997*. Munich: K. G. Saur.
Norpoth, Helmut (1992), *Confidence Regained: Economics, Mrs. Thatcher, and the British Voter*. Ann Arbor: University of Michigan Press.
Norris, Pippa (1995), 'The Politics of Electoral Reform', *International Political Science Review*, 16/1: 1–14.
—— (1996), 'Does Television Erode Social Capital? A Reply to Putnam', *Political Science and Politics*, 29: 474–80.
—— (1997a), *Electoral Change in Britain Since 1945*. Oxford: Blackwell.
—— (1997b), 'Choosing Electoral Systems: Proportional, Majoritarian and Mixed Systems', *International Political Science Review*, 18/3.
—— (1997c), (ed.), *Passages to Power: Legislative Recruitment in Advanced Industrialised Societies*. Cambridge: Cambridge University Press.
—— and Joni Lovenduski (1995), *Political Recruitment: Gender, Race and Class in the British Parliament*. Cambridge: Cambridge University Press.
—— and John Curtice (1998), 'The Media and Civic Engagement', paper presented at the *ECPR Joint Workshops*, Warwick University.
Norton, Philip (1997), 'Greater Institutionalization, Less Public Support: The British House of Commons in the 1990s', *Extensions* (Spring), 4–7.
Nozick, Robert (1974), *Anarchy, State, and Utopia*. New York: Basic Books.
Nye, Joseph S. (1997), 'Introduction: The Decline Of Confidence In Government', in Nye, Zelikow, and King (eds.), *Why People Don't Trust Government*.
—— and Philip D. Zelikow (1997), 'Reflections, Conjectures, and Puzzles', in Nye, Zelikow, and King (eds.), *Why People Don´t Trust Government*.
O'Donnell, Guillermo (1994), 'Delegative Democracy', *Journal of Democracy*, 5/1: 55–69.
—— Philippe Schmitter, and Lawrence Whitehead (1986), *Transitions From Authoritarian Rule*. Baltimore: Johns Hopkins University Press.
Olson, Jr., Mancur (1965), *The Logic of Collective Action*. Cambridge, Mass.: Harvard University Press.
Orren, Gary (1997), 'Fall From Grace: The Public's Loss Of Faith In Government', in Nye, Zelikow, and King (eds.), *Why People Don't Trust Government*.
Parker, Suzanne L. and Glenn R. Parker (1993), 'Why Do We Trust Our Congressmen?' *Journal of Politics*, 55/2: 442–53.
Parry, Geraint (1976), 'Trust, Distrust and Consensus', *British Journal of Political Science*, 6: 129–42.
—— George Moyser, and Neil Day (1992), *Political Participation and Democracy in Britain*. Cambridge: Cambridge University Press.
Parsons, Talcott (1951), *The Social System*. London: Routledge & Kegan Paul.
—— (1969), *Politics and Social Structure*. New York: Free Press.
Patterson, Samuel C. and Gregory A. Caldeira (1990), 'Standing Up For Congress: Variations in Public Esteem Since the 1960s', *Legislative Studies Quarterly*, 15/1: 25–47.
Patterson, Thomas E. (1993), *Out of Order*. New York: Alfred A. Knopf.
—— and Wolfgang Donsbach (1997), 'The News and Public Opinion', paper presented at the *Workshop on Confidence in Democratic Institutions: America in Comparative Perspective*, 25–7 Aug. Washington.

Peffley, Mark (1984), 'The Voter as Juror: Attributing Responsibility for Economic Conditions', *Political Behavior*, 6: 275–94.

Pempel, T. J. (1990), *Uncommon Democracies: The One Party Dominant Regimes*. Ithaca, NY: Cornell University Press.

Petersson, Olof (1977), *Väljarna och valet 1976)*. Stockholm: SCB/Liber.

Pharr, Susan (1997), 'Political Trust and Democracy in Japan', in Nye, Zelikow, and King (eds.), *Why People Don't Trust Government*. Cambridge: Harvard University Press.

Plasser, Fritz (1987), *Parteien unter Stress*. Vienna: Böhlau.

—— and Peter Ulram (1991) (eds.), *Staatsbürger oder Untertanen?*. Frankfurt: Lang.

Pollack, Detlef (1997), 'Das Bedürfnis nach sozialer Anerkennung: Der Wandel der Akzeptanz von Demokratie und Marktwirtschaft in Ostdeutschland', *Aus Politik und Zeitgeschichte. Beilage zur Wochenzeitung Das Parlament B13/97*: 3–14.

—— Gert Pickel, and Jörg Jacobs (1998), 'Wächst zusammen was zusammengehört? Subjektive und objektive Komponenten sozialer Ungleichheit in Ost- und Westdeutschland', in Ronald Lutz (ed.), *Armutsforschung und Sozialberichterstattung in den neuen Bundesländern*. Opladen: Leske & Budrich.

Powell, Jr., G. Bingham (1982), *Contemporary Democracies*. Cambridge, Mass.: Harvard University Press.

—— (1989), 'Constitutional Design and Citizen Electoral Control', *Journal of Theoretical Politics*, 1/2: 107–30.

Przeworski, Adam (1991), *Democracy and the Market: Political and Economic Reform in Eastern Europe and Latin America*. Cambridge: Cambridge University Press.

—— and Henry Teune (1970), *The Logic of Comparative Social Inquiry*. New York: Wiley.

Putnam, Robert D. (1993), *Making Democracy Work*. Princeton, NJ: Princeton.

—— (1995a), 'Bowling Alone: America's Declining Social Capital', *Journal of Democracy*, 6: 65–78.

—— (1995b), 'Tuning In, Tuning Out: The Strange Disappearance of Social Capital in America', *Political Science and Politics*, 28/4: 664–83.

—— (1996), 'The Strange Disappearance of Civic America', *American Prospect*, 24.

—— and Steven Yonish (1998), 'New Evidence on Trends in American Social Capital and Civic Engagement: Are We Really "Bowling Alone"?' unpub.

Raboy, Marc and Bernard Dagenais (1992), *Media, Crisis and Democracy: Mass Communications and the Disruption of Social Order*. London: Sage.

Rae, Douglas W. (1971), *The Political Consequences of Electoral Laws*, rev. edn. New Haven: Yale University Press.

Ragin, Charles (1987), *The Comparative Method*. Berkeley: University of California Press.

Rawls, John (1971), *A Theory of Justice*. Cambridge, Mass.: Harvard University Press.

—— (1993), *Political Liberalism*. New York: Columbia University Press.

Robinson, Michael (1976), 'Public Affairs Television and the Growth of Political Malaise: The Case of "The Selling of the Pentagon" ', *American Political Science Review*, 70: 409–32.

Rogowski, Ronald (1974), *Rational Legitimacy: A Theory of Political Support*. Princeton: Princeton University Press.

Rohrschneider, Robert (1994), 'Report from the Laboratory: The Influence of Institutions on Political Elites' Democratic Values in Germany', *American Political Science Review*, 88: 927–41.

—— (1996), 'Institutional Learning versus Value Diffusion: The Evolution of Democratic Values Among Parliamentarians in Eastern and Western Germany', *Journal of Politics*, 58: 442–66.

Rohrschneider, Robert (1998), *Learning Democracy: Democratic and Economic Values in Unified Germany*. Oxford: Oxford University Press.

Roller, Edeltraud (1994), 'Ideological Basis of the Market Economy: Attitudes Toward Distributional Principles and the Role of Government in Western and Eastern Germany', *European Sociological Review*, 10: 105–17.

—— (1997), 'Sozialpolitische Orientierungen nach der deutschen Vereinigung', in Gabriel (ed.), *Politische Orientierungen und Verhaltensweisen im vereinigten Deutschland*, 115–46.

Rose, Richard (1984), *Do Parties Make a Difference?* 2nd edn. London: Macmillan.

—— (1992), 'Escaping from Absolute Dissatisfaction: A Trial-and-Error Model of Change in Eastern Europe', *Journal of Theoretical Politics*, 4/4: 371–93.

—— (1995a), 'A Crisis of Confidence in British Party Leaders', *Contemporary Record*, 9/2: 273–93.

—— (1995b), 'Freedom as a Fundamental Value', *International Social Science Journal*, 145: 457–71.

—— (1997a), *Survey Measures of Democracy*. Glasgow: University of Strathclyde Studies in Public Policy No. 294.

—— (1997b), 'How Patient Are People in Post-Communist Societies?' *World Affairs*, 159/3: 130–44.

—— and Christian Haerpfer (1992), *New Democracies between State and Nation: A Baseline Report of Public Opinion*. Glasgow: University of Strathclyde Studies in Public Policy No. 204.

—— —— (1993), *Adapting to Transformation in Eastern Europe: New Democracies Barometer II*. Glasgow: University of Strathclyde Studies in Public Policy No. 212.

—— —— (1994), *New Democracies Barometer III: Learning from What is Happening*. Glasgow: University of Strathclyde Studies in Public Policy No. 230.

—— —— (1996a), *New Democracies Barometer IV: A 10-Nation Survey*. Glasgow: University of Strathclyde Studies in Public Policy No. 262.

—— —— (1996b), *Change and Stability in the New Democracies Barometer: A Trend Analysis*. Glasgow: University of Strathclyde Studies in Public Policy No. 270.

—— and William Mishler (1994), 'Mass Reaction to Regime Change in Eastern Europe: Polarization or Leaders and Laggards?' *British Journal of Political Science*, 24: 159–82.

—— —— (1996), 'Testing the Churchill Hypothesis: Popular Support for Democracy and its Alternatives', *Journal of Public Policy*, 16: 29–58.

—— —— and Christian Haerpfer (1998), *Democracy and Its Alternatives: Understanding Post-Communist Societies*. Oxford: Polity Press.

Rosenstone, Steven J. and John M. Hansen (1993), *Mobilization, Participation, and Democracy in America*. New York: Macmillan.

Rothstein, Bo (1997), 'Sociala fällor och tillitens problem', in Holmberg and Weibull (eds.), *Ett missnöjt folk*.

Ruddle, Helen and Joyce O'Connor (1995), 'Volunteering in the Republic of Ireland', in Joyce D. Smith (ed.), *Voluntary Action Research*, Voluntary Action Research: Volunteering in Europe, Second Series, Paper No. 4. London: The Volunteer Centre, 91–104.

Rustow, Dankwart A. (1970), 'Transitions to Democracy', *Comparative Politics*, 2: 337–63.

Sabato, Larry (1991), *Feeding Frenzy: How Attack Journalism Has Transformed American Politics*. New York: Free Press.

Sahlins, Marshall (1972), *Stone Age Economics*. Hawthorne, NY: Aldine.

Sakamoto, Y. (1995), 'A Study of the Japanese National Character: Ninth Nationwide

Survey', Institute of Statistical Mathematics, Tokyo, Research Memorandum No. 572.

Sampson, Anthony (1993), *The Essential Anatomy of Britain: Democracy in Crisis*. New York: Harcourt Brace.

Samuelson, Robert J. (1995), *The Good Life and its Discontents*. New York: Random House.

Sartori, Giovanni (1976), *Parties and Party Systems: a Framework for Analysis*. New York: Cambridge University Press.

—— (1987), *The Theory of Democracy Revisited*. Chatham, NJ: Chatham House.

—— (1994), *Comparative Constitutional Engineering*. London: Macmillan.

Saward, Michael (1994), 'Democratic Theory and Indices of Democratization', in Beetham (ed.), *Defining and Measuring Democracy*, 6–24.

Schmidt, Manfred G. (1998), *Sozialpolitik in Deutschland. Historische Entwicklung und internationaler Vergleich*. Opladen: Leske & Budrich.

Schmitt, Herman and Sören Holmberg (1995), 'Political Parties in Decline?', in Klingemann and Fuchs (eds.), *Citizens and the State*.

Schumpeter, Joseph A. (1952), *Capitalism, Socialism and Democracy*. 4th edn. London: George Allen & Unwin.

Sears, David O. (1975), 'Political Socialization', in Fred I. Greenstein and Nelson W. Polsby (eds.), *Handbook of Political Science*, ii. Reading: Addison-Wesley.

Shin, Doh Chull (1998), *The Evolution of Popular Support for Democracy during the Kim Young Sam Government*. Glasgow: University of Strathclyde Studies in Public Policy No. 297.

—— and Richard Rose (1997), *Koreans Evaluate Democracy: A Survey Study*. Glasgow: University of Strathclyde Studies in Public Policy No. 292.

Shlapentokh, Vladimir (1989), *Public and Private Life of the Soviet People*. New York: Oxford University Press.

Sik, Ota (1992), 'Sind Sozialismus und Demokratie vereinbar?', in Herfried Münkler (ed.), *Die Chancen der Freiheit: Grundprobleme der Demokratie*. Munich/Zürich: Piper, 81–91.

Simon, Janos (1996), *Popular Conceptions of Democracy in Post-Communist Europe*. University of Strathclyde Studies in Public Policy No. 273.

Smith, Tom (1997), 'Factors Relating to Misanthropy in Contemporary American Society', *Social Science Research*, 26: 170–96.

Starr, Harvey (1991), 'Democratic Dominoes: Diffusion Approaches to the Spread of Democracy in the International System', *Journal of Conflict Resolution*, 35: 356–81.

Sundquist, James L. (1980), 'The Crisis of Competence in Our National Government', *Political Science Quarterly*, 95: 183–208.

Svallfors, Stefan (1997), 'Political Trust and Attitudes Towards Redistribution: A Comparison of Sweden and Norway', paper presented at the annual meeting of the International Social Survey Program.

SWS-Rundschau (1992), 'Meinungsprofile: Neue Demokratien Barometer 1991', *SWS-Rundschau*. Vienna, 32: 57–88.

Sztompka, Piotr (1996), 'Trust and Emerging Democracy', *International Sociology* 11/1: 37–62.

Taagepera, Rein and Matthew S. Shugart (1989), *Seats and Votes: The Effects and Determinants of Electoral Systems*. New Haven: Yale University Press.

Taras, Raymond C. and Rajat Ganguly (1998), *Understanding Ethnic Conflict: The International Dimension*. New York: Longman.

Tarrow, Sidney (1996), 'Making Social Science Work Across Space And Time: A Critical Reflection On Robert Putnam's *Making Democracy Work'*, *American Political Science Review*, 90: 389–97.

Taylor, Charles (1985), 'Human Agency and Language', *Philosophical Papers*, 1. Cambridge: Cambridge University Press.

—— (1992), 'Wieviel Gemeinschaft braucht die Demokratie?' *Transit*, 5: 5–20.

Teixeira, Ruy A. (1992), *The Disappearing American Voter*. Washington: The Brookings Institution.

Thomassen, Jacques (1990), 'Economic Crisis, Dissatisfaction and Protest', in Jennings and van Deth (eds.), *Continuities in Political Action*.

—— (1995), 'Support for Democratic Values', in Klingemann and Fuchs (eds.), *Citizens and the State*.

Tolchin, Susan J. (1996), *The Angry American: How Voter Rage Is Changing the Nation*. Boulder, Colo.: Westview Press.

Topf, Richard (1986), 'Political Change and Political Culture in Britain 1959–87', in John Gibbins (ed.), *Contemporary Political Culture; Politics in a Postmodern Age*. London: Sage.

—— (1995), 'Beyond Electoral Participation', in Klingemann and Fuchs (eds.), *Citizens and the State*.

—— Peter Mohler, and Anthony Heath (1989), 'Pride in One's Country: Britain and West Germany', in Jowell, Witherspoon, and Brook (eds.), *British Social Attitudes: Special International Report*.

Torcal, Mariano and Jose R. Montero (1996), 'Social Capital in Spain: Exploring Political Attitudes and Behaviour Between Continuity and Change', unpub. paper.

Transparency International (1997), *Transparency International Publishes 1997 Corruption Perception Index*. Berlin: Transparency International.

Tyler, Tom R., Kenneth Rasinski, and Kathleen McGraw (1985), 'The Influence of Perceived Injustice Upon Support for the President, Political Authorities, and Government Institutions', *Journal of Applied Social Psychology*, 15: 700–25.

Ulram, Peter (1994), 'Political Culture and Party System in the Kreisky Era', in Günther Bischof and Anton Pelinka (eds.), *The Kreisky Era in Austria*. New Brunswick: Transaction Publishers.

Uslaner, Eric M. (undated), 'Faith, Hope and Charity: Social capital, Trust, and Collective Action', University of Maryland, unpub.

—— and Robert D. Putnam (1996), 'Democracy and Social Capital', prepared for the *Conference on Democracy and Trust*, Georgetown University, November.

—— (1996), 'Morality Plays: Social Capital and Moral Behavior in Anglo-American Democracies', presented to the *Conference on Social Capital in Europe*, Milan, November.

van Deth, Jan (1996), 'Voluntary Associations and Political Participation', in Oscar W. Gabriel and Jurgen W. Falter (eds.), *Wahlen und Politische Einstellungen in Westlichen Demokratien*. Frankfurt am Main: Peter Lang.

Verba, Sidney (1965), 'Conclusion: Comparative Political Culture', in Lucian W. Pye and Sidney Verba (eds.), *Political Culture and Political Development*. Princeton: Princeton University Press, 512–60.

—— and Norman Nie (1972), *Participation in America: Political Democracy and Social Equality*. New York: Harper & Row.

—— —— and Jae-on Kim (1978), *Participation and Political Equality: A Seven-Nation Comparison*. New York: Cambridge University Press.

—— Kay Schlozman, and Henry Brady (1995), *Voice and Equality: Civic Volunteerism in American Politics*. Cambridge, Mass.: Harvard University Press.

Walz, Dieter and Wolfram Brunner (1997), 'Das Sein bestimmt das Bewußtsein. Oder. Warum sich die Ostdeutschen als Bürger 2. Klasse fühlen', *Aus Politik und Zeitgeschichte. Beilage zur Wochenzeitung Das Parlament* B51/97, 13–19.

Warren, Mark E. (1996), 'Democracy and Trust', paper for the *Conference on Democracy and Trust*, Georgetown University, November.

Wattenberg, Martin (1991), *The Rise of Candidate-Centered Politics*. Cambridge, Mass.: Harvard University Press.

Weatherford, Stephen M. (1984), 'Economic "Stagflation" and Public Support for the Political System', *British Journal of Political Science*, 14: 187–205.

—— (1987), 'How Does Government Performance Influence Political Support?' *Political Behavior*, 9: 5–28.

—— (1991), 'Mapping the Ties That Bind: Legitimacy, Representation and Alienation', *Western Political Quarterly*, 44: 251–76.

—— (1992), 'Measuring Political Legitimacy', *American Political Science Review*, 86: 149–66.

Weaver, R. K. and Bert A. Rockman (1993) (eds.), *Do Institutions Matter?* Washington: The Brookings Institution.

Weil, Frederick D. (1987), 'Cohorts Regimes, and the Legitimation of Democracy: West Germany since 1945', *American Sociological Review*, 52: 308–24.

—— (1989), 'The Sources and Structure of Legitimation in Western Democracies', *American Sociological Review*, 54: 682–706.

—— (1993), 'The Development of Democratic Attitudes in Eastern and Western Germany in a Comparative Perspective', in Frederick D. Weil (ed.), *Research on Democracy and Society*, i, *Democratization in Eastern and Western Europe*. Greenwich, Conn.: JAI Press: 195–225.

Weisberg, Herbert (1981), 'A Multidimensional Conceptualization of Party Identification', *Political Behavior*, 2: 33–60.

Weisberg, Jacob (1996), in *Defence of Government: The Fall and Rise of Public Trust*. New York: Scribner.

Welzel, Christian (1997), *Demokratischer Elitenwandel: Die Erneuerung der ostdeutschen Elite aus demokratie-soziologischer Sicht*. Opladen: Leske & Budrich.

Westerståhl, Jörgen and Folke Johansson (1985), *Bilden av Sverige: Studier av nyheter och nyhetsideologier i TV, radio och dagspress*. Stockholm: SNS.

Westle, Bettina (1994), 'Demokratie und Sozialismus: Politische Ordnungsvorstellungen im vereinten Deutschland zwischen Ideologie, Protest, Nostalgie', *Kölner Zeitschrift für Soziologie und Sozialpsychologie*, 46/4: 571–96.

White, Stephen, Richard Rose and Ian McAllister (1997), *How Russia Votes*. Chatham, NJ: Chatham House.

Whiteley, Paul and Patrick Seyd (1997), 'Political Capital Formation Among British Party Members', in J. van Deth (ed.), *Private Groups and Public Life: Social Participation, Voluntary Associations and Political Involvement in Representative Democracies*. London: Routledge.

Widfeldt, Anders (1995), 'Party Membership and Party Representativeness', in Klingemann and Fuchs (eds.), *Citizens and the State*.

Wiesenthal, Helmut (1996), 'Die Transition Ostdeutschlands: Dimensionen und Paradoxien eines Sonderfalls', in Helmut Wiesenthal (ed.), *Einheit als Privileg*. Frankfurt am Main: Campus, 10–38.

Williams, Bernard (1988), ' Formal Structures and Social Reality', in D. Gambetta (ed.),
    Trust: Making and Breaking Co-operative Relation. Oxford: Blackwell.
Wright, James D. (1976), *The Dissent of the Governed.* New York: Academic Press.
Yamigichi, Toshio and Yamigichi Midori (1994), 'Trust and Commitment in the United
    States and Japan', *Motivation and Emotion*, 18: 129–66.
Zimmerman, E. (1979), 'Crises and Crisis Outcomes', *European Journal of Political
    Research*, 7: 67–115.

INDEX OF NAMES

GENERAL INDEX

accountability issues 23–4
advanced industrial societies 60–1
  confidence in political actors 61–5
  institutional confidence 65–72, 75–6, 243–7
  post-modernization 238–341
  regime performance evaluations 68–9
  respect for authority 249–50
  support for democratic principles 69–72, 236–7
  support for political community 72–4
  see also under individual countries
affective beliefs 58
affective orientations 58–9
Albania, satisfaction with regime performance 51, 230
Algeria, reversion to authoritarianism 7, 266
American National Election Study (ANES) 61–3, 66–7
Argentina 235
  institutional confidence 20, 227
  support for regime principles 17
  willingness to fight for country 42
armed forces, support for 19, 246, 252, 253
  see also regime institutions, support for
Armenia, satisfaction with regime performance 49, 51
Australia, support for political actors 65
Austria 148
  support for political actors 63
authoritarianism:
  return to 7, 31, 32, 235, 265–8
  transition from, *see* democratization
authority, attitudes towards 19, 24, 237, 239
  advanced industrial societies 249–50
  declining respect for 243–6
  post-modernization and 242–3
  predicted and observed changes 247–50
Azerbaijan:
  regime performance evaluation 46
  support from political community 39

Belarus:
  institutional confidence 20
  satisfaction with regime performance 48, 49, 51
Belgium, institutional confidence 195
Bosnia, consequences of political divisions 26

Brazil:
  satisfaction with regime performance 18
  support for regime principles 17
  willingness to fight for country 42
Britain 147
  civic engagement 259
  consequences of political divisions 26, 262, 270
  democratization 81, 148
  institutional confidence 66, 67, 194, 227
  national pride 72
  political trust 6, 181, 186
  protest potential 262
  support for political actors 61–2, 65
Bulgaria 81, 85, 88
  satisfaction with regime performance 49, 52
bureaucratization 238
Bush, George 61, 255

Canada:
  consequences of political divisions 26, 262, 270
  institutional confidence 195, 227
  support for political actors 20, 63
Central Europe 32
  democratization 265, 268
  institutional confidence 20
  satisfaction with regime performance 18, 49, 51, 53
  support for political community 39
  trajectories of support for democracy 83–8
  see also Europe; *under individual countries*; post-communist Europe
Chile:
  institutional confidence 208
  satisfaction with regime performance 230
  support for regime principles 17
China 265
  support for political community 39
Chun Doo Whan 156, 159, 162
church 239
  attendance, post-communist Europe 94, 96
  confidence in 246, 253–4
Churchill hypothesis 81–2, 85, 93
civic engagement 11, 258–61
  social trust relationship 21–2, 172–3
  see also political participation

It is not a matter of simple economic determinism, however. The five Nordic societies (all relatively rich, and characterized by the most Postmodern values of any group of countries in the world) all rank low on this variable. But the four Confucian societies also tend to rank low on this variable, despite the fact that Japan is rich, while Taiwan and South Korea are much less so, and China is somewhat relatively poor). Nevertheless, the overall correlation with economic development is strong and highly significant.

With modernization, people increasingly looked to the state, rather than to a Supreme Being, to provide security. During the past several decades in